By Honor Bound

By Honor Bound

State and Society in Early Modern Russia

Nancy Shields Kollmann

CORNELL UNIVERSITY PRESS

ITHACA AND LONDON

Copyright © 1999 by Cornell University

All rights reserved. Except for brief quotations in a review, this book, or parts
thereof, must not be reproduced in any form without permission in writing from
the publisher. For information, address Cornell University Press, Sage House,
512 East State Street, Ithaca, New York 14850.

First published 1999 by Cornell University Press.

Printed in the United States of America.

Library of Congress Cataloging-in-Publication Data
Kollmann, Nancy Shields, 1950-
     By honor bound : state and society in early modern Russia / Nancy
Shields Kollmann.
        p.   cm.
    Includes bibliographical references and index.
    ISBN 0-8014-3435-1 (cloth : alk. paper)
    1. Courts of honor--Russia--History.   2. Libel and slander-
-Russia--History.   3. Honor--Russia--History.   I. Title.
KLA285.H65K65   1999
345.47'0256--dc21   99-13343

Cornell University Press strives to use environmentally responsible suppliers
and materials to the fullest extent possible in the publishing of its books. Such
materials include vegetable-based, low-VOC inks and acid-free papers that are
recycled, totally chlorine-free, or partly composed of nonwood fibers.

Cloth printing   10 9 8 7 6 5 4 3 2 1

To Sasha and Christopher

Contents

Abbreviations

AAE	*Akty, sobrannye v bibliotekakh i arkhivakh Rossiiskoi imperii Arkheograficheskoiu ekspeditsieiu Imp. akademii nauk.* 4 vols. and index. St. Petersburg, 1836, 1838.
AI	*Akty istoricheskie, sobrannye i izdannye Arkheograficheskoiu kommissieiu.* 5 vols. St. Petersburg, 1841–42.
AIu	*Akty iuridicheskie.* St. Petersburg, 1838.
AIuB	*Akty, otnosiashchiesia do iuridicheskogo byta drevnei Rossii.* 3 vols. and index. St. Petersburg, 1857–1901.
AMG	*Akty Moskovskogo gosudarstva.* 3 vols. St. Petersburg, 1890–1901.
ASEI	*Akty sotsial'no-ekonomicheskoi istorii severo-vostochnoi Rusi kontsa XIV–nachala XVI v.* 3 vols. Moscow, 1952–64.
Chteniia	*Chteniia v Imp. obshchestve istorii i drevnostei Rossiiskikh pri Moskovskom universitete. Sbornik.* 264 vols. Moscow, 1845–1918.
DAI	*Dopolneniia k Aktam istoricheskim.* 12 vols. and index. St. Petersburg, 1846–75.
DDG	*Dukhovnye i dogovornye gramoty velikikh i udel'nykh kniazei XIV–XVI vv.* Moscow and Leningrad, 1950.
DR	*Dvortsovye razriady.* 4 vols. St. Petersburg, 1850–55.
Forschungen	*Forschungen zur osteuropäischen Geschichte.* 53 vols. to date. New series. Berlin, 1954–.
Veselovskii, ISZ	Veselovskii, S. B. *Issledovaniia po istorii klassa sluzhilykh zemlevladel'tsev.* Moscow, 1969.
KR	*Knigi razriadnye po ofitsial'nym onykh spiskam. . . .* 2 vols. St. Petersburg, 1853–55.

PRP	*Pamiatniki russkogo prava*. 8 vols. Moscow, 1952–63.
PSRL	*Polnoe sobranie russkikh letopisei*. 41 vols. to date. St. Petersburg and Moscow, 1841–.
PSZ	*Polnoe sobranie zakonov Rossiiskoi imperii*. Volume 1 in 40 vols. with 5 additional vols. of indices. St. Petersburg, 1830.
RGADA	Rossiiskii gosudarstvennyi arkhiv drevnikh aktov.
RGB	Rossiiskaia gosudarstvennaia biblioteka.
RIB	*Russkaia istoricheskaia biblioteka*. 39 vols. St. Petersburg and Leningrad, 1872–1929.
RK	*Razriadnaia kniga (knigi)* [various years] *gg*. Moscow, 1966, and other editions.
RZ	*Rossiiskoe zakonodatel'stvo X–XX vekov*. Ed. O. I. Chisti-akov. 9 vols. Moscow, 1984–94.
SbRIO	*Sbornik Imp. russkogo istoricheskogo obshchestva*. 148 vols. St. Petersburg and Petrograd, 1867–1916.
SGGD	*Sobranie gosudarstvennykh gramot i dogovorov*. 5 pts. Moscow, 1813–94.
SRIa	*Slovar' russkogo iazyka XI–XVII vv*. 23 vols. to date. Moscow, 1975–.
ZA	*Zakonodatel'nye akty Russkogo gosudarstva vtoroi poloviny XVI–pervoi poloviny XVII veka. Teksty*. Leningrad, 1986.

Terms and Abbreviations in Manuscript Citations

delo	item
f. or fond	collection
l. or ll.	*list, listy*: folio
opis'	archive description, catalog
stb.	*stolbets*: scroll
stol	desk, subsection of Military Service Chancery
v.	verso

Preface

The research that led to this book started off in a somewhat different direction. Having finished a book on Muscovite politics that focused on elite clan genealogies, I decided that the next logical step should be to study precedence (*mestnichestvo*). Precedence was Muscovy's system of assigning military rank according to clan honor—honor calculated according to clan heritage, military service, and an individual's genealogical ranking in his clan. Precedence eventually did find its way into this book in Chapters 4 and 6, but only in the broader context of its underlying theme—honor.

Knowing that Muscovite law also mentioned compensation for the more general crime of insult to honor (*beschest'e*), I explored the secondary literature, finding only a handful of articles using a small number of litigations on insult to honor. Because of this dearth of literature, I did not expect much when I looked for cases of insult in the same Moscow archive in which precedence suits are housed (RGADA, the Russian State Archive of Ancient Documents). However, I found hundreds—case upon case of Muscovite men and women reliving before judges the angers, tensions, and anxieties that compelled them to go to court to defend their good names. Dishonor suits were not an unknown—but certainly an underappreciated—historical source and seemed to me far more interesting than precedence cases. Compared with the generally faceless and dry compendia of genealogy and service records that constitute precedence cases (they are as alike "as peas in a pod," to borrow a phrase used in another context by the great Russian historian V. O. Kliuchevskii), litigations over dishonor (*beschest'e*) sparkle with real people arguing, negotiating, and working out problems in their own voices. I was drawn to look not at a single judicial institution but rather at a code of values, a social discourse, and a dynamic cultural practice.

This research has convinced me that judicial cases are a source of great potential; in RGADA alone there are thousands extant, concerning a wide range of crimes and disputes from central and provincial courts. They allow us to build history from the bottom up in a microhistorical way, which seems to me the best way to test our broad paradigms of historical change. This study attempts to move from the local level, from evidence of day-to-day litigation, to make arguments on a macro level, addressing, among other themes, the powerful paradigm of "autocracy" in Russian history.

This work owes much to many scholars who inspired me or helped me along the way. My graduate mentor, Edward L. Keenan, left me the long-standing challenge to figure out "what's really going on here" in any given Muscovite situation, which I have taken as a charge to look at social praxis at the lived level, behind the screen of received historiography. Numerous colleagues have helpfully read or discussed my ideas with me: Daniel Rowland, Eve Levin, Janet Martin, Hans-Joachim Torke, Robert Crummey, Michael Flier, Paul Bushkovitch, Terry Emmons, Paul Seaver, and Paul Robinson. Two conferences gave me lively forums at which to present my work: the Seventh International Conference on Kiev Rus' and Muscovite History, held in Berlin in 1992, and the Second Summer Workshop in Early East Slavic Culture, held at Stanford in 1993 with funding from the Social Science Research Council. At the latter, I was particularly inspired by the comments of our "outside expert," Natalie Zemon Davis, who pushed us to think about Muscovy comparatively. Valerie A. Kivelson has over the years been a good critic and reader, advising on translations, broadening my horizons with theory, and generously sharing original ideas. Each of these colleagues helped make this book better; none, of course, is responsible for its shortcomings.

Numerous institutions have underwritten my work. The History Department at Stanford University has strongly supported my research, and I have received generous leave time as well as fellowship and travel funds. I am grateful to the chairmen who presided over the years of this research: Jim Sheehan, David Kennedy, Keith Baker, and Norman Naimark. Stanford's Center for Russian and East European Studies, under Alex Dallin's leadership, generously granted me a Mellon Fellowship in 1985. I received three International Research and Exchanges Board (IREX) grants between 1986 and 1995 to support about seven months of research in Moscow and St. Petersburg; I also received Fulbright-Hays Faculty Research Abroad fellowships in 1986 and 1995. The National Endowment for the Humanities supported me in 1985–86 with an academic-year grant that got me launched and a summer stipend in 1993 that helped me work through my precedence database. Finally, I was the grateful recipient of a John Simon Guggenheim Memorial Fellowship for academic year 1994–95, during which time I wrote most of the text. I am extremely thankful to all these sources of private and public funding that have sustained my work.

I owe a particular debt to colleagues in Russia for their interest in my project and support in the archives. Aleksander Borisovich Kamenskii of the Russian State Humanities University and Iurii Moiseevich Eskin of RGADA helped make my brief stay in the summer of 1995 immensely productive. Then and in 1986, the staff of RGADA eagerly responded to my every archival request. I am grateful to them all. B. N. Floria and M. E. Bychkova have steadily shown interest in my work and provided helpful advice. R. G. Skrynnikov served as my advisor during my 1986 stay and went beyond the call of duty to help me get access to materials and to set up consultations with scholars in Moscow.

I started this research a year or so before my daughter, Sasha, was born; three years later Christopher joined us. Their coming may well have slowed the pace of this work, but their presence has so enriched my life that I suspect the book is also enriched. It is with delight that I dedicate this book to them. I cannot fail to mention as well the great comfort I received over these years of research from our loyal companions, Kira and Asta. Their trust and love have never faltered. But the greatest gift of support and encouragement came from my husband and closest colleague, Jack Kollmann. Although he will have to be satisfied with having had my first book dedicated to him, nothing has changed—he remains my constant source of support and encouragement. He knows, I hope, that none of this could have been done without him.

Introduction

This is a book about how individuals in early modern Russia—primarily in the sixteenth and seventeenth centuries—defended their personal honor and how the state participated in that process by providing legal norms and access to litigation. Honor in Muscovy was a rhetoric of personal dignity that accrued to all subjects of the tsar, regardless of social rank; only notorious criminals were denied the opportunity to litigate to defend their good name. Honor and its defense in Muscovy present the historian with a remarkably rich field of meaning. Because honor disputes involved insult, they reveal concepts of identity, social values, and interactions among individuals. Because honor was possessed by individuals in all social ranks, even by slaves, it reflects on the nature of society in Muscovy and the relations of society to the state. The book explores a wide range of aspects of early modern Russia through the prism of honor: litigation and legality, social hierarchy and community, concepts of individual and collective identity, ideology and institutions of governance.

Honor shows itself in the early Russian historical record in two arenas: in legislation and litigation over insult to honor (*beschest'e*), which was primarily verbal insult, and in litigation among members of the landed cavalry elite over precedence in service assignment (*mestnichestvo*). Such elite precedence was based on calculations of genealogy and clan service. Legislation was issued by the grand princes (tsars after 1547), and the judicial venues were the tsar's courts. Judges were grand-princely appointees—governors in the provinces or high-ranking administrators in various offices in the Kremlin. The striking aspect about defense of honor in Muscovy is its social inclusiveness: All subjects of the tsar could litigate, although, as we see in Chapter 1, the institutions of litigation also included significant defense of social hierarchy.

Its social inclusiveness might seem to distinguish the Muscovite concept of honor from commonplace notions of honor in European history. To modern minds, "honor" is associated with medieval chivalry or aristocratic dueling and politesse, not with the everyday activities of the common man or woman. In fact, nonelite groups in premodern Europe defended their honor with a vigor equal to that of noblemen, and it is in this comparative context that one should view the Muscovite defense of honor.[1] In sixteenth-century England, for example, yeoman farmers and artisans clogged the courts with suits for defamation[2]; in sixteenth- and seventeenth-century Dijon and eighteenth-century Paris, master craftsmen and artisans sought recompense for insult[3]; in Italy, courts entertained suits from prostitutes as well as noblemen[4]; in early modern Germany, guilds asserted corporate honor.[5] At the same time, across the board, insulted individuals and groups took the law

---

[1] Robert A. Nye gives a good summary of the European historical context: "Honor Codes," in Peter N. Stearns, ed., *Encyclopedia of Social History* (New York, 1994), pp. 325–27. Edward Muir describes the genesis of dueling: *Mad Blood Stirring: Vendetta and Factions in Fruili During the Renaissance* (Baltimore, 1992), chap. 8.

[2] See J. A. Sharpe, *Defamation and Sexual Slander in Early Modern England: The Church Courts at York*, Borthwick Papers no. 58 (York, n.d. [1980?]); Mervyn James, "English Politics and the Concept of Honour, 1485–1642," *Past and Present, Supplement 3* (1978); Martin Ingram, *Church Courts, Sex and Marriage in England, 1570–1640* (Cambridge, England, 1987), chap. 10; W. R. Jones, "'Actions for Slaunder'—Defamation in English Law, Language and History," *Quarterly Journal of Speech* 57, no. 3 (1971):274–83; Miranda Chaytor, "Household and Kinship: Ryton in the Late 16th and Early 17th Centuries," *History Workshop Journal* 10 (Autumn 1980):25–60.

[3] See James R. Farr, *Hands of Honor: Artisans and Their World in Dijon, 1550–1650* (Ithaca, N. Y., 1988), chap. 4; David Garrioch, "Verbal Insults in Eighteenth-Century Paris," in Peter Burke and Roy Porter, eds., *The Social History of Language* (Cambridge, England, 1987), pp. 104–19; Gregory Hanlon, "Les rituels de l'agression en Aquitaine au XVIIe siècle," *Annales: E.S.C.*, no. 2 (1985):244–68; Arlette Jouanna, "Recherches sur la notion d'honneur au XVI-ème siècle," *Revue d'histoire moderne et contemporaine* 15 (1968):597–623; Claude Gauvard, *"De grace especial": Crime, état et société en France à la fin du Moyen Age*, 2 vols. (Paris, 1991), chap. 16.

[4] See Peter Burke, *The Historical Anthropology of Early Modern Italy* (Cambridge, England, 1987), chap. 8. Guido Ruggiero chronicles insult against the state and nobility: *Violence in Early Renaissance Venice* (New Brunswick, N.J., 1984), chap. 8.

[5] On early modern Germany, see David Martin Luebke, "Serfdom and Honour in Eighteenth-Century Germany," *Social History* 18, no. 2 (1993):143–61; Susanne Burghartz, "Rechte Jungfrauen oder Unverschämte Töchter? Zur weiblichen Ehre im 16. Jahrhundert," *Journal Geschichte* 1, no. 13 (February 1991):39–45; Kathleen E. Stuart, "The Boundaries of Honor: 'Dishonorable People' in Augsburg, 1500–1800," Ph.D. dissertation, Yale University, 1993; Mack Walker, *German Home Towns: Community, State, and General Estate, 1648–1871* (Ithaca, N.Y., and London, 1971), chap. 3; Richard van Dülmen, *Kultur und Alltag in der frühen Neuzeit*, vol. 2. *Dorf und Stadt, 16.–18. Jahrhundert* (Munich, 1992), pp. 194–214; Martin Dinges, "Die Ehre als Thema der historischen Anthropologie. Bemerkungen zur Wissenschaftsgeschichte und zur Konzeptualisierung," in Klaus Schreiner and Gerd Schwerhof, eds., *Verletzte Ehre. EhrKonflikte in Gesellschaften des Mittelalters und der frühen Neuzeit* (Cologne, 1995), pp. 29–62. My thanks to Tara Nummedal for introducing me to the latter two books.

into their own hands, redressing insult with shaming rituals, physical assault, vendetta, and feud.[6] By the sixteenth century, aristocrats and the socially ambitious began to separate themselves from the rest of society through their stylized reaction to insult (the duel) and by adopting new standards of "civility."[7] Thus honor accrued to individuals and collectives, reflecting a societal understanding that people had honor and that it should be publicly defended.

Bertram Wyatt-Brown argues that the sensibility of honor as an attribute of all members of a community, which he calls *primal honor*, has its roots in a common European heritage grounded in, first, an Indo-European association of honor with family, blood, and valor (Tacitus, for example, chronicled Germanic tribes' keen sensitivity to personal affront and family honor); and second, the moderating influence of the Stoic and Christian values that emphasize personal virtue, civility, and the cultivation of self-esteem distinct from the world's estimation.[8] Other writers have seconded the idea of honor as "a pan-European moral code." James Farr noted that the thirteenth-century Spanish law code, the *Partidas*, defines as insults to honor words and acts that were also considered insults to honor in sixteenth-century France.[9] Our Russian cases resound with very similar calumnies and insulting actions.

[6]See Elizabeth S. Cohen, "Honor and Gender in the Streets of Early Modern Rome," *Journal of Interdisciplinary History* 22, no. 4 (1992):597–625; Natalie Zemon Davis, "Charivari, Honor and Community in Seventeenth-Century Lyon and Geneva," in John J. MacAloon, ed., *Rite, Drama, Festival, Spectacle: Rehearsals towards a Theory of Cultural Performance* (Philadelphia, 1984), pp. 42–57; idem, "The Reasons of Misrule," in her *Society and Culture in Early Modern France* (Stanford, 1975), pp. 97–123.

[7]See C. Stephen Jaeger, *The Origins of Courtliness: Civilizing Trends and the Formation of Courtly Ideals, 939–1210* (Philadelphia, 1985); Muir, *Mad Blood*, chap. 8; Marvin B. Becker, *Civility and Society in Western Europe, 1300–1600* (Bloomington, Ind., 1988); Mark Motley, *Becoming a French Aristocrat: The Education of the Court Nobility, 1580–1715* (Princeton, N.J., 1990); Kristen B. Neuschel, *Word of Honor: Interpreting Noble Culture in Sixteenth-Century France* (Ithaca, N.Y., 1989); Norbert Elias, *The Court Society,* trans. Edmund Jephcott (New York, 1983); Orest Ranum, "Courtesy, Absolutism and the Rise of the French State, 1630–1660," *Journal of Modern History* 52 (1980):426–51. Also see James ("English Politics"), who depicts Elizabethan "honor society" as primarily aristocratic, and Donna T. Andrew, "The Code of Honour and its Critics: The Opposition to Duelling in England, 1700–1850," *Social History* 5, no. 3 (1980): 409–34. Studies of honor as a theme in literature focus on its appeal to the elite: Julio Caro Baroja, "Honour and Shame: A Historical Account of Several Conflicts," in J. G. Peristiany, ed., *Honour and Shame: The Values of Mediterranean Society* (Chicago, 1966), pp. 113–16; F. R. Bryson, *The Point of Honor in Sixteenth-Century Italy* (New York, 1935); Curtis Brown Watson, *Shakespeare and the Renaissance Concept of Honor* (Princeton, N.J., 1960); Charles Laurence Barber, *The Idea of Honour in the English Drama, 1591–1700* (Goteborg, 1957).

[8]Bertram Wyatt-Brown, *Southern Honor: Ethics and Behavior in the Old South* (New York, 1982), chap. 2; a revised and abridged edition is *Honor and Violence in the Old South* (New York, 1986). Baroja adds a third source, the Roman concept of honor as office and title: "Honour and Shame," p. 83.

[9]Farr, *Hands of Honor,* p. 182, cites Baroja, "Honour and Shame," pp. 84–91.

Early modern Russia did not share all of the influences that shaped honor in other European countries. Its elite, for example, never reached the point of social development that drove European noblemen to invent the duel. (Muscovites first encountered the duel in the seventeenth century as a European import.) But Russia's heritage, nevertheless, was Indo-European, whether traced through the East Slavs themselves or through the Normans, who first catalyzed political formation among the East Slavs. It shared with Europe an agrarian, peasant economy. Early Russia's Orthodox Christianity shared with Catholicism a belief in human dignity, which underlay the defense of honor across the European plain. Russia was part of the pan-European culture in which reputation and status, codified as personal honor, were basic building blocks of community and identity.

The social inclusiveness of honor in theory and in the practice of litigation raises issues of its social significance. How did honor function on the local level? How did individuals use such litigation to defend or advance their status? How did honor litigation relate to broader patterns of conflict and conflict resolution? These questions provide one focus of this book: I will explore how honor litigation provided a means for individuals and communities to pursue or resolve tensions and to structure personal relations.

In Muscovy, however, more than in the European states contemporary with it, the state was closely identified with the defense of honor. The tsar's administration codified laws and provided court venues, whereas in Europe venues were myriad. The Catholic Church, local courts, and high courts shared jurisdiction over defamation according to the content of the insult.[10] In Russia also, as Chapter 4 details, the state devised precedence litigation for the elite and maintained official military and genealogical records from which to calculate relative rank. This practice eliminated the need for the elite to generate such extralegal means as vendettas and duels to defend honor. Finally, in Russia, the state itself was imbricated in the rhetoric of honor; the tsar and his representations stood at the apex of the community of honor (see Chapter 5). Thus, the second focus of this book: how honor fits into the broader array of Muscovite political institutions and concepts. I argue that the state used the defense of honor as one of many strategies to integrate the peoples of its growing and diverse empire.

I try to balance these two perspectives through a bottom-up social inquiry into the uses of honor based on the knowledge that a sense of personal dignity was ambient among East Slavs long before Muscovy consolidated power, and through a top-down examination of how the state co-opted honor for its own objectives. Neither approach should be taken as primary. Particularly to be

---

[10]Sharpe, *Defamation*, pp. 3–6.

avoided is a "statist" reading of the latter perspective as maintaining that ideas and institutions such as honor had meaning in Russia only insofar as the state created them and bestowed them on the people. Indeed, individuals and communities were adept manipulators of received discourses and institutions such as honor. Honor can and should be construed both locally and at the macro level, because both coexisted in the complex society of premodern Muscovy. To better understand how honor served both state and community, I first examine the complexity of community and the diversity of governing strategies in the sixteenth century.

Forging Structures of Governance

In Muscovy, the sixteenth century was a period of administrative consolidation over a constantly expanding realm. Like Ferdnand Braudel's "long sixteenth century" in the Mediterranean world, Moscow's sixteenth century begins earlier, with Ivan III, who served as heir presumptive with his father from c. 1448 and ruled from 1462 to 1505.[11] His administration initiated many of the key goals, strategies, and institutions that endured through the 1500s. In turn, it was a "long fourteenth century" that had prepared the ground for this sixteenth-century consolidation of power.[12] The seminal era from the 1290s to the mid-1400s was one of opportunistic reaction to the political and economic collapse of both the Golden Horde and the Teutonic Knights. Moscow's grand princes and boyar elite, like their counterparts in the Grand Duchy of Lithuania, responded by putting their houses in order domestically and by aggressively expanding their territory.[13] That Moscow's rulers reacted

---

[11]On date as heir presumptive, see Gustave Alef, "A History of the Muscovite Civil War: The Reign of Vasilii II (1425–62)," Ph.D. dissertation, Princeton University, 1956, pp. 332–35, citing *Dukhovnye i dogovornye gramoty velikikh i udel'nykh kniazei XIV–XVI vv.* (DDG) (Moscow and Leningrad, 1950), no. 52, pp. 155–60.

[12]Elsewhere I describe the fourteenth century as "formative" for the political elite: *Kinship and Politics. The Making of the Muscovite Political System, 1345–1547* (Stanford, 1987), chap. 1.

[13]For a useful survey of expansion in the early period, see I. B. Grekov and F. F. Shakhmagonov, *Mir istorii. Russkie zemli v XIII–XV vekakh* (Moscow, 1986). Despite its Stalinist interpretation, good chronological narrative and maps of Muscovite expansion into non-Slavic lands can be found in *Ocherki istorii SSSR. Period feodalizma, konets XV v.–nachalo XVII v.* (Moscow, 1955). Also for good maps, see Allen F. Chew, *An Atlas of Russian History*, rev. ed. (New Haven, Conn., and London, 1970); Martin Gilbert, *Atlas of Russian History*, 2d ed. (New York, 1993); John Channon and Robert Hudson, *The Penguin Historical Atlas of Russia* (London, 1995). M. N. Tikhomirov offers a detailed description of Muscovy's lands in the sixteenth century: *Rossiia v XVI stoletii* (Moscow, 1962).

in this way to the regional vacuum of power bespeaks no unusual messianic self-conception, no plan for world domination or nomadic spirit.[14]

Moscow's European neighbors were also gobbling up territory by the sixteenth century, even before any had developed theories of mercantilism or absolutism to legitimize expansion of land, people, and resources. The Portuguese, Spanish, Dutch, and British looked overseas for expansion, while the Habsburgs and Jagiellonians pushed toward the frontier borderlands of the steppe eastward from the Danube toward the Caspian Sea. These empires were driven variously by dynastic imperative, political pressures, and economic needs. In Muscovy's case, economic pressures were excuse enough. Within its fifteenth-century borders, natural resources were scarce and land was relatively unproductive because of poor soil, poorly timed precipitation, and a short growing season.[15] Expansion provided income from the far Northern and Siberian fur trade and from export and transit trade along major trade routes (the Volga River and the Baltic and White Seas).

For more than a hundred years, Moscow was remarkably successful in its drive to expand. The debacle of the Livonian War (1558–82) halted expansion toward the Baltic until Peter the Great's time, but expansion south and east continued with little interruption. By the demise of the Daniilovich line in 1598,[16] the realm stretched from Novgorod and Pskov northwest of Moscow eastward along the White Sea littoral to the Ob' River beyond the Ural Mountains and occupied most of the forested land north of the steppe and east of Smolensk. By the end of the sixteenth century, the Muscovite empire comprised several distinct regions. The Center was the heartland around Moscow, settled primarily by Orthodox East Slavs, where peasant agriculture and a landed cavalry elite dominated economy and society. Another region was the North, the old Novgorodian lands stretching from the Gulf of Finland to the Urals, north

[14]Arnold Toynbee popularized the view that Moscow's expansionism was a "Byzantine heritage" of imperialism: *Civilization on Trial* (New York, 1948), pp. 164–83. V. O. Kliuchevskii forged a sort of "frontier thesis" interpretation of the Russian people as constantly colonizing: "Kurs russkoi istorii," in *Sochineniia*, 5 vols. (Moscow, 1956–58), vol. 1 (1956), lect. 2. The "messianic" view is often associated with the "Third Rome" theory, but that is a misreading. The original "Third Rome" text primarily argues for the piety of the ruler; see Nikolai Andreyev, "Filofei and His Epistle to Ivan Vasil'yevich," *Slavonic and East European Review* 38, no. 90 (1959):1–31; Paul Bushkovitch, "The *Life of Saint Filipp*: Tsar and Metropolitan in the Late Sixteenth Century," in Michael S. Flier and Daniel Rowland, eds., *Medieval Russian Culture. Vol. II* (Berkeley, 1994), p. 31; David M. Goldfrank, "Moscow, the Third Rome," *Modern Encyclopedia of Russian and Soviet History* 23 (1981):118–21.

[15]On climate, see Leslie Symons, *The Soviet Union. A Systematic Geography*, 2d ed. (London and New York, 1990), chaps. 3–4, and John C. Dewdney, *A Geography of the Soviet Union*, 3d ed. (Oxford, 1979), chap. 2.

[16]The Daniilovich line was a branch of the Kievan Riurikide princely clan, descendants of Prince Daniil Alexandrovich, who died in 1303. The dynasty died out in 1598 with the death of Ivan IV's last and childless son, Fedor Ivanovich.

These spectacular wooden churches and village buildings at Kizhi illustrate the wooden architecture of the isolated villages in the Russian North, an area that Moscow conquered from Novgorod in the late fifteenth century. (Photograph: Jack Kollmann.)

of Moscow, where landed cavalrymen were few. Here forest exploitation, fishing, and hunting played a greater role in the economy than agriculture, and communities of peasants free of landlord control were the social norm. Orthodox East Slavs coexisted with converted and non-Christian Finno-Ugric peoples, as well as with non-Christian or recently converted Permian and Zyrian tribes. On the recently conquered western frontier, other Orthodox East Slavs and some Catholic East Slavs who had for several generations lived under the Grand Duchy of Lithuania fell under Muscovite suzerainty. Here cities enjoyed self-government, and nobility and bourgeoisie enjoyed corporate privileges and rights.

The steppe frontier, ever expanding to the south and east, was a land in transition, shared by communities of free Orthodox East Slavic peasants and Cossacks, increasingly joined by members of the elite who brought enserfment and central control of the land fund. The Middle Volga was populated by a variety of peoples subordinate until 1552 to the Khanate of Kazan'; the Mordvinians and Mari were Finno-Ugric, and only some were Christianized; the Tatars and Turkic Chuvash were Muslim. Late in the century and through the seventeenth century, Muscovite control expanded to the Turkic nomadic peoples of the steppe south of the Urals and to the indigenous peoples of western and eventually eastern Siberia. Siberian natives spoke a variety of indigenous languages and practiced animistic religions.

Muscovite tsars claimed sovereignty over these myriad peoples, expressing this assertion in their official titles with the words *gosudar'* and (by the end of the sixteenth century) *samoderzhets*. Both terms have been construed as claiming a sort of despotic total control, but contemporaries understood the terms to imply "sovereignty" without a connotation of servility.[17] As sovereigns of "all the Rus' lands" and beyond, Muscovy's rulers exercised their power with flexibility and pragmatic accommodation to existing social and political institutions. In so delegating and recognizing local leadership, Muscovite rulers did not divide sovereignty and thereby create political pluralism along a European legal model; they retained a patrimonial claim to unilateral sovereignty. They devolved the execution of power, however, to a startlingly wide array of institutions and practices.

Geography and demography forced their hand to some extent. In the far northern forests, settlement was dispersed and villages were tiny (averaging one to three households), with denser settlement only near major towns and monasteries, primarily in the Center. The rigors of the climate (long winter freeze, short growing season, northern latitude, infertile soil) prevented larger population accumulation.[18] S. B. Veselovskii's image of the fifteenth-century countryside is memorable: "From a bird's eye or airplane's view an area settled with numerous tiny villages must have looked like a leopard's coat, in which the background was forest, and the settlements, scattered among the fields and meadows, were spots of various size and irregular shape." Even as late as 1724, the population density of the Empire averaged fewer than ten inhabitants per square *versta* (a *versta* equals approximately two-thirds of a mile) in areas other than the provinces of Moscow (with twenty inhabitants per square *versta*) and Kiev (with ten to twenty).[19]

Governance in such conditions was difficult; add the element of physical expanse, and it became challenging indeed. As Peter Brown cautioned, writing

[17] See Isabel de Madariaga, "Autocracy and Sovereignty," *Canadian-American Slavic Studies* 16, nos. 3–4 (1982):373–74; Marc Szeftel, "The Title of the Muscovite Monarch up to the End of the Seventeenth Century," *Canadian-American Slavic Studies* 13, nos. 1–2 (1979):70–76; Marshall Poe, "What Did Muscovites Mean When They Called Themselves 'Slaves of the Tsar'?" *Slavic Review* 57, no. 3 (1998):585–608.

[18] On peasants' accommodation to the physical setting, see Janet Martin, "'Backwardness' in Russian Peasant Culture. A Theoretical Consideration of Agricultural Practices in the Seventeenth Century," in Samuel H. Baron and Nancy S. Kollmann, eds., *Religion and Culture in Early Modern Russia and Ukraine* (DeKalb, Ill., 1997), pp. 19–33.

[19] S. B. Veselovskii, *Selo i derevnia v severo-vostochnoi Rusi XIV–XVI vv.* (Moscow-Leningrad, 1936), pp. 27–28. On population density, see Gilbert, *Atlas*, p. 38.

about Byzantium, "Distance [is] the First Enemy of all extended empires. . . . Terrifyingly active and peremptory at the center, the imperial system of government found itself becalmed on a Sargasso Sea once it reached the provinces."[20] Distances were daunting in the Muscovite empire: From Moscow to Perm' in the upper Kama basin today is 1,378 kilometers by rail; to Tomsk in Western Siberia, 3,500; to Vladivostok on the Pacific, 9,297. The Volga River alone, Moscovy's major trade artery, measures over 3,500 kilometers in length. Climate added to the difficulties of communication: Encumbered by mud most of the spring and autumn, dirt roads were easily passable only in May through August; winter freeze speeded transportation, but temperatures inhibited movement. When the need was urgent, huge distances could be covered very quickly by a post system, but as a rule, central government stood at a far remove from most communities.[21]

Nevertheless Moscow's sixteenth-century rulers were obsessed with the same sorts of issues that beleaguered their European counterparts—that is, how to enlist local elites in their project of state expansion, how to expand their armies, and how to tax to pay for it all. In short, mobilization of resources was their overriding concern. Faced with an apparent dearth of bureaucratic personnel, or perhaps most accurately, of liquid resources with which to compensate a central officialdom, the state reacted by defining its job minimally, demanding only the right to mobilize fiscal, natural, and human resources; to administer high justice; and to monopolize war, peace, and foreign alliances. To accomplish these tasks, the Kremlin delegated, when possible, mundane administrative tasks to the groups best constituted to accomplish them. In most cases those groups existed; in other cases, the state created or enhanced them.

A major priority for Muscovy in the sixteenth century was the cultivation of a metropolitan (Moscow-based) elite who would execute central policy. To do so, the Kremlin both brought new clans into high status and co-opted elites from conquered areas. High-ranking clans were invited to join the court elite, provided that they converted to Orthodoxy. Princely families of the ruling Gedyminide dynasty of the Grand Duchy of Lithuania and of the Kazan' ruling house, princes from the North Caucasus, sovereign princely lines from old Rus' principalities such as Iaroslavl', Rostov, and Suzdal'—all added jewels to

---

[20]Peter Brown, *Power and Persuasion in Late Antiquity. Towards a Christian Empire* (Madison, Wis., 1992), p. 12; on "distance," Brown paraphrases Braudel (p. 17).

[21]See, for example, how quickly documents travelled from the Center to the provinces when the issue was suspected treason: N. Ia. Novombergskii, *Slovo i delo gosudarevy. Protsessy do izdaniia Ulozheniia Alekseia Mikhailovicha 1649 goda*, vol. 1 (Moscow, 1911). See also Paul Shott, "Transportation in Russia," *Modern Encyclopedia of Russian and Soviet History* 39 (1985):170–78.

the Moscow grand prince's crown.[22] Richly rewarded with status, land, and booty, these new clans and new boyars contributed to stability as the empire was assembled piecemeal. At midcentury, the government moved to bolster elite cohesion by compiling genealogical books and military musters to support the precedence (or *mestnichestvo*) system of status ranking based on family heritage and service.

Moscow's grand princes cultivated and co-opted this metropolitan elite, and delegated administrative power, by tolerating pockets of limited sovereignty. Their kinsmen received appanage principalities,[23] as did some high-ranking princely families (primarily from the Grand Duchy) called *service princes*.[24] In the midfifteenth century, a quasi-independent Tatar principality was created at Kasimov to cultivate support among dissident princes in Kazan', and a Nogai counterpart was created at Romanov in the midsixteenth century to serve similar purposes. Even the vast tracks in the Urals awarded to the Stroganov family in return for colonization and trade development were pockets of independent rule that provided Moscow an administrative machine in a

[22]On the expansion of the boyar elite, see my *Kinship and Politics*, chaps. 2–3; Ann M. Kleimola, "Patterns of Duma Recruitment, 1505–1550," in Daniel Clarke Waugh, ed., *Essays in Honor of A. A. Zimin* (Columbus, Ohio, 1985), pp. 232–58, and her "*Kto kogo*: Patterns of Duma Recruitment, 1547–1564," *Forschungen zur osteuropäischen Geschichte (Forschungen)* 38 (1986):205–20; A. A. Zimin, "Kniazheskaia znat' i formirovanie sostava boiarskoi dumy vo vtoroi polovine XV–pervoi treti XVI v.," *Istoricheskie zapiski* 103 (1979):195–241; idem, "Feodal'naia znat' Tverskogo i Riazanskogo velikikh kniazhestv i Moskovskoe boiarstvo kontsa XV–pervoi treti XVI veka," *Istoriia SSSR* no. 3 (1973):124–42; idem, "Suzdal'skie i rostovskie kniaz'ia vo vtoroi polovine XV–pervoi treti XVI v.," *Vspomogatel'nye istoricheskie distsipliny* 7 (1976):56–69; idem, *Formirovanie boiarskoi aristokratii v Rossii vo vtoroi polovine XV–pervoi treti XVI v.*, pt. 1 (Moscow, 1988), pp. 28–153; Gustave Alef, "Reflections on the Boyar Duma in the Reign of Ivan III," *Slavonic and East European Review* 45 (1967):76–123; idem, "Aristocratic Politics and Royal Policy in Muscovy in the Late Fifteenth and Early Sixteenth Century," *Forschungen* 27 (1980):77–109; idem, "The Origins of Muscovite Autocracy: The Age of Ivan III," *Forschungen* 39 (1986), 362 pp.

[23]On the appanage system, see S. B. Veselovskii, "Poslednie udely v severo-vostochnoi Rusi," *Istoricheskie zapiski* 22 (1947):101–31; S. M. Kashtanov, "Iz istorii poslednikh udelov," *Trudy Moskovskogo gosudarstvennogo istoriko-arkhivnogo instituta* 10 (1957):275–302; Tikhomirov, *Rossiia v XVI stoletii*, chap. 3; A. A. Zimin, "V. I. Lenin o 'moskovskom tsarstve' i cherty feodal'noi razdroblennosti v politicheskom stroe Rossii XVI veka," in *Aktual'nye problemy istorii Rossii epokhi feodalizma. Sbornik statei* (Moscow, 1970), pp. 273–78, and his "O politicheskikh predposylkakh vozniknoveniia russkogo absoliutizma," in *Absoliutizm v Rossii (XVII–XVIII vv.)* (Moscow, 1964), pp. 18–49 (English translation by Susan Zayer Rupp, in Nancy Shields Kollmann, ed., *Major Problems in Early Modern Russian History* [New York, 1992], pp. 79–107). In the seventeenth century, the new Romanov dynasty did not use the appanage system to support males in the family, even though a few males would have been eligible (most surviving Romanov progeny in the seventeenth century were women).

[24]On service princes, see M. E. Bychkova, *Sostav klassa feodalov Rossii v XVI v. Istoriko-genealogicheskoe issledovanie* (Moscow, 1986), chap. 2.

far-flung corner of the realm.[25] The rulers of all such lands wielded judicial authority and the right to grant immunities from their own jurisdiction to land-holders within their holdings. They had their own cavalry forces and administra-tive elites and were limited only by a prohibition against foreign alliances. These various institutions were phased out from the 1560s through the midseventeenth century as their political utility waned, but they reflect Muscovite autocrats' will-ingness to diffuse administrative authority in ways not threatening to central power. At the same time, secular and ecclesiastical landholders enjoyed broad grants of immunity from the ruler's administrative, fiscal, and judicial authority.

At the local level, Moscow used similar strategies of cultivation, co-optation, and devolution of administration.[26] In the North, they relied on existing com-munes of free peasants (*volosti*) under the supervision of governors (*namestniki*); even monasteries and cathedrals in some places participated in secular adminis-tration. Georg Michels has shown that even in the late seventeenth century, the communities of the North were far removed from central governance.[27] In the Middle Volga and Siberia, local elites were co-opted. Tatar and Siberian elites kept their indigenous institutions, laws, and practices as long as they stayed loyal; these populations were taxed through a system different from that employed in the Cen-ter, paying in furs or their equivalent. This levy was called a *iasak*, while peasants in the Center paid a "tax burden" (*tiaglo*) in cash, kind, or service. In Smolensk and other western areas, noblemen and burghers maintained their corporate priv-ileges and institutions. Such an eclectic and laissez-faire policy was a mainstay of colonial practice into the eighteenth century.[28] On the steppe frontier, governors enjoyed wide authority in the absence of local gentry, and frontier military forces straddled the social categories of peasant, townsman, and privileged cavalry. Moscow put most of its energies into the Center, however, working to forge strong provincial communities of landed gentry cavalrymen, who both constituted the army and served as a quasi-bureaucracy.

---

[25]On such independent principalities, see Tikhomirov, *Rossiia v XVI stoletii*, pp. 42–52; Kash-tanov, "Iz istorii poslednikh udelov"; Veselovskii, "Poslednie udely"; V. B. Kobrin, *Vlast' i sob-stvennost' v srednevekovoi Rossii (XV–XVI vv.)* (Moscow, 1985), chap. 2. On Kasimov, see V. V. Vel'iaminov-Zernov, *Issledovanie o Kasimovskikh tsariakh i tsarevichakh*, 4 pts. (St. Petersburg, 1863–87); Janet Martin, "Muscovite Frontier Policy: The Case of the Khanate of Kasimov," *Russ-ian History* 19, nos. 1–4 (1992):169–80.

[26]I survey these practices in "The Rus' Principalities [in the Fourteenth Century]," *The New Cam-bridge Medieval History Vol. VI* (Cambridge, England, forthcoming); "Russia," ibid., *Vol. VII, c. 1415–c. 1500* (Cambridge, England, 1998):748–70; and "Muscovite Russia, 1450–1598," in Gregory L. Freeze, ed., *Russia: A History* (Oxford and New York, 1997), pp. 27–54.

[27]Georg B. Michels, "The Violent Old Belief," *Russian History* 19, nos. 1–4 (1992):203–30.

[28]See Andreas Kappeler, *Russlands erste Nationalitäten: Das Zarenreich und die Völker der mit-tleren Wolga vom 16. bis 19. Jahrhundert* (Cologne, 1982); idem, "Das Moskauer Reich des 17. Jahrhunderts und seine nichtrussischen Untertanen," *Forschungen* 50 (1995):185–98; George V. Lantzeff, *Siberia in the Seventeenth Century* (Berkeley, 1943).

For the cavalrymen of newly conquered lands, Moscow pursued a gradual-ist policy of political integration: For the first several decades after conquest, principalities in the Center and towns such as Novgorod and Pskov in the northwest were ruled through separate "courts" (*dvortsy*) and majordomos (*dvoretskie*)[29]; only gradually over the century were these offices blended into the growing system of central bureaus.[30] An even more powerful mechanism of forging local elites, however, was the service tenure land system (*pomest'e*), grants of populated land held on condition of military service. Muscovy used these grants to create new provincial gentries or to reshape existing elites signif-icantly. The land and peasant labor needed to expand the *pomest'e* system were obtained not only through conquest, but also by transferring free peasant com-munes to newly recruited cavalrymen. From Novgorod, eight thousand men were deported to various provinces in the Center (Vladimir, Nizhnii Novgorod, Pereiaslavl', and others) and replaced with about two thousand men from Moscow. Throughout the century, such population resettlements served as a tool to populate newly conquered areas or to bolster frontier economies shat-tered by war. In the 1570s, for example, petty landholders from the Novgorod environs were moved into the newly conquered western frontier (Velikie Luki, Toropets, Dorogobuzh, Smolensk, and Viaz'ma), while others were moved to recently captured territories in Livonia. When Russian settlers were driven out of Livonia, they were resettled on the Novgorod frontier as border guards and used to restore the local economy. These relocations disrupted regional attach-ments and provided the opportunity to create new regional solidarities.[31]

[29]Zimin, "O politicheskikh predposylkakh," pp. 33–35; idem, "Lenin," pp. 284–85; idem, "O sostave dvortsovykh uchrezhdenii Russkogo gosudarstva kontsa XV i XVI v.," *Istoricheskie zapiski* 63 (1958):180–205; Gustave Alef, "Muscovite Military Reforms in the Second Half of the Fifteenth Century," *Forschungen* 18 (1973):93–101; B. N. Floria, "O putiakh politicheskoi tsentralizatsii Russkogo gosudarstva (na primere Tverskoi zemli)," in *Obshchestvo i gosudarstvo feodal'noi Rossii* (Moscow, 1975), pp. 281–90; Ia. S. Lur'e, "Rol' Tveri v sozdanii Russkogo natsional'nogo gosudarstva," *Uchenye zapiski Leningradskogo gosudarstvennogo universiteta* 36 (1939):85–109.

[30]See A. K. Leont'ev, *Obrazovanie prikaznoi systemy upravleniia v Russkom gosudarstve* (Moscow, 1961); N. P. Likhachev, *Razriadnye d'iaki XVI veka* (St. Petersburg, 1888); A. A. Zimin, "O slozhenii prikaznoi sistemy na Rusi," *Doklady i soobshcheniia Instituta istorii Akademii nauk* 3 (1955):164–76; Peter B. Brown, "Early Modern Russian Bureaucracy: The Evolution of the Chancellery System from Ivan III to Peter the Great," Ph.D. dissertation, University of Chicago, 1978, and his "Muscovite Government Bureaus," *Russian History* 10 (1983):269–330.

[31]See Janet Martin, "Mobility, Forced Resettlement and Regional Identity in Muscovy," in A. M. Kleimola and G. D. Lenhoff, eds., *Culture and Identity in Muscovy, 1389–1584*, UCLA Slavic Stud-ies, n.s. 3 (Moscow, 1997), pp. 431–49. On the *pomest'e* system, see Vincent E. Hammond, "The History of the Novgorodian *Pomest'e*: 1480–1550," Ph.D. dissertation, University of Illinois at Urbana-Champaign, 1987; V. N. Bernadskii, *Novgorod i novgorodskaia zemlia v XV veke* (Moscow and Leningrad, 1961), chap. 11, pp. 314–52; S. V. Rozhdestvenskii, *Sluzhiloe zemlevlade-nie v Moskovskom gosudarstve XVI veka* (St. Petersburg, 1897); K. V. Bazil'evich, "Novgorodskie pomeshchiki iz posluzhil'tsev v kontse XV veka," *Istoricheskie zapiski* 14 (1945):62–80; A. A. Zimin, "Iz istorii pomestnogo zemlevladeniia na Rusi," *Voprosy istorii* no. 11 (1959):130–42.

The state enlisted such local elites to carry out central policy in fiscal and criminal matters, thereby cultivating group solidarity. Loyalty to clan and region was a latent consciousness that Muscovy accentuated. In the early decades of the sixteenth century, the collection of taxes for fortification was shifted from centrally appointed governors to local elites; in the 1530s, criminal jurisdiction was transferred to locally selected boards of landed cavalrymen. In the 1550s, local collection of taxes in the Center and the North was transferred to boards of taxpaying peasants or townsmen selected by their communes.[32] Increasingly, as the state transferred peasant communes to landlords, administrative and judicial power over peasants shifted away from the central apparatus; private landlords maintained such immunities from grand-princely administration even after midcentury, when the state was revoking fiscal immunities.[33] By overseeing petty judicial issues, landlords in essence saved the state from maintaining an extensive local bureaucracy.

Through legislation on inheritance and the transfer of hereditary property, the state constituted stronger local gentry communities in the Center. From the 1550s to 1570s, edicts prohibited landholders in certain areas and most princely clans from selling patrimonial lands to individuals not of the given region or clan. The effect was to enhance what some scholars call local "corporations" of gentry who mustered to war together, maintained law and order, and dominated local offices.[34] By the seventeenth century, in the Center and on the frontier as gentry moved southward, these policies created vigorous local power networks. Valerie Kivelson has described, for example, how gentry factions dominated office-holding and local politics in seventeenth-century Vladimir-Suzdal'. Brian Davies and Carol Belkin Stevens graphically describe how frontier governors bent central policy to local conditions. Davies cites a

[32]On governors, see A. A. Zimin "Namestnicheskoe upravlenie v Russkom gosudarstve vtoroi poloviny XV–pervoi treti XVI v.," *Istoricheskie zapiski* 94 (1974):271–301; H. W. Dewey, "The Decline of the Muscovite *Namestnik*," *Oxford Slavonic Papers* 12 (1965):21–39. On local reforms, see Robert O. Crummey, "Reform under Ivan IV: Gradualism and Terror," in idem, ed., *Reform in Russia and the U.S.S.R.* (Urbana, Ill., and Chicago, 1989), pp. 12–27; N. E. Nosov, *Ocherki po istorii mestnogo upravleniia Russkogo gosudarstva pervoi poloviny XVI veka* (Moscow and Leningrad, 1957), and his *Stanovlenie soslovno-predstavitel'nykh uchrezhdenii v Rossii* (Leningrad, 1969).

[33]On immunities and fiscal policy, see S. B. Veselovskii, *Selo i derevnia*, and his *K voprosu o proiskhozhdenii votchinnogo rezhima* (Moscow, 1926); Alexandre Eck, *Le moyen âge russe* (Paris, 1933); Iu. G. Alekseev, *Agrarnaia i sotsial'naia istoriia severo-vostochnoi Rusi XV–XVI vv. Pereiaslavl' uezd* (Moscow and Leningrad, 1966); Horace W. Dewey, "Immunities in Old Russia," *Slavic Review* 23 (1964):643–59; Jerome Blum, *Lord and Peasant in Russia from the Ninth to the Nineteenth Century* (New York, 1969), chaps. 5–6; S. M. Kashtanov, *Finansy srednevekovoi Rusi* (Moscow, 1988).

[34]The legislation: *Zakonodatel'nye akty Russkogo gosudarstva vtoroi poloviny XVI–pervoi poloviny XVII veka. Teksty* (ZA) (Leningrad, 1986), no. 1, p. 29 (not before June 1550); ibid., no. 5, pp. 31–33 (1 May 1551); ibid., no. 36, pp. 55–56 (15 January 1562); ibid., no. 37, p. 56 (9 October 1572). Debate on these laws: Kobrin, *Vlast' i sobstvennost'*, pp. 68–88.

particularly striking example in which a local community complained that its new governor refused to accept the customary bribes that had previously ensured that incumbents would be beholden to local interests.[35]

These strategies allowed Moscow to develop a larger army, with attendant social stratification and tension. In the sixteenth century, Muscovy's military was primarily a cavalry, composed of a landed elite that served seasonally and provided its own equipment, horses, and training. The cavalry army grew steadily in the sixteenth century.[36] Its leadership elite—the "sovereign's court" (*gosudarev dvor*)—grew from a handful of boyars and their courts to about 3,000 men at midsixteenth century.[37] By the seventeenth century, the sovereign's court had evolved a series of ranks (*stol'nik, striapchii*, and the like), and contemporary documents distinguished these men as those "who serve from the Moscow list" (*po Moskovskomu spisku*) as opposed to those who serve from a provincial town (*po gorodu*).[38] According to the remuneration scale of the end at the century, the highest ranks received 3.5 times more land than the lowest provincial gentry. Legislation on dishonor enforced this social hierarchy.

Paralleling this growth of the Moscow-based and provincial cavalry was the creation in the sixteenth century of an expansive noncavalry army with more modern equipment and techniques. At midcentury, musketeers, artillery, and Cossack regiments numbered around 30,000, outnumbering the ca. 21,000 cavalry servitors; by the end of the century, there were about 30,000 cavalrymen, 20,000 musketeers, 3,500 artillerymen, and significant numbers of frontier Cossacks and non-Russian troops (e.g., Bashkirs, Tatars).[39] Often called in English *contract servitors*, these troops did not enjoy tax privileges or the right to own land or peasants. They straddled urban and rural society. Some, such as

[35]Valerie Kivelson, *Autocracy in the Provinces: The Muscovite Gentry and Political Culture in the Seventeenth Century* (Stanford, 1996), chaps. 2–5; Carol Belkin Stevens, *Soldiers on the Steppe. Army Reform and Social Change in Early Modern Russia* (DeKalb, Ill., 1995); Brian L. Davies, *State Power and Community in Early Modern Russia* (Cambridge, England, forthcoming); idem, "Village into Garrison: The Military Peasant Communities in Southern Muscovy," *Russian Review* 51 (1992):481–501; idem, "The Politics of Give and Take: *Kormlenie* as Service Remuneration and Generalized Exchange, 1488–1726," in Kleimola and Lenhoff, eds., *Culture and Identity*, pp. 39–67 (example in his n. 55).

[36]On the cavalry elite, see Richard Hellie, *Enserfment and Military Change in Muscovy* (Chicago and London, 1971); idem, *Slavery in Russia, 1450–1725* (Chicago and London, 1982), pp. 4–18; John L. H. Keep, *Soldiers of the Tsar: Army and Society in Russia, 1462–1874* (Oxford, 1985).

[37]On the *gosudarev dvor*, see Bychkova, *Sostav*; V. D. Nazarov, "O strukture 'Gosudareva dvora' v seredine XVI v.," in *Obshchestvo i gosudarstvo*, pp. 40–54; A. P. Pavlov, *Gosudarev dvor i politicheskaia bor'ba pri Borise Godunove (1584–1605 gg.)* (St. Petersburg, 1992).

[38]On the absence of class tension within the metropolitan or Moscow-based elite, see Zimin, "O politicheskikh predposylkakh," pp. 21–27; V. B. Kobrin, *Vlast' i sobstvennost'*, chaps. 3, 6; Pavlov, *Gosudarev dvor*.

[39]On these ranks, see Stevens, *Soldiers on the Steppe*; Kliuchevskii, *Istoriia soslovii v Rossii* in *Sochineniia*, vol. 6 (1959), lect. 17; Hellie, *Enserfment*, pt. 3, pp. 151–234; Keep, *Soldiers*, chaps. 3–4.

regiments of Cossacks, tended farm plots to supplement income; others lived off the revenues of artisanal work in the off-campaign season. These new communities created social diversity, especially on the frontiers, that blurred the more rigid social distinctions maintained in the Center.

While Muscovy aggressively cultivated its metropolitan and provincial cavalry elite as a means of expanding its military forces and of mobilizing peasant labor, it left a wide range of administrative activity in the hands of communities themselves. In towns, for example, the state cultivated a small elite of merchants (*gosti*), who served as the grand prince's factors, overseeing international trade, collecting tolls and revenues from state monopolies, and the like. They enjoyed tax and land privileges similar to the highest elite. Muscovy's urban artisans and small merchants, however, paid taxes and suffered competition from the artisans and tradesmen of landlords and ecclesiastical institutions such as monasteries who enjoyed tax immunities. Towns enjoyed limited self-government through communes (*posady*), which oversaw day-to-day governance and constituted a liaison with the grand prince's governor.[40]

Communal organization similarly provided the backbone of day-to-day administration among the peasants, whether in the far North where peasant *volosti* persisted or on landlords' properties. Landlords often governed through peasant communes and their boards of elders, with only the wealthiest among them employing bailiffs. Peasant communes had oversight in day-to-day issues of law and order, cooperative agrarian endeavors, and tax collection.[41] At the level of individuals, a wide degree of authority was left to landlords, family patriarchs, communal elders, and the church. Family patriarchs exerted authority over households of slaves, serfs, women, children, and other dependents; social welfare was left to families, neighbors, communes, landlords, parishes, monasteries, and the religious hierarchy. The Orthodox Church itself constituted a nexus of diffused power. It wielded extensive authority as a landlord over its peasant villages and urban settlements, and it acted as the societal arbiter of cultural expression, promoting a theocratic, patriarchal, and hierarchic view of society and state that complemented the ruler's assertions of autocracy. By age-old statutes and tradition, the Orthodox Church, with its law codes derived from Byzantium, had jurisdiction over all the Muscovite Orthodox pop-

[40]On townsmen, see P. P. Smirnov, *Posadskie liudi i ikh klassovaia bor'ba do serediny XVII veka*, 2 vols. (Moscow and Leningrad, 1947–48), and J. Michael Hittle, *The Service City: State and Townsmen in Russia, 1600–1800* (Cambridge, Mass., and London, 1979). On merchants, see Samuel H. Baron, "Who were the *Gosti*?" *California Slavic Studies* 7 (1973):1–40, and Paul Bushkovitch, *The Merchants of Muscovy, 1580–1650* (Cambridge, England, 1980).

[41]On peasant communes, see L. V. Cherepnin and V. D. Nazarov, "Krestianstvo na Rusi v seredine XII–kontse XV v.," in Z. V. Udal'tsova, ed., *Istoriia krest'ianstva v Evrope. Epokha feodalizma*, 3 vols. (Moscow, 1985–86), 2:250–86; Blum, *Lord and Peasant*, chap. 6; Veselovskii, *Selo i derevnia*. See Steven Hoch's argument on the tyranny of communes: *Serfdom and Social Control in Russia: Petrovskoe, A Village in Tambov* (Chicago, 1986).

ulace in crimes declared church related and nearly total jurisdiction, save for the highest crimes, for individuals living on its lands. Thus the picture is of a centralized state mobilizing only a narrow range of essential resources and services, devolving administrative authority or tolerating local autonomies as expedient. The same situation of calculated decentralization is evident in legal practice.

In legal reform, for example, Muscovite rulers moved toward standardization by issuing two law codes (1497, 1550) that served as judge's handbooks, sketching out procedure, court fees, and laws on particular issues. At the same time, however, other codes served different purposes or communities. Church courts used ecclesiastical law codes, portions of which dated back to Kiev Rus'. The *Russkaia pravda*, a compendium of East Slavic customary law dating from the Kievan era, continued to circulate in Muscovite lands, presumably for village courts (a new redaction was done in the early seventeenth century). In 1589, a version of the 1550 Moscow law code, adapted to the social structure and economic patterns of the North, was compiled but not officially sanctioned; contemporary sources also cite a separate Perm' law code (*Zyrianskii sudebnik*).[42] Thus, even Muscovy's striving toward judicial uniformity was belied by the multiplicity of judicial venues, without, apparently, interfering with its overall project of mobilization. All in all, sixteenth-century governance amounted to a patchwork quilt of forms and practices: peasant communes in the North; corporate estates in the west; *iasak*-paying tribes and indigenous elites on the Middle Volga and in Siberia; governors presiding over a motley array of Cossacks, musketeers, and siege forces on the steppe frontier; and provincial gentry and boyar elite with their dependent peasants in the Center. The Kremlin maintained its claims to high justice, taxation, and military and diplomatic affairs, and local communities bore the brunt of mundane administration.[43]

All this evidence suggests that the tsars' claim of autocracy encompassed a remarkably varied political economy. Although this approach was pragmatic and functioned in the sixteenth century, it existed in tension with the state's continued desire to mobilize resources. The better Moscow's rulers could knit together their disparate lands, the better they would accomplish their goals. They had a

[42]On codes, see Daniel H. Kaiser, *The Growth of the Law in Medieval Russia* (Princeton, N.J., 1980); idem, "Law, Russian (Muscovite), 1300–1500," in Joseph R. Strayer, ed., *Dictionary of the Middle Ages*, 13 vols. (New York, 1982–89), 7 (1986): 506–12; Hans-Joachim Torke, "Sudebnik," in idem, ed., *Lexikon der Geschichte Russlands* (Munich, 1985), pp. 370–71. Perm' code: S. K. Bakhrushin, "Komi," in *Ocherki istorii SSSR. Period feodalizma. Konets XV v.–nachalo XVII v.* (Moscow, 1955), p. 648.

[43]As difficult as it was when the prevailing orthodoxy exaggerated Muscovy's centralization, some Soviet scholars tried to argue for the diversity of Muscovy's governing strategies: Tikhomirov, *Rossiia v XVI stoletii*; Veselovskii, "Poslednie udely"; Zimin, "Lenin"; idem, "O politicheskikh predposylkakh."

hard row to hoe, however, as they tried to forge even minimal cohesion. Leaving to Chapter 5 a consideration of the strategies of integration that the state employed, one among them being the rhetoric and practice of honor, let us here reflect on what this means for an understanding of Russian autocracy.

The Nature of Autocracy

On one hand, the nature of Muscovite autocracy seems self-evident: It was despotic, nearly totalitarian. Such a conception has a long heritage. Marshall Poe has demonstrated that the trope of Muscovy as a despotic state was imposed by European (English, German) travelers to Muscovy in the sixteenth and seventeenth centuries and grew as much from their local prejudices and classical education as from their familiarity with the practice of Muscovite autocratic power. This view was sustained by nineteenth-century statist scholarship and reinvigorated in the twentieth century because of Cold War tensions between the West and Stalin's Russia.[44] The most salient feature of this approach is the sharp distinction it draws between Muscovy and Europe, which is idealized as the normative model of development.

This contrast is based by and large on abstract concepts of legality, rather than on an analysis of the practice of autocracy. It emphasizes the inadequacies of Russia's juridical development in comparison with that of Europe, particularly with regard to the rights of communities and individuals. Muscovy did not share the traditional hallmarks of the European (read French, British, and to some extent, German) path of development: There were no legal limits on the power of the tsar, and Muscovy had no enfranchised corporate bodies or representative institutions of a truly constitutional, parliamentary type. From a juridical point of view, Muscovy did not have feudalism, with its implicit guarantees of reciprocal political rights, private property, and sanctity of law. In sum, Muscovy would seem to live up to the interpretation that holds that government was arbitrary, rule uniformly administered, and society disenfranchised and passive.

On the other hand, the above description of Muscovite governance strikes a dissonant chord, inasmuch as it depicts Muscovy in terms that should sound familiar to readers of current early modern European historiography. Simply put, current work on early modern European politics is moving beyond the traditional juridical focus and evolutionary framework to explore the complexities

---

[44]Richard Pipes' *Russia under the Old Regime* (New York, 1974) is a classic statement, but his work culminates a line of interpretation that goes back to the sixteenth century. See Marshall Poe, "'Russian Despotism': The Origins and Dissemination of an Early Modern Commonplace," Ph.D. dissertation, University of California, Berkeley, 1993.

of the practice of state power. Recent work on early modern absolutism provides a good example. Once seen as a sort of totalizing vehicle for the destruction of feudal classes,[45] absolutism in Europe is now presented as an expedient amalgam of new political claims executed through the co-optation and involvement of traditional elites, corporate institutions, and mind-sets. Historians are focusing on clientelism and patronage and on personal and affective ties, finding them more significant structures of power than the once-assumed categorical shift to rational bureaucracy, "new men," and parliamentary institutions.[46] Microhistorical studies have demonstrated the tremendous diversity that early modern European monarchs presided over, tolerated, and manipulated—diversity in regional customs, in social groups and their legal statuses, in language and confessions, in deviance from official norms, and the like.[47] Such historical work is paralleled by shifts in theory away from totalizing paradigms, especially evolutionary ones, and toward the interplay of people and institutions in the *practice* of politics.[48]

Regarding the key issue of legality, the early modern European experience is proving more complex than the traditional presumptions of rule by law would indicate. Significantly, a recent study of the phenomenon of aristocracy in European history manages to avoid any mention of juridical privileges, finding the essence of aristocracy in such practices as endogamous marriage patterns, privileged access to resources and political position, distinct patterns of education and culture, and the like[49]; and scholarship since Sir Lewis Namier has exposed the extralegal machinations of politics in early modern parliamentary institutions so central to the older construction of a normative European path. Mark Kishlansky, for example, argues that parliamentary elections in England through the midseventeenth century were governed by a principle of "harmonious choice" rather than by "contest" over principle and ideology. Harmonious choice, he argues, "knit the local society together. . . . It was a ritual of

---

[45]J. Russell Major traces the demise of the old paradigm and sums up historiography in *From Renaissance Monarchy to Absolute Monarchy* (Baltimore and London, 1994); he discusses his idea of the early modern "transition from feudalism to clientelism" in "Bastard Feudalism and the Kiss . . .," *Journal of Interdisciplinary History* 17, no. 3 (1987):509–35.

[46]Nicholas Henshall sums up recent literature in a forceful argument against the old paradigm: *The Myth of Absolutism: Change and Continuity in Early Modern European Monarchy* (London, 1992). A good example is William Beik, *Absolutism and Society in Seventeenth-Century France: State Power and Provincial Aristocracy in Languedoc* (Cambridge, England, 1985).

[47]For microhistory, see Emmanuel Le Roy Ladurie, *Montaillou*, trans. Barbara Bray (New York, 1979); Carlo Ginzburg, *The Cheese and the Worms*, trans. John and Anne Tedeschi (Baltimore, 1980); idem, *The Night Battles*, trans. John and Anne Tedeschi (New York, 1985); Natalie Zemon Davis, *Fiction in the Archives* (Stanford, 1987).

[48]For critiques of evolutionary perspectives, see Robert W. Gordon, "Critical Legal Histories," *Stanford Law Review* 36 (1984):57–125, and Sherry B. Ortner, "Theory in Anthropology since the Sixties," *Comparative Studies in Society and History* 26 (1984):126–66.

[49]Jonathan Powis, *Aristocracy* (Oxford, 1984).

affirmation that bound the participants to each other and recreated their collective identity."[50] As our conceptions of early modern Europe change, with more attention to praxis, Muscovy looks more a part of an early modern European continuum.

Recent scholarship on Muscovy, for example, looks beyond both the traditional equation of autocracy with despotic power and the Soviet Marxist view of the state as the embodiment of dominant class oppression.[51] It is less tied to evolutionary schemes of development based on a model of European progress, and explores structures in an "anthropological" manner, to use Peter Burke's phrase.[52] And it presents a conception of Russian autocracy that accommodates a dynamic interaction between state and society that cannot be captured in juridical terms alone.

Tension over the nature of Muscovite political power, however, is palpable in the historiography and well exemplified by a debate between Richard Pipes and George Weickhardt.[53] Concerning the nature of private property in Muscovite Russia, Pipes argued that because the tsar could in theory always confiscate property (and often did in practice), there was no true private property and no rule by law in premodern Russia. Weickhardt, admitting the tsar's theoretical right to confiscate, pointed out that rulers did so relatively rarely and argued that confiscations were limited by law to allegations of treason, that the day-to-day practice of landholding indicated de facto private ownership, and that judicial practice demonstrated predictability and consistency. Weickhardt's argument is reminiscent of Richard Hellie's stance. Ordinarily no friend to the Muscovite centralized state (in much of his work Hellie has emphasized the slavery of the people and the "hypertrophy" of state power), he nevertheless avers that Muscovy possessed "a high degree of 'legality'": "[W]hile law and autocracy may diverge in theory, the law seems to have been applied properly most of the time. . . . [E]arly modern Russian authorities achieved explicit

---

[50]Mark A. Kishlansky, *Parliamentary Selection: Social and Political Choice in Early Modern England* (Cambridge, England, 1986), p. 226.

[51]Soviet historians did not take the European Marxist turn toward a Gramscian appreciation of cultural hegemony and a more complex model of causation (despite some parallel experimentation in the 1960s; see essays collected in Samuel H. Baron and Nancy W. Heer, eds., *Windows on the Russian Past: Essays on Soviet Historiography since Stalin* [Columbus, Ohio, 1977]). Nor did it take an Annales-type move toward material and social history grounded in a nonevolutionary scheme of historical change. On recent trends, see Kivelson, *Autocracy in the Provinces*; Stevens, *Soldiers on the Steppe*; Davies, *State Power*; Michels, "The Violent Old Belief."

[52]Peter Burke distinguishes social history from historical anthropology by the latter's lesser emphasis on change over time: *Historical Anthropology*, chap. 1.

[53]George Weickhardt, "The Pre-Petrine Law of Property," *Slavic Review* 52, no. 4 (1993):663–79; Richard Pipes, "Was There Private Property in Muscovite Russia?" *Slavic Review* 53, no. 2 (1994):524–30; George Weickhardt, "Reply," ibid.:531–38. Central to the debate is also George G. Weickhardt, "Due Process and Equal Justice in the Muscovite Codes," *Russian Review* 51 (1992): 463–80.

and noncontradictory rules that were publicized, made available, and administered as decreed."[54] Ultimately, Pipes' and Weickhardt's stances may be irrec-
oncilable, because they are based on different visions of the role of law in a
putative European historical path.

The stakes in such debates are high because of their presentist implications. For those who see autocracy as despotism, Russia's future today is
doomed, because it lacks essential legal preconditions for modern liberal
development. For those who see autocracy as less powerful in practice than
in claim, Russia's future potential is less gloomy, because its history provides
evidence of agency and voluntarism. The prognosis is somewhere in
between. Undoubtedly Russia still needs to confront its historical legacies of
serfdom, weak urban development, and minimal education and literacy,
which disadvantage it in the "European" comparison. It might be argued, however, that the absence of legal charters and corporate estates is not a categorical obstacle toward progress. Although prediction is not our task here, it is
safe to say that these presentist debates provide perhaps the deepest level of
significance of this research on honor. It is my goal here to stimulate rethink-
ing of the nature of power in Russian history by exploring the practice of
honor, a practice that contrasts the rhetoric of authority with the negotiation
of those discourses and that sees state power as comprised in large part by the
actions of individuals and social communities performing as knowledgeable
actors within received political institutions.

Sources

Source materials on honor in early modern Russia are relatively scarce; particularly lacking are narrative discussions of honor and the "honorable man"
comparable to the extensive early modern European literature on these themes.
In sixteenth- and seventeenth-century England and France, for example, humanist debates recast the concept of honor away from the medieval emphasis on
birth and military valor toward a new focus on religious piety and civic virtue.
In sixteenth- and seventeenth-century Italy, a broad literature explored the intri-
cacies of honor and insult (the "point of honor") and the proper execution of
the duel.[55] Across Europe, handbooks for the aspiring nobleman dictated standards of civility and politesse that became the hallmarks of elite "men of honor."

---

[54]Richard Hellie, "Early Modern Russian Law: The Ulozhenie of 1649," *Russian History* 15,
nos. 2–4 (1988):179; idem, *Slavery in Russia, 1450–1725*; idem, "The Structure of Modern Russian History: Toward a Dynamic Model," *Russian History* 4, no. 1 (1977):1–22.

[55]See Mervyn James, "English Politics"; Ellery Schalk, *From Valor to Pedigree: Ideas of Nobility in France in the Sixteenth and Seventeenth Centuries* (Princeton, N.J., 1986); Bryson, *Point of
Honor*; Muir, *Mad Blood*, chap. 8.

Muscovy was not a society with a habit for such learned discourse. In the sixteenth and seventeenth centuries, the rural population was primarily illiterate; the very small merchant and artisan classes displayed limited, functional literacy only. The cavalry elite similarly focused on military valor and religious piety, but did not engage in literary life. Even among the boyars, literacy was virtually unknown until the mid- to late seventeenth century. Pockets of literacy existed among monks and church hierarchs, but not among parish clergy. Outside of church and monastic scriptoria, the greatest concentration of literacy was in the Kremlin ministries, where secretaries and undersecretaries (*d'iaki* and *pod'iachie*) possessed secular (Russian chancery language)—not learned (Slavonic)—literacy and did not apply their knowledge to nonbureaucratic genres until the midseventeenth century. Most important, Muscovy lacked professions: There were no lawyers, no universities or seminaries, almost no secondary schools, and no traditions of learned country gentlemen. Printing got under way, under church supervision, in the 1620s and focused primarily on ecclesiastical works.[56] Thus, although honor was palpable to Muscovites, there was little social or institutional support for narrative reflection on it.

Some reflections on honor did appear in the church's moralistic and penitential texts, but by and large clerics devoted themselves to different genres and concerns: combating heresy in disquisitions; tracing the Russian past as a strand in the ongoing chronicle of universal Christendom in annals; developing a quasi-theocratic ideology of church and state in liturgical ritual, art, and court ceremony; and creating pietistic resources in hagiography and homilies. But clerical writers also preached moral behavior in didactic texts, such as the fourteenth-century *Emerald* and *Bee* and the later *Domostroi*, a source that merits particular attention. Produced in the midsixteenth century at either Novgorod or Moscow, the *Domostroi* shows signs of foreign provenance and Russian reworking. Some of its sixty-plus chapters outline a patriarchal and Orthodox system of values based on deference to God, tsar, family, and father, while others convey practical instruction for household managers—in other words, for women—on such matters as gardening, canning, cooking, and managing household servants. Given the low rate of lay literacy in sixteenth-century Muscovy, it is difficult to see for whom this compendium was useful, and indeed its manuscript history suggests that it circulated among a small

[56]On literacy, see Gary J. Marker, "Printers and Literacy in Muscovy: A Taxonomic Investigation," *Russian Review* 48, no. 1 (1989):1–20, and idem, "Literacy and Literacy Texts in Muscovy: A Reconsideration," *Slavic Review* 49, no. 1 (1990):74–89. On the quantity and content of printed books, see Gary J. Marker, *Publishing, Printing and the Origins of Intellectual Life in Russia, 1700–1800* (Princeton, N.J., 1985), chap. 1, and V. S. Rumiantseva, "Tendentsiia razvitiia obshchestvennogo soznaniia i prosveshcheniia v Rossii XVII veka," *Voprosy istorii*, no. 2 (1988):26–40.

readership of priests, merchants, boyars, and landed provincial gentry.[57] The code of values it depicts should be regarded as an idealized one, but as we will see in Chapter 1, it is compatible with the concerns Muscovites expressed when they complained about insults to their honor. Other, more secular primers and handbooks of deportment began to circulate in Russia only in the late seventeenth and especially the eighteenth century in response to the growth of the landed and civil service elite and the ready reception of European culture and social norms.[58] Precisely because they represent new systems of values, they do not help in analyzing honor in sixteenth- and seventeenth-century Russia.

Foreign travelers' accounts of early modern Russia are seductively attractive with regard to honor and social values. Visitors to Muscovy such as the German diplomat Sigismund von Herberstein, the Elizabethan envoy Giles Fletcher, and the German scholar Adam Olearius, to name a few, were ethnographically inclined to a surprising degree, pausing to describe daily life, dress, marriage customs, and behavior among the elite (Herberstein) and the peasantry (Olearius). But the picture they present is on the whole negative, colored by the common trope that Russia's "nobility" and people were uncultured, servile, and prone to violence, quite the opposite of contemporary European civilization.[59] A similarly rich but less tainted source is Grigorii Kotoshikhin's description of Muscovite governmental institutions and practices, written in exile for the Swedish king between 1666 and 1667. This work gives attention to court politics and the household life of the tsar and boyars and is a good source on judicial procedure, including the defense of honor.[60]

In the end, however, we are left with legal materials as our primary sources for the study of honor in Muscovy. As discussed in greater detail in Chapter 1, the laws are laconic. They give standards of compensation and punishment for

[57]Carolyn Johnston Pouncy, ed. and trans., *The Domostroi: Rules for Russian Households in the Time of Ivan the Terrible* (Ithaca, N.Y., 1994), pp. 37–49, and idem, "The *Domostroi* as a Source for Muscovite History," Ph.D. dissertation, Stanford University, 1985.

[58]Gary J. Marker, "The Petrine 'Civil Primer' Reconsidered: A New Look at the Publishing History of the 'Grazhdanskaia Azbuka', 1708–1727," *Solanus* (1989):25–39; J. L. Black, *Citizens for the Fatherland: Education, Educators, and Pedagogical Ideals in Eighteenth Century Russia* (New York, 1979), pp. 209–66; Max Okenfuss, *The Discovery of Childhood in Russia* (Newtonville, Mass., 1980).

[59]Poe, "'Russian Despotism'"; Larry Wolff, *Inventing Eastern Europe: The Map of Civilization on the Mind of the Enlightenment* (Stanford, 1994). For bibliography of travel accounts, see Marshall Poe, *Foreign Descriptions of Muscovy: An Analytic Bibliography of Primary and Secondary Sources* (Columbus, Ohio, 1995), and *Istoriia dorevoliutsionnoi Rossii v dnevnikakh i vospominaniiakh*, ed. P. A. Zaionchkovskii, 5 vols. in 13 pts. (Moscow, 1976–1989), vol. 1 (1976).

[60]Grigorii Kotoshikhin, *O Rossii vo tsarstvovanie Alekseia Mikhailovicha*, 4th ed. (St. Petersburg, 1906); English translation: "On Russia in the Reign of Alexis Mikhailovich," trans. Benjamin P. Uroff, Ph.D. dissertation, Columbia University, 1970.

insult to honor but do not define honor in either an explicit or theoretical way. Until the nineteenth century, there was no law that specifically addressed defamation by slander or libel.[61] We must turn to court cases to define honor and trace how individuals and communities used it, but these court cases too are problematic.

I have gathered a database of more than one thousand cases of precedence (*mestnichestvo*), of which some are archival but most published. A few of the precedence cases are mammoth compendia of legal precedents submitted in support of the litigants; most are telegraphically short, noting the names of the litigants and a quick, on-the-spot resolution. By contrast, suits for dishonor (*beschest'e*) are Rabelaisian in content, reflecting the raucous world of insult and injury in all possible settings. Dishonor suits in Moscow and provincial archives, most of them still unpublished, number into the thousands. I have compiled a database of more than six hundred archival and published *beschest'e* suits (for more on these sources and the database, see Chapter 1). The typical "case" consists of an initial petition and often a rejoinder by the defendant; some cases include testimony from witnesses. Very few describe full judicial procedure including the verdict: For only slightly more than one-fourth of the suits in the database do we know the resolution. The remaining cases were settled out of court, or their records have been lost to posterity. Thus, dishonor suits are generally fragmentary and brief. There are few full-blown narratives, only fleeting glimpses of the lives of men and women in all of Muscovy's regions and social statuses. Nevertheless, in the aggregate these suits give a consistent, compelling impression of how honor served Muscovites.

Given the paucity of sources other than litigation, it is not surprising that the historiography on honor in Muscovy is weakly developed. That is not the case for precedence (*mestnichestvo*), which has merited extensive attention because it represented, in many historians' views, a struggle between tsar and elite for power. On the theme of dishonor (*beschest'e*), only a few articles can be found, most of them drawing on published laws and court cases: Nikolai Lange examined standards of punishment in dishonor suits; Serge Levitsky surveyed the law; B. N. Floria analyzed the social hierarchy implicit in dishonor fines; and Horace W. Dewey surveyed the practice of dishonor litigation, linking its emergence in the sixteenth century with Muscovy's increasing

---

[61]On defamation in Imperial Russian law, see K. P. Pobedonostsev, *Kurs grazhdanskogo prava. Pt. 3: Dogovory i obiazatel'stva* (St. Petersburg, 1896), pp. 589–97; D. I. Meier, *Russkoe grazhdanskoe pravo*, 5th ed. (Moscow, 1873), pp. 178–79; two articles by V. N. [V. M. Nechaev] and K. K. [K. A. Krasuskii] on "Obida lichnaia" in *Entsiklopedicheskii slovar'* (St. Petersburg, 1897) 21a:504–7; G. Sl. [G. B. Sliuzberg], "Kleveta," in ibid. 15 (1895):332–34; V. Spasovich, "O prestupleniakh protiv chesti chastnykh lits po ulozheniiu o nakazaniiakh 1845 goda," *Zhurnal Ministerstva iustitsii* 3, pt. 2 (1860):3–44.

social stratification.[62] Two studies survey literate opinion on honor from the Kievan era through the seventeenth century, while a handful of essays trace the evolution of European-influenced laws on defamation in nineteenth-century Russia.[63] This literature does not put forward a comprehensive interpretation about the role of honor and dishonor in Muscovy, nor has it prompted debates about its significance in Russian history.

The absence of narrative disquisitions on honor may be a blessing in disguise; the theories of jurists and philosophers can obscure a messy reality. With our sources primarily judicial, the voices of individuals come through, although of course in the idiom of court practice. Only a diary, memoir, or epistolary source could give us a firmer grasp of how people internalized the concept of honor, but such sources are the exception anywhere in early modern Europe, let alone Muscovy.

Theories of Honor

Before launching into the thick of Muscovite insult and anger, it would help us to reflect in general terms on the meaning of honor in premodern societies. Richard van Dülmen wrote that "in hardly any society does honor play so great a role as in the early modern society of orders."[64] Indeed, honor was ubiquitous in early modern Europe, and this circumstance immediately sets these societies apart from our own. The sociologist Peter Berger wrote that to us moderns, the concept of honor is hopelessly antiquated: "Honor occupies about the same place in contemporary usage as chastity. An individual asserting it hardly invites admiration, and one who claims to have lost it is an object

---

[62]Nikolai I. Lange, "O nakaniiakh [sic] i vzyskaniakh za beschestie po drevnemu russkomu pravu," *Zhurnal Ministerstva narodnogo prosveshcheniia* 102 (1859):161–224; Serge Levitsky, "Protection of Individual Honour and Dignity in Pre-Petrine Russian Law," *Revue d'histoire du droit/Tijdschrift voor rechitsgeschiedenis* 40, nos. 3–4 (1972):341–436; B. N. Floria, "'Beschest'e' russkogo feodala XV–XVI vv.," *Russkoe tsentralizovannoe gosudarstvo* (Moscow, 1980), pp. 42–44; idem, "Formirovanie soslovnogo statusa gospodstvuiushchego klassa drevnei Rusi (Na materiale statei o vozmeshchenii za 'beschest'e')," *Istoriia SSSR* 1983, no. 1 (1983):61–74; Horace W. Dewey, "Old Muscovite Concepts of Injured Honor (*Beschestie*)," *Slavic Review* 27, no. 4 (1968):594–603. See also my "Honor and Dishonor in Early Modern Russia," *Forschungen* 46 (1992):131–46; idem, "Was There Honor in Kiev Rus'?" *Jahrbücher für Geschichte Osteuropas*, 36, no. 4 (1988):481–92; idem, "Women's Honor in Early Modern Russia," in Barbara Evans Clements, Barbara Alpern Engel, and Christine D. Worobec, eds., *Russia's Women: Accommodation, Resistance, Transformation* (Berkeley, 1991), pp. 60–73.

[63]L. A. Chernaia, "'Chest': Predstavleniia o chesti i beschestii v russkoi literature XI–XVII vv.," in A. S. Demin, ed., *Drevnerusskaia literatura. Izobrazhenie obshchestva* (Moscow, 1991), pp. 56–84; Helen Y. Prochazka, "On Concepts of Patriotism, Loyalty, and Honour in the Old Russian Military Accounts," *Slavonic and East European Review* 63, no. 4 (1985):481–97.

[64]Van Dülmen, *Kultur und Alltag* 2:194.

of amusement rather than sympathy." For a modern person, insult is virtually incomprehensible unless it involves material rather than merely psychological damage.[65] But to many premodern people, honor itself was a tangible good. Shakespeare, of course, is an authority: "He that filches from me my good name / Robs me of that which not enriches him, / And makes me poor indeed." But there is other, more prosaic evidence as well. In 1696, a Yorkshire woman upbraided gossipers for defaming another woman, declaring "they might as well take her life as her good name from her." And Peter Moogk notes that mideighteenth-century French Canadians were observed to be "more keen to acquire high esteem than to amass riches."[66] Honor was important in premodern terms because it acted as a symbolic language with which to communicate status and identity, as well as a social praxis with which to defend or advance same.

Most fundamentally, honor is a cultural construct that shapes both personal identity and place in community. The sociologist Erving Goffman argued that identity is constructed by inculcation with norms and attitudes that may come to seem natural in a particular group, class, or culture, but, he cautions, that are not really natural at all: "Universal human nature is not a very human thing. By acquiring it, the person becomes a kind of construct, built up not from inner psychic propensities but from moral rules that are impressed upon him from without." He calls socially constructed identity the "face" a person puts toward the world and argues that "saving face" is crucial to maintaining identity. Goffman points out that if a person is careful to save face "primarily from duty to himself, one speaks in our society of pride; when he does so because of duty to wider social units, and receives support from these units in doing so, one speaks of honor."[67] In other words, honor is personal identity socially ratified. This inescapable link between personal esteem and public

[65] Peter Berger, "On the Obsolescence of the Concept of Honour," in Michael J. Sandel, ed., *Liberalism and Its Critics* (New York, 1984), p. 149. But see William Ian Miller's essay on the honor implicit in modern social interaction: *Humiliation: and Other Essays on Honor, Social Discomfort and Violence* (Ithaca, N.Y., 1993). See also other studies on honor in the modern day: Robert A. Nye, *Masculinity and Male Codes of Honor in Modern France* (New York, 1993); Kevin McAleer, *Dueling: The Cult of Honor in Fin-de-Siècle Germany* (Princeton, N.J., 1994).

[66] Shakespeare: *Othello* 3.3.153–55. Yorkshire woman: Sharpe, *Defamation*, p. 3. On French Canada: Moogk cites Pierre F. X. de Charlevoix (1744): "'Thieving Buggers' and 'Stupid Sluts': Insults and Popular Culture in New France," *The William and Mary Quarterly*, 3d ser. 36, no. 4 (1979):534. Similarly, the title of Guido Ruggiero's article makes this point: "'More Dear to Me than Life Itself': Marriage, Honor and a Woman's Reputation in the Renaissance," in idem, *Binding Passions: Tales of Magic, Marriage and Power at the End of the Renaissance* (New York, 1993), pp. 57–87.

[67] Goffman, "On Face Work," in *Interaction Ritual* (Chicago, 1967), pp. 9–10, 45. Clifford Geertz makes much the same analysis of culture in general: "Undirected by culture patterns—organized systems of significant symbols—man's behavior would be virtually ungovernable." *The Interpretation of Cultures: Selected Essays* (New York, 1973), p. 46.

approbation puts the symbolic discourse of honor at the heart of understanding a premodern society's social structures and relationships.

Anthropologists have devoted significant attention to honor, followed more recently by historians, many of them cited above. The anthropological study of honor was launched in the 1960s, primarily by scholars of the Mediterranean region.[68] In search of fundamental social values, they put forward the linked concepts of *honor* and *shame*.[69] "Honor and shame" societies, they argued, were primarily small-scale agrarian face-to-face (or as one scholar wryly put it, in reference to endemic village squabbles, "back-to-back") communities "where the social personality of the actor is as significant as his office." Such communities tend to have loose social boundaries and to be agonistic or conflict-ridden: "Within the minimal solidary groups of these societies, be they small or large families or clans, spheres of action are well defined, non-overlapping and non-competitive. . . . [But] outside these groups . . . [honor] has to be asserted and vindicated."[70] Honor works, then, as a means to define social insiders and outsiders.

Most noteworthy in the Mediterranean is the central position of women in the social value system. Women held the key to a family's honor because of their sexual power: Promiscuity could disgrace families, whereas modesty reflected well on the family unit. Women were thus expected to cultivate "shame," whereas men's honor was calculated by their success in defending their family's women from insult. Male honor could be enhanced by sexual exploits with other men's women, married or unmarried, actions that created tension in the system. Honor is thus a tangible aspect of a family's resources, "symbolic capital" in Pierre Bourdieu's phrase,[71] and a weapon with which rivalries, ambitions, and all manner of conflict can be played out.[72]

Early modern Muscovy shows great affinities with Mediterranean honor and shame societies, and this anthropological literature is thus all the more apt

---

[68]The initial statement is in Peristiany, ed., *Honour and Shame*. Continuations of the project include David D. Gilmore, ed., *Honor and Shame and the Unity of the Mediterranean* (Washington, D.C., 1987), and J. G. Peristiany and Julian Pitt-Rivers, eds., *Honor and Grace in Anthropology* (Cambridge, England, 1992).

[69]Revisionist theory centers on Michael Herzfeld's argument that hospitality was a more central ethic in these societies than honor and shame: "'As in Your Own House': Hospitality, Ethnography, and the Stereotype of Mediterranean Society," in Gilmore, ed., *Honor and Shame*, pp. 75–89.

[70]Peristiany, "Introduction," in idem, ed., *Honour and Shame*, p. 11.

[71]Pierre Bourdieu, *Outline of a Theory of Practice*, trans. Richard Nice (Cambridge, England, 1977), pp. 171–83. Others cite the belief that honor was a zero-sum game (if you insulted someone, the honor they lost became your gain): Thomas V. Cohen and Elizabeth S. Cohen, *Words and Deeds in Renaissance Rome* (Toronto, 1993), pp. 24–25.

[72]See Christopher Boehm, *Blood Revenge: The Enactment and Management of Conflict in Montenegro and Other Tribal Societies* (Philadelphia, 1984).

for us.[73] Julian Pitt-Rivers pointed out the "complexity" of honor, the fact that it can simultaneously play different roles in society and for individuals. Chronicling some of those significances, from the personal to the social, Pitt-Rivers noted that honor can be a personal calculation of self-esteem; a socially esteemed attribute, such as chastity; an impersonal measure of achievement, such as an office or political precedence; or a means for collective definition of groups, such as families, clans, guilds, or nations. Honor can even be linked with the sacred and with political authority: A person's true honor can be construed as the essence given to him by God or by the temporal rulers who are God's worldly delegates.[74] Economic status, gender, social role, and political position all shaped definitions of honor—almost universally, it seems, standards of honorable behavior for women diverged from those for men. In some places and times, honor had a strong corporate character. In early modern Europe, for example, guilds elaborated and assiduously defended a code of artisanal honor quite distinct from honor for noblemen; whole social groups were declared "dishonorable" because their professions were considered unclean (butchers, executioners, and others).[75] European nobilities, as noted above, developed an exclusive code of honor in the early modern period in response to social change. In Muscovy, by contrast, codes of honor made few qualitative distinctions between social groups, perhaps reflecting Muscovy's absence of corporate bodies and its less complex social stratification.

It is the ambiguity, tension, and necessary dependence between the public and private aspects of honor that make it so socially versatile. Where a society accords a high value to personal honor, the state can wield the discourse of honor in its own interest. As Pitt-Rivers puts it, "transactions of honour . . . not only provide, on the psychological side, a nexus between the ideals of society and their reproduction in the actions of individuals . . . but, on the social side, between the ideal order and the terrestrial order, validating the realities of power and making the sanctified order of precedence correspond to them." Because identity is grounded in social values, "social integration" is advanced as well as "the legitimation of established power." In a similar vein, Elvin Hatch argues that people respect honor because they derive satisfaction and self-esteem from internalized social values that simultaneously affirm dominant discourses.[76]

---

[73]Those working with the Mediterranean "honor and shame" paradigm include Ramon A. Gutierrez, "Marriage, Sex and the Family: Social Change in Colonial New Mexico, 1690–1846," Ph.D. dissertation, University of Wisconsin, 1980; Patricia Seed, *To Love, Honor and Obey in Colonial Mexico: Conflicts over Marriage Choice, 1574–1821* (Stanford, 1988); Peter Burke, *Historical Anthropology*; Thomas Cohen and Elizabeth Cohen, *Words and Deeds*; Elizabeth Cohen, "Honor and Gender."

[74]Julian Pitt-Rivers, "Honor," *International Encyclopedia of the Social Sciences* 6 (1968):503–11.

[75]Farr, *Hands of Honor*; Stuart, "Boundaries of Honor"; Dinges, "Die Ehre."

[76]Pitt-Rivers, "Honour and Social Status," in Peristiany, ed., *Honour and Shame*, p. 38; Elvin Hatch, "Theories of Social Honor," *American Anthropologist* 91 (1989):341–53.

But honor is not merely a static tool of social control. It is also an independent cultural discourse that individuals can manipulate, recreate, and modify for individual or group self-interest. Cultural norms like honor, as Pitt-Rivers wrote, are

> a structure of conflicting premises within which the struggle for dominance took place. . . . The achievement of honor was not then simply a refraction or demonstration of the reality of power or precedence, as Thomas Hobbes (*Leviathan*, chapter 10) thought, but also a means of achieving or maintaining them through the control of the definition of honor.[77]

Theory on honor pushes us to look at the destabilizing and interactional roles it played. As Elizabeth Cohen noted, "honor with its norms, its rhetoric and its strong emotional charge offered a set of resources for the conduct of interpersonal strife."[78] It is particularly apt for conflict and conflict resolution because of the complementary behavior patterns it prescribes. Reminding one of Wyatt-Brown's twofold definition of "primal honor," Pitt-Rivers speaks of "two opposed—and ultimately complementary—registers" that govern behavior in Western civilization: "the first associated with honor, competition, triumph, the male sex, possession and the profane world, and the other with peace, amity, grace, purity, renunciation, the female sex, dispossession in favor of others, and the sacred." They are complementary because the person who has won dominance must adopt the opposite virtues to merit honor: generosity, magnanimity, moderation.[79]

Theorists often point out that litigation over honor can be the last step in an escalating tension between parties that can then be settled by the cathartic experience of public exposure. Honor gave disputants a symbolic system, ritualistic and ceremonial, with a familiarity to the community that advanced the cause of reconciliation. The execution of a litigation—with public declarations of insult and affront, formulaic and florid language, mediated settlements or sanctions carried out in public—could be a resolving experience. It could also be disruptive, however, if individuals litigated in order to harass. Then artificial delays or continued insults could make it a theater for compounding antagonisms. In either case, the value system and praxis of honor shaped social interaction.

[77]J. G. Peristiany and Julian Pitt-Rivers, "Introduction," in idem, eds., *Honor and Grace*, p. 4.
[78]Cohen, "Honor and Gender," p. 601.
[79]Julian Pitt-Rivers, "Postscript: The Place of Grace in Anthropology," in Peristiany and Pitt-Rivers., eds., *Honor and Grace*, pp. 242–43. Although Pitt-Rivers's gender associations are stereotypical (the sacred is often a male characteristic, as Valerie Kivelson pointed out to me), the theory of complementary registers is helpful.

Looking at the viewpoint of the insulter rather than that of the offended party, we can see further societal functions for honor. Sensitivity to honor makes insult a potent weapon. In order to avoid the humiliation of actually having to defend one's honor, individuals are more inclined to behave by society's norms. If they overstep such bounds, communities could subject them to humiliation, in charivaris for cuckolded husbands or in gestures, taunts, and defilement of private property for people whose morals were deemed by neighbors to be "loose."[80] Thus, while most of the insults uttered and brought to court in honor cases from England to Muscovy may have been uttered in hot blood in the midst of some drunken or heated dispute, others might represent the moralizing or malicious voice of the community trying to control its members.

At root, then, honor can be seen as one of the means to define and police the boundaries of community. Honor gives community members a discourse—a rhetoric and a cultural practice—with which to shape the way they interact, to identify insiders and outsiders in a community, or to pursue conflict. Other ideas and cultural practices (piety, service, or gender roles, for example) complement and complicate these patterns of interaction. Honor as a discourse reflecting social place is sensitive to social change: Conflicts over honor tend to proliferate when societal verities are at risk, when social mobility, economic change, or religious and ideological debate disrupt conventional assessments of identity and disturb the ordering of traditional communities.[81] Defense of honor, then, becomes a means of shoring up status.

All these social functions and psychological meanings of honor make their appearance in early modern Muscovy. Litigations on insult reveal the social constructs deemed appropriate for the smooth functioning of social interaction and social hierarchy in any given society. They reveal the petty tensions of life in face-to-face communities, from village courtyards to city streets to Kremlin palaces. They show how honor values bolstered the social and political status quo, providing an embodiment of an idealized image of state and society. And they demonstrate in their waxing and waning how Muscovites responded to changes in social structure and moral order as they negotiated the turbulent sixteenth and seventeenth centuries.

I explore these various issues by moving from the micro to the macro. Chapter 1 explores the definition of honor in Muscovy, and Chapter 2 links discourse

[80]David Garrioch discusses the potential gain for insulters: "Verbal Insults," p. 116. Elizabeth Cohen depicts the covert shaming of insulters: "Honor and Gender." Natalie Davis finds individuals complaining of being humiliated unjustly in a charivari: "Charivari, Honor." Peter Burke noted that public shaming might be instigated maliciously: *Historical Anthropology*, p. 108.

[81]Sharpe points out the explosion in defamation suits in England during an era of intense social change: *Defamation*. Muir links the rise of the duel and new concepts of noble honor with social change: *Mad Blood*, chap. 8.

with praxis by examining women's central place in Muscovite concepts of honor. Continuing the synchronic or "anthropological" approach and focusing on the praxis of honor, Chapter 3 uses honor litigation as a case study of Muscovite legal culture. In Chapter 4, I analyze the practice of precedence ranking in the elite based on clan honor (*mestnichestvo*). Chapter 5 then places honor in the context of the state's strategies of governance and political integration, devoting particular attention to the rhetoric of autocracy. Chapter 6 assesses change over time, examining the social and political factors that contributed to the abolition of precedence in 1682, with particular attention to the emergence of "absolutist" rhetoric and practices of power. Finally, the Epilogue traces continuities in the social significance of honor into the Imperial period of Russian history.

CHAPTER 1

Cultural Concepts of Honor

Institutions and laws to defend personal honor appeared first in Muscovite law codes and practice in the midsixteenth century. The timing is no coincidence. The protection of honor in various forms was a response to social tension, and the sixteenth century was a time of intense political and social change. I explore here the social setting in which Muscovite protections of honor emerged on the background of long-standing cultural traditions of honor and then turn to Muscovite definitions of honor in practice.

Social Tensions in Sixteenth-Century Russia

As detailed in the Introduction, the sixteenth century was in many respects the classic century of pre-Petrine Russian history. It was the century when Muscovy leapt into the status of imperial power with aggressive conquests stretching from Belarus' to western Siberia; the century when Moscow created enduring institutions of governance based on a privileged landed military elite; the century when the grand princes officially became "tsars," claiming the imperial heritage of Byzantium and of the Golden Horde; the century, according to some schemes, when "centralization" was achieved by defeating "remnants of feudal opposition."[1] However one construes it, the sixteenth century was one of consolidation of power and institution building.

---

[1]There are two variations in presenting the sixteenth century as pivotal. Most historians frame the period with turning points at approximately the midfifteenth and early seventeenth centuries: Robert O. Crummey, "Periodizing 'Feudal' Russian History," in R. C. Elwood, ed., *Russian and East European History: Selected Papers from the Second World Congress for Soviet and East European Studies* (Berkeley, 1984), pp. 17–41. See, for example, S. M. Solov'ev, *Istoriia Rossii s drevneishikh vremen*, 29 vols. in 15 bks. (Moscow, 1959–66), bk. 1, *Predislovie*; and V. O. Kliuchevskii, *Kurs russkoi istorii* in his *Sochineniia*, 8 vols. (Moscow, 1956–59), vols. 1–2 (1956–57), lects. 7, 16, 25. Those who give Ivan IV a generally positive interpretation see the midsixteenth century as climactic: S. F. Platonov, *Ivan the Terrible*, ed. and trans. J. L. Wieczynski with intro. by Richard Hellie (Gulf Breeze, Fla., 1974); and Ruslan G. Skrynnikov, *Ivan the Terrible*, trans. Hugh Graham (Gulf Breeze, Fla., 1981). Janet Martin makes a forceful argument for continuity from Kiev Rus' through the sixteenth century in *Medieval Russia, 980–1584* (Cambridge, England, 1995).

It was, however, also a century of disruption and recasting of communities. Free peasant communes were being transferred to landlords; peasants and townsmen were being recruited into petty gentry, into the contract servitor military units (musketeers, Cossacks, artillery); peasants were being burdened with serving on local tax-collection boards and with other tasks of local government, responsibilities that were generally not welcomed. Local landed elites were being recast with population transfers, new recruitment, new strictures on landholding and inheritance, and new duties presiding over local law and order in the brigandage reform of the 1530s. The boyar elite doubled in size by the midsixteenth century, with newcomers hailing from both newly arrived princely families and indigenous nonprincely families. Whole new social categories were being created—privileged merchants (*gosti*, first attested at midcentury), bureaucratic scribes (*d'iaki* and *pod'iachie*), contract servitors. More and more people were selling themselves into slavery to escape poverty. At the broadest level, the state itself was becoming multiethnic and far more socially diverse with the absorption of non-Slavic lands, although, because colonial policy did not attempt assimilation, imperial expansion may not have had any direct impact on the life experience of people in the rest of the realm, except for the highest elites.

These changes were the result of the state's concerted effort to mobilize its resources in the sixteenth century. It was an intense but not catastrophic process, one that yielded social stress and tension nonetheless. At the same time, however, the state suffered catastrophic disruption that further upset social patterns. Although the hundred years from the mid-1400s to the mid-1500s was a time of economic and demographic growth, the decades from the 1570s through the end of the century witnessed economic devastation from causes natural (famine, epidemic) and political. Ivan IV's *Oprichnina* (1564–72) wreaked havoc on gentry and peasants in the Center and the North. The Livonian War (1558–82) decimated populations in the northwest regions (Novgorod, Pskov areas). The state financed its military and bureaucratic expansion throughout the century with predatory taxation that crippled the populace. The result of these various depredations was impoverishment and depopulation; peasants fled the lands northwest of Moscow and some parts of the Center to the various frontiers or to more accommodating owners. Other peasants and poor gentry opted for personal servitude to landlords as one of the few social safety nets available to them. The state responded with limitations on peasant mobility (limitations that proved nearly impossible to enforce) and cadastral recording to bind peasants to their villages; together these strategies paved the way for enserfment. The state also intensified efforts to prevent peasants, townsmen, and poor gentry from becoming slaves voluntarily.[2]

[2]Jerome Blum, *Lord and Peasant in Russia from the Ninth to the Nineteenth Century* (New York, 1969), chaps. 8, 10, 13, 14; G. V. Abramovich, "Gosudarstvennye povinnosti vladel'cheskikh krest'ian severo-zapadnoi Rusi v XVI–pervoi chetverti XVII veka," *Istoriia SSSR* 3 (1972):63–84; N. A. Rozhkov, *Sel'skoe khoziaistvo Moskovskoi Rusi v XVI veke* (Moscow, 1899); Richard Hellie, *Slavery in Russia, 1450–1725* (Chicago and London, 1982), pp. 4–18.

The life experience of many Muscovites in the sixteenth century challenged social hierarchy and undermined personal security. Traditional communities were recreating themselves. It was in very similar circumstances of social disruption and increasing social stratification in Elizabethan England that J. A. Sharpe observed a sharp rise in defamation suits,[3] and Muscovite concerns about honor also erupted in sixteenth-century conditions. Later a resurgence of suits over honor in the last decades of the seventeenth century can be observed, when social categories again were in flux (see Epilogue). In such circumstances, honor was used as a response to social tensions from the bottom of society up and from the state down.

It was as a very practical mechanism to cope with new configurations at court, in villages, and on the frontier that honor was deployed. People did not respond to disruption with works of narrative literature pondering social change and its causes or with reflections on social structure that were comparable to medieval European essays on the "great chain of being" or early modern disquisitions on civility and honor. Rather, the state responded with the opportunity to litigate and with laconic law codes that listed scales of recompense for insult to honor. For the state, honor was a mechanism for building social stability; for individuals, it was a way to reinforce social status when communities were changing all around. Thus Muscovy's juridical institutions to defend honor can be seen as offspring of change. They were grounded, however, in East Slavic tradition and derived their strength from that link with the past.

Honor before Muscovy

Judging by the evidence of the earliest legal sources, a consciousness of personal dignity that could be publicly defended had long existed among the East Slavs. Legal sources of the eleventh to fifteenth centuries[4] protected personal dignity, although they do not use the Muscovite-era term for "honor" (*chest'*);

[3]J. A. Sharpe, *Defamation and Sexual Slander in Early Modern England: The Church Courts at York*, Borthwick Papers no. 58 (York, n.d. [1980?]), pp. 25, 27.

[4]The relevant works and their publications are the short and expanded redactions of the Russian Law (*Russkaia pravda*): *Rossiiskoe zakonodatel'stvo X–XX vekov v deviati tomakh* (RZ), 9 vols. (Moscow, 1984–94), 1 (1984):47–49, 64–73; the 1189–99 treaty of Novgorod and the Gotland towns: *Pamiatniki russkogo prava* (PRP), 8 vols. (Moscow, 1952–63), 2 (1953):124–32; a 1229 treaty of Smolensk and the Gotland towns: PRP 2:54–98; the Church Statutes of Vladimir and Iaroslav: RZ 1:139–40, 148–50, 168–70, 189–93; the Court Law for the People: M. N. Tikhomirov, ed., *Zakon sudnyi liudem prostrannoi i svodnoi redaktsii* (Moscow, 1961); the Pskov charter of 1397: RZ 1:331–42; the Novgorod judicial charter of the midfifteenth century: RZ 1:304–8; the late fifteenth-century Novgorod church judicial charter: *Akty, sobrannye v bibliotekakh i arkhivakh Rossiiskoi imperii Arkheograficheskoiu ekspeditsieiu Imp. akademii nauk* (AAE), 4 vols. and index (St. Petersburg, 1836, 1838), vol. 1, no. 103, pp. 79–80; the *Pravosudie metropolichie*: PRP 3 (1955): 426–32, 438–57.

in the pre-Muscovite period, that term was associated with military glory[5] or with the godliness attributed to saints and heavenly figures.[6] The short and expanded redactions of the Russian Law (*Russkaia pravda*) are replete with references to offenses to personal honor, which are often (but not consistently) termed injury (*obida*) or disgrace (*sram, sorom, sramota*).[7] The short redaction of the Russian Law reflects legal norms of the eleventh century, whereas the expanded redaction represents norms of earlier generations compiled by the thirteenth century and remaining in effect in the later Rus' and Muscovite lands well into the sixteenth century. In the sixteenth century, the Russian Law was edited again, indicating that this collection of East Slavic customary law complemented the mainly procedural Muscovite law codes of 1497 and 1550 and was still in use.[8]

In the Russian Law, humiliating actions were singled out for punishment. In the short redaction alone, several such affronts are identified, some not even called "injury" (*obida*): a blow of a sheathed sword or hilt of a sword (art. 4); striking with an object or back of a hand (art. 3); cutting off a mustache or beard (art. 8); threat with a sword (art. 9); a slave striking a free man (art. 17); and pushing and shoving that does not result in serious bodily harm (art. 10). Those labeled "injury" suggest affront to dignity as well as physical damage: bloody or bruising assault (art. 2); severed finger (art. 7); theft of a slave, horse, weapon, hunting dog or bird, clothing (arts. 13, 29, 37); failure to repay a debt (art. 15). In some of these cases, the fine mandated compensation over and above restitution; in others, a humiliating assault was compensated more than a less-humiliating blow (four times the fine for a blow from the back of the

---

[5]This argument is made in my "Was There Honor in Kiev Rus'?" and evokes the debate on "honor/glory" between Iurii Lotman and A. A. Zimin: *Jahrbücher für Geschichte Osteuropas* 36, no. 4 (October 1988):481–92. See also Helen Y. Prochazka, "On Concepts of Patriotism, Loyalty, and Honour in the Old Russian Military Accounts," *Slavonic and East European Review* 63, no. 4 (1985):481–97. See usages of the word *chest'* through the fourteenth century, primarily in religious and military connotations: I. I. Sreznevskii, *Materialy dlia slovaria drevne-russkogo iazyka po pis'mennym pamiatnikam*, 3 vols. (St. Petersburg, 1893–1903), 3: cols. 1571–75.

[6]L. A. Chernaia, "'Chest': Predstavleniia o chesti i beschestii v russkoi literature XI–XVIII vv.," in A. S. Demin, ed., *Drevnerusskaia literatura. Izobrazhenie obshchestva* (Moscow, 1991), pp. 56–84; on godliness, see pp. 56–57. Chernaia proposes a three-stage evolution of honor, from honor based in family (in the Kievan era), to honor associated with service rank (in the Muscovite period), to the beginnings of an assertion of honor as dignity and worth separate from worldly rank and heritage (in the Petrine period). The scheme is too categorical for the Muscovite period, inasmuch as litigation over precedence and dishonor rely on criteria of both family and rank, and because the scheme masks the intensely personal commitment individuals felt to their honor even if it were based in family, rank, and external marks of status.

[7]On *obida*: Sreznevskii, *Materialy* 2 (1895): col. 503 cites the Primary Chronicle. For further examples, see ibid.: cols. 502–6; *Slovar' russkogo iazyka XI–XVII vv.* (SRIa), 23 vols. to date (Moscow, 1975–), 12 (1987):49–51. On *sram*: Sreznevskii, *Materialy* 3 (1903): cols. 465–67, 475–78.

[8]Daniel H. Kaiser, *The Growth of the Law in Medieval Russia* (Princeton, N.J., 1980), pp. 41–46.

hand, as opposed to a bloodying assault). The expanded redaction repeats many of these clauses, although it less often awarded supplemental compensation and added compensation to the grand-princely court. Still, the Expanded Russian Law maintained the short redaction's protections against humiliating affronts and injuries. Interestingly, neither code cites verbal insult specifically but concentrates on actions detrimental to dignity.

The concept of dignity evinced in Kievan law codes was socially inclusive; the codes used subjects such as "men" (*muzhi*) or "whosoever" (*kto kogo*). A few social distinctions are evident: In the Expanded Russian Law, for example, a higher bloodwite (a monetary compensation to kinsman of a murdered person) for elite men is indicated, but all social groups had the right to avenge murder; also, different compensations were mandated for a peasant and a prince's official who were unjustly tortured (arts. 1, 19–27, 33). However, the social inclusiveness of clauses reflecting dignity is striking. The expanded redaction, for example, extends the categories of persons protected from humiliating assault beyond the norms of the short redaction to include slaves and indentured servants who suffered at the hands of their masters (arts. 56, 59–62). Other twelfth- and thirteenth-century law codes often use the terminology of "disgrace" or "shame" (*sram, sorom, sramota*) for affronts to an individual's decorum, reputation, and status as a free and law-abiding subject, while maintaining social inclusiveness. The Expanded Russian Law uses this term to refer to a freeman's compensation for the "shame" of being struck by a slave (art. 65). Twelfth- and thirteenth-century Novgorod and Smolensk trade treaties consider false arrest "shameful." These treaties and a church legal statute label as "disgrace" such offenses against women as impugning a woman's reputation and hitting a woman not one's wife,[9] uncovering a woman's hair (as insulting as damaging a man's beard in Russian Orthodox custom), and sexual offenses such as adultery.[10] Paralleling later Muscovite practice, these provisions support social breadth even while respecting social hierarchy; compensation for rape, for example, was usually calculated according to social status.[11]

Later legal sources from Novgorod, the church, and fifteenth-century Muscovy continue the defense of personal dignity. Laws protected individuals from such insults as the assault of a pregnant woman, the beating of a slave (whereupon he or she should be freed), a woman fighting or striking

---

[9]False arrest: PRP 2:125, art. 4; PRP 2:62, art. 13. Church statute: RZ 1:169, 170, arts. 25, 31.
[10]Hair, in Novgorod treaty: PRP 2:126, art. 8. Adultery, in 1229 Smolensk treaty: PRP 2:62, art. 11.
[11]Novgorod treaty: PRP 2:125–26, arts. 7, 14. Church Statute of Iaroslav: RZ 1:168, arts. 2, 3, 7. 1229 Smolensk treaty: PRP 2:62, art. 12. *Pravosudie metropolichie*: PRP 3:427, art. 7. B. N. Floria devotes considerable attention to the evolution of social distinctions in compensation awards: "Formirovanie soslovnogo statusa gospodstvuiushchego klassa drevnei Rusi (Na materiale statei o vozmeshchenii za 'beschest'e')," *Istoriia SSSR*, no. 1 (1983):61–74.

her husband,[12] and the uncovering of a woman's hair or the cutting of a man's mustache or beard.[13] Threat of harm and false arrest continued to be compensated.[14] Verbal insult and solicitude to reputation also occur in ecclesiastical and secular law codes: An early church statute claimed church jurisdiction over verbal insult, and another guaranteed compensation to women called whores.[15] Another ecclesiastical code condemned false accusation. Novgorod secular and ecclesiastical judicial charters protected the reputation of court officials and litigants from slander.[16]

Clearly legal sources—secular and ecclesiastical—of Kiev Rus', the towns of the northwest, and the principalities of the northeast through the fifteenth century evinced a concern for humiliation as well as injury in their concept of crime. They do not generalize a practice of redress for insult, either in terminology or legal definition, as consistently as did the Muscovite state in the sixteenth century. But by the fifteenth century, legal codes planted the seed of Muscovite practices by adopting a consistent terminology for dishonor based on the root word "*chest'*" ("honor"; thus "*beschest'e*" or "dishonor")[17] and linked it more and more to issues of reputation. A very early usage of "dishonor" is in a midfourteenth-century manuscript of an ecclesiastical code, the Court Law for the People, where quarreling is labeled "dishonor" (*beschest'e*).[18] Other usages date to the fifteenth century: In reworkings of the Russian Law, dishonor is associated with physical assault, although in an ecclesiastical code of that century, the *Pravosudie metropolichie*, dishonor involves reputation ("dishonor" payment is given to a tavern owner in whose establishment a murder was committed).[19] The *Pravosudie metropolichie* and a fifteenth-century reworking of the Expanded Russian Law also list compensation for "dishonor" to various secular and ecclesiastical officials without defining dishonor.[20] When early Muscovite sources use the term

[12]Assault on woman, slave beaten: *Zakon sudnyi*, p. 40. Women fight, etc., in *Pravosudie metropolichie*: PRP 3:428, arts. 35, 36.

[13]Hair, in Novgorod treaty: PRP 2:126, art. 8. Beard, in Russian Law: RZ 1:47, art. 8, and 1:69, art. 67; in 1229 Smolensk treaty: PRP 2:74, art. 19; in 1397 Pskov charter: RZ 1:342, art. 117; in *Pravosudie metropolichie*: PRP 3:427, art. 9.

[14]Threat, in Russian Law: RZ 1:47, art. 9, and 1:65, art. 24; in *Pravosudie metropolichie*: PRP 3:428, art. 25. False arrest, in Novgorod treaty: PRP 2:125, art. 4; in 1229 Smolensk treaty: PRP 2:62, art. 13.

[15]Verbal insult: RZ 1:140, art. 9. Insult to women: RZ 1:169, art. 25.

[16]*Zakon sudnyi*, pp. 33–34, 39–40. Secular charter: RZ 1:304–5, art. 6; ecclesiastical charter: AAE 1, no. 103, p. 79.

[17]Sreznevskii lists relatively few uses of the word "dishonor" (*beschest'e*) in fourteenth-century sources; it was mainly used in a religious meaning: *Materialy* 1: cols. 81–82. Later uses in Muscovite sources are frequent and reflect the meaning here described: SRIa 1 (1975):179–80.

[18]*Zakon sudnyi*, p. 42.

[19]Russian Law: PRP 1:210–11, art. b. *Pravosudie metropolichie*: PRP 3:427, art. 14.

[20]*Pravosudie metropolichie*: PRP 3:426, arts. 1–3. Expanded Russian Law: PRP 1:206, art. v.

"dishonor," it was similarly associated with verbal insult (as discussed below, in the section Muscovite Honor in Law and Litigation).

Thus pre-Muscovite legal sources reflect a societal respect for dignity, personal inviolability, and reputation. The interest of the law would seem to be to avoid violence, to maintain standards of decorum and gender roles, to protect family by punishing sexual promiscuity, and to uphold a person's good name in the community. For the individual, honor would seem to reside in honest living, sexual probity, restraint of emotions, peaceableness, and respect for social hierarchy and office. Narrative sources on honor in the pre-Muscovite and Muscovite periods suggest similar social values. If the Russian Law and subsequent legal codes defined personal dignity negatively, by identifying behavior to be avoided, we can look to prescriptive handbooks and other didactic literature such as panegyrics, hagiography, and penitentials (handbooks for clergy on the conduct of confession and penance for various sins) for a positive evaluation of those social values that made up what later came to be called "honor." Here the picture is skewed somewhat by the fact that such sources emanated from the church and prescribed perhaps an extreme code of behavior. George Fedotov, for example, remarks on the irrelevance, even the detrimental effect, of imposing an ascetic ideal on the laity.[21] Nevertheless, these works establish a prescribed ideal that was reflected to a great degree in Muscovite-era litigation.

One primary handbook of moral behavior—the *Izmaragd* or *Emerald*—circulated in the Rus' lands in the fourteenth and fifteenth centuries; in the sixteenth century, the *Domostroi* was compiled. These handbooks do not present themselves as defining the "honorable man"; the *Emerald* fits the genre of Orthodox pietistic "admonition," and the *Domostroi* is in many ways a typical early modern handbook of domestic management. The one is more pietistic, the other more practical.[22] But both present similar codes of values based in ascetic, Orthodox ideals and can be used to surmise the society's implicit standards of honor. The handbooks put religious virtues first: piety, devotion to God's word in scripture, and charity to the poor. As for worldly behavior, they stress the cultivation of inner meekness, from which stems a number of other virtues—obedience, silence, sexual probity.

Meekness and humility (*smirenie*) appear as high attributes in handbooks and other sources, such as panegyrics and hagiography. The saintly ideal, even for laymen, was the ascetic monk, but even princes were praised for meekness.

[21]George P. Fedotov, *The Russian Religious Mind, Vol. II: The Middle Ages. The Thirteenth to Fifteenth Centuries*, ed. with intro. by John Meyendorff (Cambridge, Mass., 1966), pp. 50, 55.

[22]Fedotov, *Russian Religious Mind, Vol. II*, pp. 37–40, describes the *Emerald*. On the *Domostroi*, see Carolyn Johnston Pouncy, ed. and trans., *The Domostroi: Rules for Russian Households in the Time of Ivan the Terrible* (Ithaca, N.Y., 1994), pp. 37–51.

Prince Andrei Bogoliubskii is thus hailed: "He was meek (*smiren*) and humble and simple in his wisdom and quiet and kind and loving and merciful."[23] Handbooks preached the cultivation of self-effacing virtues: "that fear which the angels have, humility and submission, meekness, mildness, soberness, obedience, attention." The *Domostroi* also accentuated meekness and subservience in its admonition to patriarchs "not to steal, live dissolutely, lie, slander, envy, offend, accuse falsely, quarrel with others, condemn, carouse, mock, remember evil, or be angry with anyone."[24] Forgiveness, kindness, Christian charity, and peacefulness assure moral perfection.

To achieve these lofty goals of deportment, obedience is to be cultivated. The *Emerald* declares, "Obedience 'is king over all good works and all virtues. Fasting leads up to the doors; alms, to heaven; charity and peace, to the throne of God, but obedience will put you at the right hand of God'." Obedience begins with filial piety; children must respect parents, and parents must instill in them such subservience. The *Domostroi* warns that if children are allowed to grow up lazy, disobedient, and undisciplined, parents' reputation will suffer: "Your house will be dishonored, your good name destroyed. You will be reproached by your neighbors, ridiculed by your enemies."[25] In turn, silence or prayer will help ensure honorable conduct.

Silence and prayer protect the pious from the temptations of sin that come from loose talk. The *Domostroi* enjoins:

> While working, engage in prayer or devout conversation or remain silent. If any work is begun with an idle or wicked word, with complaints or jokes, with blasphemy or filthy speech, from such work and from such conversations God's mercy departs. . . . Thoughtless Christians thus invite into their minds devils, who put into their minds evil, enmity, and hate. These demons arouse the Christians' thoughts to lust, anger, blasphemy, foul speech, and every sort of evil.

For women in particular, obedience and silence were cardinal virtues. The *Emerald* declares: "Listen, O wives, to the precept of God and learn to obey your husbands in silence."[26] The *Domostroi* repeats the sentiment: "Every day a wife should consult with her husband and should ask his advice on every matter. She should remember what he requires of her." Women should avoid oppor-

---

[23]Ascetic ideal: Paul Bushkovitch, *Religion and Society in Russia: The Sixteenth and Seventeenth Centuries* (New York, 1992), pp. 11–14. Bogoliubskii: *Polnoe sobranie russkikh letopisei* (PSRL), 41 vols. to date (St. Petersburg and Moscow, 1841–), 9 (1862):251 (6683).

[24]Fedotov, *Russian Religious Mind, Vol. II*, p. 53. *Domostroi*: Pouncy, *Domostroi*, p. 103.

[25]*Emerald*: Fedotov, *Russian Religious Mind, Vol. II*, pp. 55–56. *Domostroi*: Pouncy, *Domostroi*, p. 97.

[26]*Domostroi*: Pouncy, *Domostroi*, p. 101. *Emerald*: Fedotov, *Russian Religious Mind, Vol. II*, p. 77.

tunities to gossip and slander: "With her servants the mistress should never engage in idle talk or mocking speech. She should not invite market women, idle wenches, or sorcerers of any sort to the house. . . . A good woman monitors herself. . . . She refuses to listen to or to indulge in bad, mocking, or lecherous speech. . . . She should not gossip about anyone. . . . The husband and wife should never listen to gossip or believe a tale without direct evidence."[27] Penitentials also resonate this theme with persistent attention to sins of slander and lying.[28] Implicit here is a link between deportment and social stability: Loose talk is to be avoided because it invites sin and gossip and because it creates rumors and suspicions that can ruin another's reputation or set in motion angry rivalries.

Tranquillity in communities was a high virtue, particularly for the sixteenth-century *Domostroi*, perhaps reflecting the added challenges of collective life in a time of change. The *Domostroi* enjoins the good Christian to treat his neighbors with charity:

> Anyone who is good, whether he lives in a village or a town, is neighborly. He exacts reasonable rents and dues from his peasants, whether for the government or for his own chancery, at the proper time; he does not use force, robbery, or torture. . . . Merchants, master-craftsmen, and small landowners should likewise be straightforward and devout as they pursue trade, engage in crafts, or till the soil. They should not steal, rob, pillage, slander others, tell lies, curse, engage in duplicity or sharp trading practices. They should trade, work their crafts, or raise grain by means of their own honest strength.

The *Domostroi* also endorses social hierarchy: Each man should excel at his station in life, aspiring no higher than God had ordained for him. "Someone . . . who imitates other people, living beyond his means by borrowing or acquiring ill-gotten gains, will find his honor turn to great dishonor. Such a person will find himself subject to ridicule and scorn. . . . For every person must flee vainglory, flattery and ill-gotten gains and live according to his means."[29]

In addition to these prescriptions for conduct supportive of the social status quo, didactic literature prescribed another instrument of social stability: sexual probity. Eve Levin has argued that Orthodoxy among the East Slavs dwelled on sexual sin more than did Latin Catholic Christianity precisely because of a concern for the social disruption of promiscuity. Orthodox teaching on the topic was thereby tortured. Chastity was held up as a universal ideal; the necessity of

---

[27]Pouncy, *Domostroi*, pp. 131–32, 139.

[28]A. Almazov, *Tainaia ispoved' v pravoslavnoi vostochnoi Tserkvi. Vol. III. Prilozheniia* (Moscow, 1995), pp. 153, 158 and passim.

[29]Pouncy, *Domostroi*, pp. 121–123.

procreative sex within marriage was only grudgingly accepted and generally discouraged, and all other sexual behavior was roundly condemned.[30] Thus there are the frequent occasions of praise of people who, though married, live with spouses without blemish of sexual misbehavior, even without conjugal relations. Dmitrii Donskoi is praised because "before marriage he preserved his body in chastity . . . and after his wedding he also kept his body chaste, without sin. . . . He lived with his Princess Avdotiia twenty-two years in chastity and had with her sons and daughters and raised them in piety." Iuliana Lazarevskaia is praised for abstaining from conjugal relations: "Then she begged her husband to allow her to join a convent. He did not let her do so, but they agreed to live together without sexual relations."[31]

Interestingly, moralistic handbooks do not devote extensive attention to sexual conduct,[32] other than warning parents to preserve sons' and especially daughters' chastity: "Fathers must guard and protect their children, keeping them chaste and free from every sin, just as the eyelid guards the pupil and as though these were their own souls."[33] Penitentials, however, put in first place a range of queries regarding sexual sins, dwarfing by comparison the emphasis they put on transgressions such as theft, assault, murder, slander, and child neglect, which were perhaps regarded as less frequent or less socially disruptive.[34] Hagiography and panegyrics to grand princes similarly stress chastity, purity, and avoidance of all bodily passions. St. Sergii, for example, is praised: "And always in every way he deprived his body and withered away his flesh and preserved his cleanliness of body and soul without sullying it."[35] In the next chapter, I further pursue the link between sexuality, women's honor, and social stability.

The *Domostroi*'s quotation of a classic Byzantine "admonition to the young" would seem to sum up expectations for virtuous behavior for all, not just the young, judging by themes seen in law codes, didactic literature, and, as we see later in this chapter, litigation:

> Be pure in your soul and free from the passions of the body. Have a short stride, a quiet voice, and a pious word. Be moderate with food and drink, silent before your elders, obedient to those wiser than you. Be submissive to your superiors and genuinely loving to those equal to or below you. Separate yourself from all evil and carnal things. Say little, think much. Do not cut people down with words or indulge in idle conversation. Do not be impudent; blush with shame.[36]

[30]*Sex and Society in the World of the Orthodox Slavs, 900–1700* (Ithaca, N.Y., and London, 1989), chap. 1 and pp. 131–35.

[31]Donskoi: *Pamiatniki literatury drevnei Rusi. XIV–seredina XV veka* (Moscow, 1981), pp. 214–15. Iuliana: *Pamiatniki literatury drevnei Rusi. XVII vek*, 3 bks. (Moscow, 1988–94), bk. 1 pp. 100–1.

[32]Fedotov remarks on this: *Russian Religious Mind, Vol. II*, p. 99.

[33]Pouncy, *Domostroi*, p. 93.

[34]*Tainaia ispoved*, pp. 145, 159–62 and passim.

[35]*Pamiatniki literatury . . . XIV–seredina XV veka*, pp. 286–87.

[36]Pouncy, *Domostroi*, p. 98.

It would seem that ideally, honor is to be had in decorous behavior, piety, meekness, the absence of violence, and respect for family and community. What it meant to merit honor did not vary greatly from pre-Muscovite to Muscovite places and times; what changed was the public place of honor. Until the sixteenth century, law codes had not standardized the concept, nor are litigations known before Muscovy. One Novgorod birch-bark document—in which a woman complained that she and her daughter were defamed with sexual slander—suggests that in this urban republic, litigation was possible.[37] But the Muscovite state took an active role in resolving conflicts over honor and insult and focused the meaning of "dishonor" (*beschest'e*) on reputation—that is, on verbal insult—even more than on humiliating assault. Those words and deeds that people considered humiliating amounted to a paradigm of the honorable individual that paralleled the prescriptions of law codes and handbooks from the Kievan era to the sixteenth century.

Muscovite Honor in Law and Litigation

As in pre-Muscovite Rus', no Muscovite source spelled out a systematic definition of "honor." It is as if defining honor were unnecessary, because standards of proper behavior were common knowledge. In this, Muscovy differs from its early modern European counterparts. In the medieval Latin West, church law generally covered jurisdiction over insult, based on the theory that publicly uttered insult undermined the harmony of a Christian community and interfered with the church's enforcement of Christian morals. Over time, canon law established parameters for insulting word and deed. By the sixteenth century, civil courts in England, France, Spain, and elsewhere were also claiming jurisdiction over insult[38]; they based their claim on the heritage of Roman law and drew on its concept of *injuria*.[39]

---

[37]V. L. Ianin and A. A. Zalizniak, *Novgorodskie gramoty na bereste* (Moscow, 1986), p. 214.

[38]On insult breaking social harmony, see Martin J. Ingram, *Church Courts, Sex and Marriage in England, 1570–1640* (Cambridge, England, 1987), pp. 292–95; Sharpe, *Defamation*, p. 8; W. R. Jones, "'Actions for Slander'—Defamation in English Law, Language and History," *Quarterly Journal of Speech* 57, no. 3 (1971):275. On laws and concepts of honor in England, see Sharpe, *Defamation*, pp. 4–5; Jones, "'Actions for Slander'"; Ingram, *Church Courts*, pp. 294–97; Mervyn James, "English Politics and the Concept of Honour, 1485–1642," *Past and Present: Supplement 3* (1978). For France, see Arlette Jouanna, "Recherches sur la notion d'honneur au XVIème siècle," *Revue d'histoire moderne et contemporaine* 15 (1968):597–623. For Spain, see Julio Caro Baroja, "Honour and Shame: A Historical Account of Several Conflicts," in J. G. Peristiany and Julian Pitt-Rivers, eds., *Honour and Shame: The Values of Mediterranean Society* (Chicago, 1966), pp. 83–92. For Italy, see F. R. Bryson, *The Point of Honor in Sixteenth-Century Italy* (Chicago, 1935); Guido Ruggiero, *Violence in Early Renaissance Venice* (New Brunswick, N.J., 1980); Peter Burke, *The Historical Anthropology of Early Modern Italy* (Cambridge, England, 1987).

[39]Max Radin, *Handbook of Roman Law* (St. Paul, Minn., 1927), pp. 138–43.

In principle, Muscovy also had access to classical concepts of defamation: *Justinian's Digest* (midsixth century) devotes a chapter to *injuria*,[40] and later Byzantine compilations of Justinian civil law, such as the *Ecloga* (726) and the *Procheiros nomos* (870s), found their way to Muscovy in Slavic translations of the Byzantine Nomokanon (*Kormchaia kniga*).[41] But these particular aspects of the Nomokanon were not used; Muscovite secular law was not modeled on either Byzantine canon or lay law, nor did Muscovites emulate the Byzantine penchant for jurisprudence. Muscovite secular law was practical and laconic. This is not to say, however, that Muscovites had no sensitivity to defamation. As Pollock and Maitland put it so quaintly a hundred years ago concerning medieval England: "Nothing could be less true than that our ancestors in the days of their barbarism could only feel blows and treated hard words as of no account."[42] Like medieval Englishmen, Muscovites vigorously sued and won protection from insult, both verbal and physical. Their indifference to theoretical consideration of defamation bespeaks Russia's limited development of the Byzantine legal heritage rather than indifference to the principle involved.

Although no Muscovite law paused to define what constituted verbal insult or humiliating act, from references scattered throughout law codes we can extrapolate a good sense of what honor meant and test it against people's concerns expressed in litigation. Early law codes raise the issues of verbal insult and respect for high status. The Dvina Charter of 1397–98 stated: "Whoever insults a boyar verbally or beats him bloodied, or bruises him, should be sentenced by the governor to pay dishonor according to the family heritage [of the injured party]." Although the 1497 law code (*Sudebnik*) does not use the term "dishonor," it provides sanctions for "verbal insult" (*lai*).[43] The 1550 law code begins the specific treatment of "dishonor" with a clause defining recompense for insult, but it does not suggest what dishonor is. For Muscovites, insult was primarily a verbal offense: Various terms for verbal insult (*lai*, *bran'*, *neprigozhie slova*, *nepristoinye slova*) are trademarks of dishonor suits. For what those insulting words were, we have to rely on litigation. First, though, we can extrapolate from law codes—starting in 1550 through the seventeenth century—several other aspects of the meaning and use of honor in Muscovy.

[40]Justinian, *The Digest of Roman Law: Theft, Rapine, Damage and Insult*, trans. C. F. Kolbert (Harmondsworth, England, and New York, 1979), pp. 158–85.

[41]On Byzantine law, see Nicholas Oikonomides, "Law, Byzantine," in Joseph R. Strayer, ed., *Dictionary of the Middle Ages*, 13 vols. (New York, 1982–89), 7:390–93, and John Meyendorff, "Law, Canon: Byzantine," ibid., pp. 394–95. On its reception in Rus', see Daniel H. Kaiser, "Law, Russian (Muscovite)," ibid., p. 506, and P. Ivan Žužek, S.J., *Kormčaja Kniga: Studies on the Chief Code of Russian Canon Law*, Orientalia Christiana Analecta 168 (Rome, 1964), esp. pp. 88–90.

[42]Sir Frederick Pollock and Frederick William Maitland, *The History of English Law before the Time of Edward I* (Cambridge, England, 1895), p. 535.

[43]Dvina Charter: RZ 2:181, art. 2. 1497 law code: RZ 2:61, art. 53; the article is repeated in the 1550 law code: RZ 2:102, art. 31.

Legislation was concerned with defending personal dignity from verbal abuse and humiliating assault. As a rule, laws distinguished between dishonor (*beschest'e*) and physical injury (*uvech'e*) and did not consider most assault dishonoring.[44] But certain types of physical assault were deemed humiliating, particularly those related to sexual infractions and reputation: Rape was harshly punished, and assault on a woman, especially if she were pregnant, was compensated with prison and twofold dishonor fines. False accusations of illegitimate birth were also dishonoring.[45] Echoing the Russian Law and appanage-era legislation, litigation also shows that affronts to personal decorum such as pulling a woman's braid or knocking off her hat were dishonoring (just as pulling a man's beard or ripping his clothing was considered an insult).

Legislation used the concept of honor to promote peace in communities, resonating with the handbooks' concern over neighborliness and social order. By law, assaults on a house insulted the owner; conversely, a host's physically abusing his invited guests was a dishonor to them. It was considered dishonoring to be bitten by another man or attacked by dogs.[46]

In addition, laws used honor in a variety of ways that simultaneously defended reputation and curbed judicial abuses. From the 1550s on, for example, victims of insults to reputation—such as rendering a false judgment, giving false testimony, making a false arrest, submitting a false accusation to a court, planting evidence, or writing a false loan document on someone—were compensated for "dishonor."[47] Disrespect to the officers of the state was similarly dishonoring

[44]On *uvech'e* and *bezchest'e* distinguished in law codes, see 1550 law code: RZ 2:101, art. 26; 1589 law code: PRP 4:421, art. 73; 1649 law code: RZ 3: chap. 1, art. 5, p. 85; chap. 3, art. 5, p. 90; chap. 10, art. 106, p. 113; art. 136, p. 121; art. 142, p. 123; arts. 162–63, pp. 128–29; art. 199, p. 134; art. 281, p. 150; chap. 21, art. 88, p. 245; chap. 22, arts. 11, 17, p. 249.

[45]Assault on pregnant woman, in 1649 law code: chap. 22, art. 17 (RZ 3:249–50). Illegitimacy: ibid., chap. 10, art. 280, pp. 149–50.

[46]Assaults on home, in 1649 law code: chap. 10, arts. 198–200 (RZ 3:134). Host abusing guests, in 1649 law code: chap. 22, arts. 11, 12 (RZ 3:249). Bite by another man: A. A. Titov, ed., *Kungurskie akty XVII veka. 1668–1699 g.* (St. Petersburg, 1888), no. 72, pp. 249–63 (1697). Legislation on dog attack: 1649 law code, chap. 10, art. 281 (RZ 3:150). Examples of dog attacks: *Rossiiskii gosudarstvennyi arkhiv drevnikh aktov* (RGADA), f. 210, Prikaznyi stol, stb. 278, l. 596 (1641); stb. 784, ll. 131–33 (1678).

[47]False judgment: 1649 law code, chap. 10, arts. 5, 9 (RZ 3:102, 103). False testimony: 1556: *Akty istoricheskie, sobrannye i izdannye Arkheograficheskoiu kommissieiu* (AI), 5 vols. (St. Petersburg, 1841–42), vol. 1, no. 154/V, no. 5, p. 255. 1589: PRP 4:440–41, art. 212. 1649 law code, chap. 10, art. 162 (RZ 3:128–29). False arrest: 1550 law code, art. 70 (RZ 2:113). 1589, art. 103 (PRP 4:425). 1649 law code: chap. 21, art. 88 (RZ 3:244–45). False accusation, in 1550 law code, RZ 2:97–98, art. 6, 102–3, art. 33. 1582: AI vol. 1, no. 154/XX, pp. 271–72. 1589: PRP 4:414 , art. 6. Conciliar law code of 1649, chap. 2, art. 17 (RZ 3:89); chap. 7, arts. 12, 31 (pp. 94, 97); chap. 10, arts. 9, 14, 17–18, 107, 143, 171, 252 (pp. 103–4, 113, 123, 130, 145); chap. 21, art. 55 (p. 239); chap. 25, art. 4 (p. 253). 1681: *Polnoe sobranie zakonov Rossiiskoi imperii* (PSZ), in 40 vols. with 5 additional vols. of indices (St. Petersburg, 1830), vol. 2, no. 886, pp. 346–47. Planting evidence: 1649 law code, chap. 21, art. 56 (RZ 3:239). False loan document: 1649 law code, chap. 10, art. 251 (RZ 3:145).

to individual and tsar. Assaulting a serviceman in a military encampment was a dishonor to him; intentional misspelling in a document or improperly using someone's name or rank in direct address denigrated a person's social rank; assaulting a bailiff as he served papers was dishonor to him and to the tsar's administration as represented by the document. Other laws specifically upheld the orderly working of the judicial system. To employ a mediator and then not abide by his resolution was punished as a dishonor to him; quarreling in a court-room before judges was punished with a twofold dishonor fine.[48] Taking the law into your own hands also called forth punishment as well as bringing dishonor to the victim. Torturing a thief instead of turning him in to authorities, for example, was a dishonor to him.[49] Finally, a wide range of "dishonors" involved insult to the church or to the tsar and his representations. They included such offenses as quarreling in a church or in the tsar's chambers or insulting a judge.[50] Often these offenses that affected state institutions as well as individuals were punished with at least a twofold dishonor fine, as well as with any appropriate compensation, to underscore their seriousness. So, laws show us the ways in which the courts used the concept of honor. They protected individuals from insult to reputation and at the same time discouraged petty violence and disor-der in communities; they defended home and neighborhood from violence; they discouraged abuse of the judicial system; and they inculcated respect for the tsar, his representatives, and institutions.

Litigation reveals the spicy details of what Muscovites really said when they insulted one another. I have gathered a database of more than six hundred par-tial and complete litigations over honor, of which more than half are archival and the rest published. The collection seems to represent the chronological, geographical, and thematic breadth of the concept and practice.[51] The litiga-tions stem from some of the many institutions with judicial authority in early modern Russia. Functions like adjudication, tax collection, and military recruitment were generally not connected in a hierarchy of central and local offices. A few chanceries were established by the seventeenth century with pri-mary responsibility for litigation involving the landed elite (the Moscow and Vladimir Judicial Chanceries), but other offices also handled suits for these

---

[48]Mediator: 1649 law code, chap. 15, art. 5 (RZ 3:163). Courtroom: 1649 law code, chap. 10, arts. 105–6 (RZ 3:112–13).

[49]Assault bailiff: 1649 law code, chap. 10, art. 142 (RZ 3:123). Serviceman: 1649 law code, chap. 7, art. 32 (RZ 3:97). Intentional misspelling and misuse of names: 1675: PSZ 1, no. 597, p. 1000. 1680: PSZ 2, no. 812, pp. 253–54. 1685: PSZ 2, no. 1106, pp. 651–52. But cf. 1690: PSZ 3, no. 1374, pp. 66–67. Torture thief: 1649 law code, chap. 21, art. 88 (RZ 3:244–45).

[50]1649 law code, chap. 1, arts. 5–7 (RZ 3:85–86), chap. 3, arts. 1, 2, 5 (RZ 3:89–90), chap. 10, art. 106 (RZ 3:113).

[51]For further details, see my "Honor and Dishonor in Early Modern Russia," *Forschungen* 46 (1992):131–46.

ranks as well as for other social categories.[52] Judicial authority over the city of Moscow was given to the "Land" Chancery (*Zemskii prikaz*), for example, while the Foreign Affairs Chancery had jurisdiction over much of the North and over some non-Russian groups on the western and steppe frontiers.[53] At the same time, local governors in the Center, Siberia, and the steppe frontiers had broad judicial authority over all social ranks; in the North, communal institutions and even ecclesiastical offices could serve as courts. Furthermore, landlords had judicial authority over their dependent peasantry, as did the church over its clerics, monks, nuns, and secular dependents. Thus, surviving records on dishonor litigation are scattered in many archives because of their various institutional provenances.

The database for the present study represents a broad range of the possible sources of adjudication on dishonor. Approximately half (378) of its 632 cases are held in the archive of the Military Service Chancery (*Razriadnyi prikaz*), but because records from many different chanceries fell into that repository over time, it is a varied resource. The rest of the database comes from various secular and ecclesiastical juridical institutions.[54]

The collection has considerable social and geographical diversity. It gives pride of place to military servitors,[55] but urban people, ecclesiastical officials and their dependents, peasants, and slaves are also represented. Geographically, it contains numerous cases from all of Muscovy's several regions: the Center, the Novgorod lands, the western and steppe frontiers, the North (the Dvina, Perm', and Viatka lands), and Siberia, with the Center and steppe frontiers somewhat predominating.

[52]On judicial and other chanceries, see S. E. Kniaz'kov, "Sudnye prikazy v kontse XVI–pervoi polovine XVII v.," *Istoricheskie zapiski* 115 (1987): 268–85; A. V. Chernov, "O klassifikatskii tsentral'nykh gosudarstvennykh uchrezhdenii XVI–XVII vv.," *Istoricheskii arkhiv* 1, no. 1 (1958): 195–202; N. V. Ustiugov, "Evoliutsiia prikaznogo stroia Russkogo gosudarstva v XVII v.," in *Absoliutizm v Rossii (XVII–XVIII vv.)* (Moscow, 1964), pp. 134–67; Peter B. Brown, "Muscovite Government Bureaus," *Russian History* 10 (1983):269–330.

[53]Administrative records of the Foreign Affairs Chancery are held in fond 141, "Prikaznye dela starykh let" in RGADA. See my "Preface" and also the "*Predislovie*" in N. P. Voskoboinikova, ed., *Opisanie drevneishikh dokumentov arkhivov moskovskikh prikazov XVI–nach. XVII vv.* (RGADA f. 141. *Prikaznye dela starykh let*) (Moscow, 1994), pp. i–xiv.

[54]These include the State Armory (some published in *Moskovskaia delovaia i bytovaia pis'mennost' XVII veka* [Moscow, 1968], and *Pamiatniki delovoi pis'mennosti XVII veka. Vladimirskii krai* [Moscow, 1984]); local governors' courts in the Vladimir (*Pamiatniki delovoi*), Perm' (Titov, *Kungurskie akty*), the Northern Dvina, and Sol' Vychegodsk areas (*Russkaia istoricheskaia biblioteka* [RIB], 39 vols. [St. Petersburg and Leningrad, 1872–1929], vol. 12 [1890], and vol. 14 [1894]); the courts of the Metropolitan of Rostov Velikii (*Pamiatniki pis'mennosti v muzeiakh Vologodskoi oblasti. Katalog-putevoditel'*, 5 vols. in 11 pts. [Vologda, 1982–89]) and of the cathedral church of Ustiug Velikii (RIB 25 [1908]); and monasteries and churches in Novgorod, Astrakhan', Nizhnii Novgorod, and elsewhere (RIB 2 [1875]).

[55]Only 130 cases involved litigants of whom neither were in military service; in another 71 cases, a nonmilitary person was involved with a military man, leaving 431 suits between military men of various ranks.

The collection has a broad chronological range, but only a handful of such litigations survive for the sixteenth and early seventeenth centuries; they increase steadily through the seventeenth century. This pattern is attested not only in this relatively small database, but also in the approximately two thousand dishonor cases recorded in the published description of the Military Service Chancery archive. In both my database and the archive, the number of dishonor suits increased dramatically from the 1670s through the 1690s,[56] reflecting the tremendous social change of those decades. The decline in the incidence of such suits exhibited by our collection and by the archive after the 1690s is a result of institutional reorganization in the Petrine era, not lack of interest (the Epilogue discusses the continued significance of honor after Peter).

Looking at dishonor as represented in the database in the aggregate, we see that physical assault alone was rarely an occasion for dishonor. It usually accompanied verbal insult. In the 558 cases in which the type of insult can be ascertained, assault was paired with verbal abuse in 189 suits (33%); in only 45 cases, humiliating physical assault alone was dishonoring. In a majority of cases (324), insult was by word alone. Personal reputation was so highly regarded because Muscovite society gave it tangible value, according responsible position in local government to men of known good reputation (the so-called "leading citizens," *liutshchie* or *dobrye liudi*) and denying trust and honor to "known evil men" (*vedomye likhie liudi*).[57] By and large, there was a common core of insulting vocabulary, which sketches out what Muscovites considered the honorable person. Although some gender and social class distinctions are evident, they do not constitute separate discourses of honor.

Of highest concern to Muscovites were allegations of unlawful behavior. The most frequent type of insult in the litigations in the database accused men and women of thievery, criminal behavior, flight from military service, and the like.[58] This recalls both the *Domostroi*'s injunctions not to lie, cheat, or steal

---

[56]The archival description for the Military Service Chancery is *Opisanie dokumentov i bumag, khran. v Moskovskom arkhive Ministerstva iustitsii*, 21 vols. (1869–1921), vols. 9–20 (1894–1921). The chronological breakdown is the following: in both my database and the archive, fewer than 10 cases per decade from 1500 through 1619; 1620s: 44 cases in the database, 19 in the archive; 1630s: 44 [39]; 1640s: 85 [78]; 1650s: 45 [122]; 1660s: 47 [91]; 1670s: 69 [178]; 1680s: 101 [445]; 1690s: 94 [893]; 1700s: 35 [124]; 1710s: 15 [0]; 1720s: 2 [0].

[57]On "known evil men," see Horace W. Dewey, "Defamation and False Accusation (*Iabednichestvo*) in Old Muscovite Society," *Etudes slaves et esteuropéennes/Slavic and East European Studies* 11, pts. 3–4 (1966/67):113–14. The law code of 1550, arts. 52, 59–61 (RZ 2:106–8) condemns evil men, and that of 1589, art. 71 (PRP 4:421) denies them honor.

[58]*Vor*: RGADA, f. 210, Belgorod stol, stb. 138, ll. 331–46 (1638); RGADA, f. 210, Prikaznyi stol, stb. 162, ll. 13–16, 160–65 (1645); stb. 675, ll. 86–93 (1673); stb. 2749, ll. 12–38 (1701). Flight from service: RGADA f. 210, Belgorod stol, stb. 857, ll. 42–60 (1693); RGADA, f. 210, Prikaznyi stol, stb. 2686, ll. 1–14 (1702). Treason: RGADA, f. 210, Prikaznyi stol, stb. 214, ll. 150–52 (1658); stb. 346, ll. 302–4 (1660); stb. 612, ll. 58–80 (1682).

and numerous law codes concerned with false accusation of wrongdoing. Family and family reputation, and the closely related issue of sexual probity, formed the second most sensitive area. Litigation over "mother oaths," over slurs to the reputation of the family, and over accusations of adultery, loose morals, and the like was common. Here the gender difference is pronounced: Although both men and women complained of such insults, the majority of the 207 suits involving women concerned aspersions on their moral character.[59] Filial piety was also demanded of the honorable person. Parents sued children for assault and disrespect, and punishments rendered in such cases were higher than the usual monetary fines.[60] Religious piety was a given: Although it did not arise often in these cases, if a person were accused of lack of Orthodox piety, he or she could sue.[61] Again, we have seen these concerns repeatedly in didactic literature and law codes.

A third common concern was social standing. No matter how lowly in the social hierarchy, Muscovites objected if their social rank were insulted. Boyars declared that their families had never served as provincial gentry, provincial gentrymen bridled at being called musketeers, musketeers rejected the label of taxpaying city person, and even slaves objected to being called field-workers when they worked as their master's bailiffs![62] A decree even declared that one cannot use the rank of standard bearer (*znamenshchik*) as a slur.[63] Individuals sued for dishonor whenever their names, families, or ranks were insulted. Litigants protested being called "*khudoi kniazhishek*" (paltry little princeling), "*detishki boiarskie*" (little sons of boyars), and "*grivnenyi voevodishka*" (penny farthing little governor).[64] They also cried foul when it was alleged that they had been beaten for a previous crime, because corporal punishment was in practice reserved for the lowest social groups or for noto-

---

[59]Men accused of sodomy and incest: K. P. Pobedonostsev, ed., *Istoriko-iuridicheskie akty perekhodnoi epokhi XVII–XVIII vekov* (Moscow, 1887), pp. 45–46 (1703); RIB 12, no. 143, cols. 589–95 (1683). Insults to women (also see Chapter 2): RGADA, f. 210, Prikaznyi stol, stb. 139, ll. 473–94 (1635); stb. 192, ll. 143–63 (1649); K. P. Pobedonostsev, *Materialy dlia istorii prikaznogo sudoproizvodstva v Rossii* (Moscow, 1890), delo 43, p. 98 (1713).

[60]RZ 3:248 (chap. 22, arts. 4, 5). Examples: RGADA, f. 210, Prikaznyi stol, stb. 384, ll. 163–64 (1667); stb. 2574, ll. 12–17 (1701).

[61]Interestingly, rarely did people insult others by calling them "heretics" (one instance is *Delovaia pis'mennost' Vologodskogo kraia XVII–XVIII vv.* [Vologda, 1979], p. 27); they used more generic phrases such as "enemy of God": RGADA, f. 210, Prikaznyi stol, stb. 400, ll. 90–106 (1674); stb. 2686, ll. 1–14 (1702); stb. 1377, ll. 42–46 (1691).

[62]The outraged slave: AAE 2, no. 142, pp. 257–58.

[63]1646: ZA no. 318, p. 217; 1648: ZA no. 337, p. 225.

[64]A sampling includes RGADA, f. 210, Belgorod stol, stb. 174, ll. 312–15 (1644); stb. 1370, ll. 125, 136–37 (1692); RGADA, f. 210, Prikaznyi stol, stb. 153, ll. 117–25 (1652); stb. 315, ll. 1–34 (1655); stb. 787, ll. 71–79 (1678); *Moskovskaia delovaia*, pt. 2, nos. 32–33, pp. 60–61 (1639); PSZ 1, vol. 3, no. 1460, pp. 149–51 (1693).

rious crimes.[65] Finally, a wide range of miscellaneous taunts and names (e.g., "bald devil," "son of a bitch," "dog," "puppy")—the sort of "fightin' words" that could spark a brawl—could be litigated in court instead of by fisticuffs.[66]

Concerns of status rank, even precedence (*mestnichestvo*), do not constitute separate discourses of honor for separate social groups, as they did in early modern Spain, Germany, and elsewhere.[67] Rather, they are intensifications of values relevant to all. Men as well as women resented sexual slander; taxed people as well as boyars were sensitive about social rank. Nor did Muscovites engage in the rich vocabulary of insulting gesture that medieval Frenchmen or sixteenth-century Italians used, nor indulge in pasquinades, that is, satirical lampoons posted for the world to see.[68] But in content, Muscovy's concept of honor shared much in common with its European contemporaries. Research on several early modern states—England, France and French Canada, Italy, Germany, and Spain—shows women's particular sensitivity to sexual slander. Accusations of criminal behavior similarly topped the list of insults in Elizabethan England, in sixteenth-century Dijon, and in eighteenth-century Paris.[69] A thirteenth-century Spanish law code, the *Partidas*, defined a range of dishonoring words and deeds that paralleled Muscovite concerns: insulting words, blows by stick and stone, and assault on one's personal property or home.[70]

Why Muscovite concepts of honor parallel early modern European concerns is difficult to say. To some extent, one might argue that they are universal human

---

[65]The Conciliar Law Code of 1649, for example, mandated that a corrupt official should be beaten for his crime, unless he were "more honorable" (*pochestnee*), in which case he would be imprisoned: chap. 10, art. 20 (RZ 3:105). Examples: RGADA, f. 210, Prikaznyi stol, stb. 729, ll. 118–28 (1676); Pobedonostsev, *Istoriko-iuridicheskie akty*, pp. 41–51 (1705).

[66]A sampling includes RGADA, f. 210, Prikaznyi stol, stb. 1064, ll. 10–13 (1687); stb. 558, ll. 453–75 (1644); stb. 787, ll. 71–79 (1678); stb. 177, ll. 56–92 (1649; published almost in full in I. E. Zabelin, *Domashnii byt russkikh tsarei v XVI i XVII st.* Pt. 1, 4th exp. ed. [Moscow, 1918], pp. 373–82); stb. 315, ll. 1–34 (1655); stb. 1013, ll. 22–40 (1669); stb. 153, ll. 117–25 (1652); *Moskovskaia delovaia*, pt. 2, no. 14, p. 52 (1634).

[67]Spain: "Religion, World Views, Social Classes and Honor During the Sixteenth and Seventeenth Centuries in Spain," in J. G. Peristiany and Julian Pitt-Rivers, eds., *Honor and Grace in Anthropology* (Cambridge, England, 1992), pp. 91–102. Germany: Richard van Dülmen, *Kultur und Alltag in der frühen Neuzeit*, vol. 2. *Dorf und Stadt, 16.–18. Jahrhundert* (Munich, 1992), pp. 194–214.

[68]France: Claude Gauvard, *"De grace especial." Crime, état et société en France à la fin du Moyen Age*, 2 vols. (Paris, 1991), chap. 16. Italy: Peter Burke, *Historical Anthropology*, chap. 8.

[69]Ingram, *Church Courts*, pp. 297–99; Sharpe, *Defamation*, pp. 10–16; James R. Farr, *Hands of Honor: Artisans and Their World in Dijon, 1550–1650* (Ithaca, N.Y., and London, 1988), pp. 182–94; David Garrioch, "Verbal Insults in Eighteenth-Century Paris," in Peter Burke and Roy Porter, eds., *The Social History of Language* (Cambridge, England, 1987), pp. 107–13.

[70]J. C. Baroja, "Honour and Shame: A Historical Account," pp. 90–91. The *Partidas* was derived from Roman law: Charles Donahue Jr., "Law, Civil," Strayer, ed., *Dictionary of the Middle Ages* 7:422. James R. Farr sees similar insults in sixteenth-century Dijon: *Hands of Honor*, pp. 182–85.

values, but because these concepts are so bound up with defense of socially constructed institutions (such as the family and social ranks) or of socially constructed gender roles, one should be wary of such assumptions. Most likely, the
connection lies in Russia's cultural commonalties with those aspects of the European past that are said to have generated European honor consciousness: Christianity (whether in Catholic or Byzantine form) and the Germanic legacy shared
by East Slavs (through Rus'-era Vikings) and much of Western Europe.

Who Was Honorable in Muscovy

Like its Kievan and appanage-era antecedents, Muscovite law was socially
inclusive. The implicit message that honor was an attribute of all social groups
was made explicit by the 1589 law code, which identified those who were ineligible to claim protection of honor as "thieves, criminals, arsonists and known
evil men."[71] In other words, people who had harmed the community had no
honor, but everyone else shared in it. This stands in sharp contrast to early
modern Germany, for example, where whole categories of people were deemed
outcasts because they engaged in "dishonorable" professions (executioners,
barbers, butchers, and others) and where guilds defined artisanal honor sepa-
rately from the honor of other social groups.[72]

Such an inclusive definition left a remarkable array of persons considered
members in good standing of the Muscovite community. The 1550 law code,
although brief, nevertheless dispels any impression that honor was a preserve
of the elite. It details the fees for insulting persons of all secular ranks: from
taxed people and even slaves to the political elite, and to wives and daughters
of all of the above.[73] Charters of local administration in 1556 and 1561 affirm
the honor of taxpayers, both urban and rural.[74] The 1589 law code was compiled to serve Muscovy's northern hinterlands; this area by and large lacked a

[71]"A tatem, i razboinikam, i zazhigalshchikam i vedomym likhim liudem bezchestia net": PRP
4:421 (art. 71).
[72]Kathleen E. Stuart, "The Boundaries of Honor: 'Dishonorable People' in Augsburg, 1500–1800,"
Ph.D. dissertation, Yale University, 1993; Mack Walker, *German Home Towns: Community, State,
and General Estate 1648–1871* (Ithaca, N.Y., and London, 1971), chap. 3; van Dülmen, *Kultur
und Alltag*, pp. 194–214; Martin Dinges, "Die Ehre als Thema der historischen Anthropologie.
Bemerkungen zur Wissenschaftsgeschichte und zur Konzeptualisierung," in Klaus Schreiner and
Gerd Schwerhof, eds., *Verletzte Ehre. EhrKonflikte in Gesellschaften des Mittelalters und der
frühen Neuzeit* (Cologne, 1995), pp. 29–62.
[73]RZ 2:101 (art. 26). This clause is repeated in the "Consolidated" (*svodnyi*) law code of the
early seventeenth century: PRP 4:500 (art. 26).
[74]1556: AI 1, no. 165, p. 315–18. 1561: AAE 1, no. 257, pp. 280–83.

privileged landed elite and featured a trading economy of artisans, merchants, fishermen, trappers, and the like. In addition to the familiar landed cavalrymen, tsarist officials, merchants, artisans, peasants, slaves, and elected communal officers whose honor was protected in the 1550 code, the 1589 code added a diverse list of persons, including priests, monks, and other church people; registered and unregistered minstrels; beggars and street entertainers; bastards, whores, and seeresses; musketeers and Cossacks![75]

The Conciliar Law Code of 1649 was the high-water mark of definitions of dishonor compensation.[76] Its almost seventy-five articles (compared with one article in the 1550 law code and thirty-one in 1589) add church hierarchs and institutions where they had not been previously (the 1589 law code had mentioned priests, but not hierarchs or specific monasteries).[77] Case law, however, as early as the late fifteenth century, shows that clerics shared in the symbolic community of honor.[78] For secular ranks, the 1649 code aggregated groups more than the 1589 code had done, but it still identified more social ranks and more complexity in redress of insult than had previous codes. Reading the 1649 law code on compensation for dishonor is like reading a catalog of contemporary social structure. Many new ranks of military and administrative servitors appear, as well as a hierarchy of merchant ranks; taxpayers in town and country (the peasants were enserfed by now) and even vagrants (*guliashchie liudi*) are included. Without stating it specifically, Muscovite law codes from 1550 through the seventeenth century portray the entire society as united by honor.

The symbolic community of honor in theory and practice included non-Orthodox and non-Russians. The 1649 law code makes foreigners eligible for protection under all the law and defines the dishonor value of Cossacks and hetmans, who were not necessarily Russian or Orthodox.[79] A 1699 law defined the dishonor value for Greeks insulted by foreigners.[80] Several suits involving non-Russians can be found. In 1639, a member of an eminent North Caucasus family, Prince Ivan Cherkasskii (who was most likely Orthodox), said he was vul-

---

[75]PRP 4:419–21 (arts. 41–72).

[76]In 1620 and 1645, specific decrees had defined the dishonor fees for various levels of merchants: V. A. Varentsov, "Zhalovannaia gramota . . .," *Sovetskie arkhivy* 1979, no. 6, p. 60, and ZA no. 304, p. 210.

[77]Conciliar Law Code of 1649: RZ 3:106–12 (chaps. 10, arts. 27–99); 251 (chap. 23, art. 3; chap. 24, arts. 1–2).

[78]AI 1, no. 50, pp. 98–99.

[79]Access to all: 1649 law code, chap. 10, art. 1 (RZ 3:102). Cossacks: 1649 law code, chap. 23, art. 3; chap. 24, arts. 1–2 (RZ 3:251). Dishonor suits among Cossacks are common: G. N. Anpilogov, *Novye dokumenty o Rossii kontsa XVI–nachala XVII v.* (Moscow, 1967), pp. 375–77; AI 2, nos. 12 and 13, pp. 12–13; *Dopolneniia k Aktam istoricheskim* (DAI), 12 vols. and index (St. Petersburg, 1846–75), vol. 12 (1872), no. 2, pp. 2–8; "Akty Tul'skogo gubernskogo pravleniia," *Letopis' zaniatii Imp. Arkheograficheskoi kommissii* (LZAK) *za 1910 god*, 35 vols. (St. Petersburg and Leningrad, 1861–1928), vol. 23 (1911), nos. 302, 305, 330, 355, 1005 (1677–1690).

[80]1699: PSZ 3, no. 1731 (the compensation was fifty rubles).

nerable to insult because of his "foreign origin" (*inozemstvo*). In 1640, a European, calling himself a "foreigner in Moscow service" (*Moskovskii kormovoi inozemets*), successfully defended himself against the charge that he had insulted another foreigner and that man's wife. The tsar's trumpeter, the European Christopher Tsytsekler, in 1643 sued a cavalryman for verbal insult.[81] In 1687, a commander (*rotmistr*) of a new model regiment was beaten by court order for insubordination: He had called his superior officer, Mikula von Berdin, a "petty foreigner" or "petty German" (*nemchinishka*) and a "drunkard." A foreigner, Tobias Krigel', won a dishonor suit in 1711 against a soldier for false accusation. In 1720, an Armenian won a dual settlement against two Armenians (one of whom identified himself as a "newly baptized Armenian," indicating conversion to Orthodoxy), for verbal insult and for assault on him and his wife.[82]

Because some of the non-Russian and non-Orthodox disputants were European, it might be speculated that they brought with them a European consciousness of honor. But the vigor of the Muscovite practice of honor on its own terms is shown by the fact that in the seventeenth century, Siberian and Tatar natives also embraced the Muscovite concept of honor. Dishonor laws do not include subject peoples, who in contemporary sources were called *iasachnye liudi* (native peoples of the North, Siberia, and Middle Volga who paid tribute called the *iasak*) or *sluzhilye tatare* (Tatars in Muscovite service), or were identified by ethnic names (e.g., Tunguz, Mordva, Chuvash, Bashkir).[83] Cases involving these groups proliferated as the *iasak* lands were more closely integrated into the central administration. As early as 1639/40, a group of Siberian natives sued their local governors for not giving them the traditional gift of wine, but substituting beer, which, they complained, would bring "shame" (*pozor*) on them "before their brothers."[84] Here they were adapting native concepts of dignity to Muscovite legal opportunities. In 1640, to cite another example, a converted Iakut woman sued three local workers for verbal abuse; they had called her a "thief." In 1673, a Iakut sued another Iakut for assaulting his wife, raping her, and thus dishonoring her. And in 1680, two service

---

[81]1639: *Moskovskaia delovaia*, pt. 2, no. 32, p. 60. 1640: RGADA, f. 210, Prikaznyi stol, stb. 130, ll. 771–81. 1643: RGADA, f. 210, Belgorod stol, stb. 190, pt. 2, l. 516.

[82]1687: RGADA, f. 210, Prikaznyi stol, stb. 1064, ll. 10–13. 1711: *Doklady i prigovory sostoiavshiesia v Pravitel'stvuiushchem Senate v tsarstvovanie Petra Velikogo* (St. Petersburg, 1880), 1, no. 516, p. 368. 1720: RGADA, f. 239, Sudnyi prikaz, op. 1, pt. 4, delo 5761, ll. 1–20 v.

[83]Published descriptions of Siberian archives give the impression that few dishonor suits occurred among the non-Russian populace: N. N. Ogloblin, *Obozrenie stolbtsov i knig Sibirskogo prikaza (1592–1768 gg.)*, 4 vols. (Moscow, 1895–1901), 1 (1895):171–73, 199–201, and 3 (1900):89–175 passim, esp. 156–57; M. P. Putsillo, *Ukazatel' delam i rukopisiam otn. do Sibiri . . .* (Moscow, 1879). Ogloblin observed that most surviving petitions from native peoples in Siberia were collective complaints about official corruption: *Obozrenie* 3:156–57. But unpublished archival descriptions are full of dishonor suits: RGADA, f. 1103 (Arzamas), 1167 (Temnikov and Kadom), 1175 (Shatsk), and 1177 (Iakutsk).

[84]Ogloblin, *Obozrenie* 3 (1900):158.

Tatars settled a land and dishonor dispute with a trial.[85] By the end of the seventeenth century, instructions to governors in Siberia explicitly ordered them to protect local natives from insults and damages (*obidy*), and a treaty of 1689 with Mongol-Buriat tribal elders defined compensation for insult (*beschest'e*) to tsarist emissaries in numbers of camels, horses, bulls, and sheep.[86]

At the same time that Muscovite treatment of insult embraced the entire populace, it also—paralleling Kievan precedent—affirmed social hierarchy. Above all, honor was a collective attribute. Not only in the system of precedence, for example, did individuals sue to protect their family honor from the insult of one member's denigrating military assignment; whole clans sometimes petitioned the tsar to protect their family name from blemish. In 1671, the descendants of Grishka Otrep'ev, notorious in Russian history as a pretender to the throne in 1605, petitioned to change their clan name from Otrep'ev to Nelidov. Their petition enumerates examples of loyal service to the tsar by members of the clan, but laments "we serve the tsars truly and nevertheless we receive only disdain and great shame, innocently, for sixty years, because of our surname, because of the criminality of Grishka Otrep'ev." The request was granted and the new surname enrolled in the Military Service Chancery records. Similarly, the Il'in clan sued in 1654 to protect its family name from taint by association with a kinsman, Nazarka Petrov syn Il'in. He had been exiled to the steppe frontier town of Kozlov for criminal deeds; the petition alleges that there he served in positions inferior to men that his clan should not have to serve beneath. The clan petitioned to have it recorded that his infamy should not affect their honor, so that they would not suffer "disgrace and eternal shame."[87] Similarly, litigants routinely complained that insults directed at them insulted their parents and ancestors as a group, or that insulters took pains to insult the whole family, particularly a rival's mother.

Thus we should not exaggerate the degree to which honor accrued to the individual per se; defense of honor protected the dignity of social groups at the same time that individuals benefited. Not only did honor protect clans, it also protected corporate bodies by calculating dishonor compensation according to

[85]1640: RGADA, f. 1177, Iakutsk prikaznaia izba, op. 3, pt. 1, delo 223, ll. 9–12. 1673: ibid., delo 1876, ll. 49–51. 1680: RGADA, f. 1167, Temnikov prikaznaia izba, op. 1, delo 1818, ll. 1–8.

[86]Instructions to governors: PSZ 3, no. 1595 (1697), and PSZ 4, no. 1822 (1701). 1689 treaty: PSZ 3, no. 1329, sect. IX, arts. 2–4. One might also cite in this regard the definition of the jurisdiction of the tsar's criminal authority included in the first Digest of Laws of the Russian Empire. Only a few categories of recently conquered peoples were exempted; they included nomads in Siberia, the Caucasus, and Transcaucasia, and the Kalmyks on the lower Volga): *Svod zakonov rossiiskoi imperii, poveleniem Imperatora Nikolaia Pavlovicha sostavlennyi. Vol. 15. Zakony ugolovnye* (St. Petersburg, 1832), bk. 1, art. 168, notes I–III.

[87]1671: RGADA, f. 210, Moscow stol, stb. 731, l. 777. Otrep'ev was the First False Dmitrii in the Time of Troubles; he ruled briefly in 1605–6. 1654: RGADA, f. 210, Belogorod stol, stb. 1202, l. 278.

social rank. The distinctions became ever more meticulous as service ranks grew more complex. The list of social categories for which honor compensations were defined in the first such compendium (the 1550 law code) is the simplest. As noted, it makes no mention of ecclesiastical ranks at all and no explicit mention of the highest court ranks, such as boyars and *okol'nichie*. Rather, the latter are included in a general rubric of high-ranking cavalrymen (*deti boiarskie*) on "*kormlenie*" (literally, "feeding"). These are men who enjoyed annual upkeep from the tsar or from communities that they administered. They represented a social range from the tsar's personal counselors (the boyars) to governors of towns or rural cantons. Their fines were equated with their annual income. This was also true for the next level down, cavalrymen "with cash allotments," which refers to the cash grants given to the rank and file army. As a rule, these were settled on service tenure estates (*pomest'e*). In the midsixteenth century, the tsar's highest-ranking servitors, the boyars, could have received one hundred rubles as cash grant annually in addition to land allotments. Below the boyars, the military service hierarchy was divided into twenty-five ranks, with annual payments that descended to six rubles for the lowest cavalry ranks.[88] The third social group mentioned in the 1550 dishonor statute comprises the state secretaries of the tsar's "palace" (*polatnye*) and "court" (*dvortsovye*) administrations, denoting the structures then being superseded by the chancery (*prikaz*) system. As with the military ranks, the compensation scale for these tsarist officials was left flexible, in this case to be reckoned "as the tsar and grand prince will order."

All other social groups were accorded specific dishonor fees significantly lower than the privileged ranks of the military and bureaucracy. Only the tsar's "great merchants" (*bol'shie gosti*) merited sizable dishonor compensation in comparison with the military ranks (fifty rubles), and only five rubles were awarded for "tradesmen, taxed city people and all people of middling (*serednie*) ranks," as well as for a "boyar's senior servant" (in other words, an indentured servant or slave). One ruble went to a peasant and a lesser servant of a large landholder (*boiarskii chelovek molotchii*) or to a lesser (*molodchii*) taxed city person. In addition, a private lord's "deputy, bailiff and sergeant at arms" (*tiun, dovotchik, pravedchik*) were valued at their cash salaries.[89] Nevertheless, the

[88]N. E. Nosov, "Boiarskaia kniga 1556. g. . . .," in *Voprosy ekonomiki i klassovykh otnoshenii v Russkom gosudarstve XII–XVII vekov* (Moscow and Leningrad, 1960), pp. 203–4. Richard Hellie notes that by the end of the century, these many gradations had been reduced to six, with cash payments ranging from twelve to five rubles: *Enserfment and Military Change in Muscovy* (Chicago, 1971), p. 36. See a graduated scale of service tenure land awards to boyars (two hundred *cheti*—a unit of land equal to approximately 1.4 acres), provincial gentry (fifty *cheti*), and undersecretaries (eight *cheti*) in 1586/87: ZA no. 44, p. 63.

[89]1550: RZ 2:101 (art 26). For English translation, see H. W. Dewey, comp., ed., and trans., *Muscovite Judicial Texts, 1488–1556* (Ann Arbor, Mich., 1966), pp. 52–53.

social range extends from boyar to slave. The 1550 law code portrays a social order stratified by status more than by class, with greater prestige accorded to military than to nonmilitary men and as a rule greater material compensation to military men than to all but the highest civilian ranks.

The 1589 law code is in many ways not comparable to the 1550 code in its social hierarchy, because it was designed for the significantly different society of the North. Nevertheless, the same principles were applied. The 1589 code repeated the clauses of the 1550 code but made greater differentiation among merchants, according fifty, twenty, and twelve rubles, respectively, to "great, middle and lesser *gosti*." After reiterating the 1550 clauses, the 1589 code enumerated social groups more specific to the North—those associated with its communal administration and more free-wheeling society. Valued at five rubles were judges, elected communal officials, and church elders; at three rubles were peasants who traded, lent money, or were regarded as "leading citizen[s]" (*dobryi chelovek*) in rural communes (*volosti*); two rubles were mandated for "leading citizen[s]" from a smaller settlement, while "lesser" men from such a small community got one and a half rubles; two rubles also went to hundredmen (lesser communal officials) and to registered minstrels. Receiving less than one ruble was a dazzling array of humanity: communal elected officials called fiftymen and decurions, unregistered minstrels, bastards (*vybliadki*), beggars and needy souls living under the protection of the church (*klikun; kalik*), whores (*bliadi*), and wise-women (*vidmi*).[90] Receiving dishonor awards according to their incomes or "as the tsar orders" were state secretaries, priests, and other parish clerics; monks and nuns; widows and other impoverished people; and finally, the musketeers, Cossacks, infantrymen, and fortifications experts who constituted, far more than did landed cavalrymen, the military defenders of the North.[91] The 1589 code's meticulous attention to so many relatively lowly social groups shows the North to have been a relatively unstratified haven of independent communes and trading communities, devoid of the heavy social weight that the landed military elite exerted in the Center.

By the middle of the seventeenth century, social and political change had generated not only a more complex social hierarchy, but also a much more complex sense of relative prestige. Significantly, the officers of the church were given pride of place and to some extent greater compensation for insult in the 1649 Conciliar Law Code. This accords with the heightened presence of the church in seventeenth-century court life after the 1589 creation of the Patriarchate in Moscow, the reign of Patriarch Filaret (1619–33; previously a boyar, father of Tsar Mikhail Fedorovich, and the power behind the throne in Mikhail Fedorovich's early

---

[90]Beggars: SRIa 7 (1980):36, 171. Whores: SRIa 1:251. Wise-women: SRIa 2 (1975):50 (the word, *ved'ma*, may be translated "witch" in the sense of seeress or sorceress, but not of ally of the devil).

[91]PRP 4:419–21 (arts. 41–72). See commentary in PRP 4:449–53, and B. D. Grekov, ed., *Sudebniki XV–XVI vekov* (Moscow and Leningrad, 1952), pp. 463–75.

years), and the influx of reformist clerics in the post–Time of Troubles era.[92] The ways in which the 1649 code compensated church officials for dishonor were paralleled by its treatment of secular ranks, and it distinguished far more sharply than previous codes between the Moscow-based civilian elite and church hierarchs on the one hand and the provincial gentry and lesser social ranks on the other.

Breaking with sixteenth-century tradition, sanctions in the 1649 code included corporal punishment and imprisonment as well as monetary fines; progressively harsher sanctions (ranging from fines to incarceration to corporal punishment) were applied as the social disparity between insulter and insulted expanded.[93] Thus, if a member of the highest secular ranks (the conciliar or *dumnye* ranks: boyar, *okol'nichii, dumnyi dvorianin, dumnyi d'iak*) insulted the patriarch, that person was subject to a public ritual of humiliation. But if a less high-ranking military servitor of Moscow or provincial ranks or a high merchant (*gost'*) insulted the patriarch, he was to be whipped; and if a lesser merchant, taxed urban or rural person, noncavalry military man, or anyone of any lesser rank insulted the patriarch, he was to be publicly beaten and imprisoned for a month. The sanctions for insulting civilians followed similar principles: As a rule, the higher the social status of the insulter or victim, the more symbolic or monetary the fine; the lower the status of the insulter and the greater the social disparity between insulter and victim, the more corporal the punishment; the lesser the social disparity between insulter and victim, the more monetary was the sanction. The tables depict the complex code of punishments and social hierarchy schematically.[94]

Cash fines were pegged to the annual salary of landed military men and given in schedules for monasteries and the taxed social groups. For the latter, the fines ranged widely, from one hundred rubles for the privileged Stroganov family, five to fifty rubles for various ranks of merchants, five to seven rubles for taxed peasants and urban people of three grades (*stat'ii*), and one ruble for peasants on the tsar's estates and for vagrants. Cash compensation for military ranks in the seventeenth century was at least two hundred rubles for the conciliar ranks, descending to less than ten rubles for the youngest or worst-equipped men in the provincial ranks.[95]

---

[92]On reformist trends in the seventeenth century, see Bushkovitch, *Religion and Society*, chap. 3.

[93]See Nikolai I. Lange's study of punishments for insult to honor: "O nakaniiakh [*sic*] i vzyskaniakh za beschestie po drevnemu russkomu pravdu," *Zhurnal Ministerstva narodnogo prosveshcheniia* 102 (1859):161–224. See also N. Evreinov, *Istoriia telesnykh nakazanii v Rossii* (New York, 1979); A. G. Timofeev, *Istoriia telesnykh nakazanii v russkom prave* (St. Petersburg, 1897); N. D. Sergeevskii, *Nakazanie v russkom prave XVII veka* (St. Petersburg, 1887).

[94]RZ 3:106–12 (chap. 10, arts. 27–99). See a 1687 petition in which a monastery built after 1649 asked that its proper dishonor value be established: RGADA f. 210, Moscow stol, stb. 717, pt. 1, ll. 23–24.

[95]Robert O. Crummey, *Aristocrats and Servitors: The Boyar Elite of Russia, 1613–1689* (Princeton, N.J., 1983), pp. 108–10; Grigorii Kotoshikhin, *O Rossii vo tsarstvovanie Alekseia Mikhailovicha*, 4th ed. (St. Petersburg, 1906), pp. 96–97.

Aggregate social divisions according to the Conciliar Law Code of 1649

Category 1	Patriarch (art. 27)
Category 2	Metropolitans, archbishops, and bishops (art. 28)
Category 3	The four conciliar (*dumnye*) ranks (arts. 27–29, 90–92)
Category 4	Abbots, abbesses, other monastery and convent officers, monks, and nuns (art. 29)
Category 5	Moscow and provincial landed cavalrymen and high merchants (*gosti*) (arts. 30, 91, 92)
Category 6	Merchants of the two "hundreds," taxed urban and rural people, non-landed military men, and all other people (arts. 31, 92, 94)
Category 7	Priests (arts. 85–89)
Category 8	Ecclesiastical secular staff (scribes, cavalrymen, slaves) (arts. 95–98)

Sanctions for insult in increasing order of corporal severity

High-status insulter and victim

Ritual of humiliation	If a person of category 3 insults the patriarch, category 1 (art. 27)
Very high fine	If category 3 insults category 2 (art. 28)
According to the tsar's determination	If category 3 insults category 3 (art. 90)
	If category 3 insults category 4 (art. 29)

Relatively low-status victims or minimal social disparity between litigants

Fine by annual cash payment	If category 1, 2, or 4 insults category 3 or 5 (art. 83)
	If category 5 insults category 3 (art. 91)
	If anyone insults category 5 (art. 93)
Fine by schedule of fees included in code	If category 6 insults category 4 (arts. 31–82)
	If anyone insults category 6 (art. 94)
	If anyone insults category 7 (arts. 85–89)
	If anyone insults category 8 (arts. 95–98)

Greater social disparity between low-born insulter and higher-status victim

Unspecified amount of time in prison	If category 5 insults category 2 (art. 30)
Beating with bastinadoes (*batogi*)	If category 5 insults category 1 (art. 30)
Beating with bastinadoes and three to four days in prison	If category 6 insults category 2 (art. 31)
Beating with a knout and two weeks in prison	If category 6 insults category 3 (art. 92)
Public beating and a month in prison	If category 6 insults category 1 (art. 31)

The late seventeenth-century traveler Augustin Meyerberg captured the variety of Muscovite military ranks and social groups: here a merchant, a gentryman, two boyar's servants armed with bow and arrow, a musketeer, and two Tatars. It was this traditional attire that Peter I decreed Muscovites should abandon in favor of European styles. (Illustration: Augustin Meyerberg, *Al'bom Meierberga: vidy i bytovye kartiny Rossii XVII veka* [St. Petersburg, 1903]. Courtesy of Harvard College Library.)

In terms of relative status, ecclesiastical ranks were privileged over secular ones by their primacy in the 1649 code and by the harshness of sanctions for offenses against them. Meanwhile, secular society was divided between, on the one hand, landed military men and the highest merchants, and on the other hand, everyone else: the taxed, the enserfed, the dependent, and the enslaved. Furthermore, within these large groups, hierarchy was reflected in differential dishonor payments and sanctions. The effect was to accentuate the social distance between the landed military elite (Moscow and provincial) and the rest of society, thus planting the seeds of a landed nobility even when the landed cavalry was becoming militarily obsolete.[96] Also significant is the 1649 code's indifference to bondage and freedom: For purposes of honor offenses, serfs and slaves are socially aggregated with free men such as merchants and musketeers. Thus, sanctions, legislation, and cases reveal the corporate structure of Muscovite society. Although psychologically individuals suffered insult on a personal level and received compensation as individuals, socially their honor was tied up with the complex web of corporate groups of which they were a part—family, clan, town and village, landlord's properties, regiment or rank, and status and office.

Honor and Social Identity

The corporate structure of Muscovite society is revealed not only in sources having to do with honor, but also in similar documentary sources. If one surveys Muscovite literature for what might be called social theory, one does not find it. Unlike their European counterparts, Muscovites did not engage in abstract theory about society.[97] Some classical social or political theory did circulate in Russia—in translated sources (the *Secreta secretorum* or Pseudo-Aristotle, Byzantine secular law), moralistic writings (the *Domostroi*), and publicists (I. S. Peresvetov)[98]—but it was not systematized and had little social impact. The only native narrative source—setting aside foreign travelers' accounts—that might serve this purpose is Grigorii Kotoshikhin's report to the Swedish king, but it focuses on government institutions and the elite and is descriptive more than analytical. One could, in a way similar to Daniel Row-

[96]Because of these data, one recent author argues that dishonor protections existed to support the feudal class: Floria, "Formirovanie." Both Horace W. Dewey and Serge L. Levitsky provide different interpretations: Dewey, "Old Muscovite Concepts of Injured Honor (*Beschestie*)," *Slavic Review* 27, no. 4 (Dec. 1968):594–603; Levitsky, "Protection of Individual Honour and Dignity in Pre-Petrine Russian Law," *Revue d'histoire du droit/Tijdschrift voor rechitsgeschiedenis* 40, nos. 3–4 (1972):341–436.

[97]For an overview of such concepts, see Antony Black, "The Individual and Society," and Jeannine Quillet, "Community, Counsel and Representation," in J. H. Burns, ed., *The Cambridge History of Medieval Political Thought, c. 350–c. 1450* (Cambridge, England, 1988), pp. 588–606, 520–72; Arthur O. Lovejoy, *The Great Chain of Being* (Cambridge, Mass., 1936).

[98]On the *Secreta secretorum* or Pseudo-Aristotle in Russia, see D. M. Bulanin, "Tainaia tainykh," in *Slovar' knizhnikov i knizhnosti drevnei Rusi*, 3 vols. in 5 parts to date (Leningrad, 1987–), vol. 2, pt. 2 (1989), pp. 427–30. On Peresvetov, see A. A. Zimin, ed., *I. S. Peresvetov i ego sovremenniki* (Moscow, 1958). On aspects of secular and church law, see Kaiser, "Law, Russian (Muscovite)," and Žužek, *Kormčaja Kniga*. On the *Domostroi*, see Pouncy, *Domostroi*.

land's analysis of chronicles,[99] survey historical works for their implicit vision of society. But the fact remains that Muscovites did not reflect self-consciously on the collective body in which they lived. Confirming the implications of sources on honor, Muscovites did not have a collective vision, even a collective noun, for their society as an entity. They saw society in multiplicity, not unity.

This conception is evident in myriad sources. When individuals presented themselves to the tsar in petitions, for example, they cited successively the major affiliations that structured their lives. Religion—Russian Orthodoxy for the most part—was apparently so basic as not to need specification. Not surprisingly, family and household were primary sources of identity. Men used the patronymic to identify their father: "your sovereign orphan, the tailor Shestachko, son of Pavel."[100] Women identified themselves in terms of the men who were responsible for them, often adding subservient adjectives: "the poor widow, prisoner of war, from Roslovl', Luker'itsa, Aleksei Shumiatskii's humble daughter and humble wife of Stepan Makovnev."[101]

Equally important in self-identification were rank and region, the two being inextricably associated with each other because of government policy. The cavalry army mustered in regional units[102]; the state summoned elected representatives to assemblies according to territorial units.[103] Taxpaying strata in different regions enjoyed different political institutions and privileges. The peasants and townsmen of the North (the old Novgorodian lands, especially west of the Urals), for example, enjoyed a more independent local government than that of the increasingly enserfed and more bureaucratically controlled central and frontier

[99]Daniel Rowland, "Muscovite Political Attitudes as Reflected in Early Seventeenth Century Tales about the Time of Troubles," Ph.D. dissertation, Yale University, 1976; idem, "The Problem of Advice in Muscovite Tales About the Time of Troubles," *Russian History* 6, pt. 2 (1979):259–83; idem, "Did Muscovite Literary Ideology Place Limits on the Power of the Tsar (1540s–1660s)?" *Russian Review* 49, no. 2 (1990):125–55.

[100]RIB 25, no. 2, cols. 2–3 (1624).

[101]*Akty Moskovskogo gosudarstva* (AMG), ed. N. A. Popov, 3 vols. (St. Petersburg, 1890–1901), vol. 1, no. 686, p. 628 (1634).

[102]For examples, see A. A. Zimin, ed., *Tysiachnaia kniga 1550 g. i dvorovaia tetrad' 50-kh godov XVI v.* (Moscow, 1950); *Sobranie gosudarstvennykh gramot i dogovorov* (SGGD), 5 pts. (Moscow, 1813–94) 3, no. 40, pp. 171–73 (1618); idem, *Knigi razriadnye po ofitsial'nym onykh spiskam . . .* (KR), 2 vols. (St. Petersburg, 1853–55), I: cols. 781–85 (1621); SGGD 3: no. 113, pp. 381–84 (1642).

[103]For summons to select representatives to state assemblies in Galich, Novgorod, and other towns, see AAE 3, no. 105, p. 144 (1619); Iu. V. Got'e, *Akty, otn. k istorii zemskikh soborov* (Moscow, 1909), no. 10, pp. 35–36 (1636), nos. 13–15, pp. 60–62 (1648); P. P. Smirnov, "Neskol'ko dokumentov iz istorii Sobornogo Ulozheniia i Zemskogo Sobora 1648–1649 gg.," *Chteniia v Imp. obshchestve istorii i drevnostei rossiiskikh pri Moskovskom universitete. Sbornik* (*Chteniia*), 264 vols. (Moscow, 1845–1918), 1913, bk. 4, nos. 2–8, pp. 8–17 (1648); AAE 4: no. 27, pp. 40–41 (1648). Instructions of Vladimir gentrymen to their delegate: St. Petersburgskii filial arkhiva Instituta rossiiskoi istorii Rossiiskoi akademii nauk, Koll. 9, no. 2 (1648).

parts of the realm.[104] Thus, taxpayers identified the many coordinates of their town or village: "your sovereign orphan of Vazha province, Kokshenskaia district, Spaskaia commune, the poor, destroyed man Ftorushka Stepanov Timofeeva."[105] Indentured men added region to their reference to their masters: "man of Stepan Iakovlevich Miliukov of Suzdal' province, Tumakov village, Ratmanko Samuilov."[106] A provincial gentryman or a man of a lesser servitor class identified himself as "man of Suzdal'" or "man of Uglich"[107] or by region and rank ("your slave, the Cossack hundredman of the Siberian towns of Eniseisk Island, Stenka Ivanov"[108]). Musketeers or men in new-model army units did not enjoy the right to own land and serfs and were mustered by regiment, rather than region. Their self-identification reflects that: "musketeer of Mikita Dmitrievich Bestuzhev's regiment, Gavrilko Faleev" or "your slave, hundredman of the Moscow musketeers, Ganka Bibikov."[109] Foreigners serving at the court cited their occupations: "your slave, doctor Vendelinka Sibilist" and "the foreigner, master artisan of lacework, Ontoshka Tamsan [Anthony Thomson]."[110] Only for the conciliar ranks was region and rank often omitted, in tacit assertion of the tsar's personal (at least in theory) acquaintance with his advisors.

Similarly, when groups of individuals submitted collective petitions, they relied on discrete, not generalizing, descriptions of their collectivity, citing region and rank: "your slaves the *stol'niki*, *striapchie*, and Moscow gentry and *zhil'tsy* and men of all ranks and the holders of service and ancestral land (*pomeshchiki i votchinniki*) of Tula, Solova, Odoev, Dedilov and other towns."[111] Records of assemblies—called in modern historiography "Councils of the Land" (*zemskie sobory*)—similarly presented society as a compilation of ranks (*chiny*). Here, for example, is the description of what most scholars consider the last such assembly, in 1653:

---

[104]On more centrally controlled cities, see J. Michael Hittle, *The Service City: State and Townsmen in Russia, 1600–1800* (Cambridge, Mass., and London, 1979); on the North, see M. M. Bogoslovskii, *Zemskoe samoupravlenie na russkom Severe v XVII veke. [Vols. 1–2], Chteniia* (1910), bk. 1, and (1912), bks. 2 and 3; idem, "Zemskie chelobitnye v drevnei Rusi," *Bogoslovskii vestnik* 1911, nos. 1–4.

[105]RIB 14, no. 284, col. 643 (1620); another example: *Pamiatniki delovoi*, no. 133, p. 168 (1631).

[106]*Pamiatniki delovoi*, no. 132, p. 167 (1629).

[107]RIB 2, no. 176/7, col. 722 (1638); RGADA f. 210, Prikaznyi stol, stb. 122, l. 122.

[108]RIB 25, no. 206, col. 271 (1654).

[109]RGADA f. 210, Prikaznyi stol, stb. 84, l. 21 (1632); *Moskovskaia delovaia*, no. 34, p. 61 (after 1644).

[110]Doctor: AI 3, no. 237, pp. 396 (1644). Lacework: *Akty, otnosiashchiesia do iuridicheskogo byta drevnei Rossii* (AIuB), 3 vols. and index (St. Petersburg, 1857–1901), vol. 1, no. 104, col. 643 (1646).

[111]A. A. Novosel'skii, "Kollektivnye dvorianskie chelobitnye o syske beglykh krest'ian i kholopov vo vtoroi polovine XVII v.," in *Dvorianstvo i krepostnoi stroi Rossii XVI–XVIII vv.* (Moscow, 1975), no. 13, p. 340 (1694).

The Great Sovereign Most Holy Patriarch of Moscow and all Rus' Nikon, the Krutitsa Metropolitan Sylvester, the Metropolitan of Serbia Mikhailo, archimandrites and hegumens with all the Holy Council, boyars, *okol'nichie*, men in other conciliar (*dumnye*) ranks, *stol'niki*, *striapchie*, Moscow-based gentry, *zhil'tsy*, provincial gentry (*dvoriane* and *deti boiarskie*), merchants (*gosti*) and trading people and people of all other ranks of the merchant and textile guilds and of the taxpaying hundreds and of the tsar's tax-free neighborhoods and musketeers.[112]

It is thus not surprising that a word for "society" was not used in the Muscovite vocabulary. In the late seventeenth century, the Belarus' scholar Simeon Polotskii coined the word *grazhdanstvo* for "society" in paraphrasing Plutarch's civic verse, but the usage did not catch on.[113] The modern Russian word for society, *obshchestvo*, gained currency in this meaning only in the late eighteenth or early nineteenth century, again appearing first in translations of European texts.[114] When interest in social theory did develop in the late seventeenth century, it was prompted by the influx of European ideas.[115] For sixteenth- and seventeenth-century Muscovites, as reflected in dishonor scales and terminology, local ties and status groups were more significant structuring principles of lived experience than abstract concepts.

[112]SGGD 3, no. 157, p. 481 (1653).

[113]Douglas J. Bennet, "The Idea of Kingship in 17th-c. Russia," Ph.D. dissertation, Harvard University, 1967, p. 244. The term was rarely used in Muscovite sources and in the eighteenth century tended to refer to urban citizenship: SRIa 4 (1977):117, 118; *Slovar' russkogo iazyka XVIII veka*, 8 vols. to date (Leningrad, 1984–), 5 (1989):216–17; *Slovar' Akademii rossiiskoi*, 7 vols. (St. Petersburg, 1789–94), 2 (1790): col. 303.

[114]Muscovite usages of *obshchestvo* were rare: SRIa 12 (1987):193–95. The same holds for *grazhdanstvo*: SRIa 4 (1977):118. There is no entry for either *grazhdanstvo* or *obshchestvo* in the following studies of Muscovite terminology: A. L. Diuvernua, *Materialy dlia slovaria drevnerusskogo iazyka* (Moscow, 1894); G. E. Kochin, *Materialy dlia terminologicheskogo slovaria drevnei Rossii* (Moscow and Leningrad, 1937); A. A. Gruzberg, *Chastotnyi slovar' russkogo iazyka vtoroi poloviny XVI–nachala XVII veka* (Perm', 1974); H. W. Schaller, Karla Gunther-Hielscher, and Victor Glötzner, *Real- und Sachwörterbuch zum altrussischen* (Neuried, 1985). In the eighteenth century, *obshchestvo* referred both to society and to organizations: *Slovar' Akademii rossiiskoi* 4 (1793): col. 601. Even in the nineteenth century, however, the meaning of *obshchestvo* as "society" may not have been deeply established: V. I. Dal', *Tolkovyi slovar' zhivogo velikorusskogo iazyka*, 4 vols. (Moscow, 1863–66), 2:1214. On the relative lack, even in the late eighteenth century, of terminology for social estates, let alone for "society," see Gregory L. Freeze, "The *Soslovie* (Estate) Paradigm and Russian Social History," *American Historical Review* 91, no. 1 (1986):11–36; David Griffiths, "Of Estates, Charters and Constitutions," in David Griffiths and George E. Munro, trans. and eds., *Catherine II's Charters of 1785 to the Nobility and the Towns* (Bakersfield, Calif., 1991), pp. xvii–lxix.

[115]L. N. Pushkarev, *Obshchestvenno-politicheskaia mysl' Rossii. Vtoraia polovina XVII veka. Ocherki istorii* (Moscow, 1982). In the eighteenth century, interest in social and political theory continued but was not a very popular trend in publication: Gary J. Marker, *Publishing, Printing and the Origins of Intellectual Life in Russia, 1700–1800* (Princeton, N.J., 1985), esp. pp. 208–10, 230–31, and tables 1.1, 2.1, 2.2, 3.2, 3.5, 4.2, 5.1, 8.1.

Muscovites presented themselves as belonging simultaneously to several communities: kin group, household, patronage network, indenture, village, town, and social rank. They had little better understanding that they lived in a single entity, even as authorities promoted numerous practices and discourses (such as honor and religion) to create some modicum of cohesion. There is nothing surprising in this; across Europe in the medieval and early modern periods, individuals perceived self in terms of social group. Caroline Bynum has forcefully revised the idea that the twelfth century in Western Europe witnessed the discovery of the individual in a modern sense; rather, she sees the era as pre-occupied with defining new forms of group life and models for individual behavior within those groups. Bynum argues that individuality as discussed by twelfth-century theologians involved conformity to ideal types, necessarily associating self with community.[116] Other scholars of the medieval Latin West, such as Antony Black, also depict individual identity as embedded in a diversity of communities: "In fact people were related to many different kinds of groups: universal and local Church, kingdom, feudal domain, city, village, gild, confraternity, family. . . . There was no single, all-pervasive, over-arching 'society,' but a wide variety of compulsory and voluntary groups."[117] Even later, in the early modern period, when national consciousness was emerging in learned writings in Europe, local, family, and patronage links were more important in practical politics than national or generalized ideological loyalties.[118] Literate Europeans may have had access to abstract theory on society that Muscovy did not (although even that theory was diverse in opinion[119]), but the lived experience of individuals had much in common in all these premodern communities. Although Muscovites were acting within the context of a unified political arena—a multinational empire ruled by the tsar—self and group identification was local and particularistic.

Muscovites' concerns about honor express the society's living social values. Admittedly, those values were ideals as much as living realities; they were a code to which individuals aspired and not all achieved. There were, after all, real

---

[116]Caroline Walker Bynum, *Jesus as Mother: Studies in the Spirituality of the High Middle Ages* (Berkeley and Los Angeles, 1982), chap. III.

[117]Black, "The Individual and Society," p. 589.

[118]See, for example, William Beik, *Absolutism and Society in Seventeenth-Century France: State Power and Provincial Aristocracy in Languedoc* (Cambridge, England, 1985); Francis W. Kent, *Household and Lineage in Renaissance Florence* (Princeton, N.J., 1977); Jacques Heers, *Family Clans in the Middle Ages* (Amsterdam, 1977); Mark A. Kishlansky, *Parliamentary Selection: Social and Political Choice in Early Modern England* (Cambridge, England, 1986).

[119]Black continues the quote cited above thus: "and a corresponding variety of sentiments about social bonds and societal authority. Different intellectual traditions—Neoplatonic, Aristotelian and humanist, theological and juristic, realist and nominalist—produced divergent views on the individual and society." "The Individual and Society," p. 589.

criminals and "loose women" in Muscovy. This was a discourse—a social ideal and cultural practice that could be manipulated for personal ends. The insults Muscovites hurled at one another may not reflect actual social behavior as much as the common values people tried to live by. Nevertheless, these values were a part of real life: They indicate the parameters within which people could live without incurring social opprobrium or official sanction. They depict the Muscovite social community as structured by family and rank and shaped by Orthodox religious belief and by respect for the authority of the tsar. They make paramount the ideals of honesty, loyal service, piety, meekness, neighborliness, and sexual probity. Honor was a theory and practice that gave Muscovites some theoretical basis for cohesion. The concept of honor was in essence parallel to Orthodoxy as a unifying body of ideas and practice. It is to the individual's practice of honor, in general, and for women in particular, that we now turn.

CHAPTER 2

Patriarchy in Practice

Sexual slander and gendered insult were among the most important issues at stake in affronts to honor. A man or woman's own sexual probity might be assailed, a man's wife slandered, or a mother oath (*maternyi lai*) hurled. Women and sexuality were as central in the workings of honor in early modern Russia as they were in sixteenth-century Italy, England, France, the Germanys, and elsewhere. And for good reason. Sexual promiscuity had power greater than crime and cursing to shake the foundations of society—it could break up families, humiliate fathers and husbands, and produce unwanted children. Individuals jealously guarded their reputations for moral probity and exerted controls on community members to toe the line.

Women had a particularly pivotal role in maintaining the stability of family and community institutions, and thus their honor was at the heart of Muscovite honor codes. This chapter, then, extends my analysis beyond insult to explore the tapestry of community relations and values illustrated by women's involvement in honor litigations.

Honor and Shame

In the intensity of its treatment of women, Muscovy resembled the classic "honor and shame" societies associated with the Mediterranean basin. In such societies, according to anthropologists, honor is the primary shaper of individual and group behavior. Gender roles are highly articulated, and strict forms of social control enforce honor as society construes it.[1]

Honor was construed patriarchally—that is, it centered on male authority. Men achieved honor by protecting the chastity and reputations of the women

[1] See the Introduction for literature on "honor and shame," as well as the material cited in my "The Seclusion of Elite Muscovite Women," *Russian History* 10, pt. 2 (1983):170–87.

in their authority. In some settings, they also won honor by pursuing sexual exploits with other families' women, but apparently not in Muscovy. Here there was no tradition of openly kept mistresses or illegitimate offspring; men were expected to be celibate outside of marriage. Women were not only held to that expectation, but were enjoined to cultivate "shame," construed as modesty, humility, and obedience. Ironically, because this code of values focused so heavily on women's sexuality, women held the psychological upper hand. Their promiscuity could humiliate fathers and husbands, and so women were both respected and feared by men. Men often accorded honorable women exaggerated respect, but attitudes toward women were fundamentally misogynistic. Female nature was distrusted as evil and seductive, a source of social disorder.[2] Because of their inherent power, women needed to be controlled.

Control took many forms. Marriages were arranged, association with members of the opposite sex was limited and supervised, and women's bodies were covered with proper headdresses, modest hair styles, and layers and layers of fabric. At its most extreme, control meant physical seclusion and shrouding. At its most diffuse, it took the form of symbolic and tangible rewards for conformity to men's expectations.

Symbolically, "honorable" women earned the esteem of the community and family members as "good women" or "good wives." Tangibly, they merited honorable marriages and material upkeep by the menfolk bound to protect them—fathers and husbands, or lacking them, more extended male kin. The exaggerated respect they received often meant more than gallantry; it could also translate into economic benefits. In Muscovy, for example, insults to the honor of a married woman were compensated at twice the rate of insults to her husband; insult to a man's unmarried daughter at four times that rate. Patriarchy often offers such a flip side to its strictures: Women who conformed benefited in status and in material wealth[3]; within the confines of societal norms, women could carve out a sphere of authority and respect.[4]

---

[2]Discussions of such patriarchal attitudes include D. E. Underdown, "The Taming of the Scold: The Enforcement of Patriarchal Authority in Early Modern England," in Anthony Fletcher and John Stevenson, eds., *Order and Disorder in Early Modern England* (Cambridge, England,1985), pp. 116–36, and Christine D. Worobec, "Temptress or Virgin? The Precarious Sexual Position of Women in Postemancipation Ukrainian Peasant Society," *Slavic Review* 49, no. 2 (1990):227–38.

[3]Conciliar Law Code of 1649, chap. 10, art. 99 (RZ 3 [1985]:112). Roman law compensated both the father and the husband of a married woman who had been insulted: Justinian, *The Digest of Roman Law: Theft, Rapine, Damage and Insult*, trans. C. F. Kolbert (Harmondsworth, England, and New York, 1979), p. 181. Christine D. Worobec also makes this point about patriarchy's flip side: *Peasant Russia: Family and Community in the Post-Emancipation Period* (Princeton, N.J., 1991), chap. 6, pp. 175–216.

[4]For a discussion of women and patriarchy in medieval Europe, see Heinrich Fichtenau, *Living in the Tenth Century: Mentalities and Social Orders*, trans. Patrick J. Geary (Chicago and London, 1991), pp. 102–11.

Muscovite social values and their day-to-day practice give real-life illustration of the Janus-like implications of patriarchy. Moral teachings emanating from the church were fundamentally misogynistic, tracing women's evil to Eve's original sin and drawing on St. Paul's view that women should be obedient in all things to their husbands. Orthodox teachings associated sexuality with the devil and saw women as the devil's most ready accomplices in subverting humankind. Women were excoriated as temptresses, gossips, and agents of disorder. George Fedotov quotes the fourteenth-century handbook, the *Emerald*: "It is better to suffer from fever than to be mastered by a bad wife. . . . Do not entrust your secrets to a bad wife lest you perish." The sixteenth-century household handbook, the *Domostroi*, quoting Ecclesiastes, warns of social castigation for sexual impropriety: "Keep close watch over a headstrong daughter, or she may give your enemies cause to gloat, making you the talk of the town and a byword among the people, and shaming you in the eyes of the world."[5] The stringency of the dominant trend of these sources is not unique to Russia; contemporary European attitudes toward women, particularly in prescriptive handbooks, were essentially the same.[6]

But such literature also accorded women value and utility within a patriarchal paradigm. An honorable woman, for example, was praised as "her husband's crown," in the words of the Old Testament quoted by the *Domostroi*. Such women were "capable, long-suffering and silent," obedient and chaste, but most interestingly, they were also competent. The *Domostroi* paints the ideal woman as an energetic household manager: She is constantly busy at embroidering and sewing; she fetches food, tends the household garden, works into the wee hours of the night spinning, is generous to the poor, is wise and loyal, and is perspicacious in speech. Guided by her husband's advice, of course, she supervises servants, instructs daughters in embroidery and cooking, and most important, sets an example of piety that leads the whole family to salvation.

[5]George Fedotov, *The Russian Religious Mind, Vol. II: The Middle Ages. Thirteenth–Fifteenth Centuries* (Cambridge, Mass., 1966), pp. 76–77; Carolyn Johnston Pouncy, ed. and trans., *The Domostroi: Rules for Russian Households in the Time of Ivan the Terrible* (Ithaca, N.Y., and London, 1994), p. 96. See also Joan Delaney Grossman, "Feminine Images in Old Russian Literature and Art," *California Slavic Studies* 11 (1980):33–70; Eve Levin, *Sex and Society in the World of the Orthodox Slavs, 900–1700* (Ithaca, N.Y., and London, 1989), chap. 1. For overview, see Nataliia Pushkareva, *Zhenshchiny drevnei Rusi* (Moscow, 1989), and her "Sem'ia, zhenshchina, seksual'-naia etika v pravoslavii i katolitsizme: perspektivy sravnitel'nogo podkhoda," *Etnograficheskoe obozrenie* 1995, no. 3 (1995):55–69.

[6]See Maria Bogucka, "The Foundations of the Old Polish World: Patriarchalism and the Family: Introduction into the Problem," *Acta Poloniae Historica* 69 (1994):37–53; idem, "Spectacles of Life: Birth—Marriage—Death. Polish Customs in the 16–18th Centuries," *Acta Poloniae Historica* 70 (1994):29–48; Andrzej Wyrobisz, "Patterns of the Family and Woman in Old Poland," *Acta Poloniae Historica* 71 (1995):69–82. For such literature in Europe in general, see Merry E. Wiesner, *Women and Gender in Early Modern Europe* (Cambridge, England, 1993), chap. 1, esp. pp. 21–25.

Reflecting on this ideal of womanhood, the *Domostroi* effuses: "Who can find a capable wife? Her worth is far beyond coral."[7] Accordingly, strong female characters figure in hagiography of female saints as well as in secular tales. Of course, they are primarily praised for their piety, chastity, devotion to family, and charity, but they are also accorded great strength of personality and wisdom in their pursuit of piety. St. Fevroniia of Murom, for example, is credited with magical powers and is shown defying and besting the Murom boyars with her wit. Iuliana Lazarevskaia strong-mindedly tends to the poor to the detriment of her health and the neglect of weekly church services. Tatiana Suntulova outwits her perfidious suitors with clever ruses and remains faithful to her spouse.[8]

The Old Belief's treatment of women dramatically demonstrates the mixed legacy of patriarchal attitudes toward women. In the first generations, the Old Belief depended on the patronage of powerful elite women and revered the martyrdom of Boiarynia Feodosiia Morozova, but subsequent generations downplayed these women's roles and constructed a male pantheon of saintly exemplars.[9]

The practice of dishonor litigations in Muscovy, as we shall see, reflected these social values. Whether through indigenous East Slavic traditions or through Orthodox teachings to an illiterate society in sermons and the reading of saints' lives in liturgies, patriarchal attitudes were disseminated among Orthodox subjects of the tsar. We see evidence in the elite and peasant villages, the far North, the steppe frontier, and the Kremlin palace. One has to wonder why this particular social code flourished. To a great extent, a functionalist analysis works here: Misogyny and patriarchy underwrote a social system that proved stable. They created stable families on a patrilineal model, families that in turn provided labor and production; reproduction and the rearing of children; and the fulfillment of social responsibilities, such as tax payment and military service. The patriarchal system preserved itself by imposing behavior that ensured the marriageability of daughters and the purity of a wife's issue.

[7]Pouncy, *Domostroi*, pp. 102–3, 132–33. The *Domostroi* is here quoting Proverbs (12:4) and Ecclesiastes (26:1–3).

[8]On Peter and Fevronia, see R. P. Dmitrieva, ed., *Povest' o Petre i Fevronii* (Leningrad, 1972); the text is *Pamiatniki literatury drevnei Rusi. Konets XV–pervaia polovina XVI veka* (Moscow, 1984), pp. 626–47. On Iuliana, see Paul Bushkovitch, *Religion and Society in Russia: The Sixteenth and Seventeenth Centuries* (New York and Oxford, 1992), pp. 145–47; the text is *Pamiatniki literatury drevnei Rusi. XVII vek*, 3 bks. (Moscow, 1988–94), bk. 1, pp. 98–104. On Suntulova, see Basil Dmytryshyn, ed., *Medieval Russia: A Source Book, 850–1700*, 3d ed. (Fort Worth, Tex., 1991), pp. 497–503.

[9]Georg Michels, "Muscovite Elite Women and Old Belief," *Harvard Ukrainian Studies* 19 (1997):428–50; Robert O. Crummey, "The Miracle of Martyrdom: Reflections on Early Old Believer Hagiography," in Samuel H. Baron and Nancy Shields Kollmann, eds., *Religion and Culture in Early Modern Russia and Ukraine* (DeKalb, Ill., 1997), pp. 132–45.

Such utility can be seen at all social levels. In the elite, it was the patrilineal clan and the family heritage that garnered economic and political status and privileges for individuals. Elite families used marriage alliances to preserve and expand family wealth and to advance politically. At the apex of the elite, for example, the ruler's marriage and those of his closest kin determined the inner circle and hierarchy of power for generations to come.[10] Thus, elite families were particularly sensitive to family honor and reputation.

In taxpaying communities, patriarchy was no less functional. In farming and trading communities, the labor unit was the married couple and its household, capable of creating and mobilizing enough labor to feed and shelter its members and to meet state obligations.[11] Unmarried daughters drained as much production from the family as their labor contributed, so they needed to be honorably married off at the appropriate age. Sons in stable marriages contributed to the household economy until they created their own homesteads by fission or inheritance.

Particularly in Russia, where collective responsibility of the whole community for taxes, law and order, and other civil duties was regularly practiced,[12] everyone depended on the stability of the household unit. Among taxpayers, as in the elite, disobedient wives and children could cripple the family economy, and sexual promiscuity by men or women upset the stability of both family and

[10]See my *Kinship and Politics: The Making of the Muscovite Political System, 1345–1547* (Stanford, 1987), chap. 4; Robert O. Crummey, *Aristocrats and Servitors: The Boyar Elite of Russia, 1613–89* (Princeton, N.J., 1983), chap. 3; Brenda Meehan-Waters, *Autocracy and Aristocracy: The Russian Service Elite of 1730* (New Brunswick, N.J., 1982), chap. 5.

[11]Families in Eastern Europe in later centuries have been observed to follow an "extended" family and marriage pattern (early and universal marriage, multigenerational households), in contrast to the West European pattern (late marriage, two-generational households, high incidence of unmarrieds) observed from the sixteenth century (much earlier in some settings). Muscovy may resemble the West European pattern: Households appear to have been nuclear and small, and, although marriage age is usually said to have been early, Daniel Kaiser observed late marriages in early eighteenth-century Russian towns. See R. E. F. Smith, *Peasant Farming in Muscovy* (Cambridge, England, 1977), chap. 4, and Daniel H. Kaiser, "Vozrast pri brake i raznitsa v vozraste suprugov v gorodakh Rossii v nachale XVIII v.," in *Sosloviia i gosudarstvennaia vlast' v Rossii. XV–seredina XIX vv.* (Moscow, 1994), pp. 225–37. More research is needed on this issue. On family patterns, see Andrejs Plakans, "Seigneurial Authority and Peasant Family Life: The Baltic Area in the Eighteenth Century," *Journal of Interdisciplinary History* 5, no. 4 (1975):629–54; idem, "Extended Family," in Peter N. Stearns, ed., *Encyclopedia of Social History* (New York and London, 1994), pp. 253–55; Pavla Horská, "Historical Models of the Central European Family: Czech and Slovak Examples," *Journal of Family History* 19, no. 2 (1994):99–106; Katherine A. Lynch, "European Style Family," in Stearns, ed., *Encyclopedia*, pp. 247–49; Peter Laslett, *The World We Have Lost*, 2d ed. (New York, 1971); Peter Laslett with Richard Wall, *Household and Family in Past Time* (Cambridge, England, 1972). See Maria N. Todorova's critique of these ideal types: *Balkan Family Structure and the European Pattern* (Washington, D.C., 1993), chap. 8.

[12]Horace W. Dewey and Ann M. Kleimola, "Suretyship and Collective Responsibility in pre-Petrine Russia," *Jahrbücher für Geschichte Osteuropas* 18 (1970):337–54.

community. Runaway wives left household and children abandoned; unchaste and thus unmarriageable daughters became a lifelong burden on their fathers; dissolute husbands left family and dependents impoverished. Community and kin had to come to the rescue. Therefore, sexual activity had to be kept within the permitted parameters of lawful marriage, and patriarchal demands for obedience had to be honored.

Ultimately the issue was survival, particularly for poorer families living at a bare subsistence level, but for all social ranks as well. Muscovy, like most premodern societies, had few social welfare resources other than the family. Grand princes had a traditional responsibility to care for the poor, which they fulfilled by distributing alms and patronizing monasteries but not by systematic social policy. Orthodox social values mandated charity, but the church seemed unable to provide it as an institution. Although monasteries did take in some poor persons, widows, and other needy people, Russian Orthodoxy's hesychast and ascetic values, the primacy of the monastic ideal, and insufficient resources all militated against the church's being active in community outreach.[13] Communities might rally to help individuals in a crisis, but resources were scarce. Families had to depend on one another. Not surprisingly, then, individuals evoked the necessity of family when beseeching the tsar's favor. In 1618, for example, the governor of Shuia in the Vladimir region reported that a poor man, assaulted by a family of town bullies, complained that "he could not sue them because they are people with lots of family, and with friends and co-conspirators (*liudi sem'ianisty i s svoimi druzi i z zagovorshchiki*)." And in 1634, a peasant from the Northern Dvina land in the far North complained that he was helpless before the assaults of his neighbors: "I am a solitary little man alone in the world (*chelovechenko odinashno*), I farm this little plot (*pashnishko*) alone." Even for the elite, having family to draw on was an important issue. In 1639, a member of a North Caucasus clan—the Cherkasskii princes—that had been in Muscovite service for several generations nevertheless sued a scion of an old Moscow family who had insulted him, "seeing my foreign status" (*vidia moe inozemstvo*); Cherkasskii called himself "familyless" (*bezsemeinoi*). Similarly, in 1675, a boyar lamented his "kinless, helpless, defenseless" position.[14]

---

[13]Fedotov, *Russian Religious Mind, Vol. II*, chap. 2. Paul Bushkovitch's portrayal of the church confirms these observations in *Religion and Society*. Richard Hellie argues that Russians turned to slavery because of the lack of a social safety net in *Slavery in Russia, 1450–1725* (Chicago and London, 1982), pp. 377–79, 692–95. Eve Levin argues that strict regulation of marriage had the intent of providing social support in a society of shortage in *Sex and Society*, chap. 2, esp. pp. 131–35.

[14]1618: *Pamiatniki delovoi pis'mennosti XVII veka. Vladimirskii krai* (Moscow, 1984), no. 206, pp. 220–21. 1634: RIB 14 (1894), no. 328, cols. 719–21. 1639: *Moskovskaia delovaia i bytovaia pis'mennost' XVII veka* (Moscow, 1968), pt. 2, no. 32, p. 60. 1675: RGADA, f. 210, Prikaznyi stol, stb. 686, ll. 63, 64.

Beyond their rhetorical effect, these laments had more than symbolic value. Document after document describes the predicament of widows and abandoned wives left to "wander from house to house," living off the kindness of others.[15] In a particularly poignant case, a woman from Ustiug Velikii in the North reported that her estranged husband abused her even after she had left him to become a nun; he assaulted her in her convent cell, beating her so badly that she had to leave the convent and seek help. She went to her son-in-law's home, saying, "And I have no clan or tribe other than they and cannot run to anyone and rest my head anywhere."[16] Whether metaphorically or materially, in this society being without kin was not a comfortable position. Patriarchal attitudes and social institutions built around such attitudes tried to ensure that everyone had a minimal safety net to which to turn.

But one should not overdo the structuralist analysis. Patriarchy endured in Muscovy not only because it created social stability. Patriarchal social values were cultural constructs that had a life of their own even as they generally flew in the face of reality. Martin Ingram speaks of the tension stemming from "'everyman's' experience of the day-to-day conflicts between the dictates of the patriarchal ideal and the infinite variety of husband/wife relationships."[17] Women in the absence of husbands proved themselves capable of managing households, meeting the tax burden, and taking on worldly responsibility. Women owned property, managed considerable household duties, participated in family decision making, and orchestrated the elaborate negotiations and festivities associated with betrothing and marrying off their sons and daughters.[18] As we have seen, such competence at domestic tasks was consistent with patriarchal values, and in principle, an alternative, more egalitarian social code might have been more appropriate. Nevertheless, patriarchy surmounted its contradictions: Men still spoke of women as weak and inferior, curtailed their property rights, and subjected them to a range of humiliating expectations and

[15]See, for example, RIB 25 (1908), no. 159, cols. 207–8 (1638); RIB 25, no. 232, cols. 316–17 (1661); *Moskovskaia delovaia*, pt. 2, no. 126, pp. 113–14 (1686).

[16]RIB 25, no. 105, cols. 128–31 (1632).

[17]Martin Ingram, "Ridings, Rough Music and Mocking Rhymes in Early Modern England," in Barry Reay, ed., *Popular Culture in Seventeenth-Century England* (London and Sydney, 1985), p. 176. Worobec also makes this point: *Peasant Russia*, p. 185.

[18]On women's participation in economic life, see Sandry Levy, "Women and the Control of Property in Sixteenth-Century Muscovy," *Russian History* 10 (1983):201–12; on restrictions on women's landholding rights, see Ann M. Kleimola, "In Accordance with the Canons of the Holy Apostles: Muscovite Dowries and Women's Property Rights," *Russian Review* 51, no. 2 (1992):204–29. George Weickhardt, unlike Kleimola, argues that the sixteenth century witnessed the apex of restrictions on women's access to property, with gradual lessening in the seventeenth and early eighteenth centuries, in "Legal Rights of Women in Russia, 1100–1750," *Slavic Review* 55, no. 1 (1996):1–23.

controls. Patriarchy existed as a cultural code affirming men's psychological sense of superiority, regardless of its economic or social instrumentality.

Patriarchy in Defense of Women

As these values played out in Muscovite life, they imposed dual obligations on fathers, families, and communities. First was the obligation to protect and defend women's honor from the slightest insult, because slurs on women also insulted the men who had responsibility for them. Insults also jeopardized maidens' marriage chances and humiliated the family in the eyes of the village or local community. Second was the obligation to control women's behavior to prevent the humiliation that promiscuity might cause and the real burdens (such as an illegitimate child) it might impose on women's fathers, neighbors, or communities. We can see this tension even in laconic Muscovite records (primarily litigations over dishonor and related juridical documents), paralleling the richer evidence unearthed by historians of patriarchal social relations in Imperial Russia.[19]

We will survey a wide array of evidence of how patriarchal strictures prompted Muscovites to use the law to defend women or to control them, moving beyond honor litigations to other legal and cultural practices. Contrary to what one might expect, documents show considerable effort to protect women from the physical oppressions engendered by patriarchy. At the extreme, Muscovite family patriarchs defended their daughters and wives from the ultimate dishonor of rape. They lodged complaints with local authorities if their daughters were threatened with rape or if they were victims of an attempted rape. In 1638, for example, an archimandrite of a monastery in Suzdal' province reported that a gang of men had attacked one of his monastery's villages at night, stolen goods, ransacked the village, and seized a woman, who was then rescued by neighbors. He lodged the complaint against a crowd of men who had repeatedly threatened these lands. A peasant in the Ustiug Velikii area (near the midreaches of the Northern Dvina River in the North) in 1675 complained that another peasant repeatedly threatened to rape his daughter and to harm him. Similarly, a landless man complained in 1691 that "my sister Agafiia was going to fetch water and when she had not yet reached the bridge by the market, the Murom townsman Iakunka Ovchinnikov grabbed [her] and pulled her under the bridge," sexually assaulting her.[20]

---

[19]Research has focused primarily on peasant communities: see Worobec, *Peasant Russia*; Stephen P. Frank, "Popular Justice, Community and Culture amongst the Russian Peasantry, 1870–1900," *Russian Review* 46 (1987):239–65; Steven L. Hoch, *Serfdom and Social Control in Russia: Petrovskoe, a Village in Tambov* (Chicago, 1986).

[20]1638: RIB 2 (1875), no. 176 (6b), cols. 720–22. 1675: RIB 25, no. 249, cols. 340–41. 1691: *Pamiatniki delovoi*, no. 193, p. 212. Other threats of assault: RIB 25, no. 54, cols. 60–61 (1628).

Muscovites also litigated vigorously to defend reputation and uphold patriarchy when the culprits could be identified. Courts, in turn, took the accusations very seriously. In a case that began with an alleged incident in 1698 and lasted through charges and counter charges until at least 1701 (when the documentation ends), a soldier's wife accused a church deacon of assault, insult, and attempted rape. She persisted in her charges even though the deacon denied all and was supported by witnesses.[21] In another case, officials of the metropolitan of Murom and Riazan' entertained the case of Fekolka Kirilova. Sought out by church authorities because she was bearing an illegitimate child, Kirilova initially accused a worker, Ivashko Bunda, of raping her. Then she accused the priest who had raised her as an orphan in his home of raping her and of maintaining illicit sexual relations with her over several years. As the priest stood firm in his denials, Kirilova piece by piece recanted details of her testimony, eventually fully withdrawing the rape charge against the priest (although not the charge against Bunda). It is remarkable that the court so assiduously investigated the accusations of this increasingly compromised witness in a trial that lasted from May to August 1683.[22]

Courts punished severely those found guilty of rape. For example, a woman sued the son of a priest in 1689 on behalf of her thirteen-year-old niece, who had been seriously injured in a sexual assault. The case stretched from January to July, and despite the defendant's denials and the hearsay nature of the evidence against him, he was found guilty. His specific cash fine is not specified, but he agreed to pay the girl's dowry (*dogovor na veno*). The case includes excerpts of Byzantine secular law mandating that a rapist pay one-third of his property to his victim and be subjected to the physical mutilation of having his nose cut off (the latter was not ordered in this case).[23] A woman of Ustiug Velikii province in 1686 settled a case of rape and assault on her home by two men, and the judges ruled that the settlement payment should be in accord with her dishonor value.[24] In 1698, a woman sued her father-in-law, a widower priest, for numerous attempts at rape; he admitted his guilt and was banished to a monastery to await further sanctions.[25]

In an extended case from Moscow of 1687 that deserves particular attention, the boy co-tsars Ioann (b. 1666) and Petr (b. 1672) Alekseevichi and regent

[21]RGADA f. 210, Prikaznyi stol, stb 2634, ll. 1–30.

[22]*Pamiatniki delovoi*, no. 186, pp. 205–9. Eve Levin also commented on courts' willingness to investigate charges of rape: *Sex and Society*, chap. 5, esp. pp. 243–45. For further discussion of rape, see my "Women's Honor in Early Modern Russia," in Barbara Evans Clements, Barbara Alpern Engel, and Christine D. Worobec, eds., *Russia's Women: Accommodation, Resistance, Transformation* (Berkeley, 1991), pp. 60–73.

[23]RIB 12 (1890), no. 199, cols. 948–54.

[24]RIB 12, no. 166, cols. 724–30.

[25]RIB 14, pt. 2, no. 79, cols. 1280–84.

Sofiia Alekseevna gave a young woman a resoundingly favorable verdict in a suit for rape.[26] The incident unfolded when a man of service rank, Stepan Korob'in, ordered his serving man, Serezhka Morev, to find him a woman for sexual dalliance. Serezhka, with the help of a female friend Katerinka, lured a young girl, Mavrutka Ventsyleeva, to Korob'in's home under false pretenses. The court transcript continues:

> They brought this maiden, Mavrutka, from Katerinka's home, on Serezhka's horse, saying they were taking her [home] to her mother, the widow Dun'ka, but, not taking her to her mother, they took her to the home of Stepan Korob'in. . . . And he, Serezhka, dragging her, Mavrutka, to him, Stepan, to his home, gave her to him Stepan in his living quarters for sexual relations. And he, Stepan Korob'in, raped her, Mavrutka, in his home in the living quarters, and he, Stepan, having raped her, Mavrutka, cast her out of his home.

Tsars Ioann and Petr and Tsarevna Sofiia ordered Serezhka beaten and exiled to Siberia with his family for his role in the crime. They ordered that Katerinka be put on stringent surety bond rather than suffer the usual punishment of exile, because her husband was in military service and the tsars were loathe to remove him from it and unwilling to exile Katerinka alone: "for the crime of a wife, husbands are not to be sent in exile; but it was not appropriate to send her Katerinka alone from her husband." The tsars reserved their harshest punishment, appropriately, for the rapist:

> And for rape Stepan Korob'in is to be punished as well by beating with a knout, and the sum of 500 rubles is to be levied on him and, it having been collected, it is to be given over to the maiden Mavrutka for her dishonor and for her dowry, and he Stepan is to be sent under guard to Solovetskii monastery until [the tsar] orders [otherwise]. And as for the fact that he, Stepan, in his testimony and in face to face confrontation with her, Mavrutka, said that he, Stepan, engaged in sexual relations with her, Mavrutka, with her consent and [he said that] he did not rape her, and [as for the fact that] he asked for a general investigation in the community (*poval'nyi obysk*) that he said would reveal previous deceit (*plutovstvo*) by her and her mother: there is no reason to carry out such a community questioning according to his request. Even without a community questioning, his, Stepan's, guilt in this affair is clear from the investigation and from his Stepan's own testimony, since he himself, Stepan, admitted in his testimony that he had told Serezhka Morev, before they brought the maiden to him, to bring him a woman or maiden for sexual relations, and in addition Serezhka Morev in testimony said about this also that he, Stepan, had spoken with him, Serezhka, about bringing [to him] a woman or

[26]PSZ 2, nos. 1266 and 1267, pp. 905–7. For further discussion on these issues, see my "Women's Honor," pp. 67–69.

maiden. And so the plan for this unlawful sexual attack was shown to be his, Stepan's. And those people mentioned above who brought this maiden to him, Stepan, also said in testimony, and others said after torture, that he Stepan raped her, Mavrutka, in a room in his home and she, Mavrutka, implored him, Stepan, not to rape her.

And according to secular laws (*gradskie zakony*), for such unlawful activity not only punishment but penalty is ordered to be done, and it is ordered to give the maiden [a portion] from the property of him who raped her. And thus it is appropriate to punish him, Stepan, for his rape and for the dishonor of the maiden and for her dowry to collect from him that money, 500 rubles, so that other people in the future will not find it fitting to behave this way.

Soon thereafter the tsars pardoned Korob'in and rescinded his exile, but not the five hundred–ruble fine.[27]

Mavrutka Ventsyleeva's case is noteworthy in many respects. First, the crime was deemed so heinous by a high-ranking Moscow servitor that it merited the personal attention of the rulers themselves, or at least their judicial administration (it's impossible to say to what extent the co-tsars and/or Sofiia were actually involved, but the transcript bears an immediacy that strongly suggests their direct participation). Second, the defendant's wealth and social status did not carry weight in the face of the victim's and witnesses' testimonies; his seemingly universal excuse that she had participated willingly and that she was deceitful was dismissed out of hand. Third, the crime was perceived as crippling this woman's prospects for an honorable marriage, and thus the award specifically took the place of her dowry, providing her a lifetime source of support.

Accused men also felt strongly about a charge of rape; their reputations were at stake as well. For example, a church deacon was accused in 1701 of attempting to rape a woman on the street as she was returning home from a wedding. He charged her with falsely accusing him in retaliation for his having told her to leave the wedding because of her own disruptive behavior. "Now others call me a fornicator (*bludnik*) in their petitions because of her," he charged in his petition to the patriarch. The case is unresolved in the surviving record, but the witness cited by the plaintiff did not corroborate her charges.[28] For the accused man, such an accusation left him at risk of further insult; clergy were particularly vulnerable because of the tension between their sacerdotal status and their lives immersed in local village life.

Muscovites also used the law to curb abuses of male authority, notably wife beating. Orthodox teachings condoned physical punishment for women, children, and dependents, urging only that it be just and moderate. The *Domostroi*

[27]PSZ 2, nos. 1266 and 1267, pp. 905–907.
[28]RGADA, f. 210, Prikaznyi stol, stb. 2634, ll. 1–30.

enjoined: "Beat [a disobedient wife] when you are alone together; then forgive her and remonstrate with her. But when you beat her, do not do it in hatred, do not lose control." The text goes on to list items that men should not use in beatings, because they cause too much injury: "a stick or staff or . . . anything made of iron or wood." As one surety document of 1640 put it, a husband's beating of his wife should be "humane" (*po liudtski*) "to avoid injury" (*bezvech'em*).[29]

Numerous examples reveal the tensions of household life in early Russia. Litigants declared that excessive beating invalidated a husband's conjugal authority over his wife: Because of his beatings, "he lives with her illegally," one irate stepfather, a townsman of Ustiug Velikii in the North, declared of his abusive son-in-law in 1632.[30] In the city of Shuia in 1626, a husband reported that his mother-in-law had threatened him because he abused his wife. If he did not stop beating his wife—her daughter—the mother-in-law threatened to take the wife back home and send her "brother" (indicating any close male kinsman) to beat up the abusive husband.[31] A group of brothers, townsmen of Ustiug Velikii, sued in 1655 on behalf of their married sister, who was being beaten by her mother-in-law and brothers-in-law while her husband was away on a trading expedition to Siberia.[32] The wife of the executioner (*zaplechnoi master*) in Iakutsk in 1683 won permission from the metropolitan of Siberia and Tobol'sk for a divorce because of her husband's abuse of her (she declared that she feared for her life), even though she had been caught in adultery.[33]

In one especially poignant case in 1687, a father reported that he had had to rescue his daughter three times from crippling beatings by her husband and her father-in-law. The father won an out-of-court settlement whereby the guilty men agreed to support the injured woman for the rest of her life while she lived apart from her husband.[34] Also in 1687, in the Ustiug Velikii area, a peasant and his son chased down the son's runaway wife and turned her over to the court of the archbishop for questioning. She testified that she fled because the two men had beaten her, and that while in flight she had had one illegitimate child and now had formally married again, from which union she was expect-

---

[29]Pouncy, *Domostroi*, p. 143. 1640: *Akty iuridicheskie* (AIu) (St. Petersburg, 1838), no. 301 (II), p. 313.

[30]RIB 25, no. 99, col. 123. See also the complaint by a mother in 1627: RIB 25, no. 34, col. 36.

[31]1626: *Pamiatniki delovoi*, no. 128, p. 162.

[32]1655: RIB 25, no. 207, cols. 272–73.

[33]AIuB 2 (1864): no. 220, cols. 641–43. Other instances include these: In 1645, an uncle sued on behalf of his niece: RIB 14, no. 342, cols. 739–40. In 1659, a wife sued her husband: RIB 25, no. 225, cols. 305–6. In 1666, a father sued his son-in-law: *Moskovskaia delovaia*, pt. 2, no. 61, p. 74. In 1644, a mother sued on behalf of her daughter: RIB 25, no. 183, cols. 236–37. For others, see RIB 25, no. 207, cols. 272–73 (1655); *Moskovskaia delovaia*, pt. 2, no. 52, pp. 68–69 (1655); ibid., no. 58, p. 72 (1660).

[34]RIB 12, no. 183, cols. 866–75.

ing a child. She went on, however, to say that she would return to her first husband if he promised to stop beating her.[35] Although men continued to have the upper hand in a society in which they were expected to discipline dependents with physical force, women could legitimately seek protection through intermediaries or through their own actions, such as flight or taking the veil.

Women also justly complained when men reneged on promises to marry them or support them in their old age.[36] These cases are particularly revealing of the vulnerability of women, who expected to find in marriage and family both respectability and a material security for the future. For example, a "poverty-stricken widow" in 1603 in the town of Tarnask in the Kholmogory region on the White Sea sued her deceased husband's nephew and heir, who had expelled her from the household and refused to return to her her dowry or her share of her husband's property. A woman of Ustiug Velikii sued in 1629, saying that her husband and his brother had gone off to "wander" and that she had suffered prison for his debts and had finally paid them off with great hardship. Now, she reported, the two men have returned and they have been beating her, once so badly that neighbors had to rescue her from being murdered. And, she complained, the husband also fails to support her and her children now that he has returned.[37]

In a similar case, a priest sued in 1637 to recover the rest of the dowry of a woman who was apparently his ward; he had given her in marriage to the son of a local peasant. He reported that the husband and father-in-law neglected her, had cast her out, and had "wasted and drunk through her dowry." The priest promised that he would preserve what remained of it until he could marry her off again to a more acceptable man. A woman from Zavalov village in the Ustiug Velikii area complained in 1638 that her mother-in-law had not been supporting her, as she had promised, while her husband was in Siberia. So now the abandoned daughter-in-law is forced to "wander from house to house," living off her own work, alms, and the generosity of "good people."[38] In 1642, a townsman in Balkhonka, near Kazan', sued on behalf of his daugh-

---

[35]RIB 12, no. 180, cols. 856–60. Note here the fluidity of marital unions. Gregory Freeze points out that marriage was not fully institutionalized until the late eighteenth century: "Bringing Order to the Russian Family: Marriage and Divorce in Imperial Russia, 1760–1860," *Journal of Modern History* 62 (1990):709–46.

[36]In addition to those cited here, see RIB 25, no. 225, cols. 305–6 (1659); RIB 12, no. 251, cols. 1169–78 (1695); *Pamiatniki pis'mennosti v muzeiakh Vologodskoi oblasti* 4, pt. 2 (Vologda, 1984), pp. 74–75, partially published in *Delovaia pis'mennost' Vologodskogo kraia XVII–XVIII vv.* (Vologda, 1979), p. 29 (1698); RIB 14, no. 134, cols. 344–46 (1620) (this last is an upkeep agreement).

[37]1603: RIB 14, no. 221, cols. 540–41. 1629: RIB 25, no. 77, cols. 88–90.

[38]1637: RIB 2, no. 237, cols. 1016–17. 1638: RIB 25, no. 159, cols. 207–8. For a similar complaint against a mother-in-law, see *Moskovskaia delovaia*, pt. 5, no. 2, pp. 201–2 (1659).

ter, saying that her husband, a townsman of Nizhnii Novgorod, had beaten and abused her and had forced her, pregnant, into a convent (where she had had the child) and that he had kept her dowry and remarried within a week of his wife's taking of the veil. Now, the father charges, the husband is reneging on his promise to pay the convent her upkeep. A townswoman of Ustiug Velikii complained in 1661 that her husband has taken up with another woman and fails to support her, his legal wife. So now she "wanders" about the village, living off alms.[39]

Promises of marriage were particularly sensitive, inasmuch as with such an understanding a woman might consent to premarital sex. If the agreement were broken, she was left publicly humiliated, unable to make an honorable marriage and deprived of material support.[40] Orthodox practice exacerbated this likelihood with the practice of formal betrothal (*obruchenie*), which could significantly precede the wedding ceremony and which was taken as binding. In reforms of 1775, the church closed the time gap between betrothal and wedding to avoid putting affianced parties, particularly women, in awkward situations, as in these telling examples.[41] In 1646, a townswoman of Ustiug Velikii reported that a man and his father and brother had taken her to live with them on a promise of marriage to the plaintiff—he had sworn a vow on an icon, possibly a form of betrothal. Nevertheless, he had expelled her from the home when she became pregnant. Now, she asks that it be put on record that he, his brother, and father are threatening her and her child with all manner of evil. In the Vologda area in 1657, a peasant woman complained that a man had reneged on a promise to marry her, had lived with her for a year and a half, had fathered her son, and now has married another woman. Now she has no one to support her.[42] Grigorii Kotoshikhin, who wrote a description of government and mores in the court elite in the 1660s, paid particular attention to this vulnerable moment. If a prospective suitor, he wrote, wins the privilege of viewing a prospective bride in person and then insults her with "evil and shameful words, and drives other bridegrooms from her," he should be made to marry her because of the dishonor to her.[43]

---

[39]1642: RIB 2, no. 206, cols. 946–49. 1661: RIB 25, no. 232, cols. 316–17.

[40]Guido Ruggiero chronicled just such a case of breach of promise in sixteenth-century Italy: "'More Dear to Me than Life Itself': Marriage, Honor and a Woman's Reputation in the Renaissance," in idem, *Binding Passions: Tales of Magic, Marriage and Power at the End of the Renaissance* (New York, 1993), pp. 57–87. John M. Klassen also cites breach of promise in fourteenth-century Bohemian suits: "Marriage and Family in Medieval Bohemia," *East European Quarterly* 19, no. 3 (1985):257–74.

[41]V. M. Nechaev, "Obruchenie," *Entsiklopedicheskii slovar'* 42 (1897):579–80.

[42]1646: RIB 25, no. 192, cols. 249–50. 1657: *Delovaia pis'mennost' Vologodskogo kraia*, p. 7.

[43]Grigorii Kotoshikhin, *O Rossii vo tsarstvovanie Alekseia Mikhailovicha*, 4th ed. (St. Petersburg, 1906), p. 157.

Muscovites also vigorously protected women from more symbolic assaults on their well-being; here the opportunity to litigate over honor provided a public forum to enforce social values. A woman's hair—here as in many other cultures[44]—had both honorific and sexual connotations and thus became a site where conflict and tension would be played out. In the Russian language, for example, over time the verb *oprostovolosit'sia* added to its literal meaning of "uncovering one's hair" the connotation of making a fool of oneself.[45] In Muscovy, maidens wore a single braid, while married women wore two plaits covered by a kerchief or headdress. Women also dressed modestly in voluminous layers of clothes. Numerous suits for dishonor were filed because a man knocked off a woman's headdress, pulled her braids, or ripped her clothing.[46] Men were equally sensitive to affronts to their bodily dignity, protesting when their clothes were ripped or beards pulled.[47]

Men were particularly sensitive to verbal slanders about the women in their families. Repeatedly in the cases in my database, men specified that they had been insulted "with a mother oath." In 1641, for example, a military servitor (a *zhilets*) in Tula (south of Moscow toward the steppe frontier) complained that while he was getting ready to go off on military duty, a group of neighbors accosted him at his home and insulted him with a mother oath. He sued for the insult not only to him but also to his mother.[48] Men also protested when a woman was called a "bad wife" or "bad woman" (*nedobraia zhena*), which covered a range of negative connotations. In 1623, for example, a gentryman of Nizhnii Novgorod called a musketeer captain's wife a "bad woman" and tried to lift up the carriage mantle shrouding her, also a humiliation. And in 1635, Prince Dmtrii Ivanov syn Meshcherskii admitted that he had called his sister-in-law a "bad wife" and had said that her children were illegitimate; he

[44]Hair is associated with the head, which symbolized honor, and also has sexual connotations: Julian Pitt-Rivers, "Honor," *International Encyclopedia of the Social Sciences* 6 (1968):503–11, and idem, "Honour and Social Status," in J. G. Peristiany, ed., *Honour and Shame: The Values of Mediterranean Society* (Chicago, 1966), p. 25.

[45]SRIa 13 (1987):50; Vladimir Dal', *Tolkovyi slovar' zhivogo velikorusskogo iazyka*, 4th ed., 4 vols. (St. Petersburg, 1912–14) 2:1775.

[46]RIB 25, no. 63, cols. 72–73 (1628); ibid., no. 86, cols. 100–2 (1631); RIB 2 (1875), no. 206, cols. 946–49 (1642); RIB 14, no. 295, cols. 662–64 (1623); RIB 14, no. 336, cols. 729–30 (1641). RGADA, f. 210, Prikaznyi stol, stb. 262, l. 45, (1680); ibid., stb. 15, ch. 2, ll. 708–10 (1625); RGADA, f. 2160, Sevskii stol, stb. 37, ll. 10-12 (1689); *Moskovskaia delovaia*, pt. 2, no. 102, pp. 97–98 (1676).

[47]RGADA, f. 210, Prikaznyi stol, stb. 33, ll. 248–50 (1629); ibid., stb. 987, ll. 58–71 (1666); AI 4, no. 205, pp. 437–38 (1668); RGADA, f. 210, Prikaznyi stol, stb. 740, ll. 4–65 (1677). Hair and beards were also involved in honor in nineteenth-century Russian peasant communities: M. M. Gromyko, *Traditsionnye normy povedeniia i formy obshcheniia russkikh krest'ian XIX v.* (Moscow, 1986), pp. 93–99; N. A. Minenko, *Zhivaia starina* (Novosibirsk, 1989), p. 98.

[48]RGADA, f. 210, Prikaznyi stol, stb. 130, ll. 403–31.

pleaded drunkenness to excuse his bad behavior and was sentenced to perform a ritual of humiliation and to pay a large fine.[49]

Men responsible for women would protest explicit sexual slander against them. While women also suffered other insults—they were often called thieves and criminals (*vor, vorovka*)—sexual slander was by far the affront most often addressed to them. They were called bitch (*suka*), whore (*bliad', kurva*), and cheater (*plutovka*). In 1649, for example, a gentryman on the steppe frontier in Userda complained that his neighbor came to his home and called his wife and two maiden daughters whores. The two men eventually settled out of court. A brawl erupted in 1691 at the home of a Moscow boyar, Prince Iakov Nikitich Odoevskii, between a *stol'nik*, P. V. Kikin, and a state secretary (*d'iak*) Kharlampov. Kikin charged Kharlampov with accusing him of committing incest with his mother and taunting him repeatedly about it. Kikin reacted so vociferously that Prince Odoevskii sued him for the dishonor of creating such a disruption in his home, while Kikin sued Kharlampov for the dishonor to his mother. He was, as he said in his petition, "ready to die for his mother's honor." Unfortunately, the case is unresolved in the extant records.[50] Similarly, a townsman in the Kitaigorod section of Moscow in 1691 sued another for saying that he had had sexual relations with the plaintiff's maiden daughters.[51]

Muscovites also sought legal protection from the scorn of illegitimate birth. Prayers and christenings were withheld from unmarried mothers and their babies until the mothers testified that the pregnancy was caused by rape or otherwise coerced sexual relations. This issue shows the two-edged sword of patriarchy: Patriarchs sought to establish the respectability of their female dependents, while the verification procedure exerted social control, perhaps helping to deter illicit sexual activity. In 1679, for example, a landlord reported to church judicial authorities in the Riazan' and Murom metropolitanate that his servant girl, who had fled his village, had given birth. She claimed to the investigating priest that she had been raped and had had no other sexual relations. The priest then performed the required prayers and gave her the proper documentation (a *pocherevnaia pamiat'*). Similarly, in 1682, a landlord's man from the Murom area reported to the local governor that a servant girl of the

---

[49]1623: RGADA, f. 210, Moscow stol, stb. 15, ll. 320–28. 1635: RGADA, f. 210, Prikaznyi stol, stb. 139, ll. 473–94.

[50]1649: RGADA, f. 210, Prikaznyi stol, stb. 192, ll. 143–63. 1691: RGADA, f. 210, Prikaznyi stol, stb. 1998, ll. 337–71; ibid., stb. 1534, ll. 105–8.

[51]1691: RGADA, f. 210, Prikaznyi stol, stb. 1203, ll. 6–9, 140–58. Other suits involving sexual slander include RIB 25, no. 63, cols. 72–73 (1628); I. E. Zabelin, *Domashnii byt russkikh tsarei v XVI i XVII st.*, 3 bks. (Moscow, 1990), reprint publ. of 4th exp. ed. (Moscow, 1918), pp. 354–58 (1642); RGADA, f. 210, Prikaznyi stol, stb. 1013, ll. 22–40 (1669); RGADA, f. 210, Belgorod stol, stb. 1260, l. 242; K. P. Pobedonostsev, ed., *Materialy dlia istorii prikaznogo sudoproizvodstva v Rossii* (Moscow, 1890), viazka 76, delo 43, p. 98 (1713).

landlord had lived illegally with another man and had had a child. He turned in the accused couple, who reported that they had been punished in the church courts in the previous year for fornication (*bludnoe delo*). The governor then turned the man over to the church courts for further punishment.[52] A priest in the Northern Dvina area in 1690 investigated an illegitimate birth to Pelageika Prokof'ev doch'. Pelageika accused a man of raping her and then taking her as his common-law wife; he denied all. They finally reached a settlement in which he paid something toward the child's upkeep.[53] In 1696, a parish priest in the Northern Dvina area questioned a single peasant girl about an alleged pregnancy. She was forced to undergo physical examination by some widows of the village and was pronounced not pregnant. A woman in 1694 was reported to the archbishop's court in Tot'ma in the North (in the Vologda area) and questioned about her illegitimate pregnancy. She accused a young man and then a priest of raping her, then eventually recanted, naming the baby's real father, a man who had fled the area. She was beaten for her initial false accusation.[54]

Such litigation was carried on mainly by men on behalf of their dependent women. But women participated in their own defense as well. In the absence of a male superior, widows, nuns and abbesses, soldier's wives, and others might speak up for their own honor. They litigated to win social approbation and psychological reinforcement, as well as tangible compensation. Courts did indeed award women the twofold or fourfold fines they merited by law. In 1685, for example, a townsman in Kolomna near Moscow sued because another townsman had insulted his wife and two sons with a mother oath and had threatened them with a club. According to the settlement, the man was awarded the dishonor payment for townsmen of his category (seven rubles), his wife received fourteen rubles, and his two sons received seven between them, for a total of twenty-eight rubles.[55] In 1690, a provincial cavalryman of Elets (south of Moscow near the upper Don) won a case on behalf of his maiden daughter who had been beaten, insulted, and accused of stealing. He was awarded thirty-two rubles, four times his allotment of eight, but the judgment was overturned on procedural grounds.[56] In 1692, a minor sued on behalf of his widowed mother and himself for unspecified verbal abuse (*bran'*). He was awarded half his father's annual allotment of seventy-five rubles (his father had been a *zhilets*— a Moscow-based cavalry rank), and his mother received twice the allotment.[57] A shipbuilder won a settlement in 1709 for verbal insult to himself and his wife,

---

[52]1679: *Pamiatniki delovoi*, no. 174, pp. 195–96; for a similar case, see ibid., no. 183, p. 202 (1681). 1682: *Pamiatniki delovoi*, no. 218, p. 226.

[53]RIB 12, no. 212, cols. 988–90.

[54]1696: RIB 12, no. 256, col. 1229. 1694: RIB 12, no. 245, cols. 1144–54.

[55]RGADA, f. 210, Prikaznyi stol, stb. 918, ll. 18–43.

[56]RGADA, f. 210, Prikaznyi stol, stb. 2608, ll. 1–58.

[57]RGADA, f. 210, Prikaznyi stol, stb. 1561, ll. 1–28.

for the accusation that she was a criminal (*vorovka*). They received 303 rubles (twice the shipbuilder's annual allotment of 101 rubles for his wife, and 101 more for himself).[58] And in a complicated case of 1720, the litigants—all Armenians in Russian service—reached an out-of-court settlement that amounted to the plaintiff's annual allotment for himself (fifty rubles; he was a barber to Peter I's wife Catherine) and twice that for his wife. The charge was that the defendants had verbally insulted husband and wife and had beaten the man.[59] When a male litigant sued on behalf of women or other family members, it was apparently he, not the insulted dependents, who pocketed the award.

Dishonor suits demonstrate Moscow's patriarchal value system, rewarding people whose virtue was affirmed and punishing those guilty of slander. For women, this had paradoxical implications: The more women identified with these values and used these judicial protections, the more patriarchy was reinforced. To the modern mind, the system would hardly seem a welcoming ethos for women. But we should recall that to contemporaries, these gendered roles offered security in an insecure world. When women were in positions such as domestic managers, marriage brokers, propertied widows, nuns, or abbesses, they operated with a certain degree of autonomy. Living by the standards of patriarchy, women balanced control with reward and carved out spheres of independence.[60]

Enforcing Patriarchal Values

In addition to internalized values of patriarchy and opportunities to litigate over verbal and physical humiliation, communities had other ways to enforce controls on women's behavior and sexual activity, such as veiling and seclusion. This was particularly an issue for the elite, because control over women helped to maintain high status. At the same time, it was not feasible to prohibit peasant and urban women from the public square and marketplace. Indeed, veiling and seclusion of elite women the world over signified status; they "were signs that a man could afford to have servants . . . and that he occupied an economic position that allowed him to protect the honor of his family from abuse."[61] Elite Muscovite women were secluded through the sixteenth and seventeenth centuries, by all accounts more intensely in the seventeenth century. They lived in separate quarters at home, wearing shrouds or traveling in closed carriages in

---

[58]RGADA, f. 239, Sudnyi prikaz, op. 1, ch. 4, delo 5420, ll. 1–15v; published in part in Pobedonostsev, *Materialy*, pp. 45–46.

[59]RGADA, f. 239, Sudnyi prikaz, op. 1, ch. 4, delo 5761, ll. 1–20v.

[60]See the literature on women's authority in the interstices of society cited in my "Women's Honor," pp. 69–70; Worobec (*Peasant Russia*, pp. 8, 13–14, 177–78, 204–5, 215) makes this point as well.

[61]Nikki Keddie and Lois Beck, "Introduction," in idem, eds., *Women in the Muslim World* (Cambridge, Mass., 1978), p. 8.

Muscovite weddings were elaborate rituals that combined folk elements with religious liturgy;
here, in an engraving from the 1647 edition of Olearius's *Travels*, the bride is transported in a
closed carriage to the church. Olearius wrote, "Their weddings are elaborate, and the bride is conveyed to her new home with special pageantry" (trans. Samuel H. Baron). Women in the elite as a
rule traveled in similar carriages, secluded from the public gaze. (Illustration: Adam Olearius, *Oft
begehrte Beschreibung der newen Orientalischen Reise* [Schleswig, 1647]. Courtesy of Special Collections, University of Southern California Libraries.)

public. Among the cases I studied is the instance in 1623, cited in the previous
section, when a man tried to raise the mantle of a woman's carriage.[62]

Contemporaries, foreign and Russian, commented on the practice. Sigismund von Herberstein, referring to the 1520s, wrote: "No woman who walks
in the street is deemed chaste or respectable. Thus wealthy or important people
keep their women so shut up that no one can see or speak to them."[63] And in

[62]RGADA, f. 210, Moscow stol, stb. 15, ll. 320–28 (1623).

[63]Sigismund von Herberstein, *Description of Moscow and Muscovy, 1557*, ed. Bertold Picard,
trans. J. B. C. Grundy trans. (New York, 1966), p. 40. Other observers also said that strict control was
limited to the elite: Adam Olearius, *The Travels of Olearius in Seventeenth-Century Russia*, ed. and
trans. Samuel H. Baron (Stanford, 1967), pp. 168–69; Augustin Baron de Mayerberg, *Relation d'un
voyage en Muscovie*, 2 vols. (Paris, 1858), 1:140; see also S. S. Shashkov, *Istoriia russkoi zhenshchiny*,
in idem, *Sobranie sochinenii*, 2 vols. (St. Petersburg, 1898), 1: cols. 702–6, 714, 752.

the early seventeenth century, a French mercenary, Jacques Margeret, noted: "Russian women are held under close supervision and have their living quarters separate from that of their husbands."[64] Royal women were shrouded in curtains as they walked between churches in the Kremlin; at other times they rode in closed carriages.[65] For the elite, this practice protected women's value as marriage partners and procreators, as it also demonstrated the affluence and honor of the family.[66]

At the same time, one should not take seclusion as evidence of women's abject subordination. They were accorded significant respect and established spheres of independent activity compatible with the norms of patriarchy. Women, respected for their piety and moral example, often operated independently in the religious sphere. Several elite women, for example, provided safe haven and material support for persecuted Old Believers in the first generation of the Schism.[67] Women in the ruling family maintained correspondence with Eastern patriarchs, patronized monasteries and distributed alms, and interceded with the tsar for mercy in judicial cases. Most significantly, they were regarded as essential components of the functioning of the "God-dependent" community. This is strikingly apparently in Aleksei Mikhailovich's correspondence with his sisters at court, as analyzed by Isolde Thyrêt.[68] While off at battle, the tsar entreated the female members of his household for prayers for victory; he informed them of the daily military and political events as well. Clearly he saw them as involved in the fused public/private world of Kremlin politics and as playing an essential spiritual role in his godly autocracy.

Communities could also use public forums of insult as a strategy to encourage conformity to social expectations. This could occur in a number of forms. The very act of shouting insults, especially sexual innuendoes, in public forums could be construed as policing social behavior—insulting was a strategy, after all. Hurling an insult at someone publicly was an assault on his reputation, a means of forcing a reaction from the insulted person, which could redound to the benefit of the insulter. By their very nature, insults were not affronts to personal dignity unless uttered publicly, before witnesses. Thus, the very utterance lodged doubt in people's minds and forced the insulted party on the defensive. As David Garrioch argues on the example of eighteenth-century Paris, insults "were a form of socialisation, a way of teaching [the dominant] value system,

---

[64]Jacques Margeret, *The Russian Empire and Grand Duchy of Muscovy: A 17th-Century Account*, trans. and ed. Chester S. L. Dunning. (Pittsburgh, 1983), p. 31.

[65]Herberstein, *Description of Moscow*, p. 40; Olearius, *Travels*, pp. 73, 169; Mayerberg, *Relation* 2:116–18.

[66]See my "The Seclusion of Elite Muscovite Women."

[67]Michels, "Muscovite Elite Women."

[68]Isolde Thyrêt, "Life in the Kremlin under the Tsars Mikhail Fedorovich and Aleksei Mikhailovich: New Perspectives on the Institution of the *Terem*," unpubl. manuscript (1996).

and of compelling, if not real observance, at least lip-service to it." Even if an insult were brought to court and litigated, the "insulting moment" provided a site for social manipulation. "If the opponent did not join battle, the insults proclaimed the victory of the insulter and the public shaming of the victim."[69] With witnesses spreading gossip quickly through the community, an insult could become a permanent slur on one's reputation unless sternly countered. Insults worked in this way in Muscovy as well; recall the complaint cited in the previous section by a church deacon accused of rape, that "now others call me a fornicator."

In most of these cases, insults seem to have been hurled in anger in the heat of a brawl or altercation. But sometimes the elements of persistence or publicity suggest a more didactic intent to shame someone into better behavior. In 1605, for example, neighbors succeeded in driving a family out of the town of Tarnask in the Kholmogory area with repeated public insults to the wife for sexual promiscuity. Similarly, a woman walked up to a man in Moscow in 1666 and accused him of luring a servant girl and a maiden into sexual activities with others; the man was so insulted that he called her a slovenly bastard, and she sued him for dishonor. In a 1683 investigation by officials of the archbishop of Ustiug Velikii and Tot'ma into an illegitimate birth, a man yelled at another man in public, accusing him of incestuous relations with his sister, the unwed mother under investigation. Many witnesses corroborated the sexual slander. The accused sued for dishonor, saying that his sister was married to a man now in Siberia and denying any immoral activity.[70] And in Kostroma in 1694, a criminal investigator (*syshchik*) shouted out loud in church, calling another man of much higher rank (a *stol'nik*) a "bastard" (*vybliadok*) and insulting him with a mother oath. A man in 1700 assaulted a priest in church while he was performing the liturgy; the priest's wife and daughter came to his rescue and were attacked as well. Later at a compatriot's house, the man called the priest, who was his own father confessor, a "thief, criminal, and fornicator."[71] Such insults in such public settings, particularly in church or in cases of repeated harassment, might have been intentional public shaming.

The more specific the insults got, the more likely it seems that the sexual slander of which individuals complained so bitterly might have been uttered to police

[69]David Garrioch, "Verbal Insults in Eighteenth-Century Paris," in Peter Burke and Roy Porter, eds., *The Social History of Language* (Cambridge, England, 1987), pp. 104–19, quotes on pp. 113, 116, and idem, *Neighbourhood and Community in Paris, 1740–1790* (Cambridge, England, 1986), pp. 33–55.

[70]1605: RIB 14, no. 234, cols. 558–59. 1666: Zabelin, *Domashnii byt*, pp. 396–97. 1683: RIB 12, no. 143, cols. 589–95.

[71]1694: RGADA, f. 210, Prikaznyi stol, stb. 1552, ll. 30–58. 1700: RGADA, f. 210, Prikaznyi stol, stb. 2342, ll. 16–28. For another incident of insult in a church, see RGADA, f. 210, Prikaznyi stol, stb. 128, ll. 346–49 (1641).

neighbors' conduct. Note, for example, the incident in 1686 in Vologda in which a man accused his neighbor of a range of crimes, including theft and heresy, and capped off the tirade by saying before many witnesses, "your wife goes from house to house and sleeps around." The insulted man sued for dishonor; in any case, the insult had the intent of public shaming "before many witnesses." Or the instance in 1689, when a gentryman asserted that another was illegitimate, alleging that the man's mother had slept with a household servant; or one in 1655, when a man in a new-model regiment accused another man's wife of "sneaking into the cellar" for sex. Both incidents suggest self-righteous moralizing.[72]

Even if victims did defend themselves promptly, damage could be done. Christine Worobec gives a telling nineteenth-century example of a maiden whose reputation was ruined (she had been publicly shamed) because of sexual slanders that were later proven groundless and publicly recanted. Such false accusations were accordingly harshly punished, but harm had been done.[73] Choosing to insult could be done by a rival for spite or in a calculated fashion to advertise unacceptable conduct to the community. Even though such insults may have been punished as dishonor because they upset community norms for proper interaction—and even if there were no truth in them—they demonstrated and affirmed community norms and put all within earshot on notice of the unpleasant consequences of deviance.

Individuals could also adopt more ritualized forms of public shaming. In early modern Europe, a particular type of insult—called in France *tapage* or *bacchanale*—was practiced. David Garrioch explains: "This consisted of an aggrieved party—nearly always a man—stationing himself outside his opponent's door or window, shouting out insults and generally creating a nuisance, often for quite some time." The grievance that prompted the public outburst might consist of having been spurned in a love affair, or it might reflect neighbors' concern at perceived loose morals in a local household; it usually concerned sexual impropriety. Garrioch documented it in eighteenth-century Paris, Elizabeth Cohen in sixteenth-century Italy, and we see it in Muscovite sources as well.[74] There are cases of Muscovites complaining of other people publicly shouting sexual slander at them at their homes. In 1626, for example, a parish priest in Iur'ev Polskoi reported that a neighbor, apparently drunk, came to his

---

[72]1686: *Pamiatniki pis'mennosti v muzeiakh Vologodskoi oblasti*, 4, pt. 2 (1984), pp. 54–55; partial publication in *Delovaia pis'mennost' Vologodskogo kraia*, p. 27. 1689: RGADA, f. 210, Prikaznyi stol, stb. 1074, ll. 92–100. 1655: RGADA, f. 210, Prikaznyi stol, stb. 211, ll. 30–33.

[73]Worobec, *Peasant Russia*, pp. 146–48. Gromyko also cites an example in which the community rallied to reinstate an innocent girl's sullied reputation: *Traditsionnye normy*, pp. 93–99.

[74]Garrioch, *Neighbourhood and Community*, p. 44–45; Elizabeth S. Cohen, "Honor and Gender in the Streets of Early Modern Rome," *Journal of Interdisciplinary History* 22, no. 4 (1992):597–625.

home while the priest was away and stood "at the window yelling mother oaths at my wife and maiden daughter." The defendant was found guilty and beaten with bastinadoes and imprisoned for the offense.[75] Also in 1626, the townswoman Ovdotitsa in Ustiug Velikii put on record her complaint (*iavka*) against her neighbor Mariia Tarasova that Mariia wanted to bewitch her and that she "came under my window and said all manner of unspeakable insult." Mariia responded by denying the charges and suing Ovdotitsa for dishonor. A peasant of the Northern Dvina lands sued in 1653, saying that a neighbor "came under my window and insulted my mother with all manner of unspeakable insults and called her a whore and before this he has bragged of doing all sorts of unlawful things to us, murder and theft." And in 1666, Ivan Sas, a colonel in service in Belgorod on the southern frontier, insulted his commanding officer, Boyar Prince Boris Aleksandrovich Repnin; a few days later Sas came to Repnin's home and "made great noise under the window."[76]

Each of these instances is different, and none is fully elaborated, but in each case the element of publicity to enforce community norms is clear. In the last cited case, for example, the commanding officer's response to the noisemaking was to tell Sas to sue him properly in the district offices. But clearly Sas's goal was to humiliate Repnin beyond the range of the mere courthouse. In the first and third cases, the element of *tapage* is suggested, inasmuch as a wife and maiden daughter were targets of the insults, and sexual slander was explicit. In the allegations of witchcraft, the public shaming may have stemmed from enmity between neighbors, but the attempt to publicly discredit is clear.[77]

A more elaborated public shaming ritual would be a charivari, in which a large, diverse group of community members—men, women, and youth—held a family or individual up to public ridicule for gross infractions of community norms, particularly sexual norms. The form varied in different countries, as did the targeted behaviors. In usual early modern European practice, cuckolded husbands and those whose wives were perceived to dominate them were targets of ridicule; older men who upset the local marriage market by marrying much younger women often brought the wrath of the young men of the community on them. Adulterous wives were ready targets, as were young girls of dubious virtue. Charivaris were mounted to drive the implicated parties publicly through the community in some humiliating way that was symbolic of the alleged offense. Cuckolded husbands were tied backward on horses with horns fixed to their heads; girls of ill repute were paraded through town with tarred

[75]1626: RGADA, f. 210, Prikaznyi stol, stb. 17, ll. 172–73, 330–34.

[76]1626: RIB 25, no. 9, cols. 10–11, no. 10, cols. 11–12. 1653: RIB 14, no. 359, cols. 766–67. 1666: RGADA, f. 210, Prikaznyi stol, stb. 977, ll. 1–46.

[77]For another example of insult shouted in anger, see RGADA, f. 210, Prikaznyi stol, stb. 824, ll. 1–99 (1680).

clothes, bared bosom, and disheveled hair. Sometimes the humiliation took the form of marking the door and home of a suspected miscreant—tarring the door, affixing horns to the gate, breaking open the door or gate—all symbolic of easy, illicit sexual access. Always, charivaris were accompanied by noise—shouts, drums, or the singing of lewd songs, the so-called rough music. These spectacles powerfully exerted social pressure, not only forcing individuals to conform or to depart the village, but also putting the whole community on notice that such treatment awaited them should they ever transgress.[78]

Charivaris are recorded after the Muscovite era in Russian peasant communities in the nineteenth century, and they followed much the same form: a theatrical, ritualized display featuring riding backward, "rough music," and the public display of the transgressor. But their targets were more concerned with petty theft and other crimes that destabilized village communities than with sexual mores. Stephen Frank argues that collective shamings for sexual transgressions were unnecessary because husbands were expected to punish philandering wives themselves.[79]

In the Muscovite period, as far as I have been able to tell, such collective charivaris did not occur. In one intriguing dishonor case of 1651, a man in service in Mozhaisk complained that it was said he had ridden a cow and a bear "like a fool (*shutom*)," a reference to riding backward; he denied it vigorously, saying a community survey had exposed the allegation as false.[80] But this oblique reference may not refer to a ritual like charivari. It is possible that charivaris in Muscovy are hidden by the nature of the sources. As Worobec noted for the nineteenth century, charivaris were unofficial (in fact they were officially condemned by church and state alike) outbursts of community disorder that would not likely be recorded systematically.[81] They tended to be noted

---

[78]Literature on charivaris and public shaming includes Natalie Zemon Davis, "The Reasons of Misrule," and "Women on Top," in idem, *Society and Culture in Early Modern France* (Stanford, 1965), pp. 97–153; idem, "Charivari, Honor, and Community in Seventeenth-Century Lyon and Geneva," in John J. MacAloon, ed., *Rite, Drama, Festival, Spectacle: Rehearsals toward a Theory of Cultural Performance* (Philadelphia, 1984), pp. 42–57; E. P. Thompson, "'Rough music': Le charivari anglais," *Annales: E.S.C.* 27 (1972):285–312; Ingram, "Ridings"; Cohen, "Honor and Gender"; Peter Burke, *The Historical Anthropology of Early Modern Italy* (Cambridge, England, 1987), chap. 8; Underdown, "Taming of the Scold"; Ruth Mellinkoff, "Riding Backwards: Theme of Humiliation and Symbol of Evil," *Viator* 4 (1973):153–79.

[79]Frank, "Popular Justice"; Worobec, *Peasant Russia*, p. 195. Minenko also notes how accusations of thievery were insulting in eighteenth-century peasant communities: *Zhivaia starina*, p. 93.Gromyko describes public humiliation of women accused of illicit sexual activity (smearing tar on their gates, throwing soot on their clothes): *Traditsionnye normy*, pp. 93–99.

[80]*Moskovskaia delovaia*, pt. 5, no. 1, p. 200.

[81]Worobec, *Peasant Russia*, p. 22. David Garrioch and Martin Ingram both note that charivaris declined when authorities began to prosecute them as a form of public disorder, as well as when social changes undermined their impact: Garrioch, *Neighbourhood and Community*, p. 217–18; Ingram, "Ridings," pp. 189–92.

only when affronted victims of charivaris complained against the humiliation they had suffered.[82] And *tapage* amounted to a sort of charivari by individuals.

For collective shaming rituals, Muscovites seemed either to substitute the forms of individual insult that we have discussed or to rely on patriarchal control as Worobec suggests, or—a third alternative—to turn to official institutions for enforcement of norms. Elements of public shaming, after all, were deeply ingrained in Muscovite judicial sanctions, some approaching charivari-like symbolism. Grigorii Kotoshikhin reported: "men who commit crimes with other men's wives or with maidens and are caught, on the day of capture or another day they both, man and woman, no matter of what rank they are, are led through the marketplace and through the city streets together, naked, and then beaten with a knout."[83] Public processions of convicted criminals also occurred. In 1699, thieves taking advantage of a fire to steal were (in addition to harsh punishment and exile) ordered to be led publicly by the scene of the fire; and for those soldiers or townsmen who should have been fighting the fire, town criers were dispatched to announce their perfidy to the various town and soldier neighborhoods.[84] Members of the political elite who were found guilty of offenses were exposed to the reprobation of their peers in the Kremlin by being led publicly to punishment. In 1633, for example, two *stol'niki* who had sued a boyar for precedence lost their suit and were sentenced to prison for dishonoring the defendant. But as they were being led across the Kremlin grounds to prison, "in front of the Frolov Gates," it was announced to them that the tsar had bestowed mercy and canceled the sentence.[85] If members of the elite refused to accept defeat in suits over precedence, they were subjected to a public ritual of humiliation, as discussed in Chapter 4. The principle of publicity is clear here.

People also had recourse to official institutions to bring erring members into conformity with norms or to reassert norms in the face of individuals flouting them. An example of such recourse is the many notices (*iavki*) used to put deviance from norms on record in advance. Fathers, for example, could use the courts to dissociate themselves from a wayward daughter or a runaway wife, from the debts such women were compiling, or from the dishonor their wantonness heaped on the family. These notices also graphically illustrate the gendered roles imposed on men and women, husbands and wives, sons, daughters,

---

[82]For example, the public shaming discussed by Elizabeth Cohen in "Honor and Gender" and the charivaris examined by Natalie Zemon Davis in "Charivari, Honor and Community" came to light because their victims sued for defamation.

[83]Kotoshikhin, *O Rossii*, p. 116.

[84]PSZ 3, no. 1693 (1699).

[85]*Dvortsovye razriady* (DR), 4 vols. (St. Petersburg, 1850–55), 2: cols. 350–51 (1633). N. D. Sergeevskii cites other examples of "marketplace" (*torgovaia kazn'*) punishments, in which the element of publicity intensified the punishment: *Nakazanie v russkom prave XVII veka* (St. Petersburg, 1887), pp. 155–58.

and daughters-in-law. In 1621, a peasant from the Ustiug Velikii area registered with authorities his complaint that his wife had run off with another man and also with his life's savings, and that now the other man boasts he will ruin him even further with false accusations. In 1626, a peasant from Vologda registered with local authorities the complaint that his daughter-in-law had run away, stealing jewelry and clothing from the family, and then died. He wanted it recorded that he and his son had no responsibility in her death.

Also in 1626, a townsman of Ustiug Velikii served notice that his daughter-in-law was living with his son not as a good wife should, but "illegally," as he put it. She has fled the household and has threatened to commit suicide out of spite to her husband and his father. The father declared that, should she do harm to herself such as "throwing herself into water, hanging herself or running into traffic," it would not be their fault. In 1628, a peasant in the Ustiug Velikii area registered a notice about his daughter-in-law: Since her husband, his son, has gone to Siberia, the wife refuses to obey him, steals, and has left home. Now he wants to renounce responsibility for her so the girl's "clan and tribe" will have no claim against him.[86]

Similarly, a musketeer in Ustiug Velikii in 1629 registered a complaint against his wife's "drunken criminal behavior" (*pianskoe vorovstvo*): She steals from him, has physically attacked her in-laws, and has left home to live with her family, who are now threatening him with harm. He seeks to put people on notice of the possibility that they would assault him, falsely accuse him, bewitch him, or otherwise ruin him. In 1632, a merchant or artisan from Ustiug Velikii registered a complaint against his wife because "she doesn't obey me; whenever I leave the house for work, she sells our wares in the neighborhood for a loss and she does not do her work and does not live with me and she threatens me and has left me." In another such notice, a cleric from Ustiug Velikii in 1638 dissociated himself from his wife, who had taken up with another man while he himself had sat in prison because of her false accusations against him. Now that he has been released, she has fled to unknown parts. He declares himself not responsible for her future actions. Also in Ustiug Velikii in 1640, a priest served notice that his errant daughter-in-law had fled home repeatedly, "not loving her husband and not wanting to live with him, but not because she was beaten or tortured but of her own willfulness." She had recently fled again, stealing clothing and jewelry. Her father-in-law petitioned to absolve himself of responsibility for her debts and criminality.[87] These many notices publicly affirmed values as they also pragmatically protected the initiator's material interests.

[86]1621: RIB 25, no. 1, cols. 1–2. 1626: RIB 25, no. 5, cols. 6–7. 1626: RIB 25, no. 26, cols. 27–28. 1628: RIB 25, no. 61, cols. 70–71.

[87]1629: RIB 25, no. 68, cols. 79–81. 1632: RIB 25, no. 100, col. 124. 1638: RIB 25, no. 156, cols. 205–6. 1640: RIB 25, no. 174, cols. 226–27.

Parents could register complaints about their prodigal children, even bringing them to court. In 1629, an Ustiug Velikii townsman recorded a notice dis-
sociating himself from his son, who drinks, disobeys him, plays at dice, and is
falling into debt. "After this point he is no longer my son and I will have nothing to do with him." The father denied responsibility for the dissolute man's
debts and "criminality." In 1655, the eminent Moscow merchant (*gost'*) Vasilii
Shorin sued that his ward was living so recklessly and wastefully (beating his
wife, carousing with women, drinking) that "his wife and son are always in
tears." He asked that the patriarch send the dissolute husband to a monastery
"for his drunkenness and cheating . . . so that his soul will not perish." A
mother in Moscow sued her son in 1683, alleging that "he lives illegally, forgetting the fear of God and does not attend church." He goes about with
"unbaptized foreigners" and disobeys, injures, and dishonors her. In questioning, the son, apparently a follower of the Old Belief, responded, "I pray in my
home, I follow the old religion and bless myself in the old fashion," and denied
the rest of the charges. He was ordered beaten for his insults to his mother and
sent to a monastery for his apostasy.[88]

Neighbors and other non-kin also reported people to the authorities for
immoral behavior. In 1630, the abbess of a convent posted notice with the
courts of the metropolitan of Ustiug Velikii about a nun in the convent and her
daughter, who caroused: "they come here at night with unknown people and
drink and make noise and threaten and dishonor us." A gardener registered a
complaint in 1663 against a woman who had been living at his household: "she
drinks and carouses (*brazhnichaet*) and . . . goes about with unknown people"
and insults and threatens the plaintiff and his wife. Now she has left the household again, leaving her children abandoned and "dying of hunger." The petitioner declares that he will not be responsible for any harm that might come to
her while she is gone. The governor of Suzdal' was sent in 1666 to investigate
a charge of adultery. The husband was found guilty "because he failed to take
his wife away from sin and procured for her (*eiu svodnichaet uchinil*)." The
errant husband was beaten and imprisoned for his sin as well as for insulting
the governor while resisting arrest. In Tobol'sk in western Siberia, a Cossack
turned in another man with a girl in 1684 because he said they lived in sin. The
woman was beaten for her sexual license.[89] In 1695, a man registered notice
about his abusive neighbor in the Vladimir area; he reported that the neighbor

[88]1629: RIB 25, no. 75, col. 87. 1655: *Moskovskaia delovaia*, pt. 2, no. 52, pp. 68–69. On
Shorin's career, see Samuel H. Baron, "Vasilii Shorin: Seventeenth-Century Russian Merchant
Extraordinary," *Canadian-American Slavic Studies* 6, no. 4 (1972):503–48. 1683: DAI 10, no.
107, pp. 466–67. Similar complaints include RGADA, f. 210, Prikaznyi stol, stb. 2574, ll. 12–17
(1701), and ibid., stb. 384, ll. 163–64 (1667).

[89]1630: RIB 25, no. 82, cols. 96–97. 1663: *Moskovskaia delovaia*, pt. 2, no. 60, p. 73. 1666:
RGADA, f. 210, Prikaznyi stol, stb. 993, ll. 1–107. 1684: DAI 11 (1869), no. 11 (VIII), pp. 37–40.

beats his wife so badly that she has had to be rescued by neighbors, whom he now insults and threatens with an ax and falsely accuses. A wife turned in her husband, a church deacon, to the Holy Synod in 1721 because of his adultery. He was stripped of his ecclesiastical rank and told to live properly with his wife again. "And a picture of him (*persona*) should be sent to all bishoprics so that nowhere should he be allowed to serve holy liturgies." The woman he had sinned with was sent to be punished by the civil authorities.[90]

Notices (*iavki*) represent one voice protesting errant behavior and implicitly seeking community affirmation. Muscovites could also impose legal obligations on individuals, not always with good results. For example, an artisan in the tsar's Kadashevo settlement in 1660 petitioned that his niece's husband, apparently living in his household, be sent to a monastery because he had reneged on his written promise "that he will not drink and carouse and will go to church . . . and will obey me in all things." Now the man fails on all counts, "beats and tortures" his wife, and has drunk up all her dowry property. Alternatively, to police deviance, Muscovites could deploy an institution of collective responsibility—that is, surety bonds. In 1640, ten townsmen from the settlement (*posad*) of the Tikhvin monastery, for example, put up a surety bond to guarantee that a member of their community would straighten his ways:

> He will live with his mother, not insulting her or beating her, and will not beat his wife until injury without cause, and will not commit murder (*golovshchina*), and will not go out at night to buy and drink wine and beer and tobacco and will not even think of this, and will not associate with criminal people from outside of the community, and will not play dice, and he will live like all the other good townsmen live with their mothers and wives, without criminal behavior, and will discipline his wife according to her just deserts and humanely, not with intent to injure.
>
> Should he relapse into his bad ways, the guarantors will suffer whatever penalty the monastic elders decree.[91]

The absence of collective charivaris and the recourse to judicial instruments such as notices and surety bonds do not necessarily validate the statist interpretation of Russian history, that Muscovite society was passive and inert. Rather, we have seen individuals consciously using a variety of strategies to police their communities: internalized patriarchal values, male authority over women and dependents, individual insults, more ritualized forms of insult,

---

[90]1695: *Pamiatniki delovoi*, no. 200, pp. 217–18. 1721: *Polnoe sobranie postanovlenii i rasporiazhenii . . . Synoda* 1 (1869), no. 91, p. 117.

[91]1660: *Moskovskaia delovaia*, pt. 2, no. 58, p. 72. 1640: AIu no. 301 (II), p. 313, my translation. Also translated in H. W. Dewey and A. M. Kleimola, eds. and trans., *Russian Private Law in the XIV–XVII Centuries* (Ann Arbor, Mich., 1973), no. 76, pp. 248–49.

legal notices, and bonds. The use of surety bonds reminds us in fact that Muscovites often gathered their forces collectively. Surety bonds were used liberally in litigation to ensure participation in proceedings or to guarantee payment of fines; they were imposed by the state to guarantee the loyalty of high-ranking men. Responsibility for tax payment was collective in communities; village and urban communes elected collective representatives for local administration. In fact, we do well to recall how minimal was local government, how weakly felt was central control in outlying districts, and how local government was composed of members of the community in any case. These were not disengaged, inert communities dependent on the state to order their lives.

All these examples show communities and individuals struggling to do the impossible—that is, to maintain an idealized patriarchal community in which adolescents never cross the bounds from courting to illicit sex, in which illegitimate children are never born, in which all young people are married off to proper mates and stay married, in which husbands never overstep the bounds of their authority over women, and in which no wives ever commit adultery while their soldier husbands are off at war. It was an impossible goal and yet its pursuit attracted significant energies. That pursuit took forms from those as ephemeral as religious teachings and modeling of gender roles to more tangible complaints about neighbors' and kinsmen's behavior, to insults in public places and publicly imposed sanctions. Individuals sought recourse from insult by defending their honor, or that of their daughters and wives, in court. Thus the discourse of honor in a patriarchal setting both provided norms for regulating specific behavior and offered individuals mechanisms for safeguarding their reputations in their communities. The code of honor itself, in which women played a central role, was designed to ensure substantial compliance to social norms. And from that compliance came social stability—resting on a base of male authority, women's honor, and collective community norms.

CHAPTER 3

The Praxis of Honor

Muscovites of all social ranks litigated energetically to defend their honor. The courts served them because it was a traditional responsibility of a good tsar to provide justice. The community played a role in honor disputes, because insult to honor disturbed community stability and because community involvement was integral to the legal process in Muscovy, as it was in many other premodern judicial systems. Thus, the ways in which people litigated over insult are expressions of the broader legal culture. Trials over dishonor can serve as a case study of the Muscovite legal system and as a window into how communities and individuals pursued and resolved disputes. This chapter, then, explores several aspects of Muscovite legal culture by examining how honor fit into individuals' and communities' strategies of dispute resolution.

Discovering why people litigate in premodern societies, particularly over something as intangible as insult and reputation, is not as straightforward as it might seem. Because their goals in litigating rarely involved "a disinterested love for the law"[1] or a desire to enforce objective norms, disputants litigated in ways that we might not expect. Litigants very frequently, for example, did not pursue cases to conclusion, or they accepted the judgment of God in coming to resolution. They frequently settled even seemingly rock-solid cases out of court. They often invoked the authority of the community in the form of witnesses, sureties, or character references in pursuing their suits. They accepted and made use of the social, theatrical, and ritual aspects that are embedded in trial processes. Such attitudes and practices made for a legal culture of remarkable flexibility and responsiveness in early modern Russia.

---

[1]Phrase from Wendy Davies and Paul Fouracre, eds., *The Settlement of Disputes in Early Medieval Europe* (Cambridge, England, 1986), p. 234.

Circumstances of Insult and Violence

Litigation is the culmination of stress between individuals or groups, often against the backdrop of broader community tensions. Litigations over insult in particular silhouette people at a moment of crisis and show in stark relief the social system within which people live and the means they use to pursue and resolve disputes. Such litigations also highlight violence and its containment and raise the question of the level of violence in Muscovy. Most insults arose between people who were acquainted with each other. Horace W. Dewey, working with a small sample of litigations, argued that most dishonor litigations occurred between individuals of the same social rank.[2] The database used here confirms his conclusion. In 566 cases in which the social situation of litigants can be ascertained, almost two-thirds (382 cases) occurred among social equals. Less often did social superiors sue inferiors (115 instances in 566 cases), and only infrequently did social inferiors sue superiors (69 of 566 cases).[3] These statistics indicate that insults were a common byproduct of community interrelations and, further, as I shall argue in this chapter, that litigation over insult itself constituted a means of social interaction in communities. It could promote social stability or it could further disrupt it, and whether the goal was restorative or disruptive, in either case it was accomplished by willful execution of a shared discourse of community norms.

Least often in this collection of cases did insult arise among strangers encountering each other in public places. This did occur, however. Marketplaces seem to have been rife with idle insult, seemingly unprovoked, among strangers. For example, a priest of the Kholmogory diocese complained in 1579 of being insulted and assaulted by a man attempting to steal his money at market. Eleven years later, the same priest sued again for assault and dishonor on the road outside a tavern.[4] In 1687, a servant of the Siberian tsarevich Vasilii Alekseevich complained of being insulted without provocation in the marketplace by strangers.[5]

Insults often punctuated the pursuit of official duties. Military men were known to denigrate their superior officers. In 1594, for example, a Cossack

---

[2]H. W. Dewey, "Old Muscovite Concepts of Injured Honor (*Beschestie*)," *Slavic Review* 27 (1968):598.

[3]The more specific breakdowns are as follows: social equals suing each other within the Moscow-based elite (93); gentrymen (105); taxed groups, including contract servitors (158); clergy (21); and foreigners (5). Social superiors suing inferiors: Moscow-based servitors suing gentry (24), taxed people (39); gentry suing taxed people (34); and clergy suing taxed people (18). Social inferiors suing superiors: gentry suing Moscow-based servitors (9); taxed suing privileged ranks (48); and monks and parish clergy suing the military elite (12).

[4]1579: RIB 14 (1894), no. 62, cols. 117–18. 1590: RIB 14, no. 69, cols. 130–31.

[5]RGADA, f. 210, Prikaznyi stol, stb. 1061, ll. 50–51. This descendant of the Siberian Tatar ruling family, which was under Moscow's suzerainty, served in Moscow.

commander complained that his hundredman had disobeyed him, shot and assaulted people while drunk, and insulted the commander when he began an investigation into the man's misbehavior.[6] Townsmen sometimes refused the orders of the public safety and fire warden (*ob'ezzhii*). A warden in 1671 reprimanded a resident of Moscow for keeping his fire burning at night and in return suffered a hail of insults about himself, his father, and his mother.[7] Civil and military officials sometimes quarreled over jurisdiction and authority. In the 1520s, for example, a military commander accused his colleague of insubordination and insult in a dispute over lines of command. In 1636, two military commanders in Krapivna on the southern frontier accused each other of insult and insubordination. In 1687, disputants came to blows and insults when a judge accused the state secretary assigned to his court of improperly registering documents at his home, not in the chancery as required. They settled the dispute after the plaintiff won a judgment based on witness testimony.[8]

Governors and elected local officials were often insulted in the line of duty. In 1626, for example, an elected judicial official in the far northern Kholmogory region served notice on a local peasant that he should divide his land based on a recent sale. Instead, the peasant seized the deed from him, insulted and assaulted him, and stole his bag with other official documents in it. In 1644, a locally selected criminal officer (*gubnoi starosta*) repeatedly refused requests by the governor of Voronezh to help in investigations, once insulting him by calling him a "penny farthing little governor" (*grivnenyi voevodishka*).[9] Conversely, others sued for excess brutality and insult at the hands of officials, as in 1627, when a peasant in Ustiug Velikii sued the local customs and alcohol chief for assault and insult relating to a dispute over a shipment of rye. And in 1633, the archbishop of Astrakhan' and the Terek region sued the governor of nearby Chernoiarsk for theft, assault, dereliction of duty, and insult to his various officials.[10]

As common as these complaints were, the vast majority of dishonor cases occurred between private individuals in day-to-day, unofficial interaction. As we saw in Chapter 2, kinsmen frequently accused each other of insult. Parents accused children of disrespect, fathers-in-law sued daughters-in-law and vice versa for disobedience and abuse, in-laws came to insults over disputed inher-

---

[6]G. A. Anpilogov, ed., *Novye dokumenty o Rossii kontsa XVI–nachala XVII v.* (Moscow, 1967), pp. 375–77.

[7]*Moskovskaia delovaia i bytovaia pis'mennost' XVII veka* (Moscow, 1968), pt. 2, no. 76, p. 83. Other incidents with *ob'ezzhie*: RGADA, f. 210, Prikaznyi stol, stb. 1203, ll. 10–14, 20–26, 59–60, 163–66 (all 1690).

[8]1520s: S. Bogoiavlenskii, ed., "Bran' kniazia Vasiliia Mikulinskogo . . . ," *Chteniia*, 1910, bk. 3, Miscellany, pp. 18–20. 1687: RGADA, f. 210, Prikaznyi stol, stb. 1063, ll. 82–104. Other complaints against corrupt officials: AMG 1, no. 241, pp. 259–61 (1629); no. 277, pp. 309–10 (1630).

[9]1626: RIB 14, no. 301, cols. 673–74. 1644: RGADA, f. 210, Belgorod stol, stb. 174, ll. 312–15.

[10]1627: RIB 25 (1908), no. 44, cols. 46–47. 1633: RIB 2 (1875), no. 152 (2), cols. 522–25.

itances. Even more commonly in the records, neighbors fell into disputes. Banquets and weddings were classic occasions for insults to flare: Tongues were loosened by drink, and the gathering often brought together individuals who would not otherwise associate. Not surprisingly, early Rus' and Muscovite law codes defined specific punishments for affronts to guests at ceremonial occasions.[11] Examples of brawls at these occasions abound in the cases in the database. Two gentrymen, for example, fell to brawling at a wedding in Lebedian' (south of Moscow, on the upper Don River) in 1629; two Europeans (Anthony Thomson and J. Edward Rowland) at a Christmas party in 1646 fell to blows and insult in a long-simmering dispute over a debt; and in 1649, two monastic servitors who had been at a banquet got into a quarrel on the way home.[12]

Whereas insults at festive occasions seem to have arisen spontaneously, many others arose among neighbors in the context of property disputes or neighborhood tensions. In dishonor litigations, one can glimpse the petty quarrels that punctuated life in small communities, be they villages, military regiments, or the exclusive elite that assembled daily in Kremlin anterooms. Numerous litigants describe being harassed and insulted by their neighbors until they were driven from their villages. In 1635, for example, a family in Shuia in the Vladimir area allegedly so harassed its neighbors with insults, threats of assault, and stone-throwing that the neighbors filed a notice against them. In a similar case of 1619, also in Shuia, a man complained of his neighbors: "We cannot walk past their house, they sic their dogs on us, and when we try to defend ourselves they try to cut us with a knife, and they brag that they will murder us. Because of all this threat and attacks by dogs and humiliation and insult from him and his sons, I, my mother, and wife are unable to live."[13] In a rural setting in the North in 1605, a family left the village because of a neighbor's persistent sexual slander of its women. Similarly, a peasant complained in 1606 that his neighbor harassed him, telling him "You cannot flee from us, we'll have your head, you won't be able to live in this village with us."[14]

Close quarters among strangers also bred strife. A townsman on the southern frontier complained in 1696 of seven Don Cossacks who had been billeted

---

[11]RZ 1:64 (art. 6; the expanded *Russkaia pravda*); RZ 2 (1985):181 (art. 3; the 1397–98 Dvina charter); RZ 2:195 (art. 20; the 1488 Beloozero charter); RZ 3 (1985):249 (chap. 22, art. 11; the Conciliar Law Code of 1649).

[12]1629: RGADA, f. 210, Prikaznyi stol, stb. 33, ll. 248–50. 1646: AIuB 1, no. 104, cols. 643–66. 1649: *Pamiatniki delovoi pis'mennosti XVII veka. Vladimirskii krai* (Moscow, 1984), no. 152, pp. 178–79. Other disputes among dinner guests: *Moskovskaia delovaia*, pt. 2, no. 18, p. 54 (1635); RIB 14, no. 150, cols. 379–80 (1636); RIB 14, pt. 2, no. 52, cols. 993–96 (1676).

[13]1635: RIB 2, no. 176 (3), cols. 710–11. 1619: *Pamiatniki delovoi*, no. 113, p. 154.

[14]1605: RIB 14, no. 234, cols. 558–59. 1606: RIB 14, no. 242, cols. 570–72. Other similar cases of harassment by neighbors: RIB 14, no. 259, cols. 595–96 (1609); *Pamiatniki delovoi*, no. 206, pp. 220–21 (1618); RIB 25, no. 60, cols. 68–70 (1628).

in a cottage at his home. From their window they had shot the plaintiff's dog and then assaulted the plaintiff when he complained. A nun complained of abuse intended to drive her from the convent.[15] Muscovites complained frequently of large-scale assaults on their homes by neighbors, assaults that often included sexual slander and affront to the women of the targeted household. For example, a gentryman of Kashira complained in 1641 that his neighbor with his men rode up to him and his wife while they were working in the fields and set their dogs on them, attacked them, and ordered the wife to bow down in subservience to them.[16]

It often took some time before individuals went to court; repeated incidents and escalating quarrels might erupt in a final insult or assault that generated a suit. Countless plaintiffs sued over assaults—on their homes, their hayfields, or their property—that were accompanied by abusive language; they often explicitly linked those affronts to long-term disputes over the property in question. For example, two peasants in the Kholmogory area in 1627 disputed a hay meadow and fell to quarreling and insulting each other. The plaintiff alleged, "and in the past they have bragged of all manner of evil things against me and my son and my cattle, of murder and of expelling me from my home." The defendant responded in kind, saying that the plaintiff had illegally claimed the land for seven years and had repeatedly insulted and threatened him; the defendant even implied that the plaintiff was working witchcraft against him and his family. In another case, an infantryman on the southern frontier complained in 1692 that he was insulted when the men of a local landholder attacked and ransacked his home, accusing him of being a serf and thus ineligible to own property. His soldier status was affirmed by investigation in record books, thus confirming his right to own property.[17]

A good example of how neighborly relations could boil over into litigation after repeated incidents comes from 1649, when a gentryman on the southern frontier in Userda accused a neighbor of beating and insulting him, his wife, and daughters at his home. In response, the neighbor, also a gentryman, accused the plaintiff of refusing to repay money he had borrowed from the defendant's mother, accused the plaintiff's wife of not repaying grain she had

---

[15]Cossacks: *Moskovskaia delovaia*, pt. 2, no. 138, pp. 121–22. The Conciliar Law Code explicitly makes shooting a man's dog a crime: RZ 3:150 (chap. 10, art. 282). Nun: RIB 14, pt. 2, no. 30, cols. 916–18 (1625).

[16]1641: RGADA, f. 210, Prikaznyi stol, stb. 278, l. 596. Other such assaults with sexual slander for women include RGADA, f. 210, Prikaznyi stol, stb. 15, ch. 2, ll. 708–10 (1625); RIB 25, no. 18, cols. 19 (1626); RIB 14, no. 305, cols. 681–83 (1628); RGADA, f. 210, Prikaznyi stol, stb. 33, ll. 74–77 (1628); ibid., stb. 558, ll. 492–98 (1645); *Delovaia pis'mennost' Vologodskogo kraia XVII–XVIII vv.* (Vologda, 1979), pp. 53–55 (1668).

[17]1627: RIB 14, no. 304, cols. 677–81. 1692: RGADA, f. 210, Belgorod stol, stb. 1356, ll. 122–322.

borrowed from the defendant's nephew, and accused the plaintiff of refusing to pay for a sword that he had borrowed and for reneging on other debts. The plaintiff responded by suing the defendant's widowed mother for not returning dyes she had borrowed from him or the dyed cloth. When the defendant at the trial denied all on his mother's behalf, the plaintiff accused him of trampling on his grainfields. Faced with taking an oath to the truth of these various allegations, the two acrimonious neighbors settled and split the court fees.[18]

Verbal insults often served as the last straw in a bitter rivalry. In 1641, for example, two brothers, gentrymen from Kozlov on the steppe frontier, sued a fellow gentryman for dishonor and cited a pattern of harassment by him and his colleagues: "He hates us because of our income and service land grant (*pomest'e*), wanting to take them forcibly from us." A groom in the tsar's stables alleged in 1636 that an artisan in Moscow had approached him and insulted him and his mother because he was angry at a suit the plaintiff had filed against him.[19] Some defendants even charged that they had been insulted as part of enduring vendettas. In 1633, for example, a gentryman sued another for assaulting (with his kinsmen) him, his mother, and his wife at a wedding in order to avenge a long enmity with the plaintiff's son-in-law. In 1653, two gentrymen of Lebedian' on the southern frontier fell into a sword fight on the road because of a three-year-old quarrel over rights to a meadow and use of common herd land. In 1653, two gentrymen of Efremov sued each other for assault and insult, one calling the other a slave. At trial, one gentryman explained that they had had a dispute about trampled grain for three years and complained that the other had assaulted his lands repeatedly.[20]

Litigations also reveal the broader networks that structured communities, such as cliques, clans, and patronage networks.[21] In a petition of 1628, a peasant sued another peasant, calling him a "powerful (*sil'nyi*) man," who with his men had broken into the plaintiff's home, assaulted him, his wife, and his children and had torn clothing and jewelry off of his wife and daughter. He also allegedly stole a keg of beer that the plaintiff had prepared for his son's wedding. "In the past they bragged of assaulting and stealing from me, of making false accusations against me and libel and all manner of evil things," complained the plaintiff. In another case, a peasant petitioned in 1634 against a neighbor who had tried to kidnap

[18]1649: RGADA, f. 210, Prikaznyi stol, stb. 192, ll. 143–55.

[19]1641: RGADA, f. 210, Prikaznyi stol, stb. 128, ll. 346–49. 1636: *Moskovskaia delovaia*, pt. 2, no. 23, p. 56.

[20]1633: RIB 2, no. 164 (I), cols. 571–73. 1653 Lebedian': RGADA, f. 210, Prikaznyi stol, stb. 196, ll. 21–54. 1653 Efremov: RGADA, f. 210, Prikaznyi stol, stb. 196, ll. 1104–20. Many cases allege repeated harassment ("in the past he has bragged of harm to me"): *Pamiatniki delovoi*, no. 119, p. 157 (1622); ibid., no. 122, p. 159 (1623); RIB 25, no. 54, cols. 60–61 (1628).

[21]On such networks, see Valerie A. Kivelson, *Autocracy in the Provinces: The Muscovite Gentry and Political Culture in the Seventeenth Century* (Stanford, 1996), chaps. 4–6; David L. Ransel, "Character and Style of Patron-Client Relations in Russia," in Antoni Mączak, ed., *Klientelsysteme im Europa der frühen Neuzeit* (Munich, 1988), pp. 212–31.

one of his servants. Alleging that "He has previously bragged of doing evil things to me such as attacking my home and falsely accusing me and libel and murder," the plaintiff underscored his lack of powerful allies by calling himself "a solitary little man alone in the world (*chelovechenko odinashno*), I farm this little plot (*pashnishko*) alone." This image of patronage networks is vividly expressed in a 1618 suit in which the Shuia governor requested that a suit over assault and insult among factions of Shuia townspeople be judged in Moscow, not locally, because the faction leaders cannot be sued fairly in the local courts because "they are powerful (*oni sil'ny*)."[22]

Local community groups do not figure only negatively in honor disputes; they often act as potential or active allies. A man in 1688 defended himself by saying that if he had really quarreled with the plaintiff as alleged, she would have reported it to the neighbors. In 1689, a woman of Ustiug Velikii accused a priest's son of raping her niece; he responded by naming his neighbors as character witnesses, saying "My neighbors know that I have never gone out for such knavery (*plutovstvo*)."[23] Neighbors and friends frequently leaped to the rescue of victims of assault and insult, often getting embroiled in the dispute themselves. In a 1638 case, neighbors saved a servant girl from assault. In another case, a man and his servants escaped assault by a gang in the streets of Moscow in 1668 by dashing into the home of a Cossack commander. A neighbor and his men then ran over to protect them, but one of the servants nevertheless was "beaten half-dead." And in 1695, a monastic servant sued his neighbor because his family was being drawn into the neighbor's abuse of his wife. She had fled her husband's beatings to the monastic servant's home, and now the defendant was allegedly threatening them as well.[24]

This evidence brings us to a level of lived experience that is rare in Muscovite documents. We hear the firsthand testimony of litigants and witnesses; we see neighbors quarreling and communities leaping into the fray. Neither the personal acquaintanceships nor the violence at the heart of these disputes should be surprising. Neighbors quarreled and litigated because it is precisely among acquaintances that tensions develop in day-to-day interaction and that reputation is most socially important. Sociologists have theorized this; for example, F. G. Bailey writes, "Those nearest are also those with whom you interact most frequently and therefore those with whom you are most likely to have a cause for contention . . . competition takes place mainly between those who are in the same league."[25] Historians have observed it. Martin Ingram notes that 80% of defamation cases he examined in sixteenth- and seventeenth-century Wiltshire involved people

---

[22]1628: RIB 14, no. 305, cols. 681–83. 1634: RIB 14, no. 328, cols. 719–21. 1618: *Pamiatniki delovoi*, no. 206, pp. 220–21.

[23]1688: RIB 12 (1890), no. 194, cols. 918–22. 1689: RIB 12, no. 199, cols. 948–54.

[24]1638: RIB 2, no. 176 (6b), cols. 720–22. 1668: *Moskovskaia delovaia*, pt. 2, no. 63, p. 76. 1695: *Pamiatniki delovoi*, no. 200, pp. 217–18.

[25]F. G. Bailey, "Gifts and Poison," in his *Gifts and Poison* (New York, 1971), p. 19.

from the same parish: "Slander actions . . . were characteristically the product of tensions between neighbours of medium substance living cheek by jowl in the small scale communities which made up the fabric of early modern English society."[26] More was at stake than simply erasing slander from the public memory; individuals litigated to advance their social esteem as well. David Garrioch writes, regarding eighteenth-century Paris, that "Many disputes were ultimately struggles for recognition and respect from other members of the local community."[27] These considerations clearly came to bear in Muscovite society, where urban and rural communities organized collectively for administrative and some judicial purposes, where agrarian practice demanded collective cooperation, and where lineage and heritage structured hierarchy in the elite. Valerie Kivelson, for example, analyzed the frequency with which witchcraft accusations sprang up within families at points of tension (e.g., disputes over inheritance, in-law tensions).[28] In such settings, tensions easily could compound at the same time that social pressure to maintain a respectable status in the community was constant.

The brawling and disorder exhibited in these cases looks less startling when placed in a comparative context. Faced with similar data, historians of medieval and early modern Europe have been confronting the problem of violence. Admitting the high level of violence that premodern European societies countenanced, they historicize it by exploring its social meaning. Wendy Davies and Paul Fouracre, for example, see violence as social strategy in medieval Europe. It was tempered by societal pressure for restoring peace, but they caution that "We must not idealize the notion of peace. Disputes were in themselves sufficiently common to constitute in themselves part of normal social interaction; 'peace,' that is to say, was already pretty contentious."[29] A similar debate about social stability in early modern England postulates a long-term decline in public violence from medieval to early modern times.[30]

---

[26]Martin Ingram, *Church Courts, Sex and Marriage in England, 1570–1640* (Cambridge, England, 1987), pp. 303–4.

[27]David Garrioch, *Neighbourhood and Community in Paris, 1740–1790* (Cambridge, England, 1986), p. 37.

[28]"Patrolling the Boundaries: The Uses of Witchcraft Accusations and Household Strife in Seventeenth-Century Muscovy," *Harvard Ukrainian Studies* 19 (1997):302–23.

[29]Davies and Fouracre, eds., *Settlement*, p. 233. Michel Foucault has made the decline of violent punishments by states a characteristic of the transition into modernity in the European framework: *Discipline and Punish: The Birth of the Prison*, trans. Alan Sheridan (New York, 1977).

[30]Lawrence Stone, "Interpersonal Violence in English Society, 1300–1980," *Past and Present* 101 (1983):22–33. Ingram provides bibliography on the debate about stability: *Church Courts*, p. 317. Also on stability, see Ian W. Archer, *The Pursuit of Stability: Social Relations in Elizabethan London* (Cambridge, England, 1991); Anthony Fletcher and John Stevenson, eds., *Order and Disorder in Early Modern England* (Cambridge, England, 1985). For data on early modern crime and violence, see the Introduction and essays by Sharpe and Spierenburg in Eric A. Johnson and Eric H. Monkkonen, eds., *The Civilization of Crime: Violence in Town and Country since the Middle Ages* (Urbana, Ill., and Chicago, 1996).

Philippa Maddern extends the concept of violence as social praxis by examining the use of officially sanctioned violence in fifteenth-century England. She argues that violence could be socially stabilizing, because contemporaries distinguished between just and unjust violence. Inappropriate violence transgressed community standards: police brutality, women beating men, riots by the poor against the rich, or wanton rampaging by an unbridled gentry. Violence that was just—drawing legitimacy from analogy to God's just punishment of sinners—included men's chastisement of women and servants, the king's execution of criminals, and a knight's crusade against the infidel. Maddern argues that violence was not necessarily "reprehensible chaos, but the normal upholder of secure, lawful, hierarchical, godly order . . . Violence, in short, was a language of social order."[31]

Violence involving insult and assault in Muscovy can be similarly contextualized. The violence of the state's legal sanctions was "just," and that observed among neighbors and co-workers was a normal result of the stress of life in small communities. Such violence was not a measure of barbarism. Even contemporary European travelers, who reveled in relating the crudity of Muscovite manners, did not report excessive levels of popular violence. The Englishman Giles Fletcher in the late sixteenth century emphasized not violence but the people's oppressed and servile state, attributing it to abuses by officials and heavy taxation. Jacques Margeret in the early seventeenth century similarly noted that men did not carry weapons except when at war, that dueling and private vengeance were harshly punished, and that people used the courts for recourse from insult. Adam Olearius, traveling in the midseventeenth century, remarked that Muscovites love swearing and quarreling but "very rarely come to blows." Augustin von Mayerberg in the late seventeenth century attributed violence by slaves to poverty and hunger.[32] In modern scholarship, Richard Hellie attributes Muscovite violence to various physiological and social causes.[33] The

[31]Philippa A. Maddern, *Violence and Social Order: East Anglia, 1422–1442* (Oxford, 1992), pp. 234–35.

[32]Lloyd E. Berry and Robert O. Crummey, eds., *Rude and Barbarous Kingdom* (Madison, Wis., 1968), pp. 169–73, 245–46; Jacques Margeret, *The Russian Empire and Grand Duchy of Muscovy: A 17th-Century French Account*, trans. and ed. Chester S. L. Dunning (Pittsburgh, 1983), pp. 64–66; Adam Olearius, *The Travels of Olearius in Seventeenth-Century Russia*, trans. and ed. Samuel H. Baron (Stanford, 1967), p. 139 (discussion of mores, pp. 130–54); Mayerberg quoted in Richard Hellie, *Slavery in Russia, 1450–1725* (Chicago, 1982), pp. 509–10.

[33]In earlier work, Hellie accounted for Muscovite violence by reference to vitamin deficiency and considered it in line with European contemporaries: *Slavery*, pp. 505–6. But more recently, he links it to inadequate left-brain development because of a societal dearth of literacy and education and declares Muscovy disproportionately violent because of this factor: "Some Considerations on the Development of the Russian Mind and Culture (Especially Late Muscovy)," unpubl. manuscript, June 1993, and "New Interpretations of Muscovite History: Literacy," unpubl. lecture, November 19, 1994. Discussing nineteenth-century Russian peasants, Richard Pipes argued that although they were violent, they generally expressed their discontent in passive protests, such as duplicity, laziness, and drinking: *Russia under the Old Regime* (New York, 1974), pp. 155–57.

violence we see in dishonor litigations should not be condemned as a Russian moral failing but rather analyzed for what it reveals about social tensions and social interaction.

The Setting of Litigation: Ritual and Community

Individuals and communities devise many ways to resolve conflict. Third-party judicial institutions are not essential; conflict resolution can be structured by personal motivations such as "moral obligations and the persuasion of peers," in Georges Duby's phrase. It could be pursued with strategies ranging from bilateral negotiation to the intercession of mediators to feud or ordeal.[34] Current scholarship avoids a strict delineation between "stateless societies" that depend on such informal means and bureaucratically organized judicial systems, seeing instead private mechanisms of dispute resolution permeating formalized judicial processes—as we indeed see in Muscovy. Nevertheless, the structuring organization for dispute resolution in Muscovy was a "triadic" judicial institution overseen by the grand prince and his judges. Those structures developed for much the same time-honored reasons that justified the extension of princely or ecclesiastical power over private disputes in premodern Europe.

The Muscovite state provided access to litigation over personal honor not only because it proved lucrative in court fees and asserted central control over political rivals. Perhaps most important, grand princes, like European kings, played the role of judge because it was one of the oldest and most traditional expectations of rulers in the Christian tradition. In Muscovite panegyrics to good rulers, the duty of rendering justice and the restraining power of "law" on the tsar's power are central themes. By "law," authors meant more than written codes, including Christian ethics and tradition as well. Learned authors saw justice as key to social stability and urged rulers to establish a worldly administration that was just and fair. Good rulers were expected to supervise their officials to avoid corruption and abuse of the people. A fourteenth-century source linked good justice with a ruler's piety:

[34]Patrick J. Geary, "Extra-Judicial Means of Conflict Resolution," in *La giustizia nell'alto medioevo. (Secoli V–VIII)*, 2 vols. (Spoleto, 1995), 1:569-601; idem, "Moral Obligations and Peer Pressure: Conflict Resolution in the Medieval Aristocracy," in G. Duhamel and G. Lobrichon, eds., *Georges Duby: L'Ecriture de l'Histoire* (Brussels, 1996), pp. 217–22. See also Paul R. Hyams, "Feud in Medieval England," *The Haskins Society Journal* 3 (1991):1–21; Otto Brunner, *Land and Lordship: Structures of Governance in Medieval Austria*, trans. from 4th rev. ed. by Howard Kaminsky and James Van Horn Melton (Philadelphia, 1992), chap. 1; Geoffrey Koziol, "Monks, Feuds, and the Making of Peace in Eleventh-Century Flanders," in Thomas Head and Richard Landes, eds., *The Peace of God: Social Violence and Religious Response in France around the Year 1000* (Ithaca, N.Y., 1992), pp. 239–58; Simon Roberts, *Order and Dispute: An Introduction to Legal Anthropology* (New York, 1979).

Having been gods, you will die as men and will be sent to a dog's place, to hell. . . . And you in your place appoint as governors and lieutenants men who are not fighters for God, pagans, perfidious, who do not understand judging and do not consider justice, who adjudicate while drunk, who hasten the proceedings. . . . People cry to you, O prince, and you do not avenge them. . . . Under an unrighteous tsar, all the servants under him are lawless.[35]

Similar thoughts were expressed in the early sixteenth century by a secular author, the diplomat Fedor Karpov. Reflecting not theocratic ideas of God-given authority, but rather citing Aristotle, Karpov argued that societies require firm government based on justice and laws: "Social order in cities and states will perish from soulful long enduring; long-suffering in people without justice and law destroys the welfare of society and social order is debased completely; evil morals arise in states and people become disobedient to rulers because of their depraved condition."[36] Maksim Grek, a Greek transplanted to Russia, declared in the early sixteenth century that the good ruler was guided by God's law, whereas the tyrant despises the word of God, the teachings of the church, and the advice of good men.[37] The quasi-literary depiction of Ivan IV at the 1551 church council, included in the protocols of the council known as the "*Stoglav*," again links justice with piety:

Having filled yourselves with the spiritual profits of Holy Scripture, instruct me, your son; enlighten me in every sort of piety. For it is good for the tsar to be pious, for all the laws of the tsar to be just and for him [to live] completely in the true belief and in purity.[38]

As well, the theme of the law is paramount in writings attributed to Ivan Peresvetov, a publicist of the midsixteenth century: "[God aids him] who calls on God for help and who loves justice and maintains a just court: justice is the heartfelt joy of God and the great wisdom of the tsar."[39]

---

[35]*Pamiatniki starinnoi russkoi literatury*, 4 vols. (St. Petersburg, 1860–62), 4 (1862):184. All translations are mine unless otherwise noted. See a similar message in the "Instruction of Semen, Bishop of Tver'": ibid., p. 185. Also see the theme of secular administration in the eulogy to Grand Prince Mikhail Aleksandrovich of Tver' (PSRL 15, pt. 1 [2d ed., 1922]: col. 167 [6907]), and in an early fifteenth-century epistle of St. Cyril of Beloozero (AI 1, no. 16, pp. 25–26).

[36]V. G. Druzhinin, "Neskol'ko neizvestnykh literaturnykh pamiatnikov iz sbornika XVI-go veka," LZAK 21, p. 109.

[37]On his general views, see Vladimir Val'denberg, *Drevnerusskie ucheniia o predelakh tsarskoi vlasti* (Petrograd, 1916), chap. 4, pt. 4.

[38]Unpubl. translation by Jack E. Kollmann, Jr., from Rossiiskaia gosudarstvennaia biblioteka (RGB), fond 304, no. 215, fols. 30, 32v. A published text is N. Subbotin, ed., *Tsarskie voprosy i sobornye otvety o mnorazlichnykh* [sic] *tserkovnykh chinekh (Stoglav)* (Moscow, 1890), pp. 34, 37–38 (RGB manuscript included in footnote variants).

[39]A. A. Zimin, ed., *Sochineniia I. Peresvetova* (Moscow and Leningrad, 1956), p. 170.

Historical tales written in the first one-third or so of the seventeenth century about the national catastrophe known as the *"Smuta"* or "Time of Troubles" affirmed the responsibility of the good ruler to heed God's rules.[40] The tales' conservatism was echoed in the church schism that erupted in the 1660s; Archpriest Avvakum advised Tsar Aleksei Mikhailovich that "The honor of the tsardom is to love justice."[41] These ideas, didactic as they were, identified the crucial significance of a well-run judicial system: Justice for the people enhanced social stability because people had peaceable means to resolve conflict. These ideals represent the loftiest goals and perceptions of Moscow's judicial enterprise.

Few judicial systems, however, meet such high expectations, and Muscovy's was no exception. Other sources suggest a necessary corrective. Horace Dewey argued forcefully that the most pressing reason that the state issued the 1497 and 1550 law codes and charters of local government was to curb corruption by governors and judges.[42] The introduction of local administrative reforms in the 1530s is similarly linked to corrupt, ineffective local government.[43] Valerie Kivelson and others have chronicled the avalanche of seventeenth-century gentrymen's complaints against local power networks (*sil'nye liudi*), particularly as they corrupted the judicial process.[44] The first generation of recorded secular tales, in the late seventeenth and early eighteenth century, included satires on the corruption of the court system. *The Tale of Ersh Ershovich*, for example, is a dead-on parody of a trial transcript, complete with formulaic language and proper procedure, except that the judges and litigants are all fish! *Shemiaka's Judgment* depicts judges as infinitely corruptible, litigants as cunning and devious, and the process as flawed. And Muscovy's most famous "rogue," Frol Skobeev, one should remember,

---

[40]On images of the ideal tsar, see Daniel B. Rowland's excellent discussion in "Muscovite Political Attitudes as Reflected in Early Seventeenth Century Tales about the Time of Troubles," Ph.D. dissertation, Yale University, 1976, chap. 3.

[41]Avvakum: N. I. Subbotin, *Materialy dlia istorii raskola za pervoe vremia ego sushchestvovaniia*, 9 vols. (Moscow, 1875–86), 4 (1878):226, 5 (1879):143. On the context of Avvakum's views, see Daniel Rowland, "Did Muscovite Literary Ideology Place Limits on the Power of the Tsar (1540s–1660s)?" *Russian Review* 49, no. 2 (1990):149–51.

[42]Horace W. Dewey, "The 1497 Sudebnik—Muscovite Russia's First National Law Code," *The American Slavic and East European Review* 15 (1956):325–38l; "The 1550 Sudebnik as an Instrument of Reform," *Jahrbücher für Geschichte Osteuropas*, n.s. 10, no. 2 (1962):161–80; and "The White Lake Charter: A Mediaeval Russian Administrative Statute," *Speculum* 32, no. 1 (1957):74–83.

[43]A. A. Zimin, *Reformy Ivana Groznogo* (Moscow, 1960), pp. 253–58; Horace W. Dewey, "Muscovite *Guba* Charters and the Concept of Brigandage (*razboj*)," *Papers of the Michigan Academy of Science, Arts and Letters, Pt. 2: Social Sciences* 51 (1966):277–88.

[44]Kivelson, *Autocracy in the Provinces*, chap. 7; Hans-Joachim Torke, *Die staatsbedingte Gesellschaft im moskauer Reich. Zar und Zemlja in der altrussischen Herschaftsverfassung, 1613–1689* (Leiden, 1974), chap. 3; Richard Hellie, *Enserfment and Military Change in Muscovy* (Chicago and London, 1971), pp. 62–65.

was said to be a solicitor of litigations.[45] Certainly the corruption and red tape of the courts in Imperial Russia was infamous: John LeDonne described the "nightmare" of eighteenth-century litigation, with increasing and overlapping layers of courts of appeal and unclear norms of procedure, and Denis Fonvizin's satirical plays lampooned corrupt judges. Irina Reyfman argued that by the turn of the nineteenth century, noblemen turned to dueling out of complete disaffection with the judicial process.[46]

It is important, however, not to read the malaise of the modern Russian bureaucracy back into the pre-Petrine period or to take either idealized extreme at face value. The Muscovite court system had its share of corruption; the central government was aware of it and could react quickly to explicit complaints of judges' conflicts of interest.[47] The minimalism of the Center's local control, however, typically left communities at the mercy of their officials. Even so, recent scholarship has problematized the issue of judicial corruption, arguing that bribery was a reciprocal relationship and that patronage and favoritism were traditional means of governance. What moderns condemn as corruption was not viewed so pejoratively in Muscovy until it reached extremes.[48] Potential litigants had a touching, if naive, faith in the potential of the system to serve them. Kivelson presents seventeenth-century gentrymen as committed to the perfectibility of the system even in the face of abuse: "You [Sovereign] should . . . order all dishonest judges to be rooted out . . . and in their place to be chosen just people, who would be able to answer for their judgments and for their service before God and before your tsarist majesty."[49] Clearly provincial gentrymen in their petitions hoped that the system could work. The evidence of dishonor litigations, as well as of other monographic studies of seventeenth-century legal culture,[50] shows a populace unwilling to disengage, as Reyfman's

[45]N. K. Gudzii, *Khrestomatiia po drevnei russkoi literature XI–XVII vekov*, 4th rev. ed. (Moscow, 1947), pp. 371–80, 399–405 (Frol as solicitor, p. 375). It should be noted that none of the dishonor cases used here cites such "solicitors."

[46]John P. LeDonne, *Absolutism and Ruling Class: The Formation of the Russian Political Order, 1700–1825* (New York and Oxford, 1991), pp. 193–99; Irina Reyfman, "The Emergence of the Duel in Russia: Corporal Punishment and the Honor Code," *Russian Review* 54, no. 1 (1995):26–43.

[47]See my discussion in "Murder in the Hoover Archives," *Harvard Ukrainian Studies* 19 (1997):324–34.

[48]Kivelson, *Autocracy in the Provinces*, p. 161; Brian L. Davies, "The Politics of Give and Take: *Kormlenie* as Service Remuneration and Generalized Exchange, 1488–1726," in Ann M. Kleimola and Gail Lenhoff, eds., *Culture and Identity in Muscovy, 1359–1584*, UCLA Slavic Studies, n.s. 3 (Moscow, 1997), n. 55; idem, *State Power and Community in Early Modern Russia* (Cambridge, England, forthcoming), chap. 6.

[49]Kivelson, *Autocracy in the Provinces*, p. 226.

[50]M. M. Bogoslovskii, *Zemskoe samoupravlenie na russkom Severe v XVII veke*, 2 vols., *Chteniia* 1910, bk. 1 and 1912, bks. 2 and 3; idem, "Zemskie chelobitnye v drevnei Rusi," *Bogoslovskii vestnik* 1911, nos. 1:133–50; ibid., 2:215–41; ibid., 3:403–19; ibid., 4:685–96; Kivelson, *Autocracy in the Provinces*; Davies, *State Power*, chaps. 6–7.

alienated noblemen did. People seemingly regarded the judicial system as worth the risks of litigation.

Going to court over honor and reputation, after all, posed risks. It advertised the details of an insult, for example, perhaps setting them in the community memory; it risked the plaintiff's being further insulted in the course of the trial or losing the trial; it gave the insulter an arena in which potentially to win public opinion over to his side; it took the disputants away from field, service, or trade; and, perhaps most of all, it was costly.[51] Court fees in Muscovy in the midseventeenth century, for example, could amount to about one-third of a ruble per ruble value of the suit. Even though some social groups (musketeers, hetmans) were excused from some of these fees,[52] the burden could be considerable. In 1640, for example, a gentryman settled a case, agreeing to pay court fees of more than eight rubles, a significant proportion of his forty-ruble annual cash grant. Another gentryman lost a suit in 1641 and found himself liable for forty-seven rubles in dishonor fines plus five rubles in court fees, when his annual cash grant was probably only in the fifteen- to twenty-ruble range.[53] In 1685, a townsman of Kolomna, whose own dishonor value was no greater than seven rubles, was to pay between three and four rubles in court fees plus a twenty-eight-ruble fine.[54] In the seventeenth century—to cite representative values—prices remained relatively stable. For horses, prices ranged from one to five rubles; annual rent for peasants ranged from one-twentieth of a ruble to two-and-a-half rubles a year. Skilled craftsmen may have earned twenty rubles a year.[55] By these standards, fines and court fees could be burdensome.

Yet people did litigate: In my database, individuals as diverse as great boyars, Siberian Cossacks, and indentured servants went to court. That they did so suggests that plaintiffs and defendants believed that the judicial process could satisfy their goals. Some went to court because a privately pursued vendetta was not a viable option; taking the law into one's hands was harshly punished in

[51]On disincentives to litigate, see J. A. Sharpe, *Defamation and Sexual Slander in Early Modern England* (York, 1980? [n.d.]), p. 24; Robert B. Shoemaker, *Prosecution and Punishment: Petty Crime and the Law in London and Rural Middlesex, c. 1660–1725* (Cambridge, England, 1991), pp. 117, 140; Garrioch, *Neighbourhood and Community*, p. 8; Elizabeth Cohen, "Honor and Gender in the Streets of Early Modern Rome," *Journal of Interdisciplinary History* 22, no. 4 (1992):610.

[52]Conciliar Law Code of 1649 on court fees: RZ 3:118–19 (chap. 10, art. 126); ibid., 3:251 (chap. 24, art. 1).

[53]1640: RGADA, f. 210, Prikaznyi stol, stb. 130, ll. 434–41. 1641: RGADA, f. 210, Prikaznyi stol, stb. 553, ll. 92–116.

[54]1685: RGADA, f. 210, Prikaznyi stol, stb. 918, ll. 18–43. Others include 1649: RGADA, f. 210, Prikaznyi stol, stb. 192, ll. 160–63; 1672: RGADA, f. 210, Prikaznyi stol, stb. 141, ll. 85–94. 1684: RGADA, f. 210, Prikaznyi stol, stb. 1161, ll. 13–24.

[55]Robert O. Crummey, *Aristocrats and Servitors: The Boyar Elite in Russia, 1614–1689* (Princeton, N.J., 1983), pp. 109–10.

Muscovy. But most had more pragmatic goals. They understood that honor was a tangible possession that should be protected, lest the insult lower their public standing, imperil their marriage chances, or cost them in material terms. A tradesman accused of dishonesty, for example, would justly fear loss of business. Although some plaintiffs might sue solely to harass and publicly humiliate their rivals, most wanted speedy settlement and material compensation.

When litigants approached the court, they found a well-articulated judicial system. It is difficult to make comparisons to other systems. It is likely that Muscovy's court system was less bureaucratically developed than, for example, contemporary English courts. Muscovy's obsession with preserving every scrap of paper associated with a suit is testimony to a less sophisticated bureaucracy. There was no formal code of judicial procedure, even by the eighteenth century, as John LeDonne remarked.[56] There was, however, a simple hierarchy for appeals, a fairly straightforward process, effective centralization of procedures, and wide dissemination to local chancery offices of manuals of procedure (*ukaznye knigi*), culminating in the 1649 Conciliar Law Code, which devoted its longest chapter (chapter 10) to that topic. By early modern standards, this was a functioning, if not fully rational, judicial system.

Suits for dishonor were initiated by the aggrieved party, and the litigants had broad leeway in deciding how far and in what ways the trial progressed.[57] Litigation began with the filing of a petition, generally in written form, but sometimes delivered orally and followed by a written petition.[58] Petitions were filed with the relevant judicial body: in the Center and frontier, with the governors (*voevody*); in Moscow, for landed military servitors, with the various judicial chanceries (*Moskovskii* and *Vladimirskii sudnye prikazy*); for taxed citizens in Moscow, with the *Zemskii prikaz*; for workers in various chanceries, with the chancery (*prikaz*) itself (the Armory, for example); for foreigners, with various chanceries for foreigners; and in the North, with local communal officers, governors, or even cathedrals or monasteries, depending on local circumstances. Muscovy made no firm distinction between civil and criminal suits, and it used two kinds of legal procedure—the accusatory (*sud*) and the investigatory (*sysk*,

[56]European comparison suggested by George Weickhardt (personal communication); John A. Armstrong called Russia's degree of bureaucratization "premature" by Weberian standards: "Old-Regime Governors: Bureaucratic and Patrimonial Attributes," *Comparative Studies of Society and History* 14 (1972):2–29; LeDonne, *Absolutism*, p. 193.

[57]On judicial institutions and procedure, see S. I. Shtamm, "Sud i protsess," in V. S. Nersesiants, ed., *Razvitie russkogo prava v XV-pervoi polovine XVII v.* (Moscow, 1986), pp. 203–51; H. W. Dewey and A. M. Kleimola, trans. and eds., *Russian Private Law in the XIV–XVII Centuries* (Ann Arbor, Mich., 1973), pp. 41–48.

[58]On judicial process in dishonor suits, see Dewey, "Old Muscovite Concepts." A suit of 1668 indicated that a petition had initially been given orally: A. A. Titov, ed., *Kungurskie akty XVII veka (1668–1699 g.)* (St. Petersburg, 1888), no. 8, pp. 16–18.

rozysk) processes—sometimes interchangeably. The accusatory procedure was initiated by litigants and could be settled before judgment. In it, the judge functions as a mediator between sides, who present their own arguments and witnesses. Investigatory suits, by contrast, can be initiated by either litigants or state authorities and cannot be settled before judgment. In these suits, the judge plays the role of active investigator, aggressively seeking out evidence, initially by deposition of the accused and then by various types of inquiry, including the community inquest (*poval'nyi obysk*), which was a survey of a large body of witnesses in the community where the crime occurred. Over time, accusatory suits absorbed some of the procedures of investigatory suits.[59] Suits over insult illustrate both types of procedure, particularly the investigatory.

The efficacy of a litigation depended on more than the execution of bureaucratic procedure. Judicial processes were able to bring angry individuals to closure on a dispute in part because of intangibles: They provided a ritual moment, a space conducive to changing individuals' behavior, and community endorsement of the process. As Davies and Fouracre note regarding medieval Europe, the ritualized character of judicial proceedings "was the only way for legal institutions to make an impact on societies perpetually riven with antagonism and oppression. Ritual was the most effective way to channel off resentments in the direction of the idea of renewed peace."[60] Ritual was essential in largely oral societies such as Muscovy; even in this setting, where written records were scrupulously kept, the general orality of the society meant that ritual communication retained impact.[61]

Muscovite law codes protected the space of the judicial arena by explicitly forbidding disruptive behavior before judges. As the 1649 code said: "Both the plaintiff and the defendant, having appeared before the judges, are to sue and answer for themselves politely, and humbly, and without noise, and they should say no impolite words whatsoever before the judges and should not argue with each other." The 1649 code went on to levy harsh fines for litigants insulting

---

[59]Older literature stresses evolution toward "modern" legal concepts and practice: V. I. Sergeevich, *Lektsii i issledovaniia po drevnei istorii russkogo prava*, 4th ed. (St. Petersburg, 1910), pp. 599–625; V. N. Latkin, *Lektsii po istorii russkogo prava* (St. Petersburg, 1912), pp. 217–30, 485–500; M. F. Vladimirskii-Budanov, *Obzor istorii russkogo prava*, 6th ed. (St. Petersburg–Kiev, 1909), pp. 634–43. More recent work stresses a less evolutionary, more interdependent development: George G. Weickhardt, "Due Process and Equal Justice in the Muscovite Codes," *Russian Review* 51 (1992):463–80; Kollmann, "Murder in the Hoover Archives."

[60]Davies and Fouracre, eds., *Settlement*, p. 240; see also Maddern, *Violence and Social Order*, p. 67. Thomas V. and Elizabeth S. Cohen label Renaissance Italian litigations as theatre and "art": *Words and Deeds in Renaissance Rome* (Toronto, 1993), p. 30.

[61]On these themes, see M. T. Clanchy, *From Memory to Written Record: England, 1066–1307*, 2d ed. (Oxford and Cambridge, Mass., 1993), chaps. 8–9; Karl Leyser, "Ritual, Ceremony and Gesture: Ottonian Germany," in idem, *Communications and Power in Medieval Europe* (London, 1994), pp. 189–213.

each other or striking or wounding anyone in the presence of the judge; such behavior was considered a dishonor to the judge.[62] Legislation from the beginning of formalized Muscovite codes in 1497 also worked to elevate the dignity of the courtroom by inflicting punishments on corrupt judges and judicial officials and standardizing judicial fees.[63]

The ritual atmosphere of a judicial process in Muscovy was invoked from its very inception by the form of the petitions with which plaintiffs first addressed the court. Here the circumstances and specifics of an insult were spelled out and a request for resolution was made in florid, emotional, formulaic rhetoric: "Merciful sovereign, Tsar and Grand Prince Aleksei Mikhailovich, autocrat (*samoderzhets*) of all Great and Little and White Russia, favor us, your orphans. Grant, O sovereign, your sovereign trial and judgment against him Vasilii and against Peter for their robbery. Tsar Sovereign! Have mercy on us! Grant us your favor!"[64] It was heightened by the formulae with which scribes drafted petitions for litigants. Petitioners called themselves "slaves," "orphans" or "beseechers of God," symbolizing their elite, taxpaying, or clerical status, respectively. They used diminutives for their names or for their homes (*dvor* becomes *dvorishko*, *dom* becomes *domishko*) or to describe their plight ("humble little dishonor"— *beschestishko*).[65] They beseeched the tsar's personal favor, often with heart-rending details that approached tropes: "For our many services, and for the blood and deaths of our kinsmen, and for our many wounds, and for our mutilation and our time in captivity. . . . "[66] Adding to the ritual quality of a trial was the formal taking of testimony and the ritual of oath-taking, discussed in the next section. One litigation even speaks of sealing an amicable settlement with a kiss.[67] The formality of the proceedings and the respect accorded officers of

---

[62]Law code of 1649: RZ 3:112–13 (chap. 10, arts. 105–6).

[63]This is a major preoccupation of Muscovite law codes: RZ 2:54, 59 (1497 law code arts. 1, 38); RZ 2:97–98, 102, 107–9, 112 (1550 law code arts. 1, 3–7, 32, 53–54, 62, 68); RZ 3:102–6 (Conciliar Law Code of 1649, chap. 10, arts. 1, 3, 5–8, 12–13, 15–16, 22, 24, etc.).

[64]Titov, ed., *Kungurskie akty*, no. 5, p. 7 (1668).

[65]*Beschestishko*: RGADA, f. 210, Prikaznyi stol, stb. 1702, ll. 1–57 (1694). *Domishko* and similar diminutives: RGADA, f. 210, Prikaznyi stol, stb. 862, ll. 64–95 (1673); RGADA, f. 210, Prikaznyi stol, stb. 1063, ll. 82–104 (1687); *Moskovskaia delovaia*, pt. 2, no. 138, pp. 121–22 (1696).

[66]RGADA, f. 210, Moscow stol, stb. 731, l. 777 (1671). This is an interesting petition in which descendants of the First False Dmitrii petition to change their surname (Otrep'ev) to escape his infamy.

[67]RGADA, f. 210, Prikaznyi stol, stb. 2693, l. 18 (1700). This might be a reference to kissing the cross as an oath, but amicable settlements did not use oaths. It may have been a ritual kiss; on that practice in Europe, see Heinrich Fichtenau, *Living in the Tenth Century: Mentalities and Social Orders*, trans. Patrick J. Geary (Chicago and London, 1991), pp. 38–40; J. Russell Major, "Bastard Feudalism and the Kiss: Changing Social Mores in Late Medieval and Early Modern France," *Journal of Interdisciplinary History* 17, no. 3 (1987):509–35.

the court provided litigants a space in which to transcend their animosities, to speak the truth, and to defer gracefully to the weight of evidence, to the spirit of reconciliation, or to the judgment of the court.

In Muscovy, trials had an important social component. The community was present in the courtroom, not only in the form of judicial officials (many recruited locally), but sometimes in the form of representatives of the community. By fifteenth- and sixteenth-century law codes, judges—who were military servitors sent from Moscow—were required to render their verdicts in the presence of and with the participation of representatives of the community, called "men of the court" or "good men" (*sudnye muzhi; liutshchie* or *dobrye liudi*).[68] Such leading citizens were given significant say in the administration of criminal justice. They were usually the more propertied residents or the longtime settlers of a rural community, and they could be communally elected officials. They paralleled the "good men" (*boni homines, scabini*) ubiquitous in medieval European adjudication, whom Susan Reynolds regards as representative of a reservoir of "legal procedures and norms" common to European lands from England to northern Italy before 1100.[69] The responsibility of local "good men" in trials was not only to curb central officials' excesses, but—equally importantly—to exert community pressure on all parties to conform to the court's decisions. The "good men" also carried significant weight in assessing the character of fellow community members: Accused criminals considered by a community's leading members as notorious (*vedomye likhie liudi*), carrying the connotation of recidivists, were punished far more harshly than those of whom community leaders approved.[70]

This principle of community involvement in the law was also embodied in the devolution of significant administrative and judicial authority to local "elders." In the first half of the sixteenth century, local criminal affairs were given over to boards of local gentry (criminal or *gubnye* officers and their staffs), and by midcentury, fiscal administration was also given to "elders" (*starosty*) elected from the taxpayers.[71] These institutions endured into the seventeenth century in the North and only gradually faded in the Center and frontiers, remaining most

[68]On "good men," see Ann M. Kleimola, "Justice in Medieval Russia: Muscovite Judgment Charters (*Pravye Gramoty*) of the Fifteenth and Sixteenth Centuries," *Transactions of the American Philosophical Society*, n.s. 65, pt. 6 (1975):18, 35, 41, and passim, and literature cited in Dewey, "The White Lake Charter," n. 9.

[69]Susan Reynolds, *Kingdoms and Communities in Western Europe, 900–1300* (Oxford, 1984), pp. 8, 23–32, 51–59.

[70]Dewey translates the term "notorious" and "recidivist": H. W. Dewey, comp., ed., and trans., *Muscovite Judicial Texts, 1488–1556*, Michigan Slavic Materials, no. 7 (Ann Arbor, Mich., 1966), p. 87. On "notorious men," see 1497 law code, arts. 8, 39, and 1550 law code, arts. 52, 56, 59–61 (RZ 2:55, 59, 106–8), and the *Ustavnaia Kniga* of the Criminal Chancery of 1555/56, arts. 1–6 (PRP 4:356–57).

[71]Dewey, "Muscovite *Guba* Charters," p. 287; RZ 2:59 (1497 law code, art. 38); RZ 2:108–9, 112 (1550 law code, arts. 62 and 68).

active in criminal affairs.[72] Thus petitions from the North were typically addressed to a large collective judicial apparatus, such as "the church elder, the leading citizens, and all peasants" of the commune, cited in a petition of 1634 in Ustiug Velikii.[73] Similarly, in 1640 in Vologda, monastic peasants were judged by a court that included two monastic elders, an elder of the peasant commune, and elected peasants. Even in the Center, where the governor's central administration absorbed much community participation in the seventeenth century, elected officials could still play significant roles. In 1667, for example, the tsar ordered a local criminal official (*gubnoi starosta*) to execute a punishment because the local governor was a friend of the guilty party.[74]

Even as community representatives lost independent judicial influence, community interests were never absent from adjudication. The typical staffing of judicial offices with men from the community ensured that familiar faces would surround litigants at court. Many provincial governors (who were simultaneously judges) in the seventeenth century were local figures, although in principle, governors were not supposed to be appointed to their local communities. Valerie Kivelson has found that in practice, in seventeenth-century Vladimir-Suzdal', one-fourth to one-third of the governors "appear to have had long-term, multi-generational ties to the towns they governed."[75] As men of local stature, they might be expected to exert more influence on litigants than a stranger would, and they might be more adept at forging settlements or suiting punishment to the crime when members of their own community were at issue. Kivelson argues that when gentrymen petitioned in the seventeenth century for locally elected judges and local courts, they were seeking "more intimate local justice": "Judges would know the community and the character of its members and would be able to take into account the reputation, social standing and family status of litigants."[76] Lesser judicial figures—for example, the staffs of brigandage elders, court bailiffs and scribes—were also recruited from the local populace. Community inquests involved even more local people in the affair, giving them a stake in making the resolution stick. Muscovite adjudication took place in a community-aware environment. One is reminded of Susan Reynolds's comment that medieval trials were more like informal assemblies than courts.[77]

---

[72]For the further development of the principle of local representation in adjudication, see Torke, *Die staatsbedingte Gesellschaft*, chap. 2, and Kivelson, *Autocracy in the Provinces*, chaps. 4 and 6.

[73]1634: RIB 14, no. 328, col. 719. For very similar addresses, see ibid., no. 227, cols. 547–48 (1604); no. 295, cols. 662–64 (1623); no. 304, cols. 677–81 (1627).

[74]1640: *Pamiatniki pis'mennosti v muzeiakh Vologodskoi oblasti* 4, pt. 2 (Vologda, 1984), p. 24. 1667: RGADA, f. 210, Prikaznyi stol, stb. 384, ll. 163–64.

[75]Kivelson, *Autocracy in the Provinces*, pp. 141–42.

[76]Ibid., p. 226.

[77]Reynolds, *Kingdoms and Communities*, pp. 24–25.

The presence of "good men," community "elders," locals as judges and bailiffs, and local witnesses and sureties enhanced the flexibility and power of the judicial process. As Davies and Fouracre point out in regard to medieval Europe, the efficacy of adjudication "hung, not on any abstract institutional structure, but on the local community, its social attitudes and its private personal relationships." They further argue that public approbation of the court system was a principal incentive for medieval people to litigate: "The key advantage of going to court was the width of support potentially available to a party there." Litigants would "construct" the support not only of witnesses but of kin, neighbors, clients, and dependents, who would more readily step forward because of the catalytic quality of a trial. "By and large the support one received at court was available on the assumption that a lasting end to the dispute could be obtained thereby. . . . Courts were the most public, that is definitive, arena available to people . . . decisions and agreements made there were more binding than any *fait accompli* established outside them."[78] Such observations apply to Muscovy as well. Participation by members of the community as officers of the court, popular representatives, witnesses, sureties, or even spectators could advance litigants' goals, as well as shape the process to suit the community's perception of the offense and the offender. As we shall see, Muscovite litigations drew amply on community participation.

Strategies of Litigation

Once the plaintiff decided to sue, he and all the other participants in the trial made choices about the course of a trial based on political and economic calculations, on the expected results of different courses of action, and on social norms.[79] As Laura Nader and Harry F. Todd, Jr., write, "Disputes are social processes embedded in social relations."[80] In premodern settings, the purpose

[78]Davies and Fouracre, eds., *Settlement*, pp. 231, 234, 235.

[79]On law as process, see Davies and Fouracre, eds., *Settlement*, pp. 232–33; Laura Nader and Henry F. Todd, Jr., eds., *The Disputing Process: Law in Ten Societies* (New York, 1978), pp. 1–40; Laura Nader, "From Disputing to Complaining," in Donald Black, ed., *Toward a General Theory of Social Control*, 2 vols. (Orlando, Fla., 1984), 1:71–94; essays by Simon Roberts and John Bossy in John Bossy, ed., *Disputes and Settlements* (Cambridge, England, 1983), pp. 1–24 and 287–93, respectively; Jane F. Collier, "Legal Processes," *Annual Reviews in Anthropology* (1975):121–44; Sally Humphreys, "Law as Discourse," *History and Anthropology* 1, no. 2 (1985): 241–64. Good applications of this approach are Shoemaker, *Prosecution*, and Cynthia Herrup, *The Common Peace: Participation and the Criminal Law in Seventeenth-Century England* (Cambridge, England, 1987).

[80]Nader and Todd, eds., *The Disputing Process*, p. 16. See also Nader's *Harmony Ideology: Justice and Control in a Zapotec Mountain Village* (Stanford, 1990), and her "Styles of Court Procedure: To Make the Balance," in idem, ed., *Law in Culture and Society* (Chicago, 1969), pp. 69–91.

Disposition of Cases Studied

Disposition	Percentage of total	Number of cases (of 621 total)
Resolved with a judgment	27.1	168
Settled before judgment	10.3	64
Only petition or notice (*iavka*) extant	17.7	110
Unfinished, partial record	44.9	279

of litigation was rarely to test a disputed behavior against an objective legal standard or to punish deviation, as it is—at least in theory—in modern litigation.[81] Rather, as Philippa Maddern argues, the function of litigation "was less to punish criminals than to achieve certain stages in the legal process which would bring pressure to bear on defendants."[82] Litigants, in short, used the judicial process to serve their various objectives.

For many litigants, the process apparently stopped with the initial petition, judging by the high number of unresolved cases in the database. Of 621 adjudicated cases, only 168, or just over one-fourth, were resolved with a judgment and sentence (see the table).[83] This finding is paralleled by studies of litigations in many settings. Philippa Maddern found criminal verdicts in fifteenth-century England to be "very rare," amounting to approximately 11% of cases she surveyed in East Anglia; Elizabeth Cohen observed that many suits over insult initiated in Renaissance Rome "seem to have been dropped or settled in other ways," as did Martin Ingram regarding defamation suits in sixteenth- and seventeenth-century Wiltshire.[84] In many cases, of course, loss of documents explains a suit's incompleteness. But the large incidence of unresolved cases suggests that document loss is insufficient explanation; I survey possible explanations here.

As with the principle of the notice (*iavka*) discussed in Chapter 2, the public declaration of an accusation often seems to have satisfied the plaintiff, perhaps because it had a deterrent effect on misbehavers or perhaps because it satisfied

[81]Many make this point: Maddern, *Violence and Social Order*, pp. 15, 65–67; Stephen D. White, "'*Pactum . . . Legem Vincit et Amor Judicium*': The Settlement of Disputes by Compromise in Eleventh-Century Western France," *The American Journal of Legal History* 22 (1978):282; Davies and Fouracre, eds., *Settlement*, p. 237.

[82]Maddern, *Violence and Social Order*, p. 112.

[83]This finding is despite the fact that the archival documents in the sample were chosen with a bias toward resolved cases. The number of adjudicated cases is smaller than the full database of 632 because some entries are excerpts from laws or other nonadjudication material.

[84]Maddern, *Violence and Social Order*, p. 111 (quote), 33 (statistic); Cohen, "Honor and Gender," p. 608; Ingram, *Church Courts*, p. 318. For similar comments and statistics, see also Sharpe, *Defamation*, p. 7; Shoemaker, *Prosecution*, chap. 6, pp. 127–65.

community expectations that one would defend one's honor.[85] Alternatively, some plaintiffs might have been deterred from pursuit by the cost and bother of litigation; as Ingram puts it in regard to early modern England, "rancour evaporated or the money ran out."[86] Landed servitors, who were expected to litigate in Moscow, had the greatest difficulty. Numerous petitions testify to their difficulties in meeting court dates when their military obligations took them to far frontiers of the realm. It is no wonder that in the seventeenth century, provincial gentry petitioned the government repeatedly for a local judicial system to avoid the hardships—corruption, red tape, and expense—of litigation in the capital.

Many litigations at some point in the process yielded to the pressure to settle, amicably or not. Motivations to settle were powerful, perhaps because they stemmed from so many sources. At the individual psychological level, Erving Goffman argues that people acting in society conduct themselves in a primarily "accommodative" manner so that all can maintain their socially constructed identity, or "face." Individuals will often ignore or forgive an insult rather than exacerbate a tense situation.[87] On the social level, such accommodation maintains or restores stability. Community interests favored face-saving settlement, because unresolved quarrels in small communities could escalate into a headache for the whole village. Settlement generally accomplished that goal better than bringing a case to verdict. As Davies and Fouracre point out regarding a range of early medieval European cases, "In all the societies we have looked at here, no matter how violent, it was recognized that it was better for disputes to end." Thus, "The purpose of much dispute settlement was not in any strict sense justice, but the restoration of peace."[88] In many premodern European societies, litigation was frowned on as an antisocial step until reconciliation had been attempted, and settlements were often regarded as more just and more binding than pursuing the letter of the law, because both parties emerged with dignity and satisfaction.[89] In Robert Shoemaker's study of misdemeanor prosecution in seventeenth- and eighteenth-century England, for example, a significant percentage of litigants who were personally acquainted settled informally: In the cases of two judges whose notebooks survive, 82% of litigants settled informally with one, and 66% with the other.[90]

---

[85]In our database, 110 of 621 entries (almost 18%) include only a petition or notice (*iavka*), unaccompanied by further documentation, suggesting that the trial was not initiated.

[86]Ingram, *Church Courts*, p. 318.

[87]Erving Goffman, "On Face Work," in his *Interaction Ritual* (Chicago, 1967), pp. 5–46, quote on p. 44.

[88]Davies and Fouracre, eds., *Settlement*, quotes on pp. 235 and 233, respectively.

[89]Settlements as more binding: White, "'*Pactum . . . Legem Vincit*'," pp. 298–304. On the pressure to settle: Shoemaker, *Prosecution*, p. 316; Martin Ingram, "Communities and Courts: Law and Disorder in Early Seventeenth-Century Wiltshire," in J. S. Cockburn, ed., *Crime in England, 1550–1800* (Princeton, N.J., 1977), pp. 127–33; Maddern, *Violence and Social Order*, p. 15. White's essay ("'*Pactum . . . Legem Vincit*'") is an especially good analysis of the dynamics of amicable settlement.

[90]Shoemaker, *Prosecution*, pp. 91–92.

In Muscovite suits over insult, sixty-four cases (10%) were resolved by written reconciliation (the documents were termed *mirovye* or "peace-making" acts). The number may seem small, but it is significant, inasmuch as it amounts to about one-third of the number of suits that were resolved by court verdict (168, or 27%). The circumstances and terms of settlements varied. Some litigants accepted the intercession of a mediator, whose role was so valued that if litigants refused to accept his decision, they were required to pay his dishonor fine and to forfeit a surety bond they had put up as earnest money.[91] But by and large, litigants reconciled on their own, before or during a trial. For example, two gentrymen settled in 1639 the day after one had insulted the other "with a mother oath before all the town," presumably before a trial had started.[92] Two townsmen in Tikhvin settled in 1684 two days after a quarrel, with the defendant paying fees and agreeing not to sue again on this issue on penalty of ten rubles.[93] On July 12, 1686, a widow sued two men for assault, theft, and rape, and on July 16, at the trial, one witness only partially supported her version of the events. That day the three settled during the trial, with the defendants paying fees calculated according to the woman's dishonor fine, perhaps giving her thus a symbolic as well as material victory.[94]

Community pressure could no doubt come to bear in this process, inasmuch as the questioning of many witnesses made the litigation a public experience. In a 1640 case, for example, twenty witnesses testified that they had not heard the insulting words alleged in the suit of one Vladimir gentryman with another, other than that each had called the other a shirker from service (*nesluga*). The judges ruled that the reciprocal insults canceled each other out; both litigants immediately paid the court fees and did not protest the resolution. In an analogous case of the same year, a plaintiff (a foreigner in a new model regiment) lost his suit when nineteen witnesses could not confirm his allegations that another foreigner in his regiment had insulted him and his wife.[95] A *zhilets* and a post driver in Tula settled in 1640 after an inquest of

[91] A ruling about this in 1637: AAE 3 (1836), no. 277, pp. 420–21; Conciliar Law Code of 1649, chap. 15, art. 5 (RZ 3:163). An agreement stipulating such terms from 1647: St. Petersburgskii filial arkhiva Instituta rossiiskoi istorii Rossiiskoi akademii nauk, f. 62, Koll. Kablukova, no. 30. On arbitration, see Geary, "Extra-Judicial Means"; William Ian Miller, "Avoiding Legal Judgment: The Submission of Disputes to Arbitration in Medieval Iceland," *The American Journal of Legal History* 28 (1984):95–134.

[92] RGADA, f. 210, Prikaznyi stol, stb. 113, l. 141.

[93] AIu, no. 276, p. 285. A similar agreement, stipulating a fine of 100 rubles: *Moskovskaia delovaia*, pt. 4, no. 32, p. 164 (1694).

[94] 1686: RIB 12, no. 166, cols. 724–30. Other instances of settlements made during a trial: RIB 12, no. 194, cols. 918–22 (1688); K. P. Pobedonostsev, ed., *Istoriko-iuridicheskie akty perekhodnoi epokhi XVII–XVIII vekov* (Moscow, 1887), pp. 45–46 (1703).

[95] 1640, Vladimir gentrymen: RGADA, f. 210, Prikaznyi stol, stb. 130, ll. 453–65. 1640, foreigners: ibid., ll. 771–81.

the community split: forty-one supported the plaintiff, and thirty-one denied all knowledge of the alleged insult and quarrel. In another case of 1640, more than forty community members were involved as witnesses or character witnesses; although the plaintiff won the case, the two men settled after the verdict. Perhaps the plaintiff agreed to forego the fine in the interest of restoring local amity, possibly pushed by community sentiment in the presence of so many neighbors.[96]

Other juridical processes also promoted the cause of reconciliation. Routinely, defendants and even plaintiffs were put on recognizance (*poruka*), a surety bond that promised that the principal would appear at the trial or else forfeit a sum put up by his guarantors. Not only did such bonds provide a "cooling off" period in which settlement or abandonment of a suit could occur, they also brought to bear the additional pressure of the guarantors, who not only stood to lose their bond but also were denied the legal right to sue the sponsored man for dishonor in case he defaulted.[97] Robert Shoemaker argues that recognizances "often successfully resolved a dispute without further legal action; not much more than a fifth of the defendants bound over were subsequently indicted" in his large sample of misdemeanor suits.[98] Many Muscovite cases were settled after one or both of the litigants were put on recognizance. In 1625, for example, a musketeer of Briansk sued a local cleric for insulting his daughter and son-in-law. The litigants were ordered placed "on sturdy recognizance" (*krepkaia poruka*) and brought to Moscow. In the face of that expensive proposition, they promptly settled the case. Similarly, on July 24, 1672, in Voronezh, an infantryman sued his brother over a quarrel that had taken place the previous day; they each gathered sureties and named witnesses. On August 18, they settled out of court before witness testimony was taken; the brother agreed to pay court fees.[99]

Suits that were not settled early on proceeded to the collection of evidence. Plaintiffs presented their side of the story to the judge, naming witnesses or presenting relevant evidence, such as marks of injury or documents. The judge questioned the defendant, who sometimes also then sued the plaintiff for false

---

[96]*Zhilets*: RGADA, f. 210, Prikaznyi stol, stb. 130, ll. 403–20 (1640). Forty witnesses, 1640: ibid., stb. 130, ll. 421–31. A similar case of settlement after resolution: RGADA, f. 210, Prikaznyi stol, stb. 918, ll. 18–43 (1685).

[97]ZA, no. 188, par. 10, p. 150 (1628). Surety bonds were used in a wide variety of ways: H. W. Dewey, "Political *Poruka* in Muscovite Rus'," *Russian Review* 46, no. 2 (1987):117–34; H. W. Dewey and Ann M. Kleimola, "Suretyship and Collective Responsibility in pre-Petrine Russia," *Jahrbücher für Geschichte Osteuropas* 18 (1970):337–54.

[98]Shoemaker, *Prosecution*, chap. 5, pp. 95–126; quote on p. 97.

[99]1625: RGADA, f. 210, Prikaznyi stol, stb. 15, pt. 2, ll. 514–17. 1672: RGADA, f. 210, Prikaznyi stol, stb. 141, ll. 85–94. Other examples include 1689: RGADA, f. 210, Prikaznyi stol, stb. 1074, ll. 92–100, and 1698: RGADA, f. 210, Prikaznyi stol, stb. 2352, ll. 40–42.

accusation or for the "dishonor" of the present suit. Defendants had the right to exclude witnesses based on enmity or kinship; if both disputants could find a common witness (*obshchaia pravda*) or witnesses whose testimony they agreed to, that testimony would decide the case. Sometimes litigants requested, or judges ordered, a general inquest (*poval'nyi obysk*) of the community to gather evidence. According to long-standing tradition, such inquests sought character references as well as firsthand eyewitness evidence. Law codes throughout the Muscovite period fought this trend, advising that witnesses "should not testify if they have not witnessed, and having witnessed should testify truthfully."[100] But character references and hearsay continued to play a large role in inquest testimony, leading to the abolition of general inquests in 1688, a reflection of increasing judicial preference for more objective evidence (documents and individual eyewitness).[101]

Many cases show the importance of witness testimony in advancing or resolving a dispute. In 1640, for example, a group of nineteen men, identified as "common witnesses," failed to support the plaintiff's claim that a fellow foreigner in Muscovite service had insulted him and his wife. He lost the case. In 1641, a gentryman sued another for insulting him in the governor's office; a common witness testified in favor of the plaintiff, and he won the suit. Similarly, in 1676, a peasant sued a priest in the Sukhona River area in the North for insult by a mother-oath; two common witnesses—a priest and a peasant—supported the plaintiff. The priest lost the suit. In 1680, a musketeer in Rylsk lost a suit over assault on his daughters by the daughter of an artilleryman because a "common witness" of seven men failed to support him.[102]

In the absence of conclusive witness or written testimony, litigants agreed to let the judgment of God resolve their dispute through some sort of ordeal, again highlighting the ritual character of court proceedings. Although judicial duels were still countenanced into the seventeenth century,[103] in the materials covered by the database only the ordeal of oath-taking by kissing the cross is attested. The procedure was executed by a priest accompanied by representatives of the local officialdom and populace as witnesses. Both litigants attended. The one who had agreed to an oath was called to the cross three times, and on the third he was asked to swear. If he failed to appear or refused to take the

[100]1550 law code: RZ 2:120 (art. 99); 1669 Newly Promulgated Articles (on criminal law): PRP 7 (1963):406–8 (art. 28).

[101]PSZ 2, no. 1294, p. 921 (1688).

[102]1640 foreigner: RGADA, f. 210, Prikaznyi stol, stb. 130, ll. 771–81. 1641: RGADA, f. 210, Prikaznyi stol, stb. 163, ll. 503–6. 1676: RIB 14, pt. 2, no. 52, cols. 993–96. 1680: RGADA, f. 210, Prikaznyi stol, stb. 805, ll. 61–78.

[103]Horace W. Dewey, "Trial by Combat in Muscovite Russia," *Oxford Slavonic Papers* 9 (1960):21–31.

oath, his opponent won the suit. If both the litigants agreed to take an oath, they threw lots to determine who would swear first.[104]

The efficacy of oath-taking as a means of resolving disputes was, judging by these cases, apparently great. Not one of the many called to take an oath actually went through the full ritual and kissed the cross; they backed out along the way. In many cases, both litigants stated their willingness to take an oath, but did not act on it; they resolved the case on the basis of witness evidence or amicable settlement instead.[105] When they did move toward the actual oath-taking ritual, litigants either abandoned the litigation along the way or settled. In most cases, litigants settled once an oath had been ordered, before the ritual had begun, or at the first of the three summons.[106] Some cases simply stopped once an oath was mentioned.[107] Some litigants facing an oath sued for delay and then never showed up to one or another of the three summons.[108] Some cases offer interesting details. In 1641, for example, two gentrymen of Elets (south of Moscow) litigated over dishonor incurred in a property dispute. The plaintiff reported that he stood to the cross kissing three times, and at the third time, the defendant intervened and agreed to settle the case and pay the court fees. The defendant then proceeded to drag his feet on paying the fees, until it was reopened three years later and the fees were collected from the defendant's sureties. In 1642, a defendant halted the ritual at the second summons to the cross, offering to come to agreement with the plaintiff, because he "did not want to commit sin" (presumably by falsely swearing). More magnanimously,

[104]On the ritual, see the Conciliar Law Code of 1649, chap. 14 (RZ 3:159–62). Oath-taking on a cross is also mentioned in passing in the 1497 and 1550 law codes: RZ 2:60–61 (1497: arts. 48, 52, 58) and 100–1 (1550: arts. 16, 19, 27). Contemporary travelers described the ritual: Giles Fletcher in Berry and Crummey, eds., *Rude and Barbarous Kingdom*, pp. 174–75; Olearius, *Travels*, p. 228. See also H. W. Dewey and A. M. Kleimola, "Promise and Perfidy in Old Russian Cross-Kissing," *Canadian Slavic Studies* 2, no. 3 (1968):327–41. Lots were used in cases valued one ruble or less (RZ 3:162 [chap. 14, art. 10]), as occurred in a 1684 case (RGADA, f. 210, Belgorod stol, stb. 1227, ll. 1–28). Priests were forbidden to take oaths; they cast lots instead: Conciliar Law Code of 1649, chap. 13, art. 4 (RZ 3:159).

[105]Resolved by witness evidence: RGADA, f. 210, Prikaznyi stol, stb. 130, ll. 771–81 (1640); RGADA, f. 210, Prikaznyi stol, stb. 130, ll. 449–65 (1640); RGADA, f. 210, Prikaznyi stol, stb. 130, ll. 403–31 (1640); RGADA, f. 210, Prikaznyi stol, stb. 163, ll. 503–6 (1641); AIuB 1, no. 104, cols. 643–66 (1646). Resolved by settlement: RGADA, f. 210, Prikaznyi stol, stb. 113, ll. 92–100 (1639); RGADA, f. 210, Prikaznyi stol, stb. 253, ll. 186–95 (1642).

[106]RGADA, f. 210, Belgorod stol, stb. 138, ll. 331–46 (1638); RGADA, f. 210, Prikaznyi stol, stb. 130, ll. 434–41, 972–92, 449–65 (all 1640); RGADA, f. 210, Prikaznyi stol, stb. 253, ll. 153–58 (1642); RGADA, f. 210, Prikaznyi stol, stb. 192, ll. 143–55 (1649).

[107]RGADA, f. 210, Prikaznyi stol, stb. 253, ll. 121–29 (1642); RGADA, f. 210, Prikaznyi stol, stb. 264, ll. 70–78 (1650).

[108]RGADA, f. 210, Prikaznyi stol, stb. 1155, ll. 20–33 (1680). In 1653, a prospective oath-taker simply walked out on the last summons of the ritual: RGADA, f. 210, Prikaznyi stol, stb. 196, ll. 317–85.

in 1690, a defendant stopped the plaintiff from kissing the cross at the last summons and agreed to pay all court fees.[109]

Sanctions and Mercy

The ways in which litigants pursued cases display their essential confidence in the judicial system at the same time that they demonstrate individuals' subjective manipulation of the process. They pursued suits or settled as the spirit moved; they yielded to public pressure; they cowed in the face of eternal damnation with cross in hand. Until the case went to the judge, the judicial process allowed flexibility and gave wide range to achieve maximum satisfaction for all sides. When judges took the stage to decide verdicts, their ability to enforce compliance with their judgments depended in part on litigants' faith in the judge's impartiality and in the system as a whole. Judges' efficacy was also enhanced by the latitude with which they could respond to the specific circumstances of a suit.[110]

When judges resolved a suit over insult, what was particularly at issue was not the truth of an allegation, but whether in fact the insulting words had been uttered. There were some exceptions. Law codes, for example, specified that an allegation of illegitimacy was dishonoring if proven false, and indeed in one case a man's parentage was investigated to establish his legitimacy.[111] Case law also suggested that it was not dishonoring to label a man a "traitor" or "deserter" (*beglets*) if the accused had indeed fled the scene of battle; the insult was otherwise very serious.[112] Accordingly, individuals took great pains to refute allegations of dereliction of military service, pointing out their own and their families' long years of faithful service.[113] False accusation of criminal activity was in theory treated harshly: A decree of 1582 mandated execution for false accusation of thievery (a frequent insult in the suits in the database), whereas the 1589 law code declared false accusation dishonoring to the victim.[114] Defendants sometimes argued therefore that they called a plaintiff a "thief" justly because he had

[109]1641: RGADA, f. 210, Prikaznyi stol, stb. 553, ll. 92–116. 1642: RGADA, f. 210, Prikaznyi stol, stb. 253, ll. 1–7, 14–15, 71–78. 1690: RGADA, f. 210, Prikaznyi stol, stb. 2608, ll. 1–58.

[110]Torstein Eckhoff, "The Mediator, the Judge and the Administrator in Conflict-Resolution," *Acta Sociologica* 10 (1966):161–66.

[111]The law: RZ 3:149–50 (chap. 10, art. 280). The case: RGADA, f. 210, Zapisnye knigi moskovskogo stola, opis' 6a, delo 12 (1662), ll. 250v–55.

[112]Case law: RGADA, f. 210, Prikaznyi stol, stb. 130, ll. 449–65 (1640). Punishment of treason: RZ 3:86–89 (chap. 2).

[113]I. E. Zabelin, *Domashnii byt russkikh tsarei v XVI i XVII st.*, 3 bks. (Moscow, 1990), reprint publ. of 4th exp. ed. (Moscow, 1918), pp. 358–63 (1643); PSZ 3, no. 1460, pp. 149–51 (1693).

[114]1582: AI 1, no. 154 XX, pp. 271–72 (1582). 1589: PRP 4 (1956):414 (art. 6). See also Horace W. Dewey, "Defamation and False Accusation (*Iabednichestvo*) in Old Muscovite Society," *Etudes slaves et est-européennes/Slavic and East European Studies* 11, nos. 3–4 (1966/67):109–20.

been convicted of theft.[115] In practice, however, most insults were too generic to be disproved one way or the other ("son of a bitch," for example), and most slurs hurled in dishonor disputes tended not to be taken literally. Judges did not investigate criminal records when a man was called a thief (*vor*); ascertaining that the insult was uttered, they convicted the defendant.[116]

Muscovy's contemporaries followed the same principle. English law declared "It matters not whether the libel be true, or whether the party against whom it is made be of good or bad fame." French law paralleled this attitude.[117] The issue at stake was more the socially destabilizing effects of hot words and reputation-ruining slanders than literal truth. Muscovite law codes did not expressly state the principle that was at the root of European canon and civil law against defaming language, but the practice of such litigation shows similar concern: the principle that slanderous language was a breach of the common peace, an act that might engender further violence, tension, and fissures in the community.[118] Clearly the court's interest in establishing the *fact* of an utterance rather than its validity expresses this same view: Individuals could not be allowed to inflame passions, defame neighbors, and rile up kindred and community. Judicial processes provided a forum for restoring an individual's social position when threatened, for forcing apologies and reconciliation when possible, or for administering penalties when insulters refused to back down.

In imposing sentences, judges tended to follow the guidelines established by the 1550, 1589, and 1649 law codes. In the few cases before 1649 for which we know the resolution, the 1550 law code's guidelines for monetary compensation seem to have been followed. We find a boyar receiving a large cash payment in 1571 for dishonor and a diplomat paying for insulting a gentryman's wife in 1594.[119] In some cases, however, judges were harsher than the law prescribed. In 1626, for example, a landless peasant was beaten for insulting a priest, when corporal punishment was not at all recommended in the 1550 law code. Also excessively harsh was a 1635 ruling in which a gentryman was sent

---

[115]RGADA, f. 210, Prikaznyi stol, stb. 675, ll. 86–93 (1673); RGADA, f. 210, Prikaznyi stol, stb. 1203, ll. 6–9 (1691); RGADA, f. 210, Prikaznyi stol, stb. 2548, ll. 1–17 (1693).

[116]RGADA, f. 210, Prikaznyi stol, stb. 2232, ll. 1–35 (1690).

[117]Quoted in Peter N. Moogk, "'Thieving Buggers' and 'Stupid Sluts': Insults and Popular Culture in New France," *William and Mary Quarterly*, 3d ser., 36, no. 4 (1979):536.

[118]Ingram, *Church Courts*, pp. 292–95; Sharpe, *Defamation*, p. 8; W. R. Jones, "'Actions for Slaunder'—Defamation in English Law, Language, and History," *Quarterly Journal of Speech* 57, no. 3 (1971):275. Closer to the concept of sedition, the Venetian state punished insult to government and noblemen as "a form of violence against the unity of the state": Guido Ruggiero, *Violence in Early Renaissance Venice* (New Brunswick, N.J., 1980), p. 126.

[119]1571 boyar: AAE 1, no. 280, pp. 315–16, and AI 1, no. 205, pp. 341–43. 1594 diplomat: N. P. Likhachev, ed., *Biblioteka i arkhiv moskovskikh gosudarei v XVI stoletii* (St. Petersburg, 1894), app. III, pp. 49–52.

to a ritual of humiliation for insulting his sister-in-law. Perhaps here the severity stemmed from the familial relationship involved.[120] Similarly, in 1642, a *stol'nik* was corporally punished for insult to another *stol'nik*'s widow, when a cash fine should have been the sentence.[121]

After the 1649 law code was issued, the range of sentences for dishonor expanded to include incarceration and corporal punishment as well as cash fines. As detailed in Chapter 1, the type and severity of punishment varied according to the social status of the insulter and insulted parties. As a rule, after 1649, judges followed these guidelines, aided by the wide distribution of printed copies of the Conciliar Law Code (many of the suits I cite include verbatim excerpts from the code). We see in 1675 a boyar paying a *stol'nik* his cash salary for insulting him, a gentryman paying a cash fine to a peer in 1683, an infantryman paying cash to a peer in 1684, and a peasant paying a cash fine to another peasant in 1697.[122] When judges strayed from the guidelines, they did not stray far, sometimes slightly mitigating punishment. In 1666, for example, a land elder (*zemskii starosta*) was sentenced to beating by bastinadoes and a week in prison for insulting a governor, when the law required beating by knout and two weeks in prison.[123] In 1667, when a son was beaten for insult to his mother, the sentence was mitigated by his being beaten with bastinadoes, not the mandated and harsher knout.[124]

Judges could intensify sentences because of the severity of the insult. In 1650, an undersecretary was sentenced to exile in Siberia for insulting a man of the Moscow ranks by submitting false evidence in a trial against him. For dishonor in this case, the punishment would normally be a cash fine. Harsher punishments also came when the insult was accompanied by the failure to obey orders in a military or administrative setting, as in 1660 when a governor was ordered to pay a cash fine and spend three days in prison for not handing over troops to the local musketeer regiment as ordered. Normally, dishonor to musketeers by a governor would merit a cash fine alone. In a case from July 1649, the eminence of the victim, the tsar's close advisor Bogdan Khitrovo, probably accounts for the intensified punishment: A servitor was ordered beaten with a

[120]1626: RGADA, f. 210, Prikaznyi stol, stb. 17, ll. 330–34. Punishments as set down in the 1550 law code (RZ 2:101 [art. 26]) and the 1649 law code (RZ 3:110 [arts. 85–89]). 1635: RGADA, f. 210, Prikaznyi stol, stb. 139, ll. 473–94.

[121]Zabelin, *Domashnii byt*, pp. 354–58.

[122]Boyar in 1675: DR 3: cols. 1287–88; relevant article: RZ 3:111 (art. 93). Gentrymen in 1683: RGADA, f. 210, Prikaznyi stol, stb. 1086, ll. 88–150; relevant article the same. Infantrymen in 1684: RGADA, f. 210, Prikaznyi stol, stb. 1161, ll. 13–24; relevant article: RZ 3:111 (art. 94). Peasants in 1697: Titov, ed., *Kungurskie akty*, no. 72, pp. 249–63; relevant article: RZ 3:111 (art. 94).

[123]RGADA, f. 210, Prikaznyi stol, stb. 993, ll. 1–107; relevant article in 1649 code: RZ 3:110–11 (art. 92).

[124]RGADA, f. 210, Prikaznyi stol, stb. 384, ll. 163–64. Relevant article in 1649 code: RZ 3:248 (chap. 22, art. 4).

knout for insulting the *okol'nichii* Khitrovo, when by the 1649 law code, the penalty should have been a cash fine.[125]

Judges enhanced their ability to enforce judgments by the strategy of publicity. In announcing or carrying out sentences, they mandated the presence of witnesses. This practice was particularly valuable in dishonor litigations when the aggrieved party wanted to ensure that the community be made aware of his or her vindication. Corporal punishment was generally to be carried out in public view, for deterrent effect as well as to enlist community approbation. In 1640, for example, a high-ranking Muscovite servitor was found guilty of insulting a judge and was ordered imprisoned; the order was announced "at the Military Service Chancery before many people." In 1677, the military governor of Briansk was ordered imprisoned for a day and an undersecretary was ordered beaten "mercilessly" with bastinadoes instead of the knout for having submitted a document with an improper form of the diminutive for the governor's name. The presiding officer was instructed to read the judgment against the two men out loud "in the local administrative office (*s'ezzhaia izba*) before many people." And in 1687, a commander in a new model cavalry unit was ordered "beaten with a knout before the whole regiment" for dishonor and disobedience to his colonel and for drunkenness.[126] For the highest social level, public rituals of humiliation were prescribed (see Chapter 4), whereas sometimes a particular form of beating with the knout was prescribed, which involved beating the victim while he was led through town (the so-called "marketplace punishment").[127] The public nature of some sanctions attests to the utility of social pressure in adjudication: Public knowledge of unacceptable behavior shaped community opinion about an individual, enlisting, as it were, the involved community to supervise the subsequent behavior of the punished individual.

Another aspect of the system of punishments worked in a different way to pursue stability: the provision of mercy in sentencing. Again, this is not unusual in the premodern European context. In England, for example, judges often found reason to mitigate sentences, doing so, for example, in about two-thirds of the criminal convictions that Cynthia Herrup analyzed, and exerting considerable flexibility in fining for convictions in Robert Shoemaker's study of Middlesex county misdemeanors.[128] In Muscovy, mercy was proffered in the

---

[125]1650: Zabelin, *Domashnii byt*, pp. 377–79; relevant articles in 1649 code are RZ 3:110–11 (arts. 91, 93). 1660: RGADA, f. 210, Prikaznyi stol, stb. 346, ll. 98–101. Dishonor fine for musketeers: RZ 3:111 (art. 94). 1649: RGADA, f. 210, Prikaznyi stol, stb. 177, ll. 56–92 (published almost in full in Zabelin, *Domashnii byt*, pp. 398–407); relevant article: RZ 3:110 (art. 91).

[126]1640: RGADA, f. 210, Moscow stol, stb. 1037, ll. 242–47. 1677: RGADA, f. 210, Belgorod stol, stb. 854, ll. 97–100, 119–20. 1687: RGADA, f. 210, stb. 1064, ll. 10–13.

[127]See N. D. Sergeevskii's discussion in *Nakazanie v russkom prave XVII veka* (St. Petersburg, 1887), pp. 155–56, and my discussion of public shaming in Chapter 2.

[128]Herrup, *Common Peace*, chap. 7, esp. p. 165; Shoemaker, *Prosecution*, pp. 156–65.

name of the tsar and construed as his personal "favor"; it was reserved for members of the privileged elite. In 1657/58, two men of a boyar clan were ordered beaten and fined for dishonoring another boyar clan in the Kremlin; the tsar remitted the beating (but maintained the fine of 1,590 rubles). In February 1683, a *zhilets* was ordered beaten for dishonoring the tsar's palace and fined for dishonoring another *zhilets*; the tsar lessened the beating to a prison term and then released the defendant from prison when he petitioned for further mercy on the basis of his old age and ill health. Similarly, in the 1687 rape case discussed at length in Chapter 2, a military servitor was sentenced to exile to the Solovetskii Monastery in addition to paying a hefty fine in lieu of the shamed woman's dowry. The tsars rescinded the exile, but not the fine. And in a remarkable case, in the summer of 1684, Tsars Ioann and Petr Alekseevichi and regent Sofiia Alekseevna ordered a gentryman executed for insolence because he had approached them with a request to reconsider a suit that they had already personally resolved. Then they bestowed mercy, levying a fine instead. But on September 16, he again appealed, "forgetting the fear of God and despising their copious and surpassing mercy," prompting the tsars again to order him executed to deter others "in the future." On October 3, 1684, they again bestowed mercy "in honor of the tsar's many-yeared health," announcing the reprieve to the unfortunate man at the last minute "in Red Square at the execution place."[129] Thus mitigation of a verdict, in addition to minimizing hardships, worked to uphold the privilege and dignity of the elite ranks and the image of a benevolent as well as just tsar.

Mercy could also emanate from the plaintiffs themselves. An element of mercy is to be found, for example, in plaintiffs being willing to forego compensation even after they had won a suit. In 1641, for example, a *zhilets* won a suit against a post driver in Tula for insult to him and assault on his man. Then they settled the suit, with the defendant paying the court fees. On May 20, 1685, a townsman of Kolomna won a suit against a peer for insult to him, his wife, and his two sons; the defendant proved unable to pay the dishonor fine of twenty-eight rubles plus court fees, and on July 18 they settled, with the plaintiff forgiving part of the debt and receiving a deed for land for the rest. In a 1687 case, two highly ranked Moscow servitors sued for insult: The more senior of the two, a *dumnyi dvorianin* named Izvolskii, alleged that the defendant, a state secretary (*d'iak*) by the name of Poplavskii, had insulted him and

---

[129]1657/58: RGADA, f. 210, Prikaznyi stol, stb. 1421, l. 105. February 1683: RGADA, f. 210, Prikaznyi stol, stb. 621, ll. 67–88. 1687: PSZ 2, nos. 1266–67, pp. 905–7. October 3, 1684: RGADA, f. 210, Prikaznyi stol, stb. 876, ll. 1–29. The reference to the "tsar's many-yeared health" may be a generic wish for good health or may, as in modern usage, refer to the birthday celebration of one of the ruling triumvirate. But if the latter, it is difficult to establish whose birthday was intended. Regent Sofiia's birthday is closest to the dates associated with this extended trial: She was born September 17, 1657, Ioann was born August 26, 1666, and Petr was born May 20, 1672.

refused to work under him in a chancery. The defendant countersued, saying that Izvolskii had said to him, "Your worth, you farm laborer, is a penny. I'll throw you out of the chancery tomorrow," and had additionally insulted him at his home. Even though Izvolskii won the suit, for which his 365-ruble annual salary was levied on the state secretary as a fine, he agreed to settle the suit because "He [Poplavskii] has apologized to me."[130]

Even more magnanimously, winning plaintiffs occasionally petitioned for punishment to be revoked or mitigated. In 1683, for example, a gentryman, B. I. Kalachov, was ordered beaten with a knout "on the stand" (*na kozle*)[131] for insult to Boyar Prince Mikhail Andreevich Golitsyn. On November 8, this order was read to Kalachov in front of the Military Service Chancery, but, as his clothing was being removed, Prince Golitsyn's man intervened, conveying the boyar's petition for mercy, asking that Kalachov not be beaten for the sake of Golitsyn's honor. And so he was reprieved. The Golitsyns were a compassionate lot, it would seem. In March 1692, Prince Boris Alekseevich Golitsyn won a suit for insult to him and his father in the tsar's quarters against two men of the Dolgorukii princely clan. The two were ordered imprisoned for insulting the dignity of the tsar's residence and were fined more than 1,500 rubles for the younger Golitsyn and an equally large amount for the father. The tsar in his mercy pardoned them the prison sentence, but not the fine. The two Dolgorukii princes protested the imprisonment and the huge fine, saying "We had a simple and common disagreement, the type that often occurs among servitors who have an enmity," citing the Conciliar Law Code of 1649 to suggest that the punishment was excessive and declaring that the Golitsyny were out to destroy them and their clan. In July 1692 and March 1693, they petitioned the court, claiming to be unable to pay such a sum. Three years later, in May 1695, they won a reprieve from the Golitsyn family patriarch, who sent word from his deathbed that he in the name of the family forgave them the dishonor and the fine.[132]

Why would litigants make such benevolent gestures? Perhaps it had to do with individuals' sense of their own honor. Recall Julian Pitt-Rivers's remarks on honor discussed in the Introduction. He argues that in many societies, the concept of honor has "two registers"—one the adamant defense of one's honor and the other the magnanimous forgiveness of a rival once one's honor has been defended.[133] This spirit of honor, plus the fact that most Muscovites

---

[130]1641: RGADA, f. 210, Prikaznyi stol, stb. 278, l. 596. 1685: RGADA, f. 210, stb. 918, ll. 18–43. 1687: RGADA, f. 210, Prikaznyi stol, stb. 1063, ll. 82–104.

[131]This form of beating was apparently less harsh than the ordinary way of beating by the knout; see Sergeevskii, *Nakazanie*, pp. 155–58.

[132]1683: RGADA, f. 210, Prikaznyi stol, stb. 1161, ll. 70–90. 1692: RGADA, f. 210, Prikaznyi stol, stb. 1421, ll. 65–129; published virtually in full in Zabelin, *Domashnii byt*, pp. 386–94. A similar case of forgiveness in 1705: Pobedonostsev, ed., *Istoriko-iuridicheskie akty*, pp. 41–51.

[133]Julian Pitt-Rivers, "Postscript," in J. G. Peristiany and Julian Pitt-Rivers, eds., *Honor and Grace in Anthropology* (Cambridge, England, 1992), pp. 242–43.

embraced Christian values of charity to one's neighbors, contributed to the spirit of magnanimity. Particularly when it came to insult, as I have discussed in this and earlier chapters, the restoration of stable social relations by rehabilitating reputation was important to communities and individuals.

Emphasizing only the stabilizing effects of litigation creates a misleading impression. First, it would be premature to do so. One would need to examine a larger selection of different kinds of disputes in a geographically limited setting and test how different groups—men, women, the poor, the privileged— experienced the law. Historians have argued that significant social groups were excluded or disadvantaged in premodern adjudication; in particular, women and the poor suffered harsher penalties or more limited access to the courts than did propertied litigants and thus did not so readily experience the law as a stabilizing or mediating social instrument.[134] The same might have been true in Muscovy. Second, as I have suggested, Muscovites complained of judicial corruption and abuse. Finally, litigants could use courts to antagonize their rivals.[135] In suit after suit, we find litigants complaining that a party in a suit fails to cooperate, will not pursue an initiated case,[136] has left town in the midst of a suit,[137] refuses to pay a fine or fulfill the terms of a settlement,[138] harasses them with litigation, and the like. In the seventeenth-century petitions against local factions cited above, gentrymen described the depredations of these *sil'nye liudi*: "And we, your slaves, suffer great injury and losses from them in their great slanderous suits; they serve on us, your slaves, and on our slaves and peasants, summonses to court, counting on the fact that they do not pay judicial fees and they cheat us, your slaves, and our slaves and peasants deliberately." They go on to explain how wealthy landholders manipulated the court system to prevent lesser gentry from recovering runaway serfs from them. A dishonor suit from 1690 echoes these sentiments. Two Novgorodian gentrymen expressed their helplessness in suing a neighbor for his twenty-two-year

[134]Shoemaker makes this argument forcefully: *Prosecution*, chap. 8 and Conclusion. Scholars also argue that where litigation is expensive or the preserve of the elite, the disenfranchised often resort to private vengeance, such as "house scorning" under cover of night, anonymous pasquinades, and the like: Cohen, "Honor and Gender"; Garrioch, *Neighbourhood and Community*, p. 47.

[135]Ingram cites decades-long suits: *Church Courts*, p. 315. David Garrioch remarks that insults were often the culmination of long-simmering tensions: "Verbal Insults in Eighteenth-Century Paris," in Peter Burke and Roy Porter, eds., *The Social History of Language* (Cambridge, England, 1987), p. 115.

[136]RGADA, f. 210, Prikaznyi stol, stb. 16, ll. 123–30 (1629); *Moskovskaia delovaia*, pt. 2, no. 96, p. 94 (1675); RGADA, f. 210, Belgorod stol, stb. 1260, ll. 131–37 (1687); RGADA, f. 210, Prikaznyi stol, stb. 1203, l. 67 (1690); ibid., stb. 1367, ll. 52–57 (1691); Pobedonostsev, *Istoriko-iuridicheskie*, pp. 5–41 (1703).

[137]RGADA, f. 210, Prikaznyi stol, stb. 121, ll. 233–35 (1638); ibid., stb. 130, ll. 487–94 (1640); ibid., stb. 431, ll. 60–109 (1682); ibid., stb. 1425, ll. 45–77 (1691).

[138]RGADA, f. 210, Prikaznyi stol, stb. 11, ll. 230–32 (1624); ibid., stb. 553, ll. 92–116 (1641); ibid., stb. 729, ll. 118–28 (1676); ibid., stb. 679, ll. 159–62 (1691); ibid., stb. 1497, ll. 11–23 (1692).

pattern of false accusations and harassment of them: "And we cannot sue him for dishonor; he is too wealthy."[139]

Insult and dishonor suits could be a spiteful strategy of negotiating local tensions. A long-simmering dispute between a gentryman of Zemliansk by the name of Plotnikov and a local undersecretary named Okulov, for example, apparently boiled over in April 1682 when the two fought and exchanged insults at Plotnikov's home. Okulov said Plotnikov and his family had long been harassing people in the village, and Plotnikov called Okulov a thief and murderer and charged him with assaulting and insulting his sister and her property. The transcript dryly records that "The trial could not be concluded because all the parties were quarreling among themselves." When the case was referred to Moscow, Okulov was ordered to cease his work in Zemliansk until the charges were investigated. The case dragged on at least three more years, with new charges and countercharges. As far as extant documentation shows, it was never settled.[140] The tsar's courts imposed penalties, collected bond from recalcitrant individuals' sureties, or confiscated property, but nonetheless, many such litigants managed to obstruct justice. In several cases, losing defendants, for example, dragged cases on without paying the fines for a year and a half—or three, eight, fifteen, seventeen, even eighteen years.[141] They requested overly harsh sentences or continued insults and threats after losing a case.[142] All in all, litigation could be an avenue for exacerbating personal and local stresses.

Muscovy's was not a perfectly equitable judicial system, but social institutions can always be manipulated in these ways. The relevant question is the degree of satisfaction individuals found in these processes. I have argued here that as a rule, individuals were more interested in winning public acknowledgment of their honor and a speedy resolution to a dispute than they were in harassing rivals. For most litigants, the judicial process seems to have worked well enough. Plaintiffs felt they would receive satisfaction, and defendants participated in the

---

[139]Petition from February 1637: P. P. Smirnov, ed., "Chelobitnye dvorian i detei boiarskikh vsekh gorodov v pervoi polovine XVII v.," *Chteniia* 1915, bk. 3: doc. no. I, p. 38; also cited in Kivelson, *Autocracy in the Provinces*, p. 225. 1691 case: RGADA, f. 210, Prikaznyi stol, stb. 1292, ll. 1–25.

[140]RGADA, f. 210, Prikaznyi stol, stb. 830, ll. 1–94.

[141]A year and a half: RGADA, f. 210, Prikaznyi stol, stb. 1223, ll. 66–135 (1690). 3 years: RGADA, f. 210, Prikaznyi stol, stb. 1522, ll. 1–53 (1690). 8 years: RGADA, f. 210, Prikaznyi stol, stb. 2481, ll. 10–51 (1692). 15 years: RGADA, f. 239, opis' 1, chast' 4, delo 5364, ll. 1–53v (1704). 17 years: RGADA, f. 239, opis' 1, chast' 4, delo 5714, ll. 1–40v (1705). 18 years: K. P. Pobedonostsev, *Materialy dlia istorii prikaznogo sudoproizvodstva v Rossii* (Moscow, 1890), viazka 779, delo 14, p. 161 (1720).

[142]Excessive punishment: RGADA, f. 210, Prikaznyi stol, stb. 1421, ll. 65–129 (1692). Continued insults and threats: RIB 25, no. 33, cols. 34–35 (1627); RIB 25, no. 86, cols. 100–2 (1631); *Moskovskaia delovaia*, pt. 2, no. 14, p. 52 (1634); RGADA, f. 210, Prikaznyi stol, stb. 161, ll. 38–42 (1644).

system because those who flouted it risked punishment. For all concerned, failing to appeal to justice posed even greater losses. Without recourse to the court, communities could be rife with feuds, vendettas, and unresolved tensions that affected daily life for many. Going to court offered sufficient flexibility that could meet the needs of individuals, communities, and the state.

Trials concerning insult to honor are particularly illustrative of the legal process at work for two reasons. First, insult to honor created moments when community relations were crystallized. Insult was often the culminating point in a simmering dispute: To really get at one's rival, one publicly shamed him or her. Second, honor litigations necessarily mobilized communities. Because honor is as public as it is private—an insult without witnesses has no ramifications on the accused's social standing—resolution of the affront needed a public forum. The more witnesses who could be called forth to reject the slander and the more public the process, the more secure the individual and the community emerged in the protection of their common norms. If the state had not lent courts, laws, and legal procedure to regulate this process, communities would have invented their own rituals, forums, or acts of violence to accomplish the task.[143] The state was involved, however, fulfilling the traditional duty of medieval rulers as judges. Individuals took advantage of a system that was as a rule "legal": predictable, limited, and publicly defined. In the process, the state gained some symbolic and some real benefits as well.

---

[143]See Christopher Boehm's study of vendettas in a society with weak state power: *Blood Revenge: The Enactment and Management of Conflict in Montenegro and Other Tribal Societies* (Philadelphia, 1984). See Edward Muir's marvelous study of vendetta culture in early sixteenth-century Italy and the transition to the ethos of the duel: *Mad Blood Stirring: Vendetta and Factions in Fruili during the Renaissance* (Baltimore, 1992).

CHAPTER 4

Honor in the Elite

In July 1650, the governor and military commander on the southern frontier, Prince Petr Grigor'evich Romodanovskii, assigned a gentryman from Poshekhon'e, Prince Vasilii Sheleshpanskii, to serve as a hundredman (*sotennyi golova*). She-leshpanskii refused to accept his orders because the assignment would make him subordinate to Romodanovskii's deputy, Fedor Glebov. Romodanovskii imme-diately threw him into prison for insubordination, and from prison Sheleshpan-skii in turn petitioned the tsar for redress of the shame of serving below Glebov. The tsar responded promptly. He scolded Romodanovskii for impris-oning Sheleshpanskii: "It is not for you to award yourself compensation for dis-honor." And he ruled in favor of Prince Sheleshpanskii: "The Glebovy have never outranked the princes from the Beloozero area. The Sheleshpanskie princes are high-born people (*liudi rodoslovnye*)" (with the implication that the Glebovy were not). But the tsar instructed Sheleshpanskii to serve as ordered, presumably to minimize disruption in the field and presumably with no nega-tive precedent set against the family honor. For good measure, he reminded Romodanovskii of the customary deference to high birth: He was to select "upstanding, exemplary" (*dobrye, ikonnye*) men, but not "people of eminent patrimony, people with honor (*otecheskie deti, liudi chestnye*), so as to avoid insult to them (*oskorblenie*)."[1]

This sharp encounter between the tsar and his general and between a man of princely heritage and a nonprince of lesser family heritage sets in relief some of the key themes of precedence. Men had the right to protect their family heritage

---

[1] RGADA, f. 210, Belgorod stol, stb. 147, ll. 48–49 (7158). In this chapter, Muscovite-style dates (reckoned from the purported beginning of the world with each year starting in September) will be included for ease of locating citations in source publications. Thus, 7158 was the year extending from September 1, 1649, to August 31, 1650.

as they moved through the ranks in their mandatory, lifelong military service careers; the tsar alone had the authority to resolve claims about place and honor, and he did so with verve and dispatch. In more complicated disputes, formal adjudication based on written evidence of family heritage or service careers took the place of the tsar's seemingly snap judgment shown here. The important thing is that complaints were addressed and, as a rule, expeditiously resolved. Although seniority in some form in court or military functions was observed in many other monarchies, nothing quite like Muscovy's system of precedence was practiced elsewhere.[2]

The Forms of Precedence Litigation

The scholarly literature on precedence is copious, as befits an institution so closely associated with elite status and with the ruler's discretion in governance.[3] Here I will give only an overview of the institution and its historiography before turning to an analysis of the social origins and long-term significance of precedence.

Precedence litigations were disputes over service assignment that arose among leaders of the tsar's army. In theory, only members of the leadership corps were eligible—that is, those men serving from "the Moscow list" (*Moskovskii spisok*), who acted as generals, governors, and diplomats. As Sheleshpanskii's suit indicates, lesser military ranks could not participate: Provincial gentrymen (*deti boiarskie, dvoriane*) and military men not of the traditional cavalry formations (i.e., musketeers, artillery, new model infantry, and cavalry) did not have "place." Nor did men in nonmilitary status, with few exceptions: The tsar's state secretaries (*d'iaki*) and merchants were by and large excluded.

Disputes over precedence could erupt in the Kremlin at the announcement of assignments at the Military Service Chancery (*Razriadnyi prikaz*); in audience with the tsar himself; or in the field when orders were changed, troops

---

[2]Iu. M. Eskin notes that even the comparativist N. P. Pavlov-Sil'vanskii failed to find European counterparts to precedence : "Mestnichestvo v sotsial'noi strukture feodal'nogo obshchestva," *Istoriia SSSR* 1993, no. 1:40. Nevertheless, general similarities to hierarchical consciousness are clear and remarked by historians: A. I. Markevich, "Chto takoe mestnichestvo?" *Zhurnal Ministerstva narodnogo prosveshcheniia*, no. 204 (1879):262–71; A. N. Savin, "Mestnichestvo pri dvore Liudvika XVI," in *Sbornik statei, posv. V. O. Kliuchevskomu* (Moscow, 1909), pp. 277–90; Robert O. Crummey, "Reflections on Mestnichestvo in the 17th Century," *Forschungen* 27 (1980):269–81.

[3]In addition to the specific studies cited in this chapter, general surveys of precedence include A. I. Markevich, *O mestnichestve* (Kiev, 1879); idem, "Chto takoe?"; idem, *Istoriia mestnichestva v Moskovskom gosudarstve v XV–XVII veke* (Odessa, 1888); V. O. Kliuchevskii, *Kurs russkoi istorii* in *Sochineniia*, 8 vols. (Moscow, 1956–59), vol. 2 (1957), lect. 27; S. O. Shmidt, "Mestnichestvo i absoliutizm (postanovka voprosa)," in his *Stanovlenie rossiiskogo samoderzhaviia. Issledovanie sotsial'no-politicheskoi istorii vremeni Ivana Groznogo* (Moscow, 1973), pp. 262–307; V. I. Buganov, "'Vrazhdotvornoe' mestnichestvo," *Voprosy istorii* 1974, no. 11:118–33; Eskin, "Mestnichestvo v sotsial'noi strukture."

were transferred, or two armies were joined (*skhod*). Disputed assignments were usually military but could also be administrative, diplomatic, or even ceremonial—such as seating at a reception or banquet, placement in a procession, or service as a *rynda* (one of a group of honorary bodyguards of the ruler). Plaintiffs sued for the sake of their entire clan, which would suffer reduced honor should the given family member be forced to serve in the subordinate role. Disputes were to be settled by a reckoning of the relative status of the litigants, based on two aspects of the litigants' family heritage. One was the genealogical status of one family in comparison with the other; the other was the relative seniority of service positions held by the litigants or by their ancestors. In theory, the staff of the Military Service Chancery took the factors of clan service and genealogy into consideration before making assignments, but disputes did arise. With all the generations of litigants' families deemed fair game, with the fallibility of previous generations' rank assignments regarding seniority, and with litigants using personal copies of service records, precedents to support each side could easily be found. Resolution was not always easy.[4]

The stakes were high: One man's service below a perceived inferior created a precedent that could reduce the status of his entire clan. Individuals resorted to dramatic gestures to avoid such humiliation. Such an incident is the celebrated case of 1650 when *okol'nichii* Prince Ivan Ivanovich Romodanovskii was ordered to sit in a lesser position than *okol'nichii* Vasilii Vasil'evich Buturlin at a banquet with Tsar Aleksei Mikhailovich and Patriarch Iosif in the Kremlin. Romodanovskii refused to sit at table, at which point the tsar ordered him forcibly taken to his seat. He then slid off the bench and was lifted up and held in place through the banquet. His recalcitrance reflected his unwillingness to accept an earlier defeat in a precedence suit against the same Buturlin. For this stubbornness, he was briefly imprisoned and sent to perform a ritual of humiliation before Buturlin (such rituals are discussed in the Precedence in Practice section).[5] In a similar incident in 1614, Boyar Prince Boris Mikhailovich Lykov declared that he would rather be executed than sit at table below an inferior. For this, he too was sent in humiliation to his rival.[6] Finally, equally recalcitrant was Prince Grigorii Afanas'evich Kozlovskii, who refused in 1691 to sit at table below an inferior even though precedence had been abolished nearly a decade earlier. Rather than attend, Kozlovskii pleaded illness but was brought forcibly in a simple, undignified cart to the palace—he had hidden away his coach and horses. As a sign of his recalcitrance, he wore black clothing and refused to

---

[4]Ann M. Kleimola makes the point about the malleability of argumentation: "Boris Godunov and the Politics of Mestnichestvo," *Slavonic and East European Review* 53, no. 132 (1975):355–69.

[5]The case: DR 3 (1852): col. 153, and PSZ 1, no. 28, p. 225 and note. A similar incident is described by Grigorii Kotoshikhin, *O Rossii vo tsarstvovanie Alekseiia Mikhailovicha*, 4th ed. (St. Petersburg, 1906), p. 46.

[6]The case: DR 1: cols. 109, 129–30, and *Razriadnye knigi* (RK) *1598–1638 gg.*, ed. V. I. Buganov (Moscow, 1974), pp. 300–2 (1614).

remove it and get out of the cart. He was then forcibly carried to the palace, wrapped bodily in a rug. When deposited at the banquet table, he lay supine and was then held in sitting position in his assigned place. For all this recalcitrance, he was demoted from boyar rank to provincial service.[7] Men risked their personal status in passionate defense of their families' honor.

Two strategies were used in arguing superior status in those precedence litigations that got to the stage of argument (as we shall see, many did not progress that far). The one that has received almost exclusive attention from historians was a complex reckoning of relative status, although in actual practice it was rarely used. When men of equally high clan status contested rank, the argument could be carried out by comparison of individual service careers and clan genealogy, contrasting the relative status of the service and of the genealogical position within the clan of the plaintiff (or of one of his kinsmen) with that of the defendant (or a kinsman). In such cases, calculations could become complicated. The plaintiff, for example, could cite instances in which he or an ancestor had served with the defendant or his ancestor; then he would compare not the valor of the service, but the hierarchical relation of the ranks held. The plaintiff might then go on to calculate how many places in their clans separated him and his opponent from the ancestors whose service had been mentioned. If the plaintiff were more senior in his clan than the defendant in his, and (or) if the plaintiff's ancestor had served in a position higher than that held by the defendant's ancestor, then the plaintiff claimed that he should serve in a position higher than that held by the defendant.[8] In other words, a man had a place both in the seniority system of his clan and in comparison with other families, "*v svoem rodu i v schete.*"[9]

Precedence presupposed the ability to calculate a man's place in his family so that it could be compared accurately with another man's place in his family. The rule used for such calculation was expressed in this way: "The son of the first brother has long been equal in status to the fourth [brother]."[10] According to

---

[7]Complex records of this case: RGADA, f. 210, Zapisnye knigi moskovskogo stola, opis' 6a, delo 25, ll. 72–74; RGADA, f. 210, Moscow stol, stb. 1162, ll. 19v–20v, 22v, 25v, 27v; PSZ 3, no. 1401, pp. 100–2; M. P. Pogodin, "Dela po mestnichestvu," *Russkii istoricheskii sbornik* 5 (1842), no. 14, pp. 342–46; "Poslednii pretendent mestnichestva . . ." *Moskvitianin* 1841, pt. 1, nos. 1–2, pp. 476–81.

[8]On the mechanics of precedence: D. A. Valuev, "Vvedenie," *Simbirskii sbornik* (Moscow, 1844); P. I. Ivanov, "O mestnichestve," *Russkii istoricheskii sbornik* 2 (1838):i–xv; A. P. Zernin, "Sud'ba mestnichestva . . .," in N. A. Kalachov, ed., *Arkhiv istoriko-iuridicheskikh svedenii, otn. do Rossii* 3, sect. 1 (1861):1–138; M. D. Khmyrov, *Mestnichestvo i razriady* (St. Petersburg, 1862); M. Pogodin, "O mestnichestve," *Russkii istoricheskii sbornik* 3 (1838), bk. 1, pp. 268–83; ibid., bk. 2, pp. 370–97. See also *Vremennik OIDR* 6 (Moscow, 1850), Miscellany (*Smes'*), p. 16.

[9]M. E. Bychkova, ed., "Novye rodoslovnye knigi XVI v.," in *Redkie istochniki po istorii Rossii*, fasc. 2 (Moscow, 1977), p. 135.

[10]On this principle, see RK *1559–1605* (Moscow, 1974), p. 106; D. A. Valuev, ed. "Razriadnaia kniga ot 7067 do 7112 goda," in *Simbirskii sbornik* (Moscow, 1844), p. 43; Markevich, *Istoriia mestnichestva*, pp. 257, 409–20.

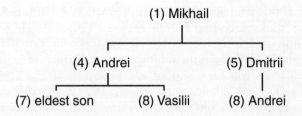

this rule, fourth, fifth, and later brothers were considered to have the same rank in the clan as their first, second, and later nephews. In other words, each first son was numbered three ranks or "places" (*mesta*) junior to his father, and his younger brothers were one rank apart from each other. Many members of a clan in various branches could thus have the same place in relationship to their common progenitor. If a clan founder was numbered one, his three sons were numbered four, five, and six; the first two sons of the eldest son (number four) were numbered seven and eight, while the first two sons of the second brother (number five) were numbers eight and nine, and so on (for one family's genealogical rankings, see the genealogy above). This sequencing order was similar to that used for succession to boyar position in those few clans who had the traditional right to inherit boyar status at court; boyar succession was also collateral but could include more than four sons if so many survived to adulthood. Collateral succession among the Rus' elites descended from the system of succession of the Riurikide clan of Kiev Rus'; the Moscow ruling family was a noted and significant exception.[11]

The four-man principle was probably suggested by the typical biological pattern of survival in elite clans. Seldom were there more than four eligible brothers in one lineage of one clan alive at one time; the fourth brother who survived to take his turn in boyar succession was a rarity. Furthermore, the ranking system described above replicated the common experience of demographic survival in clans. Men who were ranked the same in a clan would have been about the same age and would have had approximately the same experience in service.[12] Thus this abstract rule, mimicking demographic reality, allowed comparison of men in two families, a much more challenging task than comparing military service assignments. There the comparison was fairly straightforward, because the relative importance of most military ranks remained stable until the seventeenth century. Then military reform added many new roles for the traditional elite, and indeed such expansion was one of the causes of the demise of precedence.

[11]See discussion in my *Kinship and Politics* (Stanford, 1987), pp. 59–70, and my "Collateral Succession in Kievan Rus'," *Harvard Ukrainian Studies* 14, no. 3/4:377–87. Janet Martin traces the consistency of dynastic succession, noting the Muscovite exception, in *Medieval Russia, 980–1584* (Cambridge, England, 1995), chaps. 2, 4, 6, 8, 12.

[12]V. O. Kliuchevskii makes this point: *Kurs* 2:148.

Let us look at this strategy of litigation in practice. An argument based on service careers took place in 1583/84 between Prince A. D. Khilkov and Fedor Mikhailov syn Laskirev, one of the few in this collection that was actually won by the plaintiff. Even then, however, the distinction is fine, because for Khilkov, this suit was for dishonor occasioned by claims Laskirev made in a different suit. The vigilance with which clans safeguarded their reputations against smear is thus illustrated. Laskirev had been assigned to serve under S. V. Godunov in a diplomatic audience, and he sued Godunov for place. In his suit, he presented excerpts from military service books that mentioned Khilkov's grandfather, father, and other kin in positions subordinate to members of Laskirev's clan. Khilkov got wind of it and immediately protested to correct the record. In his suit, he defended his clan's seniority to the Laskirevy in two ways: First, he disputed the veracity of Laskirev's military service rosters, and second, he pointed out that on two occasions cited in the Godunov-Laskirev suit, two different Laskirevy had not protested having to serve under two different Khilkovy. The judges checked out the military service citations and could verify none of Laskirev's, whereas Khilkov's claims by and large checked out. The judges also cited as significant the Laskirevy's previous failures to sue. Khilkov won the suit.[13]

The Laskirev-Khilkov suit did not turn on genealogical considerations, but rather service rank; a case of 1598 between two members of the Zvenigorodskii princely clan illustrates genealogical calculations. Prince Vasilii Andreev syn Zvenigorodskii and his cousin Prince Andrei Dmitreev syn Zvenigorodskii were fifth and fourth military commanders in Smolensk, respectively, and Prince Vasilii protested his subordinate assignment. Investigation into the genealogies found that the plaintiff and defendant shared the same genealogical ranking with respect to their common grandfather, Prince Mikhail Zvenigorodskii. The plaintiff was the second son of his father, who was a first-born son; thus, because the grandfather was ranked number one, the son was ranked three places lower, or four, and the grandson-plaintiff was ranked three more places lower for his generation, plus another place lower as second son, or eight (see the genealogy). For the defendant, Prince Andrei, because the grandfather was number one, his father (a second son) ranked five, and he himself as a first son was ranked three places lower, or eight, like his cousin the plaintiff Prince Vasilii. The judges, having laid out these relationships, therefore decreed that the two men were to be written "mixed" (*meshaiuchi*), or alternating in the documents, with no fixed precedence given to one or the other.[14]

---

[13]Pogodin, *Dela* 2, no. 3, pp. 61–66.

[14]RK *1475–1598*, ed. V. I. Buganov (Moscow, 1966), pp. 539–40, and RK *1550–1636*, 2 vols. in 3 pts., ed. L. F. Kuz'mina (Moscow, 1975–76), 2:135–36, and RK *1598–1638*, p. 62 (all 7106). On the term "mixed," see E. A. Vasil'evskaia, "Terminologiia mestnichestva i rodstva," *Trudy Moskovskogo gosudarstvennogo istoriko-arkhivnogo instituta* 2 (Moscow, 1946):11.

In actual practice, however, cases rarely came to such detailed elaboration. The second strategy, unremarked by historians but much more frequently invoked in cases, was grosser in format and became more and more common as less eminent families rose to higher service ranks, beginning in the late sixteenth century. As noted above, in theory only "high-born" families had "place" and could seek a reckoning.[15] These were the families who served from Moscow, held the highest administrative and military ranks, and were recorded in official genealogical (*rodoslovnye*) books. Inferior clans were those who served from a provincial town (*po gorodovomu spisku*), often holding positions such as locally elected elders for criminal affairs, state secretaries and undersecretaries, and those in service to monasteries or church prelates. Thus, if a plaintiff believed that his opponent was of such lowly status, he simply proved the ancestry, without detailed genealogical reckonings or comparisons of service records. As early as 1589, litigants stated confidently that the tsar had issued an order forbidding non–high-born (*nerodoslovnye*) people from suing high-born people. In that year, for example, a man from the Olfer'ev clan lost a suit and was told: "The Olfer'evy are *nerodoslovnye liudi* and such people never have reckoning of place with high-born people (*rodoslovnye*)." The principle persisted: In 1673, a member of the Khrushchov clan sued the Karkadinov family and was resolutely told, "In relation to you, the Karkadinovy are honorable and high-born people; [they are] princes of Smolensk, and in relation to them you are not high born. And a non–high-born person has no reckoning nor place with high-born men and will not in the future have it."[16] These categories were broadly used in litigation, with plaintiffs asserting that their rival's family hailed from the provinces; had served the church, not the tsar; had never had "honor"; and the like. Such calculations even came to outrank service. One litigant was told, for example, "The Boriatinskie princes are honorable and high-born people (*liudi chestnye i rodoslovnye*), and you are a man of lowly heritage (*nerodoslovnyi*), and although your ancestors have served in military campaigns higher than the Boriatinskie, you can still serve less then they."[17] And recall the tsar's solicitude toward high-born clans expressed in Prince Sheleshpanskii's suit, summarized at the beginning of this chapter: The tsar instructed the local governor not to place high-born families in assignments that might humiliate them.

---

[15]The terminology translated as "high-born" was various: *rodoslovnye* implies enrolled in official genealogical books; *narochitye* means eminent; *otecheskie* refers to patrimony (*otechestvo*).

[16]1589: RK *1550–1636* 2:58 (7097). A litigant in 1635 also mentions the rule: DR 2: col. 444 (7143). 1673: DR 3: col. 905 (7182).

[17]Of the myriad examples, here are a few: RK *1598-1636*, p. 310, and DR 1: cols. 138–40 (7122); KR 1: cols. 86–88, and DR 1: col. 217 (7123–24); RGADA, f. 210, Prikaznyi stol, stb. 2537, ll. 16–32 (7132); DR 1: col. 890 (7135); DR 2: col. 452 (7143); DR 2: cols. 500–1 (7144). Boriatinskie: DR 2: col. 453 (7143).

Litigation for precedence based on family heritage and service became common and routinized by the midsixteenth century. The practice flourished in the sixteenth century: Iurii M. Eskin has identified 1,624 cases from the late fifteenth century to the abolition of precedence in 1682, unevenly distributed.[18] Even taking into account loss of archival documents, the ballooning of the institution from the 1570s through 1590s is striking. While Eskin recorded forty to fifty cases per decade in the 1540s–60s, in the 1570s, he identified 305. Such high numbers of litigations persisted until the Time of Troubles, when the pace began to decline, particularly after the midseventeenth century.[19] The boom in litigation in the late sixteenth century responds to the expansion of the service corps and to the disruptions in the elite caused by the *Oprichnina* (which created in essence a parallel elite, for whom status had to be created when the *Oprichnina* was abandoned in 1572).[20]

The seventeenth-century decline had many causes. First was deliberate policy: More and more campaigns, ceremonial occasions, and ranks were declared "without place" (*bez mest*), that is, inapplicable for purposes of precedence calculations. As a result, as Robert Crummey noted, precedence applied only to "the court nobility in particular situations" and left the government wide latitude in governance.[21] Second was the increasing complexity of establishing relative ranking. Clans had died out over time, except in junior lines not covered by genealogical books, leading by the late seventeenth century to a cynical sense that the tsar could raise and lower individuals at will.[22] The problem was compounded by the fact that genealogical books were not actively compiled after the 1620s, itself a reflection of a change in the significance of family in politics. Finally, litigation declined because of disillusionment with the system. The

---

[18]Iu. M. Eskin, *Mestnichestvo v Rossii. XVI–XVII vv. Khronologicheskii reestr* (Moscow, 1994). His publication includes 1,720 items, but 96 of them are laws, not litigations.

[19]My research on precedence is based on a database that is about one-third smaller than Eskin's; in a decade-by-decade breakdown, that proportion generally holds true, except for the 1570s, 1600s, and 1650s–60s. The numbers of cases in my and Eskin's databases respectively are the following: undated (in my database), 11; pre-1500, 0/16; 1500s, 5/7; 1510s, 3/5; 1520s, 4/1; 1530s, 5/9; 1540s, 30/51; 1550s, 24/52; 1560s, 23/43; 1570s, 62/305; 1580s, 211/262; 1590s, 156/245; 1600s, 58/175; 1610s, 108/153; 1620s, 128/146; 1630s, 84/108; 1640s, 72/119; 1650s, 40/93; 1660s, 24/61; 1670s, 23/39; 1680s, 4/14; 1690s, 2/13.

[20]On the political tensions of the 1580s and precedence, see Iu. N. Mel'nikov, "Mestnichestvo i politicheskaia bor'ba v Rossii v 80-x godakh XVI v.," Candidate dissertation, Institute of the History of the USSR of the Academy of Sciences of the USSR, Moscow, 1979.

[21]Crummey, "Reflections," pp. 275–80. Eskin (*Mestnichestvo*) identified "without place" decrees in 1552, 1554, 1570, 1573, 1584, 1591, 1597, 1598, 1601, 1609, 1611, 1614, 1616, 1619, 1621, 1632, 1638–42, 1645, 1646, 1648, 1650, 1651, 1654, and 1678. He also records declarations that certain kinds of service were permanently "without place," such as service in flanks in the armies (1550), as urban fire wardens (*ob'ezzhie*) (in 1600, 1601, 1603, 1604, 1616, 1617, 1619, 1620, 1621, and 1648), as bannermen (*znamenshchiki*) (1646, 1655), and in cross processions (1679).

[22]V. O. Kliuchevskii, *Boiarskaia duma drevnei Rusi*, 5th ed. (Petrograd, 1919), pp. 366–68.

seventeenth century witnessed the widening of the social basis of precedence. Provincial gentrymen and state secretaries were engaging in the system,[23] making it less and less an instrument of social exclusivity for the upper elite.[24] At the same time, as will be discussed in Chapter 6, government service was changing radically: New men were flooding into service, old families were moving into nonmilitary service, and military and bureaucratic service patterns were meshing. In such a context, precedence appeared more and more antiquated. It was abolished as a basis for service assignments in 1682.

Interpretations of Precedence

A system in which the grand prince is seemingly bound to accept the predetermined relations of family status contradicts the idea that the Muscovite tsar had "autocratic" power. Thus precedence has long been a litmus test for historians. Did precedence limit autocracy? Did it preserve elite privilege against ambitious monarchs or, conversely, put a feudal brake on the progress of more rational principles of state service? These questions represent some of the range of opinion on precedence since its abolition. Surveying the historiography is illuminating, but not for understanding precedence in its own terms. Because most discussions of precedence interpret it on a macrohistorical level, analyzing the historiography turns into a survey of the great debates about state and society in Russian history.

Few historians have found anything good in precedence. M. M. Shcherbatov perhaps made the most concerted effort for a positive interpretation. In his late 1780s essay on "the corruption of morals" in Russia, he praised precedence for fostering estate pride and downplayed its negative effects. Echoing Montesquieu, he argued that institutions like precedence established the balance of power between ruler and noblemen necessary for stable government.[25] But his argument for balance of powers was a rare one. Most scholarship, statist-dominated, condemned precedence as an obstacle to progress. In the early works of the statist school, precedence plays a pivotal role in the dialectical struggle that was said to have raged from Ivan III's time to Peter I (roughly 1450–1700) between "state relations" and the "kinship principle." K. D. Kavelin in 1847 argued that Ivan III began the introduction of public, "juridical" values in political life but was

[23]John L. H. Keep, "The Muscovite Elite and the Approach to Pluralism," *Slavonic and East European Review* 48, no. 111 (1970):217.

[24]On precedence claims by state secretaries, see S. K. Bogoiavlenskii, "Prikaznye d'iaki XVII veka," *Istoricheskie zapiski* 1 (1937):226–28; Iu. M. Eskin, "'I Vasilii skazal, to de Artemii zamyslil vorovskii . . .'," *Istoricheskii arkhiv* 1993, no. 2, pp. 189–209; and A. A. Novosel'skii, "Praviashchie gruppy v sluzhilom gorode XVII v.," *Uchenye zapiski RANION* 5 (1929):315–35.

[25]Prince M. M. Shcherbatov, *On the Corruption of Morals in Russia*, trans., ed., and intro. by A. Lentin (Cambridge, England, 1969), pp. 131–35.

stymied in his goals by aristocratic opposition that forced him to respect precedence in appointing officers. Kavelin argued that only Peter I succeeded in destroying the aristocracy and the retrograde attitudes it represented.[26]

S. M. Solov'ev gave precedence a similarly prominent place in a Hegelian scheme of evolution. Writing from the 1850s through 1870s, Solov'ev saw precedence as the outgrowth of the aristocratic pretensions of the increasingly numerous princes in Muscovite service. He condemned it for preventing the healthy development of estate (*soslovie*) consciousness in Russia, and he identified the new classes that arose in the wake of the Time of Troubles as the bearers of the "state principle," who ultimately forced the abolition of precedence.[27] A different take on the statist approach that has had staying power was exemplified by M. N. Karamzin, who argued that precedence was an expedient tool used by rulers against aristocracy. He saw precedence as a manifestation of the aristocracy's excessive pride and a threat to the state, but one that was tolerated by rulers like Ivan IV and Boris Godunov because precedence quarrels themselves undermined the aristocracy.[28] In these views, the state was unambiguously a positive force and aristocracy a retrograde one.

The Slavophile critics of these early statists rejected both their evolutionary dynamic and their positive appraisal of post-Petrine institutions and society. But, showing their Romanticism, they also condemned precedence, not because they favored the state, but because they saw it as an overly juridical and formal mechanism that disrupted their idealized organic balance of state and elite and thus helped to foster, even in Muscovite times, an "internal disintegration" that led to Peter I's "betrayal" of traditional Russian culture.[29]

Much of the debate on precedence was publicistic and allegorical, implicitly contributing to current discussions about Russian political development. Late nineteenth-century historiography was no less instrumental but tended to be more liberal than statist; it saw in precedence an opportunity for pluralistic development missed by a somnolent or selfish elite.[30] Both N. I. Kos-

---

[26]K. D. Kavelin, *Sobranie sochinenii. Vol. 1: Monografii po russkoi istorii* (Moscow, 1897), cols. 5–66.

[27]S. M. Solov'ev, *Istoriia Rossii s drevneishikh vremen*, 29 vols. in 15 bks. (Moscow, 1960), bk. 3, vol. 5, p. 309; ibid., bk. 4, vol. 7, pp. 14–17; ibid., bk. 4, vol. 7, pp. 292–95; ibid., bk. 5, vol. 9, pp. 256–74; ibid., bk. 7, vol. 13, pp. 60–64; ibid., bk. 7, vol. 13, pp. 247–53. See also his "O mestnichestve," *Moskovskii literaturnyi i uchenyi sbornik na 1847 god* (Moscow, 1847), pp. 263–316.

[28]Richard Pipes, *Karamzin's Memoir on Ancient and Modern Russia: A Translation and Analysis* (New York, 1969), pp. 110, 112–13; N. M. Karamzin, *Istoriia gosudarstva rossiiskogo*, 5th ed., I. Einerling, ed., 3 bks. (St. Petersburg, 1842–43), bk. 2, vol. 8, chap. 3, col. 68; ibid., bk. 3, vol. 9, chap. 4, cols. 159–60; ibid., bk. 3, vol. 10, chap. 4, cols. 155–56, quote on p. 156.

[29]K. S. Aksakov, "On the Internal State of Russia," in Marc Raeff, ed., *Russian Intellectual History: An Anthology* (New York, 1966), pp. 231–51; I. V. Kireevskii, "On the Nature of European Culture and Its Relation to the Culture of Russia," ibid., pp. 175–207.

[30]Eskin makes this point: "Mestnichestvo v sotsial'noi strukture," pp. 39–40.

tomarov and V. O. Kliuchevskii lamented the boyars' inability to move Russia toward pluralism and progress and blamed precedence.[31] Kliuchevskii condemned it for allowing the elite to perpetuate clan exclusivity over estate solidarity and for sowing suspicion and senseless quarreling in the elite.[32] He declared that precedence not only harmed the aristocracy and Muscovy's military preparedness, but also impeded historical progress in general for Russia. Echoing Karamzin, but with different value judgment, Kostomarov saw precedence as deleterious to the aristocracy (in that it prevented the boyars from consolidating as an estate) and regretted that it benefited the state by giving rulers a tool with which to manipulate the aristocracy.[33] A. I. Markevich was the undisputed dean of studies of precedence, author of two immense volumes chronicling the historiography and the history of the institution. Writing in 1879 and 1888, he attempted a more positive evaluation, arguing that precedence was abolished by the initiative of the aristocracy as a step in its conscious transformation from an old-style kinship-based elite to a new-style juridical estate.[34] At the turn of the century, the great historians N. P. Pavlov-Sil'vanskii and S. F. Platonov both displayed liberal proclivities in condemning precedence for obstructing the emergence of new classes and political pluralism,[35] an approach by and large paralleled from a Marxist point of view by M. N. Pokrovskii.[36] His work set the standard for the Soviet line on precedence, which saw it as an obstructionist tool of the "feudal" aristocracy in its struggle against centralization or against the rising gentry. S. O. Shmidt's work is less hackneyed; he, for example, pointed out the ritualistic

---

[31]Among juridical historians, the views of M. F. Vladimirskii-Budanov on precedence were essentially the same as Kliuchevskii's, while V. I. Sergeevich was more supportive of state authority and construed precedence as a positive phenomenon, inasmuch as it encouraged men to serve loyally and thus promoted the consolidation of the state. M. F. Vladimirskii-Budanov, *Obzor istorii russkogo prava*, 6th ed.(St. Petersburg and Kiev, 1909), pp. 115–27, esp. pp. 125–27; V. I. Sergeevich, *Lektsii i issledovaniia po drevnei istorii russkogo prava*, 3d ed. (St. Petersburg, 1903), pp. 112–28, esp. p. 126. M. A. D'iakonov's view is also similar to Kliuchevskii's: *Ocherki obshchestvennogo i gosudarstvennogo stroia drevnei Rusi*, 4th ed. (Moscow and Leningrad, 1926), pp. 225–32.

[32]Kliuchevskii, *Kurs*, vol. 2, lect. 27, pp. 139–56, esp. pp. 154–56; ibid., vol. 3 (1957), lect. 44, pp. 72–74; idem, *Boiarskaia duma*, pp. 207–16, 283–89, 366–68, 379–84, 523–26.

[33]N. I. Kostomarov, *Sobranie sochinenii. Istoricheskie monografii i issledovaniia*, bk. 5, vols. 12–14 (St. Petersburg, 1905), pp. 34–35, 42–48, 53–68, esp. pp. 62–63.

[34]Markevich, *Istoriia mestnichestva*, chap. 2; "Chto takoe?" pp. 262–71, esp. pp. 268–69 and 271. See also his *O mestnichestve*.

[35]N. P. Pavlov-Sil'vanskii, *Gosudarevy sluzhilye liudi. Proiskhozhdenie russkogo dvorianstva* (St. Petersburg, 1898), pt. 2, chap. 3, esp. p. 91; pt. 3, chap. 1, esp. p. 149. S. F. Platonov, *Lektsii po russkoi istorii*, 9th ed. (Petrograd, 1915), pp. 168–71, 436–38.

[36]M. N. Pokrovskii, *Izbrannye proizvedeniia*, 4 bks. (Moscow, 1966), pp. 281–82, 292–95, 440–42, 569–70.

and patriarchal aspects of precedence and associated its emergence with the development of absolutism.[37]

A fresh perspective on precedence is embodied in the work of A. E. Presniakov, writing in 1917, and S. B. Veselovskii, writing in the 1930s and 1940s. They proceeded from the assumption of a consensual community of self-interest of ruler and elite. They saw precedence as an outgrowth of the importance of kinship ties in Muscovite society, of the traditional value given to hierarchy, and of the consultative relationship between ruler and elite. Both regarded such patrimonial relationships as healthy; they lauded the relative lack of conflict between Muscovite sovereigns and boyars and condemned the consolidation of the autocratic state as detrimental to Muscovy's evolution toward a more pluralistic and democratic order.[38]

Recent scholarship on precedence reflects the less tendentious, more complex analysis of Muscovite politics and society that we find in Presniakov, Veselovskii, and Shmidt. Ann Kleimola follows Shmidt's lead in identifying precedence as beneficial to autocracy, but she also makes the comment that precedence helped to integrate new families into power in a way not disruptive of political stability.[39] Robert Crummey concurs that precedence was a phenomenon associated with Muscovy's transition to a new political structure, but also suggests that historians have exaggerated its importance and argues that precedence was primarily significant as a psychological compensation to Muscovite boyars for the obligation of full-time service.[40] Iu. M. Eskin and Iu. N. Mel'nikov take a sociological approach, comparing the social function of precedence for the Muscovite elite with that played by primogeniture and entail in other European "feudal" societies—that is, it allowed the elite to maintain family and clan solidarity by guaranteeing them access to the

---

[37]Vasil'evskaia, "Terminologiia"; A. A. Zimin, "K istorii voennykh reform 50-x godov XVI v.," *Istoricheskie zapiski* 55 (1956):344–59; idem, "Istochniki po istorii mestnichestva v XV-pervoi treti XVI v.," *Arkheograficheskii ezhegodnik za 1968 god* (Moscow, 1970), pp. 109–18; V. B. Kobrin, "Iz istorii mestnichestva XVI veka," *Istoricheskii arkhiv* 1 (1960):214–19; *Ocherki istorii SSSR. Period feodalizma. Konets XV v– nachalo XVII v.* (Moscow, 1955), p. 295; Shmidt, "Mestnichestvo i absoliutizm"; the essay was first published in *Absoliutizm v Rossii (XVI–XVIII vv.)* (Moscow, 1964). Two essays follow Shmidt's lead: Buganov, "'Vrazhdotvornoe'"; Hugh F. Graham, "Mestnichestvo," *Modern Encyclopedia of Russian and Soviet History* 22 (1981):8–13.

[38]A. E. Presniakov, *Moskovskoe tsarstvo* (Petrograd, 1918), chaps. 3–5, 10; S. B. Veselovskii, *Issledovaniia po istorii klassa sluzhilykh zemlevladel'tsev* (hereafter Veselovskii, ISZ) (Moscow, 1969), pp. 103–4, 469–76.

[39]Ann M. Kleimola, "Boris Godunov"; idem, "Status, Place and Politics: The Rise of Mestnichestvo during the *Boiarskoe Pravlenie*," *Forschungen* 27 (1980):195–214; idem, "The Changing Face of the Muscovite Aristocracy. The 16th Century: Sources of Weakness," *Jahrbücher für Geschichte Osteuropas* 25 (1977):481–93, esp. pp. 481–86; idem, "Up Through Servitude: The Changing Condition of the Muscovite Elite in the Sixteenth and Seventeenth Centuries," *Russian History* 6, pt. 2 (1979):210–29, esp. p. 216.

[40]Crummey, "Reflections." See also Keep, "Muscovite Elite."

lucrative rewards of high rank.[41] Different as they are, these recent works share an appreciation of the complexities of interaction between sovereign and elite; they move away from evolutionary schemes of development to a structural quest for the social functionality of institutions like precedence. Here I will extend that approach by looking at aggregate trends in the resolution of precedence cases. Those trends will return us to the great question posed by the historiography—that is, whether precedence served autocrat or elite. First, however, we look at the social foundations of the emergence of precedence as revealed in its earliest sources.

Sources of Precedence

At the most general level, precedence litigations were a natural outgrowth of status consciousness at the court. As in other medieval and early modern monarchies, court life was ordered by hierarchy. Heinrich Fichtenau, in his magisterial study of "mentalities and social orders" in early Europe, gives pride of place to hierarchical ordering as a fundamental consciousness of medieval society. Social ordering by rank and seniority found its justification in Christian interpretation of God's creation of the natural order; the hierarchies of Roman antiquity and of the Roman and Byzantine churches perpetuated these ideas for both Europe and the Rus' lands.[42]

That rank and hierarchy were structuring principles at the Muscovite court is not at all surprising. We see them in the earliest fourteenth- and fifteenth-century sources: Boyar signatories on grand-princely treaties and wills, for example, maintain a fairly consistent order over several decades.[43] Diplomatic audiences observed meticulously scripted protocols wherein successive stages of greeting and escorting the envoy ever closer to the ruler were staffed by men of increasingly higher status, culminating in the boyars, who sat in specific honorific order to the grand prince's right and left.[44] Sometimes determining relative rank was so complex that it imperiled the occasion. For example, a large Muscovite delegation to the Grand Duchy of Lithuania in

[41]Eskin, "Mestnichestvo v sotsial'noi strukture"; idem, "Mestnichestvo i maiorat," in *Chteniia pamiati V. B. Kobrina* . . . (Moscow, 1992), pp. 203–5; Mel'nikov, "Mestnichestvo i politicheskaia bor'ba," chap. 2.

[42]Heinrich Fichtenau, *Living in the Tenth Century: Mentalities and Social Orders*, trans. Patrick J. Geary (Chicago and London, 1991), chap. 1.

[43]On these lists of signatories, see my "The Boyar Clan and Court Politics: The Founding of the Muscovite Political System," *Cahiers du monde russe et soviétique* 23, no. 1 (1982):16–17.

[44]The elaborate protocols of audiences are included in *Sbornik Imp. Russkogo istoricheskogo obshchestva* (SbRIO), 148 vols. (St. Petersburg–Petrograd, 1867–1916), vols. 35, 41, 53, 59, 71, 95, and *Pamiatniki diplomaticheskikh snoshenii drevnei Rossii s derzhavami inostrannymi. Pt. 1: Snosheniia s gosudarstvami evropeiskimi* (St. Petersburg, 1851).

Adam Olearius described the grandeur of the Holstein ambassadors' reception and depicted it in the 1647 edition of his *Travels*. The tsar was flanked by four ceremonial bodyguards (*ryndy*); his boyars sat in strict order of precedence along the walls. "Along the walls around to the left [and right], and opposite the Tsar, sat over fifty distinguished

and splendidly dressed boyars, princes and state counselors," (trans. Samuel H. Baron). (Illustration: Adam Olearius, *Oft begehrte Beschreibung der newen Orientalischen Reise* [Schleswig, 1647]. Courtesy of Special Collections, University of Southern California Libraries.)

1495 was ordered to proceed "without regard to place,"[45] presumably because the task of establishing hierarchy among fifty-odd servitors was almost impossible. Conversely, an instruction to Muscovite envoys in Lithuania in 1503 bids the envoys to respect the seniority of the main envoy as symbolic of the grand prince himself. Indeed, the arrogance (*vysokoumie*) of Prince Semen Ivanovich Riapolovskii—who had apparently refused to defer to the senior diplomat in an earlier embassy—was held up to the 1503 envoys as an example of extreme public insult to the grand prince. Contemporary Lithuanian magnates similarly recognized, and probably empathized with, the Muscovite system of hierarchical place ranking: Writing to Muscovite boyars at a tense moment in a dynastic crisis of the 1490s, Lithuanian magnates demurred at addressing them by name, because "We do not know your places at this time, who is sitting above whom in the presence of your sovereign."[46]

But precedence developed a more intense and formalized system of determining rank than in other comparable premodern states. It eventually culminated in the compilation of extensive official and unofficial genealogical and military service records. Why precedence in Muscovy took so formalized a turn can only be answered speculatively. One factor may have been the concentration of power and resources in the hands of the grand prince: Because Muscovy had so relatively underdeveloped an urban and agrarian economy, and because natural resources and land were increasingly claimed as state monopolies, status at court mattered more than in a setting where aristocrats could depend on their own estates, business involvements, local political activity, or engagement in other spheres for wealth and status. Also, the speed with which the Muscovite elite grew might have forced a more bureaucratic solution to social tensions.[47]

Unquestionably, the tensions caused by expansion in the elite provided impetus for precedence to emerge, just as later moments of social turbulence (the *Oprichnina*, the Time of Troubles) occasioned a spurt of litigation.[48] The story of the expansion of the Muscovite elite is a familiar one.[49] After the ruling dynasty's victory in the midfifteenth-century dynastic war and during the grand principality's rapid territorial expansion from the 1470s through 1510, new families came to the court in waves. Established Muscovite clans, generally but

[45]*Pamiatniki diplomaticheskikh snoshenii Moskovskogo gosudarstva s Pol'sko-Litovskim. Vol. 1: 1487–1533*, ed. G. F. Karpov, in SbRIO 35 (1882), no. 31, p. 169.

[46]*Vysokoumie*: SbRIO 35, no. 76, p. 428 (1503). Lithuanians: SbRIO 35, no. 70, p. 334 (Aug. 1502).

[47]Markevich puts forward a similar list of preconditions for precedence: *Istoriia mestnichestva*, pp. 213–14.

[48]Mel'nikov, "Mestnichestvo i politicheskaia bor'ba," chap. 3; Crummey, "Reflections," p. 273.

[49]Veselovskii, ISZ; Oswald P. Backus, *Motives of West Russian Nobles in Deserting Lithuania for Moscow, 1377–1514* (Lawrence, Kans., 1957); A. A. Zimin, *Formirovanie boiarskoi aristokratii v Rossii vo vtoroi polovine XV–pervoi treti XVI v.* (Moscow, 1988); M. E. Bychkova, *Sostav klassa feodalov Rossii v XVI v. Istoriko-genealogicheskoe issledovanie* (Moscow, 1986).

not exclusively nonprincely, were faced with new families whose backgrounds commanded instant respect: scions of ruling dynasties from Russian principalities, from the Grand Duchy of Lithuania, and from Tatar khanates. Rapidly the newcomers were absorbed into the leadership corps; some were so prestigious they were given the semiautonomous status of "service princes" discussed in the Introduction. In the disruption of Ivan IV's minority (1533–47), some of these princely newcomers won hereditary boyar status. It was this upheaval in power relations that sparked frequent disputes over precedence and a corresponding routinization of the process of litigation in the 1530s and 1540s.[50] But the regularization of litigations was made possible by the gradual compilation of sources recording genealogy and relative rank at court in the fifteenth century; this documentary production was also occasioned by disruptions in the status quo and expressed a growing genealogical and rank consciousness in the elite.

A dispute in the 1460s mobilized a range of sources that show how tension over status had built up over the century.[51] The litigants were the boyars Vasilii Fedorovich Saburov and Grigorii Vasil'evich Zabolotskii[52]; Saburov testified that Zabolotskii had tried to sit in a more honorable seat ("higher," *vysshe*) than he at an official banquet, and contended that he, Saburov, was ranked "a place higher" than Zabolotskii, because his father had been ranked "several places" higher than Zabolotskii's father. Saburov referred for confirmation to the expertise of "the old boyars Gennadii Buturlin and Mikhail Borisovich Pleshcheev."[53]

From these "old boyars," the court obtained several documents that testify to ongoing record keeping in the fifteenth century. They were essentially lists recording boyars' relative status. One submitted document, the "Memo" of Petr Konstantinovich Dobrynskii (active at court in the 1430s and 1440s until he suffered disgrace in 1445), lists women who were boyars' wives around 1418,

---

[50]Zimin, "Istochniki"; Kleimola, "Status."

[51]The case is published in M. A. Korkunov, ed., *Pamiatniki XV veka. Akty iz dela o mestnichestve Saburova s Zabolotskim* (St. Petersburg, 1857). A. A. Zimin ("Istochniki," pp. 112–14) reserved judgment about the authenticity of the case, but historical evidence contained in the case checks out, and other historians have accepted it: Korkunov, *Pamiatniki*; Markevich, *Istoriia mestnichestva*, pp. 235, 237–43; idem, *O mestnichestve*, pp. 775–84; N. P. Likhachev, *Razriadnye d'iaki XVI veka. Opyt istoricheskogo issledovaniia* (St. Petersburg, 1888), pp. 101–19.

[52]The case is undated, but the years of military service of the principals and the signatories on the judgment charter that is the central source for the case indicate that it took place around 1462–64. On the boyar service of V. F. Saburov, G. V. Zabolotskii, and four signatories of the charter—Prince Ivan Iur'evich Patrikeev, Fedor Davydovich, Prince Vasilii Ivanovich Obolenskii, and Ivan Ivanovich Vsevolozh—see my *Kinship and Politics*, pp. 233, 240, 225, 201, 222, and 240, respectively. Gennadii Buturlin died by 1462–66 (*Akty sotsial'no-ekonomicheskoi istorii severovostochnoi Rusi kontsa XIV–nachala XVI v.* [ASEI], 3 vols. [Moscow, 1952–64], vol. 1, no. 308, p. 219), and M. B. Pleshcheev is not mentioned after 1467–74 (ASEI 1, no. 370, p. 270).

[53]The case's judgment charter: Korkunov, *Pamiatniki*, pp. 17–18; Likhachev, *Razriadnye d'iaki*, pp. 106–8.

when Prince Iurii Patrikeevich married the daughter of Grand Prince Vasilii Dmitrievich[54]; a related memo associated with Gennadii Buturlin lists the boyars whom Prince Iurii Patrikeevich "bypassed" (*zaekhal*) in status at the time of his arrival in 1408.[55] The "old boyar" Pleshcheev contributed a list of boyars in the 1420s and the colorful "*kika*" tale (referring to a married woman's headdress), which includes a hierarchical ranking of fifteenth-century boyars and relates an incident at the all-important wedding of Prince Iurii Patrikeevich in 1418. Patriarch of the Saburov clan Fedor Sabur allegedly insisted on sitting higher than Prince Fedor Khovanskii, the elder brother of the groom, despite Khovanskii's protest that his brother was about to become brother-in-law of the sovereign. To this implication that Prince Iurii's success in marriage should raise his entire clan in status, Fedor Sabur replied, "He has status only because of marriage; you have no marriage tie to bring you such status" (*u togo Bog v kike, a u tobia Boga v kike net*—literally, "He has God in his wife's headdress, but you have no God in your wife's headdress").[56] The tale showcases the tensions that later persisted in the precedence system, countering claims to status based on marriage and kinship with claims based on service heritage. Its colorful qualities prompted A. A. Zimin to label it "legendary,"[57] but it shows the principles of status and growing genealogical consciousness at court nonetheless.

These various lists of hierarchies at the fifteenth-century court reveal how disruptive was the arrival of Prince Iurii Patrikeevich. Within ten years of his arrival in Moscow, this scion of a branch of the ruling Gedyminide line pulled off the coup of marrying into the grand-princely family; by the next generation, Patrikeev in-laws of the grand prince had displaced the previous inner circle of boyars and endured in power to the end of the century.[58] The ranking lists cited by the "old boyars" Buturlin and Pleshcheev indicate that the established elite rallied to the challenge of new blood by compiling records of seniority at court.

An added impetus to the compilation of such records may have been demographic growth in the core boyar clans that made face-to-face means of reckoning seniority too difficult. Other disputes over place apparently occurred in the fifteenth century. The "Letter" of Gennadii Buturlin and the "*kika*" tale

[54]PSRL 24 (1921):232; Karamzin, *Istoriia*, bk. 2, vol. 5, chap. 2, n. 254, col. 109.

[55]The two memos are printed in PSRL 24:232, and RK *1475–1598*, p. 17. Buturlin's memo reproduces the boyar signatories of Grand Prince Vasilii I's will of 1406–7: DDG 20, p. 57. Another list, the "Letter" of Gennadii Buturlin, is published in Korkunov, *Pamiatniki*, pp. 18–19, and Veselovskii, ISZ, pp. 23–24.

[56]The Pleshcheev list: Korkunov, *Pamiatniki*, p. 20, and Veselovskii, ISZ, p. 24. The "*kika*" tale: Korkunov, *Pamiatniki*, p. 21, and Veselovskii, ISZ, p. 25. For explanation of this use of the phrase, "*Bog v kike*," to indicate success achieved through marriage alliances, see S. M. Solov'ev, "Neskol'ko ob'iasnitel'nykh slov po povodu drevneishogo mestnicheskogo dela," *Moskovskie vedomosti* 1857, no. 53, p. 239.

[57]Zimin, "Istochniki," p. 114. But others accept it: Markevich, *O mestnichestve*, p. 783; Veselovskii, ISZ, p. 25; Korkunov, *Pamiatniki*.

[58]See my *Kinship and Politics*, pp. 133–40.

make reference to previous suits between other clans,[59] and the fact that a formal judgment charter was issued in the 1460s dispute suggests that the elite was outgrowing the intimate size that earlier might have made disputes relatively easy to adjudicate. With the waves of princely newcomers from the 1470s on, the threat to the status quo was all the more intense.

Other early litigations show increasing complexity in argumentation and procedure. In 1469, a dispute over precedence in military service is mentioned but not elaborated.[60] In 1500, on the eve of a major battle, Boyar Iurii Zakhar'ich, younger brother of the powerful boyar Iakov Zakhar'ich, protested being assigned in the rear guard (*storozhevyi polk*) under Prince Daniil Vasil'evich Shchenia in the center regiment (*bol'shoi polk*); his dissatisfaction appeared to be not with Prince Daniil but with the rear guard.[61] The grand prince and his adjudicating boyars, however, turned him down, citing instances from military service records showing that the rear guard was not harmful to one's honor and arguing that there was not a formal hierarchy among the regiments (as was indeed established in the 1550s[62]).

Genealogical considerations were paramount in a case from 1504, in which P. M. Pleshcheev sued Petr Grigor'evich Loban Zabolotskii for refusing to serve with him.[63] Pleshcheev argued that he was higher because his clan was higher than the Saburovy and the Osteevy, who were in turn higher than the Zabolotskie. He cited as evidence two documents from the 1450s and the 1460s judgment charter. Petr Loban countered that his status was higher because of his position in his clan; he was the second son of his father, while Pleshcheev was the third son. Pleshcheev won the case with his argument based on the public status of his ancestors in addition to his genealogical position in his clan and among clans. This suit introduces some of the elements that characterize mature precedence litigations: a generally accepted hierarchy of clans, more specific reference to individuals' genealogical position in their clans, and recourse to documentary records. In order for cases to be litigated on these complex terms, more systematic records were needed.

Not surprisingly, more formal records evolved to help the established families hold their own against expanding old and arrivé new clans. The first effort to compile a genealogical record of status relations apparently was made in the 1490s or early in the sixteenth century[64]; we find it appended to the Typogra-

---

[59]Korkunov, *Pamiatniki*, pp. 18, 19, 21; Veselovskii, ISZ, pp. 23–25.

[60]K. N. Serbina, ed., *Ustiuzhskii letopisnyi svod* (Moscow and Leningrad, 1950), p. 87.

[61]RK *1475–1598*, pp. 30–31. A. A. Zimin and A. I. Markevich both suggest that this case was not precedence "in the strict sense of the word," because men were not arguing about clan honor but about service assignments: Zimin, "Istochniki," p. 111; Markevich, *Istoriia*, p. 246.

[62]RK *1475–1598*, pp. 125-26.

[63]The case is published in Likhachev, *Razriadnye d'iaki*, pp. 103–8.

[64]The list of the grand princes of Kiev, Vladimir, and Moscow, for example, ends with Ivan III's last son Ivan (b. 1490) and grandson Dmitrii (b. 1483, d. 1509). Veselovskii discusses these princely genealogies: ISZ, pp. 12–13.

phy chronicle.[65] It was not fully systematic or comprehensive but made an effort in that direction. The Typography genealogical articles are a varied collection of princely and boyar family trees; lists of boyars, including some of the "old boyars'" materials just discussed; and miscellaneous narrative tales about boyars and princes. The items in the collection fall into several groups representing different eras of compilation. The oldest group would seem to be the collection of a few hierarchical lists of boyars and *boiaryni*, the two "memos" discussed above, and several brief genealogies of nonprincely Moscow boyar clans. The genealogies generally do not extend beyond the 1440s and sometimes end as early as the 1420s. One might associate the compilation of this group with the era of the dynastic war (1430s and 1440s), judging by the individuals included and the many passing references made to events of the war. The tension created within the elite by the defection in that war of some Moscow boyars and the influx of other clans likely prompted compilation of these genealogies. Other sources included in the Typography articles testify to further efforts of genealogical compilation going on in the fifteenth century.

At the same time that Muscovite boyar families were compiling their genealogies in the early and midfifteenth century, sovereign princely families in the major centers of Northeast Rus' and the Grand Duchy of Lithuania were doing likewise.[66] In the first decades of the fifteenth century, for example, chronicles in Novgorod and Rostov included newly compiled family trees of princes of Moscow, Rostov, Beloozero, and Novgorod.[67] A prototype of the Typography collection's

[65]PSRL 24:227–34. The collection is written on different paper than the chronicle to which it is appended; its paper dates from ca. 1504, whereas the chronicle's paper dates from the 1520s–30s. Its hand is different from the two hands exhibited in the chronicle, and its author used cinnabar far more frequently. The manuscript is Gosudarstvennyi istoricheskii muzei, Manuscript Division, Collection of the Synod Library, no. 789, with the genealogical materials on fols. 319–39. The manuscript and its "seventeenth-century" binding is described in T. N. Protas'eva, ed., *Opisanie rukopisei Sinodal'nogo sobraniia (ne voshedshikh v opisanie A. V. Gorskogo i K. I. Nevostrueva).* Pt. I: Nos. 577–819 (Moscow, 1970), p. 137, and M. N. Tikhomirov, *Kratkie zametki o letopisnykh proizvedeniiakh v rukopisnykh sobraniakh Moskvy* (Moscow, 1962), p. 142.

[66]On Gedyminide genealogies and the Grand Duchy's rise to power, see M. E. Bychkova, "Pervye rodoslovnye rospisi litovskikh kniazei v Rossii," in *Obshchestvo i gosudarstvo feodal'noi Rossii* (Moscow, 1975), pp. 133–40; PSRL 17 (1907); A. L. Khoroshkevich, "Istoricheskie sud'by belorusskikh i ukrainskikh zemel' v XIV–nachale XVI v.," in V. T. Pashuto, B. N. Floria, and A. L. Khoroshkevich, *Drevnerusskoe nasledie i istoricheskie sud'by vostochnogo slavianstva* (Moscow, 1982), pp. 69–150; S. C. Rowell, *Lithuania Ascending: A Pagan Empire within East-Central Europe, 1295–1345* (Cambridge, England, 1994), chap. 2; N. N. Ulashchik, *Vvedenie v izuchenie belorussko-litovskogo letopisaniia* (Moscow, 1985); M. D. Priselkov, "Letopisanie Zapadnoi Ukrainy i Belorussii," *Uchenye zapiski Leningradskogo gosudarstvennogo universiteta. Seriia istoricheskikh nauk* 7, no. 67 (1940), pp. 5–24.

[67]A. N. Nasonov, ed. and intro., "Letopisnyi svod XV v. (po dvum spiskam)," in *Materialy po istorii SSSR*, 7 vols. (Moscow, 1955–59), 2 (1955):277–82, 320–21; *Novgorodskaia pervaia letopis' starshego i mladshego izvodov*, ed. M. N. Tikhomirov and A. N. Nasonov (Moscow and Leningrad, 1950), pp. 464–77. The compendium's dating is V. L. Ianin's: *Novgorodskie posadniki* (Moscow, 1962), pp. 24–25.

Muscovite grand-princely genealogy was composed for the 1440s Sofiia First chronicle; it is accompanied by lists of metropolitanates and dioceses that were also included in the Typography collection.[68] A Muscovite chronicle edited in 1477 developed this growing tradition of dynastic genealogy by including a large collection of princely family trees from Moscow, Iaroslavl', Rostov, and Tver', as well as the list of Tatar khans. These various princely family trees were taken into the Typography compendium, in part, no doubt, because by the end of the fifteenth century, the relevant princely lines had emigrated to Muscovite service.[69]

It is possible that the Typography collection was assembled by a particular faction for self-glorification. Perhaps it was intended to showcase princely families from Rostov, Tver', Suzdal', and Smolensk. Their entries here are lengthy compared with the generally brief boyar genealogies—they lead up to the 1470s and 1480s. Or perhaps its patrons were the two nonprincely boyar clans that received the most extended treatment in the document (Vsevolozh-Zabolotskii, Kobylin-Koshkin). The collection, however, is so motley as to be a poor showcase for the pretensions of any of these candidates. Nor is it a comprehensive reflection of the current power hierarchy during the dynastic conflict of the 1490s; significant players in the crisis such as the Patrikeev princes, the Koshkin boyars, and some Obolenskii princely boyars were left out.[70] The collection looks most like an early attempt to systematize records of hierarchy, at a time when other efforts of compilation—chronicles and military service books, for example—were also taking place at the Kremlin court.[71] Because the manuscript itself has some suggestive paleographical links with the grand-princely chancery,[72] perhaps we should best see the Typography compilation in that official context.

[68]PSRL 5 (1851):90–91. They were then included in grand-princely chronicles of the 1490s: PSRL 27 (1962):298, 367.

[69]PSRL 28 (1963):141–42 (compilation of 1497); Ia. S. Lur'e, *Obshcherusskie letopisi XIV–XV vv.* (Leningrad, 1976), pp. 140–41.

[70]On the dynastic crisis, see my "Consensus Politics: The Dynastic Crisis of the 1490s Reconsidered," *Russian Review* 45, no. 3 (1986):235–67.

[71]Military service books are discussed below; on fifteenth-century Muscovite chronicle compendia, see Lur'e, *Obshcherusskie letopisi*, and idem, *Dve istorii Rusi XV veka* (St. Petersburg, 1994).

[72]*De visu* inspection of the Typography chronicle manuscript shows the watermark to be a papal tiara, very similar to K. Ia. Tromonin, *Iz'iasneniia znakov, vidimykh v pischei bumage . . .* (Moscow, 1844), nos. 616 and 618, dated 1538, and to N. P. Likhachev, *Bumaga i drevneishie bumazhnye mel'nitsy v Moskovskom gosudarstve* (St. Petersburg, 1891), nos. 643 (1521) and 639 (1499). The shield is very similar to E. Laucevicius, *Popierius Lietuvoje XV–XVIII a.*, 1 vol. with album (Vilnius, 1967), no. 2132 (1533, 1532) or no. 2131 (1514, 1518, 1520). It is also close to Tromonin, no. 816 (1513) and no. 819 (1538). Thus, 1520s–1530s, a slightly different dating than that offered by Protas'eva and Tikhomirov (1510s–1520s). But the watermarks on the Typography genealogical collection are different: a shield of the city of Paris that can be identified with N. P. Likhachev, *Paleograficheskoe znachenie bumazhnykh vodianykh znakov*, 3 vols. and addendum (St. Petersburg, 1899), nos. 2943–44 (1504), and a sunburst identified as Likhachev, *Znachenie*, nos. 2941–42 (1504). Significantly, the dated paper on which Likhachev found the city of Paris and sunburst marks was a grand-princely charter: RGADA, fond 135, no. 1, sect. IV, item 17, fols. 2, 7. This might indicate that the compilation was done at the Kremlin court.

By the 1530s and 1540s, such compilation efforts had reached fruition. Genealogical records were being compiled at the court in a more comprehensive and systematic manner. In the 1530s, a lengthy collection of princely genealogies was appended to the Resurrection chronicle, and by the 1540s, at least two different collections of family trees of Moscow princely and boyar clans were compiled and disseminated. These deserve the name "genealogical books (*rodoslovnye knigi*)," because they updated all clans to the present generation and used a standardized format.[73] Such compilations were associated with the court: M. E. Bychkova links one of the two 1540s redactions with the Shuiskii princes, who won primacy among the boyars briefly in Ivan IV's minority. At roughly the same time, namely the late fifteenth and sixteenth centuries, the court was also compiling military service records. Muster rolls of the officers in some campaigns of the early and midfifteenth century had been included in Muscovite chronicles; by the 1480s, they were being integrated into formalized books (*razriadnye knigi*).[74] That one of the impetuses for compiling these books was the need to verify status rankings in the elite on the basis of service is indicated by the fact that *razriadnye knigi* include sources that fixed status relationships at the most politically sensitive moments in court life. Those sources were rosters of attendants at weddings in the ruling family, where great boyars and their wives were called on to perform ceremonial duties in order of importance by their seniority and political power.[75]

In the 1550s, these parallel efforts at genealogical and military muster compilation culminated in two official editions: the Sovereign's Military Muster Roll and Sovereign's Genealogy (*Gosudarev razriad*; *Gosudarev rodoslovets*).[76] These, especially the military muster, continued to be the recognized authorities, even though alternative redactions of both types of books (with more campaign rosters and more clans included) were compiled long thereafter—through the 1620s for genealogical books and in different forms through the seventeenth century for military musters. With such sources, suits could be argued on complex genealogical and service considerations; precedence in a mature form was

---

[73]Resurrection chronicle: PSRL 7 (1856):231–59; see also M. E. Bychkova, *Rodoslovnye knigi XVI–XVII vv. kak istoricheskii istochnik* (Moscow, 1975), pp. 148–49. 1540s genealogical books: Bychkova, ed., "Novye rodoslovnye knigi."

[74]Publication of earliest redaction: RK *1475–1605 gg.*, 4 vols. in 10 pts. to date (Moscow, 1977–). Concerning it: V. I. Buganov, *Razriadnye knigi poslednei chetverti XV–nachala XVII v.* (Moscow, 1962).

[75]These rosters (*svadebnye razriady*) were distributed by date in the earliest edition (RK *1475–1605*) but assembled at the beginning of the 1550s edition (RK *1550–1636*). On such sources, see Russell Martin, "Royal Marriage in Muscovy, 1500–1725," Ph.D. dissertation, Harvard University, 1996.

[76]N. P. Likhachev, *"Gosudarev Rodoslovets" i rod Adashevykh* (St. Petersburg, 1897), and *Razriadnye d'iaki*; Bychkova, *Rodoslovnye knigi*; Buganov, *Razriadnye knigi*; D. N. Al'shits, "Razriadnaia kniga Moskovskikh gosudarei XVI v.," *Problemy istochnikovedeniia* 6 (1958):130–51.

emerging.[77] The elite and the state had created an effective instrument for dealing with the social disruption occasioned by their persistent empire-building.

It is remarkable that the elite took recourse to litigation rather than to private vendetta or dueling. Dueling was in fact not an available option at this time: It developed in Italy as a fashion for the elite only around the sixteenth century and then spread gradually through Europe.[78] In some ways, of course, as Robert Crummey has observed, precedence functioned as a bloodless duel, containing conflict without risk of life.[79] Feuding and private vengeance, conversely, present a more intriguing case. Muscovy certainly had elements that could have supported private violence, such as a strong consciousness of personal honor and the strong societal importance of family and clan. Such violence does not, however, seem to have been a recourse for elite families. The reason is probably to be found in the intimate association of disputes over rank with state service. The government was involved from the start, and feuding is often associated with situations in which central government was weak and patrimonial clans strong. Accordingly, feuding and vendetta are best curtailed by social and attitudinal changes, as well as by the criminalization of the practices and the development of legal avenues to deal with insult.[80] Muscovy had both the coercive power to prevent private vendetta and a legal system capable of resolving disputes to the satisfaction of litigants, as we have seen in Chapter 3.

The preferability of legal recourse was brought home to the elite periodically when political instability opened the door to vendettas, such as in the dynastic war of the 1430s–40s, when Grand Prince Vasilii II and his cousin Prince Vasilii Kosoi were reciprocally blinded in their bitter struggle for the throne. The period of boyar rule in the 1530s–40s witnessed the arrests and murders of several leading boyars in the Shuiskii and Bel'skii princely clans and within their factions. And Ivan IV's bloody *Oprichnina* can be construed as the unleashing—willful or unintended—of private vendettas among boyar factions. Experiences such as these undoubtedly had a cautioning effect on families anxious to avenge an insult. The indifference of Muscovites to dueling even when the practice was known in the seventeenth century from contact with Europeans probably also bespeaks the elite's indifference to the idea of exclusive, corporate status. Not until the late seventeenth century do we see stirrings of the idea that the upper

[77]Most scholars consider suits before the 1530s not "precedence" proper: Zimin, "Istochniki"; Kleimola, "Status"; Shmidt, "Mestnichestvo i absoliutizm"; Buganov, "'Vrazhdotvornoe'."

[78]Edward Muir, *Mad Blood Stirring: Vendetta and Factions in Fruili during the Renaissance* (Baltimore, 1992), chap. 8; V. G. Kiernan, *The Duel in European History: Honour and the Reign of Aristocracy* (Oxford, 1988); Kevin McAleer, *Dueling: The Cult of Honor in Fin-de-siècle Germany* (Princeton, N.J., 1994).

[79]Robert O. Crummey, *Aristocrats and Servitors: The Boyar Elite in Russia, 1613–1689* (Princeton, N.J., 1983), p. 138, and his "Reflections," p. 281.

[80]Muir, *Mad Blood*, esp. chap. 8; Christopher Boehm, *Blood Revenge* (Philadelphia, 1984); Keith M. Brown, *Bloodfeud in Scotland, 1573–1625* (Edinburgh, 1986).

elite should be distinguished as an aristocracy—a trend that would have been promoted by a socially exclusive ritual such as dueling.

Precedence developed in response to social tensions that, if left unchecked, could have threatened the success of Moscow's project to expand in territory and power. It constituted a legal solution to a social and political problem and is best understood as one of many strategies that the state evolved in its drive to mobilize resources (and to keep stability while so doing). It does not seem to have been a rearguard defense by an entrenched elite to safeguard its ancient rights, as some historians argue. There were no such ingrained rights, no age-old aristocracies in Muscovy. There was a small band of boyar families that had been tied by bonds of personal service and loyalty to the Moscow grand princes, constituting the roots of an elite that grew suddenly and precipitously from 1450 or so. Precedence norms evolved with the elite itself, in a fluid situation of constant growth and invention of solutions to emerging problems. The question remains, however, of how precedence functioned over the long term to serve the elite and state.

Precedence in Practice

To answer that question, I turn to litigation for evidence of actual practice. The source basis is a collection of 1,076 cases, which numbers about one-third fewer than the approximately 1,620 cases that Iu. M. Eskin has identified, but which is proportionally equivalent in chronological distribution.[81] The database represents most cases from the published versions of military service musters, the principal Muscovite repositories of records of precedence disputes, and numerous archival cases.

Analysis of the patterns of almost two centuries of litigation is surprising and striking. In terms of historiographic interpretations, these patterns support Veselovskii's and Presniakov's understanding of Muscovite politics as patrimonial and discredit the ideas that the elite used precedence for upward mobility or that the autocrat was hobbled by it. Simply put, most of the time in precedence suits, plaintiffs lost and the status quo of clan hierarchy was affirmed. But, significantly, the tsar turned plaintiffs down in a variety of ways to cushion the blow (see the table), deftly limiting disaffection among losers and asserting his authority over the disposition of his men. Thus precedence was a quintessentially patrimonial institution, allowing the ruler to pursue policy while appeasing his men in the most personal and familiar of terms.

Of the 1,076 cases in the database, in only approximately 1% (14 cases) did the plaintiffs win outright, and four of these are associated with the Buturlin

[81]Eskin, *Mestnichestvo v Rossii*; see nn. 18–19 above.

Resolution of Precedence Cases

Resolution	Percentage of total* (number of cases of 1,076 total)
Plaintiff wins trial	1 (14)
Plaintiff appeased without trial	24 (254)
Plaintiff told to "serve as ordered"	12 (132)
No follow-up recorded	14 (155)
Plaintiff is refused (loses case)	48 (521)
When plaintiff loses case	
With trial	15
With no trial	85

*Percentages are rounded to nearest whole number.

clan, whose precedence records have long been regarded with suspicion.[82] That outright vindications were rare, however, should not imply that precedence did not satisfy litigants and resolve tensions. It did so in a more consensus-building fashion, often by preemptively removing the source of tension. In approximately 24% (254 cases) of the cases in the database, the tsar appeased the plaintiff without recourse to trial. Within that 24%, several expedients were used. Usually the tsar declared the disputed service relationship "without place" ("*bez mest*," i.e., setting no precedents for future litigation); sometimes he reassigned the disputants without further need of a suit on the issues; and occasionally he declared the men equal (*mestniki*).[83] Let us look at these strategies in turn.

Tsars declared litigants *bez mest* in many ways, not only by literally pronouncing the fact. Apparently simply accepting and recording the petition also made a disputed service assignment "without place": We find many instances of the tsar agreeing to record the petition or explicitly declaring service "without place."[84] In 1649, Prince A. M. Volkonskii, for example, was assigned to accompany the Swedish ambassador, while Iakov Zagriaskoi served the Habsburg ambassador. At the time, Volkonskii regarded his ambassador as lesser, but did not sue because, as he noted in his later petition, this was "the tsar's

[82]The four cases in which Buturliny win: RGB, f. 256, no. 340, ll. 351–66v; RGADA, f. 210, Raznye stoly, stb. 38, ll. 1–37; RK *1475–1605* 1, pt. 1, p. 167 (7027), and 1, pt. 2, p. 312 (7052). Skepticism on Buturlin-related records or comments on how they proffer information not otherwise corroborated: Mel'nikov, "Mestnichestvo i politicheskaia bor'ba," appendix 6; A. A. Zimin, "Sostav boiarskoi dumy XV–XVI vekakh," *Arkheograficheskii ezhegodnik za 1957 god* (Moscow 1958), p. 50, n. 108; Buganov, *Razriadnye knigi*, pp. 26–29, 42, 129, 241.

[83]On *mestniki*, see Vasilevskaia, "Terminologiia," pp. 11–12.

[84]RK *1475–1598*, pp. 280–81 (7085); RK *1475–1598*, pp. 456 (7099), 515 (7105), 517 (7105); RK *1598–1638*, pp. 82–83 (7107); RK *1475–1605* 1, pt. 2, pp. 197 (7034), 293 (7049), 317 (7053).

Tsar Mikhail Fedorovich is depicted consulting with the patriarch and boyars over plans for his marriage in this drawing taken from a late seventeenth-century illustrated manuscript, which was based on contemporary chronicle accounts of the wedding. Here they agree to declare his 1624 wedding "without place," that is, setting no precedents for *mestnichestvo* disputes. (Illustration: P. P. Beketov, *Opisanie v litsakh torzhestva, proiskhodivshogo v 1626 goda* . . . [Moscow, 1810]. Courtesy of Rare Book and Manuscript Library, Columbia University.)

affair." But when the two ambassadors attended services at the Kremlin on Palm Sunday and Volkonskii's ambassador was publicly listed below Zagriaskoi's, then he found the service unbearable. Volkonskii sued, and the tsar readily agreed to call this service "without place."[85]

Reassignment was also an easy way out for the tsar; it was frequent in the 24% of cases in which plaintiffs were appeased without trial. For example, in 1613, five men were assigned to be ceremonial bodyguards (*ryndy*) to the tsar. The fifth sued the third, and the tsar dismissed them all and selected four different men. Similarly, a state secretary who sued another state secretary in 1628

[85]Pogodin, *Dela 5*, no. 13, pp. 340–41; RGADA, Zapisnye knigi moskovskogo stola, opis' 6a, delo 12, ll. 201–1v (7170).

over precedence was replaced rather than being made to serve.[86] Sometimes clarifying the assignment did the trick. In 1586, E. I. Saburov was sent as first military commander (*voevoda*) to Toropets, where Prince V. K. Shish Pronskoi was already serving as governor (*namestnik*). Saburov protested serving under him. The tsar immediately elaborated: Saburov was to have sole authority on military affairs (*delo ratnoe*) and Pronskoi was to have administrative authority (*namesnicheskoe*), essentially making the men equal.[87] Thus a campaign or ceremonial occasion could proceed as planned without participants fearing an insult to their honor and eternal shame to their clan.

In a less conciliatory mechanism, the tsar instructed the litigants to serve as ordered, generally without benefit of "without place" reassurance, and promised them a litigation after the service was over. This meant that service would go ahead, but it put the burden on the litigants to pursue their grievances. This formulation occurred in approximately 12% of the database cases (132 cases), with approximately one-half mentioning that the suit occurred but not giving the resolution, and records for the other half failing to mention whether a suit subsequently occurred. In approximately 14% of the cases (155 cases), no follow-up whatsoever is recorded. Certainly, in some cases, loss of documents explains the absence of information. But, as with dishonor litigations, these statistics might indicate that litigants chose not to pursue their suits, even though failure to follow through was regarded as admission of inferior status. Such was stated explicitly in a 1619 suit between Boyar Prince D. I. Mezetskii and I. A. Pleshcheev. Mezetskii failed to pursue the suit, and the military service muster notes that "To Ivan Pleshcheev, it was clear that he was made equal (*rozveden*) with Mezetskii and he did not petition further for a trial."[88] Why not pursue a case? Perhaps because the procedure was tedious and expensive; perhaps because if the suit were lost, it could result in the clan's being publicly humiliated; or perhaps, most saliently, because hopes for victory were slim. The calculation that litigants probably made was that if they sued and succeeded in getting appeased (as we recall happened in 24% of the suits in the database), their clan was in some way vindicated, and they would come out ahead. If that did not occur, pursuit was essentially pointless and risky.

Nevertheless, many persevered, and they were generally disappointed. Almost one-half of the cases in the database (521 cases) were lost by the plaintiff. Approximately 15% of the time, he lost after a trial based on the sort of genealogical and service calculations spelled out earlier. But in approximately 85% of the cases that were lost, no such litigation was involved. The most frequent outcome of a petition about precedence was for the tsar, or a spokesman

---

[86]*Ryndy*: DR 1: col. 110 (7122). State secretary: DR 2: col. 16 (7137).
[87]RK *1559–1605*, p. 216 (7094).
[88]DR 1: cols. 409–10 (7127).

acting in his name, to reject the plaintiff summarily. The tsar might point out that the disputed service was not eligible for precedence calculations. In 1625, for example, *stol'nik* Prince V. G. Romodanovskii was assigned to summon an ambassador to the table at a ceremonial banquet, while *stol'nik* Prince F. B. Tatev was to serve at the table. Romodanovskii considered his role inferior to Tatev's and thus insulting, but the tsar refused his suit, saying that traditionally there was no application of precedence in this particular sort of service. Similarly, R. F. Khrushchov was assigned in 1658 to serve under Prince G. G. Romodanovskii; when Romodanovskii informed him that he had given L. P. Liapunov authority over the fortress while Romodanovskii went to inspect another outpost, Khrushchov protested serving under Liapunov. But the tsar responded that this service would not set a precedent regarding place; all orders would continue to be addressed to Romodanovskii, and Khrushchov would not be considered serving under Liapunov for purposes of "place."[89]

Often the clarification took the form of reminding the litigants of the 1550 rule that defined the relative place of the command positions in the flanks of the army on campaign and declared many of the relationships to be "without place." (For example, the first commanders of the advance, right, left, and rear guards were to rank lower than the chief of the central unit.[90]) In 1551, when Boyar Prince V. I. Vorotynskii protested serving as second in command of the "great" (*bol'shoi*) or central regiment while Boyar Prince P. M. Shcheniatev was first in the right flank, the tsar responded that according to the rule, "The second in command in the great regiment has no affair with the commanders of the right, forward, and rear flanks; they are to be without place and no calculations of place (*shchet*) will be given." But for good measure, he added that in any case, the Vorotynskii princes could serve below the Shcheniatev princes.[91]

Indeed, often the tsar asserted immediately that a particular family outranked another and that the suit was completely out of line. For example, in 1564, another Vorotynskii, Boyar Prince Alexander Ivanovich, protested serving first in the forward flank when Boyar Prince I. I. Pronskoi was first in the more prestigious right flank. The tsar—the redoubtable Ivan the Terrible—retorted to him, according to the written record: "You should know your own measure and serve by my order in my service." Case dismissed. Similarly, in 1630, when assignments were being given out "at the hand of the tsar," *stol'nik* Prince I. A. Khilkov protested serving first in the main flank of the auxiliary army when *stol'nik* Prince M. M. Temkin-Rostovskii was first in the main flank in the major army.

[89]1625: DR 1: cols. 696–97 (7133). 1658: RGADA, f. 210, Moscow stol, stb. 299 (I) (3), ll. 47–50.
[90]RK *1475–1598*, pp. 125-26 (7058).
[91]1551: RK *1475–1605* 1, pt. 2, pp. 403–4 (7059); RK *1475–1598*, pp. 132–33 (7059); RK *1550–1636* 1, p. 14 (all 7059). Other examples include RK *1475–1598*, p. 154 (7064); DR 2: col. 452 (7143).

Joining the two armies together (*skhod*) for battle formation would put him subordinate. Tsar Mikhail Fedorovich refused him on the spot, telling him he was suing inappropriately (*ne po delu*): "The Khilkovye have no primacy over (*ne soshlos' s*) the Temkiny." Similarly, in 1631, V. P. Chevkin sued I. I. Pushkin, again over the touchy issue of two armies joining together and service assignments made "at the hand of the tsar" thereby being rearranged. Pushkin countersued for this dishonor, saying that "The Chevkiny have always served as captains under my father and uncles; Chevkin himself served under me and my cousin Boris Grigor'evich Pushkin, and now he sues at the instigation of my enemies." Tsar Mikhail Fedorovich (according to the written account) turned to Chevkin in anger and distress (*kruchina*), saying that he sued "inappropriately, not in accordance with his rank" (*ne delom, ne po svoei mere*). Again, case dismissed.[92]

The tsar dispatched Boyar I. P. Sheremetev's suit against Boyar Prince N. I. Odoevskii in 1645 with similar aplomb. Three days after the disputed service, Mikhail Volosheninov, the Conciliar State Secretary (*dumnyi d'iak*) of the Military Service Chancery, announced to Sheremetev in the tsar's anteroom before many people that he had sued inappropriately: "Your kinsmen under previous tsars without fail served with the Odoevskie and never sued about it." For dishonor to Odoevskii, he was ordered imprisoned. In a similar case involving less eminent litigants, the resolution was the same but the punishment harsher: The losing plaintiff, N. V. Kaftyrev, was beaten with bastinadoes and imprisoned for dishonor to Prince N. V. Meshcherskoi.[93]

Frequently, the principle that decided cases was that provincial families have no "place" versus elite families. For example, in 1625, D. D. Shenkurskoi was assigned to serve under I. V. Izmailov in Mozhaisk. But Shenkurskoi protested that his kinsmen "have served well": His great-grandfather was a mayor of Novgorod and served second to Prince V. Paletskii as governor of that city under Vasilii III and Ivan IV, and his kinsmen "never served under Ivan Izmailov in any circumstances." But Izmailov sued for insult, and the judges concurred: "The Izmailovy of old under many sovereigns served in high honor (*v chesti*) in many places as military commanders." They pointed out that Ivan Izmailov's brother Artemii held the high rank of *okol'nichii* and that Ivan and his brothers have "had the honor of serving as *stol'niki*." But the plaintiff's father served in Kostroma in provincial service (*s gorodom*), and "The Shenkurskie never served in any high honor nor anywhere as military commanders." So the judges imprisoned Shenkurskoi for dishonor to Izmailov (one source says he was also beaten with bastinadoes) and told him to serve as ordered.[94]

[92]1564: RK *1475–1598*, p. 210 (7072). 1630: DR 2: cols. 124, 128 (7138). 1631: DR 2: col. 196 (7139).

[93]1645: DR 2: cols. 750–51 (7153). Kaftyrev: DR 2: cols. 749–50 (7153).

[94]1625: KR 1: cols. 1155–56, and DR 1: col. 661 (both 7133).

Sometimes the tsar lost patience with an insistent litigant who refused to wait until after service was over for his hearing; then he would punish the plaintiff for his disobedience, sometimes regardless of the merits of the case. For example, Prince S. I. Shekhovskoi sued in 1638 over serving as second commander in the main flank when *stol'nik* Prince S. I. Velikii-Gagin was second in the rear guard. He was refused because the whole campaign had been declared "without place," yet still he persisted. The tsar retorted that he had sued "acting like a criminal" (*svoim vorovstvom*) and could in fact serve far inferior to Prince Velikii-Gagin—he and even his father could serve below Velikii-Gagin and even below his son! For dishonor to the defendant, he was imprisoned, and for disobedience he was exiled to Siberia. Similarly, if less harshly, M. A. Ziuzin and B. I. Pushkin were sent in 1648 to Sweden as ambassadors, and Ziuzin sued over his inferior rank. He cited many cases from the 1550s through the 1640s in which Pushkiny served under his ancestors. Pushkin countersued for dishonor: "Even Mikita's great-grandfather Grigorii Ziuzin could serve less than me. They are lowly [literally, 'young'] people and not high born (*liudi molodye i nerodoslovnye*); you cannot even find precedents in service where they served with us (*sluchaev na nikh pisat' ne nakovo*)." And he cited "the tsar's order that low-born do not sue high-born people, nor receive a trial with them." Indeed, when the case came to trial, it was verified that the Pushkiny were included in the Sovereign's Genealogy, but not the Ziuziny. The judges ruled in Pushkin's favor on the basis of the service record he had put forward; for dishonor, the plaintiff was ordered imprisoned and then sent in humiliation to Pushkin after imprisonment. But even after that, Ziuzin refused to serve as ordered and so was imprisoned again, and his patrimonial and service-tenure lands were confiscated. The properties were restored when he was released from a long imprisonment, by which time, the military service muster book noted, he had managed to avoid carrying out the disputed service.[95]

Losing a suit for precedence was not without risks. It required at the very least that the plaintiff serve in the disputed place, thus setting an official precedent that could in the future be used against his clan. If the defendant countersued for the dishonor of the plaintiff's allegations, losing litigants might be compelled to pay a hefty dishonor fine or suffer corporal punishment as determined in the guidelines established by law. Litigants risked further punishment if they were recalcitrant. Litigants who refused to accept the verdict and to serve as ordered could be fined, imprisoned, beaten, or even suffer confiscation of property and exile. Yet much of the punishment that the tsar meted out to stubborn litigants was exemplary; the threat of imprisonment was often enough to enforce compliance. Frequently the harshest sentences were miti-

[95] 1638: DR 2: cols. 590–91, 599–600 (7147). 1648: RGADA, f. 210, Moscow stol, stb. 218, ll. 95–206; DR 3: cols. 87–88 (7156).

gated by the tsar's mercy after being announced, and prison sentences were brief enough to make a point without causing undue suffering. They ranged from "a day and a night" to three days, rarely longer.[96]

For particularly recalcitrant litigants who refused to accept their subordinate status after a suit over precedence, the tsars could decree a ritual of public humiliation called being "surrendered by the head" (*vydacha golovoiu*). It was reserved generally for men in the highest ranks and for the most extreme cases. The ceremony is so peculiar to modern eyes, and yet so powerful in the Muscovite context, that a long narrative description by the seventeenth-century Muscovite state secretary, Grigorii Kotoshikhin, deserves to be quoted.

> And those men who do not wish to serve under boyars are sent to the boyars at their home "by the head" for having dishonored a boyar. And on the day when the tsar orders some boyar or *okol'nichii* or *stol'nik* sent by the head to a boyar for dishonor, or when a *dumnyi dvorianin* or *dumnyi d'iak* or *stol'nik* is sent to an *okol'nichii*, that day the boyar or *okol'nichii* does not appear before the tsar but news is sent to him that the men who had not wanted to serve under him were being sent to him by the head. And he awaits him. And such men are sent to them with a state secretary or an undersecretary; and bailiffs, seizing those men by the arms, lead him to the boyar's home and do not permit him to ride on horseback. And when they have led him to the home of the man with whom he had not wanted to serve, they place him on the lowest staircase and the state secretary or undersecretary orders that the boyar be informed of their arrival. . . . And the boyar goes out on to the porch to the state secretary or undersecretary, and the state secretary or undersecretary begins to deliver his speech, proclaiming that the Great Sovereign has ordered and the boyars have decided that this man, who did not want to serve with him, be brought to him, the boyar, by the head for having dishonored a boyar. And that boyar expresses his humble thanks for the tsar's favor and he orders that the man whom they had brought be released to his own home. But in releasing him to his home, he orders that he [the loser] not mount his horse in the courtyard nor lead his horse into the courtyard. And the man whom they have sent by the head to him, as he is walking from the tsar's palace to the boyar's courtyard, and when he is in the boyar's courtyard, insults him and dishonors him with all manner of abuse. But that man [the winner] does nothing to him in response to his wicked insulting words and he cannot, since the tsar sends that man to him because of his dishonor, out of love for him, but for no other purpose, not so that the man would kill or injure him. And anyone who inflicted such malicious dishonor and assault on such a man sent to him would be himself punished doubly, because he dishonors not the man who has been sent to him but actually the tsar himself. And that boyar [the winner] to whom they bring [the loser] gives them [the attendants]

[96]Threat of prison: RK *1550–1636* 1, p. 348 (7091); RK *1475–1598*, p. 338 (7091). "A day and a night": RK *1475–1598*, p. 371 (7094). One day: DR 1: col. 222 (7124); RGADA, f. 210, Dopolnitel'nyi otdel, delo 18, l. 36 (7125). Two days: DR 3: col. 63 (7155). Three days: DR 1: col. 157 (7123); DR 3: col. 44 (7154); DR 3: col. 92 (7156). One week: RK *1550–1636* 2, p. 293 (7124).

generous gifts, and on the next day that boyar goes to the tsar and, having arrived, humbly thanks the tsar for his favor, for having ordered that his rival be sent to him by the head.[97]

What makes this ritual so powerful is that it acts out simultaneously vindication and graciousness, thereby enforcing social hierarchy and stability in the elite. It gave public satisfaction to the winner of the suit by forcing the loser to proceed on foot to his rival's courtyard and prostrate himself before him. But it also worked to restore consensus among the boyars in a sort of Durkheimian catharsis, as the ceremony allowed the vanquished to declare again his claims against the winner and as the norms of the ritual explicitly denied the winner the right to respond. Being surrendered by the head allowed the loser a venting of spleen to balance the winner's victory. Each, in theory, walked away satisfied, ready to bury their animosity and cease whatever disruption their quarrel was causing the tsar. The ritual was a social drama that resolved conflict in a way that restored traditional values.[98]

These immediate responses, in particular the speedy determinations of the general relationship of clans, show a system flexible enough to respond to conflict and resolve it expeditiously. In light of this evidence, the old arguments—that precedence inhibited the tsar's autocratic authority or that, conversely, it kept the aristocratic elite too busy to conceive of the idea of corporate rights—seem off the mark. The system described here was a utilitarian means of conflict resolution that functioned because the players were committed to this very personal and patrimonial system. The strongest leitmotif in these suits is the tsar's knowledge of his men and his confidence in his authority. Tsars present themselves as stern but fatherly patriarchs. When provoked, they respond with a mixture of anger and distress; the verb used is *kruchinit'*, meaning to cause grief, sorrow, and distress, as well as to provoke to anger. It conveys both long-suffering patience and frequent loss of temper, as the tsar goes about his job of schooling his children. Mikhail Fedorovich, for instance, left many examples of how he personally kept his troops in line with firm discipline and occasionally a sharp tongue.

At a banquet in 1613, for example, Boyar Prince B. M. Lykov sued for place against the tsar's uncle Boyar Ivan Nikitich Romanov. The tsar "was distressed at Prince Boris," repeating to him many times that he could sit lower than

---

[97]Kotoshikhin, *O Rossii*, pp. 44–45.

[98]For further details, see my "Ritual and Social Drama at the Muscovite Court," *Slavic Review* 45, no. 3 (Fall 1986):486–502. Diane Claire Margolf details a similar, but not so public, French example: "The Paris *Chambre de l'Edit*: Protestant, Catholic and Royal Justice in Early Modern France," Ph.D. dissertation, Yale University, 1990. For ritual humiliation in medieval contexts, see Fichtenau, *Living*, pp. 36–38, and Geoffrey Koziol, *Begging Pardon and Favor: Ritual and Political Order in Early Medieval France* (Ithaca, N.Y., 1992).

Romanov, as he had in the past. Lykov replied that "It would be better to be executed than to serve lower than Romanov," but if the tsar should order him to serve lesser because of Ivan Nikitich's kinship with the tsar, then he would serve. Mikhail Fedorovich retorted that Lykov could be less than his uncle Ivan Nikitich "by many measures aside from my kinship with him." He admonished Lykov not to distress him further and to sit at the table. Lykov refused again and returned home; the tsar sent after him and ordered him "surrendered by the head" to the tsar's uncle. Similarly, D. B. Voeikov sued B. G. Pushkin in 1626 and was harshly rebuffed by the Conciliar State Secretary of the Military Service Chancery, F. F. Likhachev, who called him and another litigant "petty gentrymen" (*detishki boiarskie*) and promised harsh punishment if they sued again. But Voeikov repeated his suit, and Tsar Mikhail Fedorovich himself chewed him out: According to the extant record, the tsar insulted him "with a mother oath," also repeated the "petty gentryman" (*synchish boiarskii*) label, and declared "If you sue again, I will order you publicly shamed (*opozoriti*)!" In a suit of 1618, Mikhail Fedorovich told a plaintiff that he was acting like a cheat (*plutal*), pointing out that he was from a lowly family of provincial gentrymen from Kashira (*liudi molodye, Koshirenia*). In 1622, he turned down a suit, threatening "great disgrace and merciless punishment" should the plaintiff sue again; when he did sue again, the tsar refused him "with great anger" (*s velikoiu kruchinoiu*) and ordered him imprisoned.[99]

Tsar Mikhail Fedorovich was not unique. In 1580, Ivan IV threatened execution to a recalcitrant litigant, whom he said "was talking nonsense, not knowing a thing (*bredit, ne znaia*)"; he called another a cheat (*plutaet*). In 1585, Tsar Fedor Ivanovich told a litigant that he played the fool (*duroval*) by bringing suit.[100] The examples can be multiplied.[101] Some of this language may have been penned by scribes, but most accounts quote a tsar directly at audiences and at banquets and seem to represent his real participation. Sometimes judges themselves took on the role of disciplinarian. In two cases of 1623, for example, the judges "expressed great distress and anger (*kruchinilis'*)" and called one litigant a "slave" and berated another with insults (*laiali*).[102]

In these cases, the tsars exhibit what has been called in the European context "zealous anger"—that is, an extreme response by a lord or sovereign calculated to set right the imbalance caused by human pride. Kings and lords frequently

[99]Lykov: DR 1: col. 109, 129–30; RK *1598–1638*, pp. 300–2 (both 7122). Voeikov: DR 1: cols. 794–95 (7134). 1618: DR 1: col. 311 (7126). 1622: DR 1: cols. 501–2 (7130).

[100]*Bredit*: RK *1475–1598*, p. 309 (7089). *Plutaet*: RK *1475–1598*, p. 308 (7089). *Duroval*: RK *1475–1598*, p. 353 (7093).

[101]From Aleksei Mikhailovich's time: DR 3: cols. 287 (7160), 361 (7161), 479 (7163), 482 (7163); RGADA, f. 210, Moscow stol, stb. 262, ll. 140–45; PSZ 1, vol. 1, no. 156, pp. 363–64 (7160). From Fedor Alekseevich's time: RGADA, f. 210, Belgorod stol, stb. 933, ll. 39–40 (7187); RGADA, f. 210, Moscow stol, stb. 1032, ll. 51–65 (7187).

[102]Slave: DR 1: col. 546 (7131). *Laiali*: DR 1: col. 547 (7131).

chastised their vassals for disrespect or pretensions to power; their anger shocked subordinates into restoring established social hierarchies.[103] The power of the outburst was in its evocation of the righteous anger of the Old Testament God; high emotion was justified by the responsibilities of lordship.

Sovereigns throughout this period also explicitly declared their authority over rank assignments. In 1500, Ivan III informed a recalcitrant general that "You are not serving Daniil [the defendant], you are serving me and my affairs." Ivan IV in 1558 told a plaintiff that he was acting like a fool (*duruet*): "We send our servitors [literally, slaves] on our service where it is appropriate." Mikhail Fedorovich instructed a Conciliar State Secretary to inform a plaintiff that he was reassigned, but not because his claim for precedence was justified; rather, the tsar can choose to send anyone anywhere he wants. On another occasion, he assured a litigant "According to my sovereign order, the boyars [in charge of assignments] assign as military commanders those who can serve with each other." In another suit, he informed two litigants that they were both low born and had no "place"—"Where the tsar orders them to serve, they will serve." Tsar Aleksei Mikhailovich said the same thing in 1660 in refusing a suit: "We assign our generals knowing who can be with whom."[104] Clearly, the ruler and his bureaucracy had the last word in this system.

Tsarist authority worked because servitors accepted the system and because rulers wielded their power with flexibility and empathy. Families tried to respect the tsar's prerogative to set their "place." We have seen above, for example, Prince Lykov agreeing to serve if the tsar made an explicit exception. Many other suits are prefaced by plaintiffs' earnest assurance that they were "ready to serve as assigned, but . . .," followed by their apologetically pointing out to the ruler what seemed to them an unjust assignment.[105] In other cases, litigants turned to the tsar confident of vindication: "The tsar knows our family status," they declared.[106] They had reason to hope on the tsar's judgment because, as we have seen, there was great latitude available for assignments. The "without place" rule was liberally used for whole campaigns and types of service and readily applied to appease disputing servitors (in approximately one-fourth of these cases, recall, some form of appeasement carried the day).

---

[103]Richard E. Barton, "Lordship in Maine: Transformation, Service, and Anger," *Anglo-Norman Studies* 17 (1995):41–63, and his "'Zealous Anger' and the Renegotiation of Aristocratic Relationships in Eleventh- and Twelfth-Century France," in Barbara H. Rosenwein, ed., *Anger's Past: The Social Uses of an Emotion in the Middle Ages* (Ithaca, N.Y., 1998), pp. 153–70.

[104]Ivan III: RK *1475–1605* 1, pt. 1:61–62, and RK *1475–1598*, p. 30 (both 7008). Ivan IV: RK *1475–1598*, p. 169 (7066). Mikhail Fedorovich: KR 2: cols. 94–95, and DR 1: cols. 929, 946–47 (7135, 7136); KR 2:12 (7136); DR 1: cols. 575–76 (7132). Aleksei Mikhailovich: RGADA, f. 210, Zapisnye knigi Moskovskogo stola, opis' 6a, delo 11, ll. 332–34 (7169).

[105]DR 2: col. 443 (7143); KR 2: col. 547 (7142); DR 2: col. 350 (7142); DR 2: col. 420 (7143).

[106]DR 1: cols. 984, 990–996 passim (7136).

Further, the tsar bestowed mercy to moderate the system, as he did in all litigation. Not often, but in cases of very harsh punishment, he lessened the sentence, often citing the reconciling influence of saints' celebrations or the intercession of holy or respected individuals. In 1623, for example, Tsar Mikhail Fedorovich in great anger sentenced a recalcitrant suitor to demotion to provincial service, but then, on the occasion of the holy day of Metropolitan Peter, he reinstated him to rank. Similarly, in 1625, he forgave a sentence of imprisonment and disgrace after the intercession of his father, Patriarch Filaret, on the occasion of the holy day of Metropolitan Aleksii. In 1633, the tsar ordered two *stol'niki* reprieved as they were being led to prison. In 1640, the tsar ordered two litigants to be released from the service of which they had complained because "They are young and do not understand campaigns in the field," even though they were still punished for the dishonor of their suit. In 1669, two recalcitrant litigants, who had "deeply angered" Tsar Aleksei Mikhailovich and "caused great harm to the Tsar's affairs," were nevertheless spared execution and instead exiled to their country estates "after the intercession of the tsar's children." In 1672, a *stol'nik* ordered beaten with bastinadoes was pardoned and imprisoned instead.[107]

The expeditiousness with which cases were resolved also suggests something of the functionality of precedence. It did not tie up the government with interminable suits on the eve of important battles. As A. I. Markevich remarked long ago, complaints were often decided on the spot by rejection or deferment. Robert Crummey concurs, noting that precedence worked efficiently and that the government had ample flexibility to work around it when necessary.[108] Thus, even though its critics declared that it harmed Muscovy's military preparedness, and Peter I later roundly condemned it in 1719 (almost 40 years after its abolition), precedence probably did not play a negative role in military readiness or governance.[109]

In light of this evidence, we might raise anew the question of *cui bono*: Whom did precedence benefit? Winners in suits clearly won defense of their status and perhaps even scrambled up the status hierarchy by dint of the victory. But winners were so few as to be unimportant. Perhaps the many plaintiffs who were rebuffed in their efforts to claim higher place might have gained social esteem in the process, because filing the suit was a means of asserting that the

---

[107]Metropolitan Peter: DR 1: cols. 575–76 (7132). Filaret's intercession: DR 1: col. 680 (7133). Turned away from prison: DR 2: cols. 350–51 (7142). "Young": DR 2: cols. 624, 626 (7148). Intercession of children: RGADA, f. 210, opis' 15, Raznye stoly, stb. 133 (II), l. 432 (7177). Pardoned to prison: DR 3: col. 896 (7180). Markevich argued that "the majority" of sentences issued in precedence were forgiven, which is a high estimate: *Istoriia*, p. 483.

[108]Markevich, *Istoriia*, pp. 492–93 (although he makes a harsher judgment in "Chto takoe?"); Crummey, "Reflections," pp. 275–80.

[109]PSZ 1, vol. 1, no. 905 (1682), pp. 371–73; PSZ 1, vol. 5, no. 3384 (1719).

two families were on a par. By and large, however, the benefits of precedence would seem to have redounded not to those who initiated suits, but to the defendants that consistently won. Precedence most often worked to affirm traditional status relationships as reflected in the original service assignments that fell under dispute, and thus it affirmed the social status quo. It also affirmed not only the tsar's power but the whole patrimonial political system.

Precedence consolidated the elite around the ruler because it simultaneously gave established families assurance of their social status, offered hope to aspiring families for higher prestige, and gave the ruler a forum in which to display his benevolence as well as his authority. Precedence allowed ambitious men to aspire to status while hardly hindering the ruler's discretion in service assignment or jostling old families from high status. When change in the status hierarchy came, as it did continually, it resulted not from aggressive litigation, but from the more traditional means by which elites were renewed across the European stage—mortality of and within clans, grand princes welcoming new families to the elite, and the elite expanding with military and bureaucratic reform and growth. An important part of the equation unquestionably was that the rapid expansion of the bureaucracy and military in the sixteenth and especially seventeenth centuries gave sovereigns a range of options. They could tolerate precedence in order to cultivate an aristocratic elite within the elite while not tying their hands or limiting social mobility. Aspiring families could enjoy lucrative leadership positions even if they never did succeed in winning the cachet of "place" in the precedence system[110]; gradually that cachet dissipated as well. The grand princes, then, could get the best of both worlds by offering ambitious men the opportunity to litigate while neither threatening the social status quo nor denying other avenues to up-and-comers.

One could perhaps argue that precedence, in fact, enhanced "autocracy"— some might even say "absolutism." But each term should be used cautiously. These litigations show that political relations—even in the seventeenth century, when the bureaucracy and empire it served were growing by leaps and bounds—were personal and face to face. Like French monarchs of this same time,[111] Russian tsars could use court rituals such as precedence disputes to keep their men in line and to enunciate standards of behavior and social status. In a fast-growing government, precedence litigations, regardless of how much the tsars might have preferred not to be bothered with these cavils, kept the sinews of the patrimonial political system flexible. If one takes "autocracy" or "absolutism" to connote a dynamic system of interdependencies between ruler and myriad elites and social groups, then precedence was indeed a tool of building "autocracy." To avoid quibbling over definitions, one might best think of precedence as a strategy in the maintenance of traditional political stability. As Anthony Giddens and Michael Mann have stressed in their theories of premodern social systems, large centralized states in premodern conditions cannot hope to create deep and broad social cohesion. Means of communication were simply insufficient. The key to success was the cultivation of an elite willing to execute the policies of the center.[112] Most fundamentally, such cultivation took the form of material rewards and high social status. Precedence can be seen as a key strategy for building a loyal elite and for responding to social change; the result was a strong and flexible state.

[112]These theories are discussed in Chapter 5: Anthony Giddens, *A Contemporary Critique of Historical Materialism, Vol. 1: Power, Property and the State* (Berkeley, 1981); idem, *The Nation-State and Violence: Volume Two of A Contemporary Critique of Historical Materialism* (Berkeley and Los Angeles, 1987); Michael Mann, *The Sources of Social Power, Vol. 1: A History of Power from the Beginning to AD 1760* (Cambridge, England, 1986).

CHAPTER 5

Strategies of Integration in an Autocracy

Muscovite rulers were faced with the same problems of governance that confronted medieval and early modern rulers in Western Europe. They had limited resources in manpower and finances and limited means of communication (even after printing was accepted, literacy was required to make it a tool of governance). Population was widely dispersed and heterogenous in dialect, confession, social status, and privileges. In such circumstances, rulers were hard pressed to integrate their realms, and in fact strove for nowhere near the degree of social and political cohesion that states seek today. To achieve stability through societal acceptance of their rule, premodern leaders adopted strategies from coercive to co-optative—fulfilling the traditional mandate of providing justice was one. Concepts and institutions of honor can be seen, from the state's point of view, as a strategy of governance, one that provided a discourse and a cultural praxis uniting the tsar's territory around a common set of social values. Honor contributed to Muscovy's social and political integration in tandem with a broad array of other strategies. Those strategies constituted the political practice of the realm. This chapter, then, explores the issue of social cohesion in premodern conditions and in so doing confronts the meaning of autocracy in action for Muscovites.

Theoretical Discourses about Cohesion

We might define social cohesion or integration as societal acceptance of the governing authorities that is sufficient to create stability and to allow those governing bodies to pursue their goals. F. G. Bailey remarked how even the seemingly strongest of regimes fall apart when societal consensus evaporates: "To a surprisingly large extent people can be ruled only in so far as they are willing to accept orders. . . . Consent, of course, means more than merely willingness to accept a particular command. It means accepting the pattern of statuses which divide people into high and low."[1] Social cohesion involves both command and

[1]F. G. Bailey, "Gifts and Poison," in his *Gifts and Poison: The Politics of Reputation* (New York, 1971), pp. 15–16.

acceptance, ideology and practice. Perceptions of how cohesion is achieved and actual practice dialectically influence each other: A society's formal discourse about how it is unified may create conditions for greater or lesser cooperation with strategies of building cohesion, and vice versa. In this section, I look theoretically at how cohesion might be achieved and contrast to those ideas the ways in which Russians have described cohesion in their state over time.

How to create social cohesion is a problem that has troubled rulers and philosophers since the time of Aristotle and Plato. Great social theorists have carved out two approaches to the problem, points of view implicit in the pairings of those two ancient philosophers and of others who followed—Hobbes and Rousseau, Hegel and Kant, Marx and Weber.[2] One approach focuses on coercion, based on an assumption of natural competition and conflict in the human condition. Variations on this theme are myriad, but a most influential modern version of this Hobbesian view has been the Marxian one, wherein each age is permeated by a dialectical tension between the dominant class's efforts to maintain its control and the struggle of subordinate classes to overthrow it.[3] The other common paradigm emphasizes consensus, based on an assumption that integrated harmony can be achieved in human societies. Again, many variations have been articulated. Often this image of society is linked to an evolutionary perspective, as in Ferdinand Tönnies's contrast between "traditional" societies (*Gemeinschaft*)—founded on personal interaction, affinitive relationships, and ascribed status—and modern societies (*Gesellschaft*)—characterized by individualism, territorial association, and contractual relations.[4] A most influential exponent of this vision was Emile Durkheim, who saw at the heart of social stability normative consensus—that is, the internalization and acting out by individuals of moral values conducive to social cooperation and the maintenance of the social system.[5]

[2]Peter Burke provides a helpful overview of trends in social theory: *History and Social Theory* (Ithaca, N.Y., 1992), esp. chap. 3.

[3]Marx's dialectical and materialist vision has continued to be advanced: Nicholas Abercrombie, Stephen Hill, and Bryan S. Turner, *The Dominant Ideology Thesis* (London, 1980).

[4]Horace M. Miner, "Community-Society Continua," *International Encyclopedia of the Social Sciences* 3 (1968):174–80. See Anthony P. Cohen's excellent critique of this concept: *The Symbolic Construction of Community* (London and New York, 1985), pp. 21–38.

[5]Emile Durkheim, *The Division of Labor in Society*, trans. George Simpson (New York, 1933); idem, *The Elementary Forms of the Religious Life*, trans. Joseph Ward Swain (London, 1915), esp. pp. 257–58. On Durkheim, see Anthony Giddens, *Capitalism and Modern Social Theory: An Analysis of the Writings of Marx, Durkheim and Max Weber* (Cambridge, England, 1971), pt. 2, pp. 65–118. A major exponent of consensus theory was Talcott Parsons: *The Social System* (Glencoe, Ill., 1951); idem, *The Evolution of Societies*, ed. and intro. by Jackson Toby (Englewood Cliffs, N.J., 1977); idem, "Social Systems," in *International Encyclopedia of the Social Sciences* 15 (1968):458–73. See Ralf Dahrendorf's critique of Parsons's stress on consensus: *Class and Class Conflict in Industrial Society* (Stanford, 1959), p. 163. Parsons's approach is explored in Lewis A. Coser, "Conflict: Social Aspects," and Laura Nader, "Conflict: Anthropological Aspects," in *International Encyclopedia of the Social Sciences* 3 (1968):232–42.

Much twentieth-century social theory has tried to reconcile these approaches. Max Weber balanced the coercive force of the state with systems of legitimation and status as building blocks of social cohesion.[6] The revisionist Marxist Antonio Gramsci argued that modern societies are stabilized by the "cultural hegemony" of the ideology of the dominant class.[7] Modern social anthropology stresses both the restorative power of ritual and ideology and the possibility of dynamic interaction between rulers and ruled in such ceremonial moments or discourses: Max Gluckman finds "the peace in the feud"; Victor Turner sees rites of passage as transformative and reconciling; and Clifford Geertz argues that ideology as expressed in cultural praxis creates moments of interactive communication.[8] Current theory in sociology and anthropology, as well as postmodernist critiques,[9] balance the coercion-consensus tension by reference to human agency. They thus look to "praxis"—that is, the willful (in Anthony Giddens's term, "knowledgeable") interaction of individuals with the institutions and ideas that shape their experience. Sherry Ortner summarizes: "Society is a system . . . the system is powerfully constraining, and yet . . . the system can be made and unmade through human action and interaction."[10]

[6]Anthony Giddens, *Capitalism and Modern Social Theory*, chap. 11.

[7]David Forgacs, ed., *An Antonio Gramsci Reader: Selected Writings, 1916–1935* (New York, 1988), chap. 6; Geoff Eley, "Reading Gramsci in English: Observations on the Reception of Antonio Gramsci in the English-Speaking World, 1957–82," *European History Quarterly* 14, no. 4 (1984):441–77; idem, "Nations, Publics and Political Cultures: Placing Habermas in the Nineteenth Century," unpubl. manuscript, 1990. Raymond Williams makes the same point in *Marxism and Literature* (Oxford and New York, 1977), p. 110.

[8]Max Gluckman, "The Peace in the Feud," in *Custom and Conflict in Africa* (Glencoe, Ill., 1959), pp. 1–26, and his *Politics, Law and Ritual in Tribal Society* (Oxford, 1965). Victor Turner, *The Forest of Symbols* (Ithaca, N.Y., 1967); idem, *The Ritual Process* (Chicago, 1969); idem, *The Drums of Affliction* (Ithaca, N.Y., 1968); idem, *Dramas, Fields and Metaphors: Symbolic Action in Human Society* (Ithaca, N.Y., 1974). On these concepts, see Edmund R. Leach, "Ritual," *International Encyclopedia of the Social Sciences* 13 (1968):520–26. Clifford Geertz, "Religion as a Cultural System," in his *The Interpretation of Cultures: Selected Essays* (New York, 1973), pp. 87–125. See also "Deep Play: Notes on the Balinese Cockfight," in his *The Interpretation of Cultures*, pp. 412–54. Anthony P. Cohen provides numerous illustrations of symbolic behavior maintaining community: *Symbolic Construction*.

[9]Foucault and Habermas are also keenly interested in cultural hegemony and the problem of power, but primarily concerning modern society: Michel Foucault, "Truth and Power," in Paul Rabinow, ed., *The Foucault Reader* (New York, 1984), p. 61; Jürgen Habermas, "The Public Sphere: An Encyclopedia Article (1964)," *New German Critique* 3 (1974):49–55; idem, *Communication and the Evolution of Society*, trans. and intro. by Thomas McCarthy (Boston, 1979), chaps. 3–4. On Habermas, see Robert Wuthnow, "The Critical Theory of Jürgen Habermas," in Robert Wuthnow, James Davison Hunter, Albert Bergesen, and Edith Kurzweil, *Cultural Analysis: The Work of Peter L. Berger, Mary Douglas, Michel Foucault and Jürgen Habermas* (London and New York, 1984), pp. 179–239.

[10]Sherry B. Ortner, "Theory in Anthropology since the Sixties," *Comparative Studies in Society and History* 26 (1984):159.

Anthony Giddens and Michael Mann, among others, are of particular interest here because they focus on premodern societies.[11] Following Foucault and others, they see power as diffused throughout society; accordingly, they hold that social integration cannot be fully controlled by the center. The claims of premodern governments are broad but their ability to exercise such claims shallow. Thus, when Mann and Giddens turn to strategies of central control, they identify a variety of means that are coercive *and* consensus-building. Giddens speaks of military power, or the threat thereof; bureaucratic control over those social resources deemed important to the dominant classes; and inculcation of generally personalized theories of legitimation, for the elites in particular. Underdevelopment of transport and communication as well as of literacy, education, and media means that neither economic control nor normative consensus alone can create and sustain societal integration.

Keenly aware of the limited resources in premodern conditions, these sociologists also argue that states focus cohesion-building strategies mainly on the elite because its support is most crucial to administrative control and because it is the most accessible by the limited means of communication in premodern conditions. What they describe, in sum, is not top-down social control but something more interactive. The family and household turn the social values of religious and secular ethics into personal goals; locally based office holders amass power by enforcing laws and moral expectations; factions within communities assemble power bases using central bureaucratic offices; and individuals and institutions that enforce social values or policy in turn benefit from rewards in the form of land, status, access, and so on. The permeation of social structures and cultural practices with a discourse that both encourages conformity and allows the possibility of negotiation and gratification creates loosely bound community and dynamic stability.[12] Thus theoretical considerations of social cohesion now see it as a process of interaction between, on the one hand, received discourses and limits imposed by institutions and culture and, on the other hand, individuals appropriating and manipulating those institutions. My discussion of how individuals and communities used honor for local concerns takes this approach, stressing individuals' "knowledgeable" manipulation of dominant discourses.

[11]Michael Mann, *The Sources of Social Power, Vol. 1: A History of Power from the Beginning to AD 1760* (Cambridge, England, 1986); Anthony Giddens, *A Contemporary Critique of Historical Materialism, Vol. 1: Power, Property and the State* (Berkeley, 1981), and his *The Nation State and Violence: Volume Two of A Contemporary Critique of Historical Materialism* (Berkeley, 1987). See also Charles Tilly's *Coercion, Capital and European States, AD 900–1992* (Cambridge, Mass., and Oxford, 1992).

[12]See a discussion of stability in early modern England in this vein: A. J. Fletcher and J. Stevenson, "Introduction," in idem, eds., *Order and Disorder in Early Modern England* (Cambridge, England, 1985), esp. pp. 31–40.

Russians writing on cohesion in their society have run the same theoretical gamut from coercion to consensus to an appreciation of the interdependence of the two. It is important to recall, however, that most of what has been written on this topic is didactic, whether emanating from the pen of a sixteenth-century chronicler bent on impressing Orthodox hierarchs, or of a nineteenth-century "Westernizer" convinced of the "enlightenment" of Peter I's reforms of "backward, stagnant" Muscovy. But it is useful to survey this literature as evidence of trends in ideology and as a theoretical ideal to juxtapose against practice, which I turn to in the second half of this chapter.

No explicit theoretical discourse about society was present in Muscovite times, but one can glean different visions of societal unity from numerous texts. The coercion and the consensus models coexisted in contemporary Muscovite portrayals of Muscovite society and politics, but it is fair to say that the image of premodern Russia as bound together by coercive central control has enjoyed a dominance in most modern interpretation. The reasons can be found in Muscovite texts. The coercion model made a late but dramatic impact on Muscovite texts starting in the late fifteenth and sixteenth century, when the theme of the Muscovite ruler as "autocrat" emerged. It was a trend propelled by a conjunction of events: the fall of Constantinople in 1453, the demise of the Golden Horde, Moscow's phenomenal territorial expansion. Starting in the early sixteenth century, learned writers brought the stern dictum of the sixth-century Byzantine scholar, Agapetus, to their aid:

> Though an emperor in body be like all other, yet in power of his office he is like God, Master of all men. For in earth, he has no peer.[13]

In the compilative projects he directed at midsixteenth century, Metropolitan Makarii constructed an image of Muscovy as heir to Byzantium and its ruler as Godlike in his power.[14] In his *Great Menology* (*Velikie minei chetii*), compiled in 1552, Makarii included historical and hagiographic texts that portrayed Muscovy as "the center of God's world" and assigned its ruler responsibility for defending the realm and the faith against all heathens—domestic heretics, Catholics, and Muslims.[15] *The Book of Degrees* (*Stepennaia kniga*), compiled

---

[13]Agapetus, chap. 21, quoted in Ihor Ševčenko, "A Neglected Byzantine Source of Muscovite Political Ideology," *Harvard Slavic Studies* 2 (1954), p. 147.

[14]David B. Miller, "The *Velikie Minei Chetii* and the *Stepennaia Kniga* of Metropolitan Makarii and the Origins of Russian National Consciousness," *Forschungen* 26 (1979), p. 279; Ševčenko, "A Neglected Byzantine Source," pp. 156–59.

[15]See Douglas Joseph Bennet, Jr., "The Idea of Kingship in 17th Century Russia," Ph.D. dissertation, Harvard University, 1967, pp. 3–5; Ševčenko, "A Neglected Byzantine Source," pp. 163–64; Miller, "*Velikie Minei Chetii*," p. 279; on the *Great Menology*, see ibid., chap. 1.

in the early 1560s under Makarii's direction, included a eulogy to Vasilii III depicting his "autocratic" rule thusly:

> His imperial heart and mind are always on guard and deliberating wisely, guarding all men from danger with just laws and sternly repelling the streams of lawlessness so that the ship of his great realm would not sink in waves of injustice. . . . For truly you are called tsar . . . who are crowned with the crown of chastity and draped in the purple robe of justice.[16]

Although the most immediate audience for these views was other churchmen and any literate members of the secular elite (of whom few were literate before the seventeenth century), this representation of power and omnipotence was portrayed in court rituals from the late fifteenth century. Their import was not lost on outsiders such as foreign diplomats, many of whom were already predisposed by classical training to see Muscovy in categorical terms. Sigismund von Herberstein, an early sixteenth-century Habsburg envoy, said about the Muscovite grand prince: "In the sway which he holds over his people, he surpasses all the monarchs of the whole world." Several decades later, the Englishman Giles Fletcher likened Muscovite government to Turkish despotism: "The manner of their government is much after the Turkish fashion . . . plain tyrannical, as applying all to the behoof of the prince." Aristotle's concept of tyranny was invoked by the German traveler Adam Olearius in the midseventeenth century: "The Tsar . . . alone rules the whole country . . . he treats [his people] as the master of the house does his servants."[17] Their constructions of early modern Russia as "a dominating and despotic monarchy" became a powerful trope in the hands of seventeenth- and eighteenth-century European political theorists, as Marshall Poe has persuasively demonstrated.[18] From their works, this idea migrated back to Russia.

[16]PSRL 21, pt. 2 (1913):610–11. All translations mine unless otherwise indicated. On this source, see also Ševčenko, "A Neglected Byzantine Source," pp. 159–63; Michael Cherniavsky, *Tsar and People: Studies in Russian Myths* (New Haven, Conn., and London, 1961), pp. 46–49; Miller, "*Velikie Minei Chetii,*" pp. 336–37; M. D'iakonov, *Vlast' moskovskikh gosudarei* (St. Petersburg, 1889), pp. 168–71. On the *Book of Degrees*, see Miller, "*Velikie Minei Chetii,*" chap. 2.

[17]Sigismund von Herberstein, *Notes upon Russia*, trans. and ed. R. H. Major, 2 vols. (London, 1851–52), 1:30; Giles Fletcher, "Of the Russe Commonwealth," in Lloyd E. Berry and Robert O. Crummey, eds., *Rude and Barbarous Kingdom: Russia in the Accounts of Sixteenth-Century English Voyagers* (Madison, Wis., 1968), p. 132; Adam Olearius, *The Travels of Olearius in Seventeenth-Century Russia*, trans. and ed. Samuel H. Baron (Stanford, 1967), p. 173. For similar comments, see also Antonio Possevino, S. J., *The Moscovia*, trans. Hugh F. Graham (Pittsburgh, 1977), p. 9, and Jacques Margeret, *The Russian Empire and the Grand Duchy of Muscovy: A 17th-Century French Account*, trans. and ed. Chester S. L. Dunning (Pittsburgh, 1983), p. 28.

[18]The phrase is Olearius's: Baron, ed., *The Travels*, p. 173. Marshall T. Poe, "'Russian Despotism': The Origins and Dissemination of an Early Modern Commonplace," Ph.D. dissertation, University of California, Berkeley, 1993.

Peter I's adoption of a European rhetoric of absolutism at the turn of the eighteenth century and the vigorous cult of Peter that ensued guaranteed that this theme of omnipotent autocracy and slavish society endured through the eighteenth century.[19] Not surprisingly, reinforced by Western images of Russia as exotic,[20] this patrimonial vision dominated the debates about Russia in nineteenth-century social thought. The statist school, for example, gave primacy to the state and dismissed society as inert (S. M. Solov'ev, Boris Chicherin). Similarly, with the spread of Marxist historiography in Russia from the late nineteenth century, the coercion paradigm became the canon. However much modified by Stalinism and Russian nationalism, Soviet historical theory maintained that societies are unified by a specific form of political control arising from the dominant mode of production in a given era. Soviet Marxist scholarship saw pre-Petrine Russia, as well as much of Imperial Russia, as ordered and stabilized by the economic and political institutions of the state acting in the interests of the feudal class.[21] In response, in this century a variety of anti-Marxist versions of the same model were developed that posited the primacy of political—rather than social and economic—forces in coercion. Such a trend, not coincidentally paralleling the rise of the totalitarian interpretation of the Soviet state, depicts early Russia variously as an "Oriental despotism" or a "patrimonial" or "hypertrophic" state, or otherwise emphasizes instruments of political

---

[19]For immediate predecessors to Petrine political thought, see Bennet, "The Idea of Kingship," chap. 4, reprinted in Nancy Shields Kollmann, ed., *Major Problems in Early Modern Russian History* (New York, 1992), pp. 385–420. On political thought in Peter's time, see Sumner Benson, "The Role of Western Political Thought in Petrine Russia," *Canadian-American Slavic Studies* 8, no. 2 (1974): 254–73; A. Lappo-Danilevskii, "Ideia gosudarstva i glavneishie momenty eia razvitiia v Rossii so vremeni smuty i do epokhi preobrazovanii," *Golos minuvshogo* 2, no. 12 (1914):24–31; Marc Raeff, *The Well-Ordered Police State* (New Haven, Conn., 1983); Cherniavsky, *Tsar and People*, chap. 3; Marc Raeff, "The Enlightenment in Russia and Russian Thought in the Enlightenment," in J. G. Garrard, ed., *The Eighteenth Century in Russia* (Oxford, 1973), pp. 25–47; James Cracraft, "Empire Versus Nation: Russian Political Theory under Peter I," *Harvard Ukrainian Studies* 10, nos. 3/4 (1986):524–41.

[20]See Larry Wolff's discussion of eighteenth-century constructions of "Eastern Europe," which includes Russia in the analysis: *Inventing Eastern Europe: The Map of Civilization on the Mind of the Enlightenment* (Stanford, 1994).

[21]A stellar example is the collectively written official history of the Soviet Union published by the Academy of Sciences in the late Stalinist years: *Ocherki istorii SSSR*, 8 vols. (Moscow, 1953–58). For discussions of Soviet revisionism within this canon, see James P. Scanlan, *Marxism in the USSR: A Critical Survey of Current Soviet Thought* (Ithaca, N.Y., 1985), chap. 5, and also his essay, "From Historical Materialism to Historical Interactionism: A Philosophical Examination of Some Recent Developments," in Samuel H. Baron and Nancy W. Heer, eds., *Windows on the Russian Past: Essays on Soviet Historiography since Stalin* (Columbus, Ohio, 1977), pp. 3–23. Also relevant is Samuel H. Baron, "Feudalism or the Asiatic Mode of Production: Alternative Interpretations of Russian History," in Baron and Heer, eds., *Windows on the Russian Past*, pp. 24–41.

control and coercion.[22] These ideas are now enjoying vogue in post-Soviet Russia, where historians have been embracing Herbert Spencer, Arnold Toynbee, Richard Pipes, the Eurasianists, and the "totalitarian" model.[23]

But the primacy of this interpretation has by and large been driven by outside factors, among them clergy anxious to elevate Muscovy in the Orthodox world, intelligents swayed by the cult of Peter and the West, and Cold War tensions. It does not correspond well to countervailing ideas in writings of Muscovite times, nor to Muscovite practice. Muscovite texts and their Kievan predecessors overwhelmingly argue for a "consensus" vision of autocracy. From Kievan times to the seventeenth century, chronicles, other historical writings, and some documentary texts consistently depict the body politic as a harmonious, Christian community united under a tsar who was legitimized by God and limited by "law" and tradition.[24] Chronicles and tales stemming back to Kievan times (generally composed by monastic authors) asserted that politics was based on love and friendship between the ruler and his elite. A chronicler quoted Grand Prince Vladimir I (ca. 980–1015) and commented:

[22]Karl Wittfogel, *Oriental Despotism* (New Haven, Conn., 1957); Arnold Toynbee, "Russia's Byzantine Heritage," in his *Civilization on Trial* (New York, 1948), pp. 164–83; Richard Pipes, *Russia under the Old Regime* (New York, 1974); Richard Hellie, "The Structure of Modern Russian History: Toward a Dynamic Model," *Russian History* 4, no. 1 (1977):1–22; Alexander Yanov, *The Origins of Autocracy: Ivan the Terrible in Russian History*, trans. Stephen Dunn (Berkeley, 1981); Hélène d'Encausse, *The Russian Syndrome: One Thousand Years of Political Murder*, trans. Caroline Higgitt (New York, 1992). The Eurasianists fit this interpretation as well; see G. E. Orchard, "The Eurasian School of Russian Historiography," *Laurentian University Review* 10, no. 1 (1977):97–106, and N. V. Riasanovsky, "The Emergence of Eurasianism," *California Slavic Studies* 4 (1967):39–72.

[23]V. B. Kobrin and A. L. Iurganov speak of "despotic autocracy" in the sixteenth century, and Evgenii Anisimov calls Peter I the founder of the "totalitarian state" in Russia: Kobrin and Iurganov, "Stanovlenie despoticheskogo samoderzhaviia v srednevekovoi Rusi (K postanovke problemy)," *Istoriia SSSR* 1991, no. 4:54–64; Anisimov, *The Reforms of Peter the Great: Progress through Coercion in Russia*, trans. John T. Alexander (Armonk, N.Y., 1993), p. 296. *Otechestvennaia istoriia* has been running a discussion on totalitarianism: 1993, no. 1. Interest in the Eurasianists is indicated by recent publications: L. V. Ponomareva, ed., *Evraziia: Istoricheskie vzgliady russkikh emigrantov* (Moscow, 1992); *Puti Evrazii: Russkaia intelligentsiia i sud'by Rossii* (Moscow, 1992); *Evraziiskie issledovaniia (almanakh "forum")* (Moscow, 1994); *Evraziistvo: Rossiia mezhdu Evropoi i Aziei* (Moscow, 1994). Social theory is also getting attention: S. I. Zhuk, "Maks Veber i sotsial'naia istoriia," *Voprosy istorii* 1992, nos. 2–3, pp. 172–77. Also in vogue is A. S. Akhieser's theory of Russia's unique, cyclical historical path: *Rossiia: Kritika istoricheskogo opyta*, 3 vols. (Moscow, 1991). See the broad range of post-Soviet approaches in Christine Ruane, ed., "Current Problems of Historical Theory," in *Russian Studies in History* 35, no. 3 (1996–97).

[24]Daniel Rowland has argued these points elegantly: "The Problem of Advice in Muscovite Tales about the Time of Troubles," *Russian History* 6, pt. 2 (1979):259–83, and his "Did Muscovite Literary Ideology Place Limits on the Power of the Tsar (1540s–1660s)?" *Russian Review* 49, no. 2 (1990):125–56.

"With silver and gold I cannot win a retinue, but with a retinue I can win silver and gold, just as my grandfather and my father won silver and gold with their retinues." For Vladimir loved his retinue and consulted them about the administration of his land, about wars and about the law of the land.[25]

Muscovite texts perpetuated this trope. An early sixteenth-century chronicler put these words into Grand Prince Dmitrii Donskoi's mouth as a deathbed peroration to his men:

> You know my customs and my ways, for I was born and grew up before your eyes, and with you I ruled, and held my patrimony. . . . I had for you deep honor and love, and under you I held cities and great power; I loved your children, and against none of you did I do evil, neither did I take by force, nor did I offend you, nor subjugate you nor rob you, nor dishonor you. But I honored you and loved you and held you in deep honor. I shared your joy and your anguish, for you are not called my boyars, but the princes of my land.[26]

Secular documents also iterated these pieties. In his will of 1353, Grand Prince Semen Ivanovich instructed his heirs: "And you should not heed evil men, and if anyone tries to breed discord among you, you should heed our father, Bishop Aleksii, as well as the old boyars who wished our father and us well."[27] Several fifteenth-century wills also contained the warm sentiment addressed in Dmitrii Donskoi's second testament (1389): "My sons, those of my boyars who take to serving my princess, care for those boyars as one man."[28] The 1550 law code states that boyars should be involved in the creation of new legislation; this was no constitutional guarantee but a statement of their traditional role of advising the tsar and sharing in his judgments.[29] The implication of these sources

[25]*Povest' vremennykh let*, ed. V. P. Adrianova-Peretts, 2 vols. (Moscow, 1950), p. 86 (6504). Other examples: PSRL 2 (1908): cols. 551 (6680), 653 (6695).

[26]PSRL 11 (1897):114 (6897), unpubl. trans. by Allison Katsev. Two fifteenth-century eulogies to grand princes of Tver' similarly depict them as routinely consulting their boyars: PSRL 15, pt. 1 (2nd ed., 1922): cols. 169–70 (6907); N. P. Likhachev, ed., "Inoka Fomy slovo pokhval'noe o blagovernom velikom kniaze Borise Aleksandroviche," *Pamiatniki drevnei pis'mennosti i iskusstva* 168 (1908) p. 53. Later compositions with the same theme: PSRL 13:76 (7042; composed early 1500s); SGGD 2 (1819), no. 51, pp. 80–81 (1584); SGGD 3 (1822), no. 16, pp. 81–82 (1613).

[27]DDG, no. 3, p. 14.

[28]DDG, no. 12, p. 36. See also DDG, no. 21, p. 59; DDG, no. 22, p. 61; DDG, no. 61, p. 198.

[29]RZ 2 (1985):120 (art. 98). It therefore set no new precedent when in 1606 and 1610 prospective tsars Prince Vasilii Shuiskii and the Polish king agreed to consult the boyars or even the entire community before new laws could be made: 1606: AAE 2 (1836), no. 44, p. 102. 1610: AAE 2, no. 165, p. 283, and SGGD 2 (1819), no. 199, pp. 394–95. See also Robert O. Crummey, "'Constitutional' Reform during the Time of Troubles," in idem, ed., *Reform in Russia and the U.S.S.R.* (Urbana, Ill., and Chicago, 1989), pp. 28–44.

is that the ruler should be open to all well-intentioned advisors, symbolizing his openness to all society. Exclusivity in power was condemned; full access to the ruler and harmony in the community was the goal.

Narrative literary texts also broadened the themes to create an ideal image of society as a godly community united in its responsibility to God and tsar. Texts that chronicled the Time of Troubles, as Daniel Rowland has shown, confronted directly the responsibility of ruler, boyars, and people. They depicted the realm as governed by pious advice and unanimous agreement, and they attributed the Time of Troubles to the breakdown of righteous communication—the rulers heeded evil counselors and thus fell into corruption, and the cowardly people failed to admonish and guide the ruler back to righteousness:

> And because of the foolish silence of all the world when they did not dare to tell the tsar about the truth, about the destruction of the innocent, the Lord darkened the sky with clouds.[30]

Unanimity of ruler and people—through the mediation of spiritual and secular leaders—should prevail. This theme is constantly stressed in the Protocols of the 1551 church council. In a speech attributed to Ivan IV, he beseeches the church hierarchs:

> Do not hesitate to speak in unanimity words of piety concerning our Orthodox Christian faith, concerning the well-being of God's holy churches, concerning our pious tsardom, and concerning the ordering of all Orthodox Christian dominions . . . assist me, all of you together and in unanimity.[31]

In sum, rulers were expected to rule by God's justice; to patronize the church; to be fair and devoted to the poor and to their men; to heed good advice from the church, the counselors, and the people; and to lead their subjects to salvation by pious example. A ruler is God's ordained mediator between sacred and secular; in Daniel Rowland's terms, social relations were "God-dependent," with earthly mortals merely acting out their parts in the Christian drama of salvation. Social cohesion, in other words, was the product of Christian commitment.

In this context, the midsixteenth-century Agapetan elevation of the tsar's image was a dramatic exception, even going beyond Agapetus's intention. The conclusion of Agapetus's Chapter 21 quoted above, for example, which praises the ruler as "like God, Master of all men," makes clear the author's distrust of exalting a ruler to excess:

---

[30] Avraamii Palitsyn, *Skazanie* (Moscow and Leningrad, 1955), p. 253.

[31] Unpubl. trans. by Jack Kollmann from RGB, fond 304, no. 215, fols. 19v, 23. A printed edition that includes this manuscipt in its variants is N. Subbotin, ed., *Tsarskie voprosy i sobornye otvety o mnorazlichnykh* [sic] *tserkovnykh chinekh (Stoglav)* (Moscow, 1890), pp. 20, 24–25.

Therefore as God, be he never chafed or angry; as man, be he never proud. For though he be like God in face, yet for all that he is but dust which thing teaches him to be equal to every man.[32]

This idea found resonance in sixteenth-century Muscovite texts as well: Metropolitan Filipp (d. 1569) used a full reading of Agapetus's text to chastise Ivan IV, culminating with this challenge: "Or have you forgotten that you are also of this earth and also need the forgiveness of your sins?"[33] A "God-dependent" vision of social cohesion and social relations was the dominant one in Muscovite sources.

The Muscovite consensus model of social integration appeared in nineteenth-century social thought, prompted by European organicist and Romantic visions of the premodern past. Whether with opprobrium or with approval, scholars and intellectuals as disparate as Petr Chaadaev, the Slavophiles, and "Westernizer" Hegelian-influenced historians such as Johann Ewers and S. M. Solov'ev presented pre-Petrine Russia as integrated and harmoniously unified.[34] Proposals for a cohering central principle ranged from the social—Solov'ev's kinship principle, *rodovoe nachalo*[35]—to the ideal—the Slavophiles' celebration of Christian communalism (*sobornost'*) or Chaadaev's condemnation of Orthodoxy as turgid and Muscovy as stagnant.[36] But these were generally static visions of society. The social emphasis of late nineteenth-century historiography, in authors such as V. O. Kliuchevskii, S. F. Platonov, and A. E. Presniakov, addressed that weakness to some extent by examining the interaction of mate-

---

[32]Quoted in Ševčenko, "A Neglected Byzantine Source," p. 147.

[33]Quoted by George P. Fedotov, *St. Filipp: Metropolitan of Moscow* (Belmont, Mass., 1978), p. 121; also see Cherniavsky, *Tsar and People*, p. 49, and Ševčenko, "A Neglected Byzantine Source," p. 173. See also Rowland, "Did Muscovite Literary Ideology," pp. 143–45, and Paul Bushkovitch, "The *Life of Saint Filipp*: Tsar and Metropolitan in the Late Sixteenth Century," in Michael S. Flier and Daniel Rowland, eds., *Medieval Russian Culture, Vol. II* (Berkeley, 1994), pp. 29–46.

[34]On the European context, see Donald N. Levine, "Cultural Integration," *International Encyclopedia of the Social Sciences* 7 (1968):372–73. See A. N. Tsamutali on such theories in Russian history writing and publicistics: *Bor'ba techenii v russkoi istoriografii v polovine XIX veka* (Moscow, 1979), and his *Bor'ba techenii v russkoi istoriografii vo vtoroi polovine XIX veka* (Leningrad, 1977).

[35]S. M. Solov'ev, *Istoriia Rossii s drevneishikh vremen*, 29 vols. in 15 bks. (Moscow, 1960), vol. 1, bk. 1, pp. 55–59.

[36]Representative statements by Slavophiles include I. V. Kireevskii, "On the Nature of European Culture and Its Relation to the Culture of Russia," in Marc Raeff, ed., *Russian Intellectual History: An Anthology* (New York, 1966), pp. 175–207, and K. S. Aksakov, "On the Internal State of Russia," in ibid., pp. 231–51. Also on the Slavophiles, see Andrzej Walicki, *The Slavophile Controversy: History of a Conservative Utopia in Nineteenth-Century Russian Thought*, trans. Hilda Andrews-Rusiecka (Notre Dame, Ind., 1975). For Chaadaev, see *Peter Iakovlevich Chaadaev: Philosophical Letters and Apology of a Madman*, trans. with intro. by Mary-Barbara Zeldin (Knoxville, Tenn., 1969). On Chaadaev, see Andrzej Walicki, *A History of Russian Thought from the Enlightenment to Marxism*, trans. Hilda Andrews-Rusiecka (Stanford, 1979), chap. 5, pp. 81–91.

rial and social forces in shaping the exercise of power. But a trend toward a social interpretation of autocratic power was cut short by the cacophony of competing visions of premodern "despotism" in the twentieth century. Only since the 1970s has some Western, generally American, scholarship been questioning the image of "autocracy" as total power and looking at the interdependencies implicit in premodern power structures.[37] Here, I contribute to that discussion by examining the strategies the Muscovite government used to foster social cohesion. I find, paralleling the trend of theory, that those strategies used both coercion and consensus, and that cohesion can best be comprehended as a result of the reception and engagement in prescribed norms and institutions.

Coercive Strategies of Integration

In the Introduction, I stressed the minimalism of the state's goals and activities and the fragility of its direct instruments of power. The diffusion of power discussed there—the conscious policy of tolerating regional and other pockets of authority and difference—was a strategy of social cohesion itself inasmuch as it reduced tension between state and society and conserved central resources for the exercise of power where it mattered most. Muscovy's rulers—the tsar and his inner circle of boyars—chose their battles wisely, setting as their primary task the exploitation of the human and material resources of the realm. To increase those resources, they preferred extensive means (territorial expansion) to intensive (e.g., mining, patronage of improved agriculture and industrial production). In turn, they were forced to busy themselves with essential tasks, such as the cultivation of the elite, the expansion and modernization of the army, and the creation of networks of fiscal and political governance. Very traditionally, Moscow's rulers also asserted judicial authority over the highest crimes, particularly those such as murder and theft, crimes which were seen as depriving the ruler of his just resources. As they undertook to unify their realm, tsars and boyars used strategies identified in modern theoretical literature: the considered use of violence; the inculcation of cultural hegemony through ritual and symbolism; and the provision of cultural practices, such as honor, that were

---

[37]The present work, like my previous publications, falls into that trend. One can also cite Edward L. Keenan, "Muscovite Political Folkways," *Russian Review* 45 (1986):115–82; Robert O. Crummey, *Aristocrats and Servitors: The Boyar Elite of Russia, 1613–1689* (Princeton, N.J.,1983); Valerie A. Kivelson, *Autocracy in the Provinces: The Muscovite Gentry and Political Culture in the Seventeenth Century* (Stanford, 1996); John LeDonne, "Ruling Families in the Russian Political Order, 1689–1725," *Cahiers du monde russe et soviétique* 28, nos. 3–4 (1987):233–322, and his *Absolutism and Ruling Class: The Formation of the Russian Political Order, 1700–1825* (New York, 1991).

open-ended enough to allow individuals to manipulate that discursive area for their own gain as well. In the next sections, let us examine these in turn, moving along the continuum from coercion to reward to ideology.

Quite rightly, recent social theory gives due emphasis—some scholars even give primary emphasis—to the underpinning importance of violence in maintaining social cohesion. There is no question that the Muscovite state used harsh violence systematically to attain its objectives when other means failed. The oft-quoted ravages of the *Oprichnina* represent an excess inasmuch as the sacking of Novgorod, the executions of boyars, and the rampages in the countryside accomplished no apparent goal and are universally condemned even by historians who venture to see some purpose in the *Oprichnina* as a whole.[38] Plenty of examples of brute force, however, are to be found. Moscow, for example, invaded the city-state of Novgorod in 1478, arrested and deported much of the local elite, executed leaders of the anti-Muscovite opposition, and instituted direct rule by governors chosen from the cream of the Moscow boyars. The conquest of Tver' in 1485 was equally violent, and that of Kazan' and Siberia no less bloody; colonial authorities did not hesitate to use military force to put down the periodic uprisings in the Middle Volga and Siberia.

It should be noted, however, that Moscow also accomplished territorial expansion without resorting to extreme destructive force. Rostov Velikii and Riazan' were added by marriage and inheritance, for example. Cowed by the conquest of Novgorod, Pskov capitulated with far fewer punitive consequences in 1510; even in Novgorod, the military annexation was preceded by repeated Muscovite attempts to secure Novgorodian loyalty without the use of force.[39] The selective use of force acted prophylactically, exerting a threat that functioned as social control. The threat of violence was also embodied in the establishment of Muscovite garrisons at all key strategic points, even the most far-flung outposts of empire.

The political elite and rulers of Moscow also readily wielded violence against those of their number who threatened the political status quo. Tensions over succession to the throne came to civil war in the 1440s–50s. Thereafter, the rulers and boyars kept their potential rivals—grand-princely brothers, nephews, in-laws—under control by imprisonment and execution, as well as by more benign policies, such as forcible tonsure or the forbidding of marriages, thereby occasionally ending clan lines (the Mstislavskii clan, which died out in 1622, is

---

[38]Such views are easily accessible in English: S. F. Platonov, *Ivan the Terrible*, trans. Joseph Wieczynski (Gulf Breeze, Fla., 1974); R. G. Skrynnikov, *Ivan the Terrible*, ed. and trans. Hugh F. Graham (Gulf Breeze, Fla., 1981).

[39]V. N. Bernadskii, *Novgorod i novgorodskaia zemlia v XV veka* (Moscow and Leningrad, 1961), pt. 2, pp. 200–352; also see N. N. Maslennikova, *Prisoedinenie Pskova k Russkomu tsentralizovannomu gosudarstvu* (Leningrad, 1955).

the most eminent example). Boyars themselves resorted to violence when rulers were weak, as in the minority of the 1530s–40s and very likely in the *Oprichnina*, but such occasions were dangerous aberrations. As a rule, violence within the ruling elite was used in limited, specific formats.[40] Tsars frequently put members of the elite in "disgrace" (*opala*), banishing them from the sight of their "bright eyes," but the sanction was usually only for a day or two. Similarly, imprisonment for members of the elite because of precedence suits was brief (one to three days), an action more to inspire fear than to punish.

Muscovite rulers also used corporal sanctions to enforce the law in criminal cases. The death penalty was prescribed in the sixteenth century for recidivist offenders. In the 1649 Conciliar Law Code, a range of punishments from incarceration to beatings to execution was prescribed for criminal *and* civil offenses. In Chapter 1, we saw how prescriptions of corporal sanctions for insult to honor privileged social superiors over subordinates. Similarly, the threat of arbitrary confiscation of property was real for merchants and the landed elite, although relatively rarely invoked.[41] Other examples of coercive measures to enforce social control include the state's increasing involvement in the seventeenth century in enforcing enserfment by pursuing runaway peasants and its willingness to prosecute Old Believers—not for doctrinal errors, but for their perceived disobedience to the tsar's authority (i.e., defying the tsar and avoiding taxes and military service). Again, however, one must add that once the precedent of the use of violence in the law was established, actual violence need not have been systematically meted out for the desired effect of social control. As we have seen in Chapters 3 and 4, sentences of corporal punishment for the elite were often rescinded, and sanctions for recalcitrant servitors often took the form of exemplary punishments—rituals of humiliation or brief imprisonment.

Given the great emphasis that has been accorded to the brutality of Muscovite government—stemming probably first from lurid descriptions of the *Oprichnina* in the contemporary European press[42]—the degree of violence in this state should not be exaggerated. Muscovy, like other premodern societies, chose strategies that were appropriate to the difficulties they faced (small elite, minimal bureaucracy, huge imperial territory, diversity of populace). These strategies included systematic and sporadic violence by officials; the threat of violence represented by administrators and garrisoned troops; the exercise of law and judicial institutions; and bureaucratic control, taxation, recruitment,

---

[40]On the measured use of violence and the treatment of appanage princes, see my *Kinship and Politics: The Making of the Muscovite Political System, 1345–1547* (Stanford, 1987), chaps. 4–5.

[41]For debates on how frequently such prerogatives were invoked, see the debate between Pipes and Weickhardt cited in the Introduction.

[42]Andreas Kappeler, *Ivan Groznyj im Spiegel der ausländischen Druckschriften seiner Zeit* (Bern and Frankfurt, 1972).

and other means of resource exploitation. Muscovy used violence selectively and prophylactically as an example for the populace.[43]

Bureaucratic measures of social control were, after all, also coercive. They fall into Giddens's "surveillance" category—that is, the systematic identification and registration of productive resources by the state. With the conquest of Novgorod, Moscow began cadastral surveys of populated lands in order to distribute land in conditional tenure; cadastres continued in newly conquered territories and in the aftermath of crises such as the *Oprichnina*, the Livonian War, and the Time of Troubles. Quite rightly, scholars have seen the registration of peasants in cadastres and subsequent prohibitions against moving from one's registered community as a key step toward enserfment.[44] At the same time, a central bureaucratic (*prikaz*) system was evolving that involved itself primarily in the registration of military servitors (the *Razriad*), foreign relations (*Posol'skie dela*), the provisioning of the cavalry (*Pomestnyi prikaz*), and the collection of revenues (the *Prikaz bol'shogo dvortsa* and its successors that collected taxes and customs revenues to support administrative and noncavalry forces). All these strategies integrated the realm by forcible subordination to the political power of the center.

Cultivating the Elite with Material Reward

Side by side with coercive measures that functioned negatively to prevent deviance, the state worked positively to attract the loyalty of its subjects. Material reward for the targeted elite was a particularly effective way to enhance cohesion; recall Giddens's and Mann's point that it was essential for premodern states to cultivate elites because elite power was essential for exerting local control and for enforcing central policy. The elite enjoyed a wide array of rewards,

---

[43]On such institutions of coercion in Muscovy, see Ann M. Kleimola, "The Muscovite Autocracy at Work: The Use of Disgrace as an Instrument of Control," in William E. Butler, ed., *Russian Law: Historical and Political Perspectives* (Leyden, 1977), pp. 29–50; Horace W. Dewey and Ann M. Kleimola, "Suretyship and Collective Responsibilty in pre-Petrine Russia," *Jahrbücher für Geschichte Osteuropas* 18 (1970):337–54; Horace W. Dewey, "Political *Poruka* in Muscovite Rus'," *Russian Review* 46, no. 2 (1987):117–34; Brenda Meehan-Waters, "Elite Politics and Autocratic Power," in A. G. Cross, ed., *Great Britain and Russia in the Eighteenth Century: Contacts and Comparisons* (Newtonville, Mass., 1979), pp. 229–46.

[44]On cadastres and enserfment, see S. M. Kashtanov, *Finansy srednevekovoi Rusi* (Moscow, 1988), chap. 2; Jerome Blum, *Lord and Peasant in Russia from the Ninth to the Nineteenth Century* (New York, 1965), chap. 13; S. B. Veselovskii, *Soshnoe pis'mo*, 2 vols. (Moscow, 1915–16); V. O. Kliuchevskii, "Kurs russkoi istorii," in his *Sochineniia v vos'mi tomakh* (Moscow, 1956–59), vol. 3 (1957), lect. 49; Richard Hellie, *Enserfment and Military Change in Muscovy* (Chicago and London, 1971), chap. 5.

continuing traditions of governance by largesse, which I. Ia. Froianov—in an argument reminiscent of Georges Duby's description of early medieval European kingdoms as based on gift-giving—has described as paramount in Kiev Rus'.[45] So also in Muscovy. At ceremonial moments, such as the conquest of Kazan' in 1552, the resolution of the Time of Troubles in 1613, and even the failed Crimean campaign in the 1680s, rulers lavished "fur coats, great French goblets and gold beakers," "horses and weaponry," "money and clothing," and, of course, land on their loyal followers.[46] More systematically, Ivan III (ruled 1462–1505) and his successors established the principle that the cavalry would be supported by grants of land in conditional tenure (*pomest'e*), to be supplemented with sufficient cash to purchase horses, weapons, and armor. A lesser level of privilege and reward was accorded noncavalry forces, such as artillery, musketeers, and new model infantry, as they were developed, in the form of tax privileges and access to communally owned land. At the same time, the principle was enforced that only cavalry members could own landed property—either in conditional or hereditary (*votchina*) tenure—with a few exceptions (the highest merchant and bureaucratic ranks and the church as an institution). The ultimate reward for the landed cavalry was enserfment of the peasantry, which provided the landed elite a steady means of support, even while its service obligations were being reduced and thus its raison d'être was fading. Not coincidentally, enserfment was paralleled by a process of transforming de facto—and by the early eighteenth century, de jure—conditional land tenure into hereditary.[47]

Government policy in the sixteenth century, and to a lesser extent the seventeenth, consolidated the landed cavalry elite territorially, as discussed in the Introduction. Janet Martin has argued persuasively that the mass resettlement of servitors to the Center from conquered areas (e.g., Novgorod, Viaz'ma, Pskov) and from the Center to the western frontier over the sixteenth century broke down regional loyalties and created the basis for reconstructed local communities with stronger loyalties to the tsar.[48] Legislation on the devolution of

---

[45]Georges Duby, *The Early Growth of the European Economy*, trans. Howard B. Clarke (Ithaca, N.Y., 1974), chap. 3; I. Ia. Froianov, *Kievskaia Rus'. Ocherki sotsial'no-politicheskoi istorii* (Leningrad, 1980), chap. 4.

[46]Quotations refer to Ivan IV's distribution of "48,000 rubles" worth of gifts to his men after the conquest of Kazan': PSRL 29 (1965):115–16 (7061). Distribution of "earned estates" after the Time of Troubles: Ann M. Kleimola, "'In accordance with the Canons of the Holy Apostles': Muscovite Dowries and Women's Property Rights," *Russian Review* 51 (1992):204–29. Largesse after the Crimean campaigns: Lindsey Hughes, *Sophia, Regent of Russia, 1657–1704* (New Haven, Conn., and London, 1990), pp. 231–32.

[47]On the cavalry elite, see Hellie, *Enserfment*; John L. H. Keep, *Soldiers of the Tsar: Army and Society in Russia, 1462–1874* (Oxford, 1985); Blum, *Lord and Peasant*. On nonelite military forces, see Keep, *Soldiers*, chaps. 3–4.

[48]Janet Martin, "Forced Resettlement and Provincial Identity," in Ann M. Kleimola and Gail Lenhoff, eds., *Culture and Identity in Muscovy, 1359–1584*, UCLA Slavic Studies, n.s. 3 (Moscow, 1997), pp. 431–49.

patrimonial property had the apparent intent of creating and bolstering regional "corporations" of landed gentry by forbidding land to be sold outside of the members of a given region or extended clan. The creation of gentry control over local criminal affairs (the *guba* system) from the 1530s on similarly forged bonds of local association and connections with the center. In the seventeenth century, regional loyalties were further intensified as service requirements were decreased and local elites became adept at consolidating their patrimonial and service tenure lands in their home regions and monopolizing local offices.[49]

In the juridical realm, the practice of precedence (*mestnichestvo*) and the genealogical and service record keeping it entailed defined the privileged elite and worked to keep it circumscribed. The elite's privileged status is also demonstrated by the law's tendency to abjure corporal punishment for high-ranking persons and to diminish corporal sanctions for them when prescribed. Granted, these juridical tendencies did not constitute legal enfranchisement; no charter of privileges guaranteed their status. Winning a Magna Carta, however, is a high standard to set in defining an enduring elite; by other measures—access to political office, economic privilege, endogamy, and to some extent lifestyle— Muscovy's landed servitors have the characteristics of other corporate, cohesive aristocracies.[50]

Institutional formats for integrating more and more individuals and families into the highest echelons of government also developed over the sixteenth and seventeenth centuries, thus expanding the benefit of the very generous amounts of land and cash awarded to the Moscow-based ranks. At the tip of the elite, one can cite the time-honored (going back to the fourteenth century) practice of grand princes marrying women from Moscow boyar families rather than from foreign dynasties. Even when, as was the rule in the seventeenth century, tsarist brides were chosen from relatively insignificant families, these brides' clans were connected by clientage and marriage to more powerful cliques.[51] A similar practice of building elite loyalty was the willingness of the boyar elite to absorb newcomers, provided they converted to Orthodoxy and intermarried with the boyar clans. Not only princes from the Grand Duchy of Lithuania (the Glinskie, Bel'skie, and Mstislavskie, for example), but also Tatar princes from Kazan' (Tsarevich Peter in the first half of the sixteenth century), the North Caucasus (the Cherkasskie), and Siberia joined the Muscovite elite in the sixteenth and seventeenth centuries.

Access to the highest ranks of decision making, status, and reward—that is, the conciliar or *dumnye* ranks—expanded in these centuries as well, paralleling a gen-

---

[49]Kivelson, *Autocracy in the Provinces*, chaps. 2–5.

[50]Jonathan Powis persuasively defines noble status in the European context without once mentioning legal charters: *Aristocracy* (Oxford, 1984). Kivelson argues that provincial servitors constituted a "gentry" despite the absence of legal incorporation: *Autocracy in the Provinces*, chap. 1.

[51]See my *Kinship and Politics*, chap. 4; Crummey, *Aristocrats and Servitors*, chaps. 3–4.

eral expansion of ranks and offices. From a handful of roles in a fundamentally patrimonial household administration, the court grew by the late seventeenth century to a clutter of largely honorific titles such as *stol'nik*, *striapchii*, and *zhilets*, each held by up to hundreds of men at a time; their main function seems to have been to spread the distribution of rewards all the more broadly.[52] Until the mid-sixteenth century, there were fewer than twenty boyars or *okol'nichie* at the court. Growth was steady in the next century, with about twenty-five to thirty-five men in four conciliar ranks until midcentury, but by 1690, there were 153 men in the four ranks (fifty-two boyars, fifty-four *okol'nichie*, thirty-eight *dumnye dvoriane*, and nine *dumnye d'iaki*).[53] Parallel growth in lesser ranks was even greater.[54] These strategies served dual purposes. To some extent, they were a response to the increased need for administrative personnel in an expanding empire. But they also created a privileged Moscow-based elite that served as a magnet for lesser elites and as a broad basis of political support for autocracy.

Ideology Enacted Symbolically in Honor

Having moved down the spectrum from coercive mechanisms to the use of reward, we come to the realm of ideas and cultural practices that encouraged identification and cooperation with the community as a whole. These practices were based on the prevailing image of Muscovy as a "God-dependent" community; the idiom of expression was Christian. The Orthodox Church provided a cultural package of theocratic values, visual symbols, and rituals that provided a potentially cohering common belief system. One can debate the degree to which Orthodoxy was internalized in sixteenth- and seventeenth-century Russia—as in pre-Reformation Europe, practicing Christians in early Russia combined Christianity with an eclectic set of values and cultural practices and resisted attempts to reform the faith.[55] Nor did it include non-Orthodox sub-

---

[52]See Crummey, *Aristocrats and Servitors*; V. O. Kliuchevskii, "Istoriia soslovii v Rossii," in *Sochineniia* 6 (1959):276–466; Keep, *Soldiers*. Grigorii Kotoshikhin details the responsibilities of each rank: *O Rossii vo tsarstvovanie Alekseia Mikhailovicha*, 4th ed. (St. Petersburg, 1906), chap. 2.

[53]See my *Kinship and Politics*, table 1, p. 76; Crummey, *Aristocrats and Servitors*, appendix A, pp. 175–77.

[54]Hellie, *Enserfment*, appendix, pp. 267–73.

[55]See Eve Levin, "Supplicatory Prayers as a Source for Popular Religious Culture," in Samuel H. Baron and Nancy Shields Kollmann, eds., *Religion and Culture in Early Modern Russia and Ukraine* (DeKalb, Ill., 1997), pp. 96–114; idem, "*Dvoeverie* and Popular Religion," in Stephen K. Batalden, ed., *Seeking God: The Recovery of Religious Identity in Orthodox Russia, Ukraine, and Georgia* (DeKalb, Ill., 1993), pp. 31–52; Georg Michels, "Myths and Realities of the Russian Schism: The Church and Its Dissenters in Seventeenth-Century Muscovy," Ph.D. dissertation, Harvard University, 1991; idem "The Solovki Uprising: Religion and Revolt in Northern Russia," *Russian Review* 51, no. 1 (1992):1–15.

jects. Nevertheless, the theocratic image of society as a community of believers and the ruler as God-ordained constituted one systematic code widely available for expressing political and social relations.

Another inclusive code that embraced non-Orthodox subjects was the protection of honor. Simultaneously, it promoted a discourse that encouraged behavior supportive of the status quo and provided practical opportunity for individuals to pursue personal needs or resolve local conflicts. Chapters 2, 3, and 4 demonstrated how individuals used litigation over honor to exacerbate long-standing conflicts or to catalyze tension into a cathartic resolution. The interactive "praxis" of honor gave honor dynamic power as a force of social cohesion. The theory of honor itself, however, also played such a role by focusing attention on the tsar as centerpiece of the whole society defined by honor. Reflecting on contemporary Muscovite ideas about honor, detailed in Chapter 1, we can see that honor encapsulated the ideal tenets of social behavior, at least from the ruler's point of view.

To be honorable was to obey the laws, to respect one's social status, to serve the tsar loyally, to revere God, and to live modestly and with sexual propriety. As I've suggested in Chapter 1, honor accrued to all subjects of the tsar, Orthodox and non-Orthodox, East Slavic and not. The only individuals who had no honor were those whose criminal behavior had in effect excommunicated them from the social whole: "thieves, criminals, arsonists and known evil men."[56] But the discourse of honor did not stop at enveloping individuals in the symbolic community of do-gooders. Honor had a concrete, physical dimension, which demarcated the parameters of the honorable community and located its center in the tsar himself. The spatial symbolism of honor in Muscovy transformed the concept of honor into a figurative glue binding all of society.

Far from being distinct from the social order, the tsar himself was its apex and its most honorable member. He claimed extensive protection of his own honor and bequeathed it to state institutions that patrimonially represented him. The tsar's representatives and representations, although inanimate objects, could become subjects of litigation over honor. Documents, seals, and money became the objects of increased protections in the Conciliar Law Code of 1649 in its Chapters 2, 3, 4, and 5; this helps explain why a man was awarded compensation for insult to honor when he was called a minter (*denezhnyi master*, implying counterfeiter) and why officials were punished for inaccuracies or omissions in the tsar's title.[57] The tsar's palace itself was deemed to have honor. For insults and assaults occurring in the tsar's presence or palace, a twofold dishonor fine

---

[56]PRP 4 (1956):421 (art. 71; 1589).

[57]Counterfeiter: RGADA, f. 210, Prikaznyi stol, stb. 876, ll. 1–29 (1683); ibid., stb. 1203, ll. 6–9, 140–58 (1691). Tsar's title: RGADA, f. 210, Novgorod stol, stb. 12, ll. 44–45 (1628); ibid., stb. 272, ll. 3–10 (1677); RGADA, f. 210, Belgorod stol, stb. 652, pt. 1, l. 388 (1670); ibid., stb. 854, ll. 97–100, 119–20 (1677).

was levied, one for the insult to the individual and one for the insult to the tsar himself or to his physical representation, the palace (but the whole payment went to the aggrieved party). Similarly, churches were equally hallowed, enjoying increased fines for affronts on their premises.[58] This is reminiscent of the honor attributed to physical location elsewhere: Thomas Cohen has argued, for example, that early modern Italian cities identified sites, such as certain palaces, as symbols of their municipal dignity and took affront when rivals mocked and desecrated pictures of that special edifice.[59]

The tsar's honor radiated down to his representatives. Officials claimed dishonor when they were not obeyed in service or were treated disrespectfully. The Conciliar Law Code of 1649 made specific provisions to protect the honor of judges before whom litigants behaved impolitely. Judges frequently complained that they had been falsely accused of favoritism in the making of judgments.[60] Dishonor suits arose when private quarrels broke out in front of judges and officials in Moscow chanceries or their provincial equivalents (*s'ezzhie* and *prikaznye izby*) or when litigants or subordinates directly insulted presiding officials.[61] Similarly, as we saw in Chapter 3, officials sued when insulted in performing their duty in the army, as fire wardens (*ob'ezzhie*), or in local administration.

Because officials represented the tsar's honor, their abuses of power were harshly punished, and individuals had the right to claim that abuse of power was dishonoring.[62] Men complained of beatings or imprisonment by a corrupt governor or state secretary and of having been coerced for bribes.[63] They were

---

[58]RZ 3:85–86 (chap. 1); 89–91 (chap. 3). I. E. Zabelin publishes numerous cases of affronts in the palace: *Domashnii byt russkikh tsarei v XVI i XVII st.*, 3 bks. (Moscow, 1990), reprint publ. of 4th exp. ed. (Moscow, 1918), pp. 348–408.

[59]Thomas V. Cohen, "The Lay Liturgy of Affront in Sixteenth-Century Italy," *Journal of Social History* 25, no. 4 (1992):864.

[60]The law: RZ 3:112–13 (chap. 10, arts. 105, 106). Judges complain: RGADA, f. 210, Moscow stol, stb. 1037, ll. 242–47 (1640); RGADA, f. 210, Prikaznyi stol, stb. 746, ll. 118–40 (1676); stb. 431, ll. 269–89; stb. 787, ll. 25–33 (1679).

[61]Quarrels before judges or in government offices: RGADA, f. 210, Prikaznyi stol, stb. 163, ll. 503–6 (1641); stb. 729, ll. 118–28 (1676); stb. 1090, ll. 99–127 (1686); stb. 1075, ll. 54–59 (1686); *Moskovskaia delovaia i bytovaia pis'mennost' XVII veka* (Moscow, 1968), pt. 5, no. 1, pp. 200–1 (1651). Insults to officers: RGADA, f. 210, Prikaznyi stol, stb. 122, ll. 113–208 (1636); stb. 346, ll. 302–4 (1660); stb. 788, ll. 193–206 (1674); stb. 2693, ll. 1–59 (1700); RGADA, f. 210, Belgorod stol, stb. 1286, ll. 437–40 (1679).

[62]For legislation against official corruption, see Horace W. Dewey, "Defamation and False Accusation (*Iabednichestvo*) in Old Muscovite Society," *Etudes slaves et est-européennes/Slavic and East European Studies* 11, pts. 3–4 (Fall–Winter 1966/67):109–20; the law code of 1550: RZ 2:97 (arts. 1, 3, 4, 5), 98 (art. 7), 102–3 (arts. 32, 33), 107 (art. 53), 113 (art. 70); the Conciliar Law Code of 1649, chap. 7, art. 11 (RZ 3:94); the Conciliar Law Code of 1649, chap. 10, arts. 1, 5 (p. 102), 7, 12 (pp. 102–3), 15, 16 (p. 104), 24 (p. 106), 146 (p. 124), 149, 150 (pp. 124–25).

[63]A sampling includes RGADA, f. 210, Prikaznyi stol, stb. 84, ll. 21–24 (1632); stb. 263, ll. 512–13 (1649); stb. 264 (ll. 70–78 (1650); stb. 1086, ll. 1–38 (1684); stb. 580, ll. 1–103 (1666); RGADA, f. 239, Sudnyi prikaz, opus 1, pt. 4, delo 5364, ll. 1–53v. (1704); AIu, no. 61, pp. 102–3 (1679).

insulted when documents were falsified against them or when defendants or witnesses testified falsely against them; they found insult in an official's favoring the other party in a suit because of enmity, corruption, or personal affiliation (*svoistvo*) or in an official's improperly and maliciously enrolling a plaintiff in service in a regiment below his dignity.[64] Most symbolically, the tsars jealously guarded the dignity of the Kremlin.

The Kremlin was a sacred space, its grounds and palaces marked as more and more hallowed the closer one approached the person of the tsar. Legislation from the midseventeenth century on defined with increasing hierarchy the physical limits of access to the Kremlin grounds enjoyed by various ranks. Only the highest ranks could ride into the Kremlin (others had to approach on foot), and even boyars had to dismount at some distance from the portico leading into the tsar's palace. The courtyard closest to the tsar's rooms was closed to all but specially authorized guards and confidants.[65]

The closer to the tsar one came, the more honored the space and the more privileged the individuals admitted to it. The tsar's presence and quarters were therefore charged sites, where individuals felt all the more keenly any affronts to their dignity, particularly because they were surrounded by witnesses from equally exalted ranks. From Cathedral Square, privileged servitors climbed the stairway next to the Palace of Facets or Faceted Chamber (*Granovitaia palata*) to the Red (or Beautiful) Portico (*Krasnoe kryl'tso*). This was a narrow walkway off which were anterooms and a small Golden Palace (or Golden Chamber), with the Cathedral of the Annunciation (*Blagoveshchenskii sobor*) at one end and the Palace of Facets at the other. At the rear of the Palace of Facets was the *Postel'noe kryl'tso* (Tsar's Palace Portico or Boyars' Mezzanine), which was the largest staging area for courtiers in attendance. It contained the stairway by which the most privileged ranks could enter the rooms of the tsar.[66] Courtiers were assigned to attend the tsar in the palace around the clock; incidents typically broke out at various staging points where courtiers gathered.

The *Postel'noe kryl'tso* and the anterooms of the tsar's chambers were the frequent scene of hot words. In 1639, for example, Prince Ivan Araslanov syn Cherkasskii alleged that Prince Ivan Lykov assaulted him in the anterooms and insulted his whole family, while Lykov countered that Cherkasskii had insulted

[64]Malicious enrollment: *Moskovskaia delovaia*, pt. 5, no. 5, pp. 207–10 (1671). Other examples of false testimony and the like: RGADA, f. 210, Prikaznyi stol, stb. 33, ll. 74–77 (1628); stb. 145, ll. 211–14 (1643); stb. 634, ll. 11–14 (1683); stb. 1425, ll. 1–44 (1689); AAE 1, no. 280, pp. 315–16 (1571).

[65]See Kotoshikhin, *O Rossii*, pp. 29–31; PSZ 1: no. 116 (1654), 468 (1670), 901, 902 (1681); and Zabelin, *Domashnii byt*, pp. 326–31.

[66]On the layout of the Kremlin, see the three maps of the Kremlin appended to *Istoriia Moskvy*, 6 vols. in 7 pts. (Moscow, 1952–59), vol. 1; Zabelin, *Domashnii byt*, pp. 115–56; commentary by Benjamin Uroff in Grigorii Kotoshikhin, "*On Russia in the Reign of Alexis Mikhailovich*: An Annotated Translation," Ph.D. dissertation, Columbia University, 1970, pp. 370–75.

him and his family, calling them "insignificant princelings" "before the *stol'niki, striapchie,* and *dvoriane*" gathered there. Another case speaks of insult "before many eminent people" in a Kremlin courtyard.[67] The publicity value that rivals got from the populated setting may account for the colorfulness of the slanders heard. In a case of 1643, a *zhilets* complained that another *zhilets* and his uncles had called him and his family "thieves, traitors, field hands" and had "chased my sons around the Beautiful Portico." Witnesses reported that the plaintiff had responded by calling the defendants "sons of bitches" or "grandsons of bitches" and "little field hands" (*stradnichonki*).[68] In 1646, a Prince Myshetskii alleged that at the *Postel'noe kryl'tso,* two servitors had called him and his family "slaves of boyars," "sons of grooms," "thieves, forgers," while witnesses testified that the two servitors had called him "Prince Scribe" and his son "Prince Undersecretary." Some complained of being called "drunkard" or "Prince Drunkard," while others complained of their social status being denigrated.[69]

As seriously as servitors took affronts in the hallowed halls of the Kremlin, equally seriously did the tsar regard such incidents in his home. They were immediately investigated and punished harshly.[70] The 1649 Conciliar Law Code decreed that for incidents in the tsar's palace, a guilty party should be imprisoned for two weeks for verbal insult and for a month or more for physical assault, and should be executed for fatal blows.[71] Cases bear out the principle of strict sanctions. In 1642, for example, a *stol'nik* was ordered "beaten with bastinadoes mercilessly" for insulting another *stol'nik*'s wife at the *Postel'noe kryl'tso* "as the tsar was walking from the Annunciation Cathedral beyond the gateway on the Feast of the Holy Trinity." Perhaps because of the nearby presence of the tsar, the harshness of this sanction exceeded the later 1649 standards, which would have mandated imprisonment.[72] In several cases, the letter of the law was followed: prison "for the honor of the palace" and a cash dishonor fee for the winning party.[73] In others, norms were exceeded: In 1674, a *striapchii* was severely punished for hitting another *striapchii* in the

----

[67]1639: *Moskovskaia delovaia,* pt. 2, nos. 32, 33, pp. 60, 61. "Eminent people": RGADA, f. 210, Prikaznyi stol, stb. 1425, ll. 1–44 (1689).

[68]Zabelin, *Domashnii byt,* pp. 358–63.

[69]1646: Zabelin, *Domashnii byt,* pp. 370–73. Drunkard: Zabelin, *Domashnii byt,* pp. 379–80 (1651); RGADA, f. 210, Prikaznyi stol, stb. 1013, ll. 22–46 (1669). Calling someone below their social status: Zabelin, *Domashnii byt,* pp. 373–74 (1648), 375–77 (1650); RGADA, f. 210, Moscow stol, stb. 245, ll. 244–324 (resolution published in PSZ 1, no. 75, p. 263) (1651).

[70]The investigatory (*sysk*) framework was mandated for insults in the tsar's presence or palace by the 1649 Conciliar Law Code (RZ 3:89–90 [chap. 3, art. 1]), as litigants sometimes reminded the court (Zabelin, *Domashnii byt,* p. 384 [1675]).

[71]RZ 3:89–90 (chap. 3, arts. 1–5).

[72]Zabelin, *Domashnii byt,* pp. 354–58.

[73]Zabelin, *Domashnii byt,* pp. 374–75 (1649), 375–77 (1650); RGADA, f. 210, Moscow stol, stb. 245, ll. 244–325 (1651); resolution in PSZ 1, no. 75, p. 263; RGADA, f. 210, Prikaznyi stol, stb. 1223, ll. 66–135 (1690); RGADA, f. 210, Prikaznyi stol, stb. 2481, ll. 10–51 (1692).

head with a stone "at the sovereign's palace in front of him, the Great Sovereign." He was sentenced to be beaten with bastinadoes "instead of the knout" and to pay a fourfold dishonor fee, when the 1649 Law Code would have demanded long imprisonment and a twofold dishonor fee for such an offense.[74]

Such incidents also offered the tsar scope for bestowing his mercy, which he often did to spare a high-ranking servitor the humiliation of imprisonment, while maintaining the cash compensation to the victim, thus gratifying both sides. Such was the outcome, for example, of the 1692 case cited in Chapter 3 in which a family of the Golitsyn princes forgave a thousand-ruble dishonor fee. In this case, the tsar had already canceled the order to imprison the two Dolgorukii princes "for the honor of the palace" (they had insulted the Golitsyny in the tsar's very chambers).[75] In one case, the tsar reduced from beating to imprisonment a sentence for hitting a man with a brick in the Golden Palace or Chamber (*Zolotaia palata*), and in another, a man was ordered "beaten with bastinadoes mercilessly" and demoted to provincial service for resisting imprisonment, to which he had been ordered for saying "impolite words" in the tsar's palace. "Not even in simple homes is it appropriate to say such things," he had been told at sentencing. The beating was rescinded, but not the demotion.[76]

Insults in the tsar's sacred space illustrate sharply the utility rulers and subjects made of the discourse of honor. Individuals chose that space to get the most effect out of their antagonisms; plaintiffs rushed to defend their honor before others; rulers exalted their dignity by punishing insults in their home with some of the harshest sanctions available, and they co-opted servitors with mitigating acts of mercy. The flexibility and manipulability of the discourse of honor for all its participants is dramatically demonstrated here.

Ritual and Ceremony

Symbolic communication and ritual were also wielded deftly to promote cohesion. Without making too sharp a distinction, one might distinguish ceremony from ritual by ritual's more transformative power: While ceremony demonstrated political or social relations, ritual could catalyze and transform them. It had "an element of magic."[77] Both, however, constitute a language perceptible to members of the given society, and they serve as particularly

---

[74]DR 3 (1852): col. 1079 (partial publication in Zabelin, *Domashnii byt*, pp. 383–84). Relevant legislation: RZ 3:90 (chap. 3, arts. 2, 5).

[75]RGADA, f. 210, Prikaznyi stol, stb. 1421, ll. 65–129; published almost in full in Zabelin, *Domashnii byt*, pp. 387–94.

[76]Hit with brick: RGADA, f. 210, Prikaznyi stol, stb. 621, ll. 67–88 (1683). Demotion: PSZ 2, no. 1097, pp. 642–43 (1684).

[77]Karl Leyser discusses this distinction: "Ritual, Ceremony and Gesture: Ottonian Germany," in his *Communications and Power in Medieval Europe* (London, 1994), p. 190.

important means of communication in societies in which orality rather than literacy predominated, as in Muscovy. Most court ceremony simultaneously communicated the image of the grandeur of the tsar *and* his intimacy with his boyars. Grand princes always appeared surrounded by advisors. Diplomatic receptions consistently described the ruler receiving envoys with the secular and sometimes the church hierarchy present[78]; in 1488, Ivan III is recorded as refusing to negotiate with a Habsburg envoy without his boyars present.[79] Robert Crummey has argued that visual depictions of rulers and boyars—found in chronicle illustrations, scenes in biographical saints' icons, and similar sources—depicted comradely, not distant and lordly, relations between them.[80] Sixteenth-century Kremlin fresco cycles depicted the realm allegorically as a heavenly army, an image sure to appeal to the boyar elite.[81]

Receptions, banquets, and rituals at court seem to have become more frequent and lavish over the sixteenth and seventeenth centuries,[82] most likely in response to the strains imposed by rapid political expansion in the elite and the empire. Karl Leyser argues, for example, that the tenth-century Ottonian court heightened its use of ritual as a response to perceived social crisis and in response to a decrease in the use of literacy at court.[83] A similar strategy was at work in Muscovy: The challenges of building and administering an empire and managing its growing elite called forth, as we have seen, new strategies of governance, new institutions of social control, and new practices of social hierarchy such as precedence. Not surprisingly, new rituals were also devised in the sixteenth century to demonstrate power relations and integrate elite and people. Elaborate wedding rituals, with assigned roles for members of the high-

[78]SbRIO 41 (1884), 53 (1885), 59 (1887), 71 (1892), 95 (1895). For foreign sources, see Berry and Crummey, eds., *Rude and Barbarous Kingdom*, pp. 129–38; Olearius, *Travels*, pp. 56–78; Bonner Mitchell and Russell Zguta, trans. and eds., "A Sixteenth-Century 'Account of Muscovy' Attributed to Don Felippo Prenestain," *Russian History* 8, pt. 3 (1981):390–412. See coronations described in 1498 (PSRL 8 [1859]:234–36) and 1547 (PSRL 29 [1965]:49–50); for seventeenth-century court rituals, see Robert O. Crummey, "Court Spectacles in Seventeenth-Century Russia: Illusion and Reality," in Daniel Clarke Waugh, ed., *Essays in Honor of A. A. Zimin* (Columbus, Ohio, 1983), pp. 130–58.

[79]*Pamiatniki diplomaticheskikh snoshenii drevnei Rossii s derzhavami inostrannymi*. Pt. 1 (St. Petersburg, 1851): col. 1. A few of countless references to such consultations of boyars and hierarchs with a grand prince: M. D. Priselkov, comp., *Troitskaia letopis'. Rekonstruktsiia teksta* (Moscow and Leningrad, 1950), pp. 364, 369, 372, 378, 380, 384, 386, 392–93, 397, 401, 408, 410, 418, 420, 426, 428, 451–52, 457; PSRL 8 (1859):245, 256, 264, 278, 280, 281, 285–86, 287, 290; PSRL 26 (1959):198, 199, 223, 225, 245.

[80]Crummey, "Court Spectacles."

[81]Daniel Rowland, "Biblical Military Imagery in the Political Culture of Early Modern Russia: The Blessed Host of the Heavenly Tsar," in Flier and Rowland, eds., *Medieval Russian Culture, Vol. II*, pp. 182–212.

[82]For a general survey of ritual at court in the Muscovite period, see Richard S. Wortman, *Scenarios of Power: Myth and Ceremony in Russian Monarchy* (Princeton, N.J., 1995), chap. 1.

[83]Leyser, "Ritual, Ceremony and Gesture."

est elite, began to be recorded and replicated in Ivan III's time; the ceremony of coronation was tried out in a moment of political crisis in 1498 and became a regular ritual from 1547.[84] Over the course of the sixteenth and seventeenth centuries, grandiose liturgical rituals that brought the ruler and his elite outside the Kremlin gained currency; at Epiphany and Palm Sunday, the tsar, church hierarchy, and court elite processed in symbolic dramas that simultaneously acted out theological mysteries and demonstrated the political order.[85]

In addition to demonstrating political relations, court ritual experiences also engaged members of the elite and, quite pragmatically, gave more and more of them opportunity to participate at court. New honorific roles were created to enhance their participation, such as the custom (new in the sixteenth century) of stationing four men, drawn from the highest boyar families, around the tsar's throne at audiences. Called *ryndy*, they wore white caftans and tall hats and carried ceremonial axes. Ritual displays of the elite certainly had the intent of impressing foreign visitors, who duly noted their awe at the splendor and size of the tsar's retinues at court or lining the streets when they first rode into Moscow.[86] But these displays also recreated the community in a cathartic way for its participants and potentially exerted a cohesive force.

Grand princes also regularly used ritual to engage the populace beyond the confines of the Kremlin elite. In processions of the cross, pilgrimages, and military campaigns, tsars acted out the hierarchies and bonds of a "God-dependent" community. In traversing their lands in a ritual manner, rulers "take symbolic possession of their realm," demonstrating its "symbolic center"—that is, its leading ideas and institutions, to use Clifford Geertz's formulation.[87] Muscovite rulers were peripatetic. Their frequent pilgrimages took them to favored

[84]On marriage records, see my *Kinship and Politics*, chap. 4, and Russell Martin, "Royal Marriage in Muscovy, 1500–1725," Ph.D. dissertation, Harvard University, 1996. On the 1498 coronation and its context, see my "Consensus Politics: The Dynastic Crisis of the 1490s Reconsidered," *Russian Review* 45, no. 3 (1986):235–67.

[85]Michael S. Flier, "Breaking the Code: The Image of the Tsar in the Muscovite Palm Sunday Ritual," in Flier and Rowland, eds., *Medieval Russian Culture, Vol. II*, pp. 213–42; idem, "The Iconology of Royal Ritual in Sixteenth-Century Muscovy," in Speros Vyronis, Jr., ed., *Byzantine Studies: Essays on the Slavic World and the Eleventh Century*, (New Rochelle, N.Y., 1992), pp. 53–76; Paul Bushkovitch, "The Epiphany Ceremony of the Russian Court in the Sixteenth and Seventeenth Centuries," *Russian Review* 49, no. 1 (1990):1–18.

[86]On *ryndy*, see Margeret, *The Russian Empire*, p. 54; Jerome Horsey, "Travels," in Edward A. Bond, ed., *Russia at the Close of the Sixteenth Century* . . . (London, 1856), p. 198. On splendid retinues, see Olearius, *Travels*, pp. 56–78 passim; Mitchell and Zguta, trans. and eds., "The Sixteenth-Century 'Account'," pp. 407–11.

[87]Clifford Geertz, "Centers, Kings, and Charisma: Reflections on the Symbolics of Power," in his *Local Knowledge* (New York, 1983), pp. 121–46, and also in Sean Wilentz, ed., *Rites of Power: Symbolism, Ritual, and Politics since the Middle Ages* (Philadelphia, 1985), pp. 13–40. See also Victor Turner, "The Center Out There: Pilgrim's Goal," *History of Religions* 12, no. 3 (1973):191–230; Victor Turner and Edith Turner, *Image and Pilgrimage in Christian Culture: Anthropological Perspectives* (New York, 1978), esp. chap. 1.

monasteries in circuits around the Muscovite heartland, sometimes extending as far north as Beloozero; hunting expeditions took them to summer residences in Kolomenskoe and elsewhere in the Moscow environs.[88] During such outings, they distributed alms to the poor, offered amnesties to prisoners, dined with local dignitaries, and worshipped at local monasteries and shrines, thereby tangibly changing the communities they visited. The effect on beholders of such rituals and images is not recorded, and it undoubtedly varied among individuals. Some perhaps took it as imposed ideology, others might have been transported to greater heights of adulation and political loyalty. In any case, ritual was, in Edmund Leach's phrase, "communicative,"[89] and the message these rituals communicated was that the realm was united from tsar to peasant by Christian piety and humility.

A description of Ivan IV's triumphant entrance in 1562 into Polotsk provides a particularly good example of symbolic communication through ritual. Polotsk had been ruled by the Grand Duchy of Lithuania since the fourteenth century, but it was once part of Kiev Rus' and was now claimed by Moscow as ancient "patrimony." The fact that the chronicle description may well embellish what actually occurred is less important to us than its idealized imagery of sanctification and community. Setting off on the Polotsk campaign in November 1561, the tsar began by establishing his links with legitimizing figures of the Muscovite past: He venerated icons and tombs sacred to the royal family housed in Kremlin cathedrals. Among the sites venerated were the ancient and revered icon of the Vladimir Mother of God (brought to Muscovy from Vladimir, but originally from Kiev) and the tombs of St. Peter and St. Iona (saint-metropolitans closely associated with the grand-princely family) in the Dormition Cathedral. He then visited the tombs of his ancestors in the Archangel Michael Cathedral across Cathedral Square. Then, with his male kin, the church hierarchy, and the court elite, he joined a procession of the cross on foot to the Church of SS. Boris and Gleb (saintly princes, patrons of the Riurikide dynasty since Kievan days) outside the Kremlin in order to venerate icons associated with his ancestor Dmitrii Donskoi's victory over the Tatars in 1380. In doing so, he left the closed environs of the Kremlin for the domain of the people and thus broadened the social impact of his procession.

Ivan IV then took with him on campaign several revered icons, including a bejeweled gold cross said to have been housed originally in Polotsk. In January, in the recently conquered Velikie Luki on the way to Polotsk, on the eve of joining battle, the tsar took part in prayers and processions of the cross around the perimeter of the town. Going on foot to demonstrate his humility, he wor-

---

[88]See my "Pilgrimage, Procession and Symbolic Space in Sixteenth-Century Russian Politics," in Flier and Rowland, eds., *Medieval Russian Culture, Vol. II*, pp. 163–81.

[89]Leach, "Ritual."

On the eve of his wedding, Tsar Mikhail Fedorovich is described as processing among Kremlin monasteries and cathedrals to pray at revered shrines. Here, in the Cathedral of the Archangel Michael, he venerated graves of his ancestors. (Illustration: P. P. Beketov, *Opisanie v litsakh torzhestva, proiskhodivshogo v 1626 goda . . .* [Moscow, 1810]. Courtesy Rare Book and Manuscript Library, Columbia University.)

shipped and dined in a monastery while the perfidious Grand Duchy forces fired on his party from across the Western Dvina River. When the city had been taken in February, the tsar entered on foot in a procession of the cross, repeatedly falling on his knees at the sight of icons and of cross processions sent to greet him, and heard the liturgy in the city's main Orthodox cathedral. In the evening, the tsar feasted with his kinsmen and generals as well as with church hierarchs and military leaders from the conquered city, whom he favored with gifts in a gesture of reconciliation.

Then the tsar sent word back to Moscow that he had regained his "patrimony" "with God's help" and with that of SS. Peter, Aleksii, Iona (sainted metropolitans, especially patronized by the grand-princely family), and a list of more than twenty named saints associated with many regions of his realm (e.g., Novgorod, Rostov, Beloozero), thereby demonstrating Polotsk's integration into the tsar's dominions.[90] He ordered bells rung in celebration in Moscow and services sung in thanksgiving and, in a show of largesse, sent gifts to the leading Moscow boyars and the metropolitan of the church. In a spirit of reconciliation, the tsar bestowed fur coats on more than five hundred Polotsk city leaders, giving them freedom to join his service or to leave to serve in the Grand Duchy. As the tsar returned home in March, he was welcomed by emissaries from Moscow at various points, where he stopped to worship or to banquet with his men and relations. Arriving in Moscow, he was met with a procession of the cross led by Metropolitan Makarii at the same Church of SS. Boris and Gleb from whence the tsar had departed. Here the tsar worshipped, gave thanks, and then entered Moscow on foot humbly with the procession. Throughout the account, Ivan is presented as God's humble servant, as generous comrade to his men, as judicious protector of Russia's heritage, and as benevolent ruler and reconciler. The symbolism of his activities stressed the (somewhat fictive) "organic" unity of Polotsk with Muscovy, drawing the new region into Muscovy by a combination of coercion, largesse, and historical symbolism.[91]

Muscovite rulers also defined the "symbolic center" of their realm with aggressive building projects. Ivan III (ruled 1462–1505) and Vasilii III (ruled 1505–33) transformed the Kremlin from an ensemble of mostly wooden structures to an exquisite stone ensemble, glittering with gold leaf and onion domes and magnificent in the magnitude and variety of its edifices. The new buildings demonstrated Moscow's imperial conquests by including elements of Novgorod and Pskov architecture; they proclaimed Moscow's cosmopolitan status with the Renaissance details on the Italian-built Archangel Michael Cathedral.[92] And the centerpiece of it all, the Cathedral of the Dormition or *Uspenskii sobor* (1479), became a ubiquitous symbol of the legitimacy of Muscovite rule, not only because it was explicitly copied from the Vladimir Dormition Cathedral and thus symbolized historical continuity, but also because it became the canonical style in which grand-princely–patronized churches were thereafter constructed throughout the realm. Cathedrals copying the massive Kremlin model were built in Iaroslavl' (1506–16), in Moscow at the Novodevichii Convent (1524), in Rostov (early sixteenth century), in Pereslavl'-Zalesskii (1557), in Vologda (1568–70), at the Trinity–St. Sergii Monastery outside Moscow (1559–85), and elsewhere. Grand princes also left visual images of

[90]Significantly, Polotsk's patron saint, Evfrosiniia (d. 1173), was not mentioned (PSRL 13:360, 361), although manuscript survival would suggest that her cult continued to flourish in the sixteenth century. This was perhaps an oversight of a Muscovite chronicler unaware of local traditions or an intentional demotion of a cult judged too vigorous. On her vita, see E. M. Voronova, "Zhitie Evfrosinii Polotskoi," in *Slovar' knizhnikov i knizhnosti drevnei Rusi*, 3 vols. in 5 pts. to date (Leningrad, 1987–), 1:147–48. Thanks to Eve Levin for raising this issue.

[91]PSRL 13:346–49, 357–65 (7071). For descriptions of a similar processions in 1552 (Kazan') and 1562 (Velikie Luki), see my "Pilgrimage."

[92]N. Ia. Tikhomirov and V. N. Ivanov, *Moskovskii kreml'. Istoriia arkhitektury* (Moscow, 1967).

The Kremlin ensemble established Moscow's symbolic center. Its architecture symbolically co-opted the political legitimacy of the Grand Principality of Vladimir, demonstrated Moscow's conquests of neighboring areas, and displayed Muscovy's foreign contacts with its Italianate flourishes. The central Cathedral of the Dormition set an architectural pattern that was then disseminated throughout the tsar's realm. (Photograph: Jack Kollmann.)

their authority in the form of new churches and monasteries built to commemorate military victories (Sviazhsk, 1551; Kazan', 1552; Narva, 1558) or to establish new centers of grand-princely patronage (Mozhaisk, 1563; Pereslavl'-Zalesskii, 1564). In this, Muscovite rulers were not alone: Sixteenth-century European rulers also assiduously disseminated their particular imperial style in architecture, iconography, and ritual to announce their power in their realms.[93]

These ritual moments promoted both political legitimacy and social cohesion by "inventing tradition," to invoke Eric Hobsbawm and Terence Ranger. They argued that nation-states build community by constructing myths and festivities based on history—accurate or generously interpreted.[94] Here we have seen Muscovite rulers and ideologues, for example, consciously evoking or inventing tradition by calling on a pantheon of previous grand princes and by celebration of cults of saints particularly associated with the grand-princely family.[95] Similar strategies, aimed at promoting territorial unity of the tsar's lands, included the promotion of cults of miracle-working icons from the provincial hinterlands. These venerated objects were transported with special ceremony to Moscow, where they were copied and returned with equal fanfare to their hometowns. By such co-optation, such venerations created a sacral link between center and periphery.[96] The church's recognition of numerous local saints' cults from the midsixteenth century similarly co-opted regional energies into the central community of faith.[97] The process was also going on in narrative texts—a prime example is Metropolitan Makarii's historical compilations, the *Book of Degrees* (*Stepennaia kniga*) and *Great Menology* (*Velikie minei chetii*), which situated Muscovy in the chronology of universal Christendom.[98] Similarly, the prolif-

[93]See Richard Bonney, *The European Dynastic States, 1494–1660* (Oxford, 1991), chap. 9. Janet Martin also cites the political symbolism of architecture: *Medieval Russia*.

[94]Eric Hobsbawm and Terence Ranger, eds., *The Invention of Tradition* (Cambridge, England, 1983).

[95]Günther Stökl, "Staat und Kirche im Moskauer Russland. Die vier Moskauer Wundertäter," *Jahrbücher für Geschichte Osteuropas* 29 (1981):481–93.

[96]See, e.g., PSRL 30 (1965):190; 13:305 (7066). This is a fascinating practice, deserving of further study. See examples of veneration of local icons in Moscow: 1395: PSRL 23 (1910):134; 26 (1959):282–85 (both 6903). 1401: PSRL 23:138; 11:184–85 (both 6909). On these relics, see also PSRL 23:136–37 (6906). 1456: PSRL 25 (1949):273–74 (6964). 1514: PSRL 8:254; 34:11 (both 7022). See examples of restoration and copying of local icons in Moscow: Vladimir: PSRL 30:141 (7022); PSRL 34 (1978):11, 13 (7022, 7026, 7028); A. A. Zimin, ed., *Ioasafskaia letopis'* (Moscow, 1957), pp. 173–74 (7026), 180–81 (7028). Rzhev: PSRL 23:205; 20:411 (both 7039); PSRL 34:173; 29:36 (both 7048). Viatka: PSRL 34:189 (7062, 7068); 13:254 (7063), 273 (7064). Novgorod: PSRL 30:174 (7069).

[97]Paul Bushkovitch, *Religion and Society in Russia: The Sixteenth and Seventeenth Centuries* (New York and Oxford, 1992), chap. 4.

[98]Miller, "*Velikie Minei Chetii.*"

eration of genealogical tales in the fifteenth century, of both the dynasty and boyar clans, mixed historical fact with "invented" traditions in the form of mythic ancestries dating back to ancient Rome. Celebrating a common past, even if a fictive one, gave a theory of community to a disparate realm.

Political Practices of Cohesion

Beyond the realm of ideas, Muscovite rulers supported a number of cultural practices that involved individuals directly in a dialogue with the established powers. One such practice was petitioning, the expectation that individuals could directly address the ruler with requests and grievances and that the ruler personally was the font of largesse and justice. The petition was the documentary form of all official bureaucratic requests for action. In their formulaic salutations and conclusions, petitions describe the personal relationship of individuals to the ruler: "To the Tsar, the Sovereign and Grand Prince of all Rus' Aleksei Mikhailovich, your slave, the kinless, helpless Ivashko Pronskoi petitions. . . . Tsar! Favor me, kinless and defenseless! Do not order me to be in dishonor from such lowly people."[99] Through most of Muscovite history, individuals had the right to petition the sovereign directly, analogous to the "petitionary order" that Geoffrey Koziol describes at the heart of early medieval French politics.[100] Only beginning in 1649 were Muscovites enjoined from giving petitions to the tsar, and the frequent repetition of this directive suggests how ingrained was the expectation of direct, physical access to the ruler.[101] By the very act of transcribing one's concerns in the form of a personal request for favor, individuals bolstered the pillars of autocratic legitimacy and also initiated processes that often satisfied their grievances.

Another social practice that emanated from the hegemonic discourse was consultation and collective judgment. As previously noted, in theory, Muscovite sovereigns were expected to consult the people, and the people had a moral obligation to advise the tsar. And in practice, rulers did defer to this expectation. In doing so, they paralleled consultative activities practiced by European rulers from medieval kings to absolute French monarchs; the practice, in other words,

[99]RGADA, f. 210, Prikaznyi stol, stb. 686, ll. 63, 64 (1675). The petitioner is the Boyar Prince Ivan Petrovich Pronskoi, in boyar rank from at least 1652 to 1683 (Crummey, *Aristocrats and Servitors*, p. 190).

[100]Geoffrey Koziol, *Begging Pardon and Favor: Ritual and Political Order in Early Medieval France* (Ithaca, N.Y., 1992).

[101]Valerie Kivelson discusses this point with reference to 1648: "The Devil Stole His Mind: The Tsar and the 1648 Moscow Uprising," *American Historical Review* 98, no. 3 (1993):755. The texts: PSZ 1: nos. 1 (chap 10, art. 20; see also chap. 1, arts. 8–9); 2: no. 1092; 3: no.1707; 4: no. 1748; 5: no. 3261; 6: nos. 3838, 3947 (1649, 1684, 1699, 1700, 1718, 1721, 1722, respectively).

did not necessarily limit monarchical power.[102] Usually this process of consultation was confined to the Kremlin: Tsars consulted their boyars or a smaller "inner circle" on day-to-day affairs; at ritual events, they were attended by the patriarch, other church hierarchs, and the assembled boyars in a symbolic demonstration of collective judgment. But it could be expanded to involve society: Tsars could instruct governors to assemble the populace and solicit complaints and petitions, which were then to be acted on locally by the governor or sent to Moscow for action. Or it could be done in more ritualized venues, as when the tsar formally summoned all his boyars and hierarchs to discuss such issues as his decision to be married (1547) or church reform (1551).

The logical extension of this mandate was the tsar's summoning of a much broader social representation when the policy to be considered had a wider impact. Such large assemblies met sporadically from the midsixteenth to the midseventeenth century. They generally considered only one issue posed by the ruler, such as the settlement of war and peace, tax increases, or legal reform. Deliberation was collective, and consensus was the goal; these gatherings offered advice to the ruler, not a decision per se. Some assemblies were summoned with ample advance warning and called forth elected representatives from all social groups save the enserfed peasants; others were cobbled together from those servitors who happened to be in Moscow for muster. Surviving sources reflect the informality of this practice: Few such assemblies are documented by formal charters or records of deliberations, and some are known only from passing references in chronicles.[103]

Contemporary sources described only the process of assembling and consulting and did not label these activities with any collective noun, as later historians did (calling them *zemskie sobory*, or "councils of the land"[104]). These were not parliamentary institutions, as scholars, especially in the Soviet era, have construed them.[105] True parliamentary institutions exhibited several key

---

[102]Susan Reynolds, *Kingdoms and Communities in Western Europe, 900–1300* (Oxford, 1984), chaps. 1, 2, 8, esp. pp. 21–32; Nicholas Henshall, *The Myth of Absolutism: Change and Continuity in Early Modern European Monarchy* (London and New York, 1992).

[103]L. V. Cherepnin over-assiduously compiled all possible references to such assemblies: *Zemskie sobory Russkogo gosudarstva v XVI–XVII vv.* (Moscow, 1978).

[104]Hans-Joachim Torke notes that the term originates with Konstantin Aksakov: "Continuity and Change in the Relations between Bureaucracy and Society in Russia, 1613–1861," *Canadian Slavic Studies* 5, no. 4 (1971):461.

[105]Cherepnin's *Zemskie sobory* is a classic statement of this position. See critiques by Edward L. Keenan in *Kritika* 16, no. 2 (1980):82–94, and Peter B. Brown, "The *Zemskii sobor* in Recent Soviet Historiography," *Russian History* 10, pt. 1 (1983):77–90. For similar, less institutional, approaches, see Richard Hellie, "*Zemskii sobor*," *Modern Encyclopedia of Russian and Soviet History* 45 (1987):226–34; Hans-Joachim Torke, *Die staatsbedingte Gesellschaft im moskauer Reich. Zar und Zemlja in der altrussischen Herschaftsverfassung, 1613–1689* (Leiden, 1974), chap. 4; idem, "Reichsversammlung," in idem, ed., *Lexikon der Geschichte Russlands* (Munich, 1985), pp. 317–19.

characteristics: fixed regularity of meetings; representative, not mass member-ship; multicameral structure; and real authority over legislation and/or the fisc.[106] Lacking these traits, Muscovite assemblies nevertheless filled an impor-tant niche in the political structure.

Consultative assemblies like these offered arenas for political activity on many levels. Following Durkheim, they can be seen as cathartic rituals of com-munication, giving physical embodiment to the theoretical godly community of the realm and inspiring participants to identify with it. More tangibly, they provided channels of communication of central policy to the provinces and venues of acceptable challenge to government policy. Hans-Joachim Torke, for example, has chronicled how the government responded to some of the collec-tive grievances advanced by gentry and merchants in the seventeenth century; Valerie Kivelson accounts how provincial gentry internalized the tenets of this political code and conducted political protest accordingly; Richard Hellie chronicled the role of the 1648 council in the compilation of the 1649 Concil-iar Law Code.[107] These assemblies were not merely top-down avenues of imposed ideology or empty ceremony. They were spheres in which significant contestation and negotiation could occur within the symbolic framework of consultative autocracy.

Many strategies, including the willingness not to interfere, worked together to create social stability in Muscovy. I should not exaggerate the degree of social stability that Muscovy achieved; like many premodern societies, it was a violent place. Most of the time, individuals related to the state in the unwel-come venues of taxation and recruitment or not at all. It was not a very admirable system, as few premodern systems would be to modern eyes. The state's ability to control territory, people, and resources came at great cost— enserfment and the diversion of resources from high culture, education, and social welfare to the needs of war and the support of a privileged elite. This was a calculus with which most premodern rulers were comfortable, however. Accepting these ground rules, one can conclude that Muscovite society achieved enough cohesion to allow the state to accomplish its essential tasks. Cohesion came from a combination of factors: coercive control; tolerance of local autonomies; distribution of rewards; effective dissemination of unifying ideas in laws, texts, and ritual; and the ability of individuals to interpret and manip-ulate the dominant ideas and institutions to their own ends within bounds acceptable to the state.

[106]For a comparative study, see Stanisław Russocki, "The Parliamentary Systems in 15th-Cen-tury Central Europe," *Poland at the 14th International Congress of Historical Sciences in San Francisco* (Wrocław and Warsaw, 1975), pp. 7–21.

[107]Torke, *Die staatsbedingte Gesellschaft*, chap. 3; Kivelson, *Autocracy in the Provinces*, chaps. 7 and 8; idem, "The Devil Stole His Mind"; Richard Hellie, "Ulozhenie Commentary—Preamble," *Russian History* 15, nos. 2–4 (1988):181–224.

Honor and its praxis provided a particularly potent means for individuals to pursue their self-interest within the framework of state-affirming institutions. By combining values that ratified the social totality and institutions sanctioned by the tsar with individual initiative, litigations on honor gave society an arena in which people and government both benefited. This connection should not be romanticized; individuals need not have liked the state to manipulate its values and institutions.[108] But in so engaging with those values and institutions, they reinforced the dominant culture to some degree. Precisely because institutions of honor fostered a dynamic relationship between daily life and the normative consensus asserted by the dominant culture, they were one source of stability for Muscovy's far-flung, multinational empire. They are emblematic of the flexibility that made autocracy viable in Muscovy: Autocracy worked not by isolating the ruler and his men in their power, but by involving society in the exercise of that power.

[108]Giddens makes such ambivalence a central aspect of his definition of social cohesion: *A Contemporary Critique . . ., Vol. 1*, pp. 45–46.

CHAPTER 6

Toward the Absolutist State

In January 1682, Tsar Fedor Alekseevich, surrounded by the ecclesiastical hierarchy, boyars, and scores of courtiers, ceremoniously ended the preference given to family heritage and service in the assignment of military rank and office (*mestnichestvo*). He burned records of precedence disputes and decreed harsh punishment for anyone who dared again to sue a colleague over "place." At first glance, this desecration of a Muscovite institution that had endured 150 years seems a momentous step, rejecting the centrality of honor in the Muscovite scheme of social values in favor of some new ethos. But that was not the case. It was not in the realm of social values that the abolition of precedence signified a transformation. Honor remained a paramount concern for Russians of all ranks, and the government remained equally willing to defend it. The abolition of precedence grew out of deep changes in state and elite in the seventeenth century, changes that created a more dynamic elite and strengthened autocracy without fundamentally disturbing traditional patrimonial values. It was a culmination and affirmation of seventeenth-century change, rather than a radical break with the past.

Here I examine seventeenth-century change in three areas—service patterns and composition of the elite, the mentality of the elite, and changing conceptions of the nature and purpose of power—in order to set the context for the abolition of precedence in 1682. I range widely into the Petrine era to demonstrate continuities of old and new, continuities in the social importance of honor, and continued development of the complementary ideas of autocracy and elite.

Forging a New Elite

The seventeenth century started as a time of political restoration. The story is a familiar one. The initial decades after the Time of Troubles were devoted to stabilizing the western border with Sweden and with the Commonwealth of Poland–Lithuania. By midcentury, Muscovy was moving aggressively beyond these tribulations. The empire expanded east across Siberia to the Pacific, south into the steppe, and southwest to Ukrainian lands, bolstered by the Thirteen Years' War (1654–67), in which left-bank Ukraine and Kiev came into the Russian fold under the continued control of the Zaporozhian Cossack Hetman.

To meet the challenge of the early modern European "military revolution," military reform proceeded apace. War on the western frontier mandated large infantry armies recruited from the populace, equipped with firearms and uniforms, and trained in modern tactics and soldierly discipline.[1] Although it had dabbled with modifications in the traditional "feudal levy" army since the mid-sixteenth century,[2] Muscovy moved systematically to transform its armed forces from an old-fashioned cavalry to a large-scale, modern infantry army during the Thirteen Years' War. Russia entered the war in 1654 with an army of forty thousand and ended the war in 1667 with more than one hundred thousand; within those numbers, the proportion of new-model troops increased from 7% to 79% at the expense of many categories of traditional forces.[3]

Concomitantly, institutions and spheres of governance grew to serve the expanding state; the realm was subdivided into military administrative districts, presaging the 1708 *guberniia* reform.[4] The number of chanceries burgeoned from forty-four in 1626 to fifty-three in 1656 and fifty-nine in 1677, leveling to fifty-three in 1682 and fifty-five in 1698 after some consolidation of offices. Consolidation did not mean downsizing. The number of state secretaries (*d'iaki*) in Moscow and in the provinces grew steadily from 78 in 1626 to 116 in 1656, 139 in 1677, 140 in 1682, and 154 in 1698. The total number of bureaucratic officers—judges, state secretaries, and undersecretaries—in

---

[1] On the military revolution, see Michael Roberts, "The Military Revolution, 1560–1660," in his *Essays in Swedish History* (London, 1953), pp. 195–225; Geoffrey Parker, *The Military Revolution: Military Innovation and the Rise of the West, 1500–1800* (Cambridge, England, 1988); Michael Howard, *War in European History* (Oxford, 1976); David B. Ralston, *Importing the European Army: The Introduction of European Military Techniques and Institutions into the Extra-European World, 1600–1914* (Chicago, 1990).

[2] Survey of reforms: John L. H. Keep, *Soldiers of the Tsar: Army and Society in Russia, 1462–1874* (Oxford, 1985), chaps. 3–4; Richard Hellie, *Enserfment and Military Change in Muscovy* (Chicago and London, 1971), chaps. 9–12; A. V. Chernov, *Vooruzhennye sily Russkogo gosudarstva v XV–XVII vv.* (Moscow, 1954).

[3] Chernov, *Vooruzhennye sily*, pp. 167–68.

[4] S. K. Bogoiavlenskii and S. B. Veselovskii, "Mestnoe upravlenie," in *Ocherki istorii SSSR. Period feodalizma. XVII vek* (Moscow, 1955), pp. 384–94. On the military districts, see Chernov, *Vooruzhennye sily*, pp. 170–72, 187–98; Peter Bowman Brown, "Early Modern Russian Bureaucracy: The Evolution of the Chancellery System from Ivan III to Peter the Great, 1478–1717," 2 vols., Ph.D. dissertation, University of Chicago, 1978, pp. 496–500.

Moscow's chanceries grew even faster: in 1626, 656; in 1656, 762; in 1677, 1,601; in 1682, 1,816; and in 1698, 2,762.[5] The growth of the bureaucratic apparatus was paralleled by a movement to regularize such work more explicitly than ever before. In rules issued from 1658 through the 1670s, the hours of work of state secretaries and boyars were defined; by the late 1670s, chanceries were being consolidated by function, and the drawing up of regularized budgets was mandated.[6] The result for the populace was more taxation, more government, and more control. The seventeenth century was one of jarring bureaucratization and state intervention, in comparison with the more laissez-faire policies of the sixteenth century.[7]

For the landed elite, the century was one of challenges and opportunities. On the one hand, the traditional raison d'être of the elite's privileges—its military service—was being eroded by military reform: Old-style troops were being eased into the new regiments so thoroughly that by 1680, the army had twice as many infantry as cavalry. Only a small group of wealthy families (10% of the whole army) remained old-style cavalry.[8] The elite was becoming militarily obsolescent. But the state moved consistently to preserve it as a privileged group, because doing so turned the elite into a de facto local bureaucracy and because such a policy avoided disruptive social unrest in a politically essential class. To accomplish this, over the century the government pursued various strategies, including redistribution and restoration of land to the upper elite and gentry,[9] enserfment, and numerous policies designed to make the servitor class a closed estate. For example, some laws prevented people of nongentry

---

[5]N. F. Demidova, *Sluzhilaia biurokratiia v Rossii XVII v. i ee rol' v formirovanii absoliutizma* (Moscow, 1987), pp. 23–24, Tables 1, 3, and 2, respectively.

[6]Defining hours: PSZ 1, nos. 237 (1658), 461 (1669), 477 (1670), 582 (1674); PSZ 2, no. 621 (1676). Budget: PSZ 2, nos. 802 and 842 (both 1680). Chancery reform: Brown, "Early Modern Russian Bureaucracy," pp. 485–500.

[7]This is a key theme of Kivelson's work: Valerie A. Kivelson, *Autocracy in the Provinces: The Muscovite Gentry and Political Culture in the Seventeenth Century* (Stanford, 1996), pp. 249–50, 261–65, and idem, "The Devil Stole His Mind: The Tsar and the 1648 Moscow Uprising," *American Historical Review* 98, no. 3 (1993):733–56.

[8]On the fate of the gentry army, see Hellie, *Enserfment*, pp. 198, 211–25. On the frontier, see Carol Belkin Stevens, *Soldiers on the Steppe: Army Reform and Social Change in Early Modern Russia* (DeKalb, Ill., 1995), chap. 1; Chernov, *Vooruzhennye sily*, chap. 7; Keep, *Soldiers*, pp. 80–87.

[9]For general discussions of state policy toward land and servitors in the seventeenth century, see Iu. V. Got'e, *Zamoskovnyi krai v XVII veke* (Moscow, 1906); idem, *Ocherk istorii zemlevladeniia v Rossii* (Sergiev Posad, 1915), pp. 58–101; Jerome Blum, *Lord and Peasant in Russia from the Ninth to the Nineteenth Century* (New York, 1969), chaps. 11–12; Hellie, *Enserfment*, chap. 3; A. A. Novosel'skii, "Feodal'noe zemlevladenie. Boiarstvo, dvorianstvo i tserkov'," in *Ocherki istorii SSSR. ... XVII vek*, pp. 139–64; E. Stashevskii, *Ocherki po istorii tsarstvovaniia Mikhaila Fedorovicha*, pt. 1 (Kiev, 1913); M. F. Vladimirskii-Budanov, *Obzor istorii russkogo prava*, 6th ed. (St. Petersburg–Kiev, 1909), pp. 547–73. Specific legislation: ZA, no. 86, pp. 93–94 (1618/19), 173, p. 142 (February 7, 1628).

background from serving in cavalry ranks or receiving service land grants[10]; others limited the transfer of land to specified groups of kinsmen, servitors from a given province, and the like; others tightened clan control over the transfer of patrimonial land.[11] These steps continued the sixteenth-century policy, discussed in the Introduction, of forging regional solidarity by limiting rights of land transfer. Still other laws sharpened the social distinctions between foreigners and nonforeigners in cavalry service and closed access to gentry status and landholding to semiprivileged groups, such as contract servitors.[12]

Similar dynamics were at work in women's landholding rights, whereby the state tried both to limit women's rights to inherit patrimonial property and to maintain families' economic viability by giving women broader control or usage rights over service-tenure lands and purchased hereditary estates. Women's landholding rights actually expanded over the seventeenth and early eighteenth century, reflecting the growing de facto corporate status of the landed elite. As George Weickhardt writes of the eighteenth century: "Owning land . . . [became] merely a prerogative of membership in the noble class rather than a means of equipping and provisioning servitors. . . . It thus made little sense by the eighteenth century to continue to deprive women of control over land or to prohibit some land from passing out of clan control by allowing inheritance by wives and daughters."[13]

In essence, the militarily obsolescent elite was being turned into a local landlord class, a de facto estate lacking only juridical status. Servitors were accorded more and more authority over their peasants and over their service-tenure land, which was approaching the legal status of patrimonial land.[14] Service requirements were lessened. In 1632, obligations for some—perhaps all—servitors were reduced from six months to four months annually, and servitors with fewer than fifteen adult male peasants were exempted from service. In 1642, gentry-

[10]AMG 1, no. 40, p. 65 (1601); AMG 1, no. 44, p. 78 (1606); see also Hellie, *Enserfment*, pp. 48–49, 53–54.

[11]ZA nos. 85, p. 93 (August 27, 1618), 156, p. 129 (before July 11, 1627), 230, p. 169 (March 7, 1636), 239, p. 177 (April 1, 1637), 271, p. 190 (June 29, 1639); Blum, *Lord and Peasant*, pp. 183–85; Hellie, *Enserfment*, pp. 56–57.

[12]Foreigners: ZA nos. 79, p. 85 (1615/16), 198, p. 156 (no later than May 8, 1630), 224, pp. 165–66 (no later than April 30, 1635). Close access: Chernov, *Vooruzhennye sily*, pp. 156–69; Hellie, *Enserfment*, p. 211.

[13]George Weickhardt, "Legal Rights of Women in Russia, 1100–1750," *Slavic Review* 55, no. 1 (1996):1–23, quote on p. 22; Ann M. Kleimola, "'In accordance with the Canons of the Holy Apostles': Muscovite Dowries and Women's Property Rights," *Russian Review* 51, no. 2 (1992): 204–29.

[14]On peasants as chattel: Novosel'skii, "Feodal'noe zemlevladenie," and Blum, *Lord and Peasant*, chap. 14. On the convergence of service-tenure and patrimonial land tenure, see Hellie, *Enserfment*, pp. 53–58; Vladimirskii-Budanov, *Obzor*, pp. 561–73; Got'e, *Zamoskovnyi krai*, pp. 382–84. Relevant legislation on landholding is published in PRP 7 (1963):35–129, and RZ 4 (1986):290–310 (1714).

men with fewer than fifty adult male peasants were excused from service, opening the window of exemption much wider, and in 1653, the service obligation
was lowered to three months.[15] The government also bolstered the economic
viability of the gentry by awarding them, over the course of the 1620s, prefer-
ential rights—such as lower prices for grain, freedom from billeting troops, and
lower taxes for their peasants—and by allowing men who had joined the Cossacks in the Time of Troubles to regain their previous status, even gentry rank.[16]

A more vibrant local nobility developed in the provinces. Valerie Kivelson
points out that gentry in the second half of the seventeenth century took advantage of growing state willingness to allow them to send proxies for military service so that they could stay home and tend their estates. John Keep estimates
that by the end of the century, about only one in five provincial gentrymen was
actively engaged in military service; the rest dwelled full time on their estates.[17]
At the same time, the Moscow-based elite was making great inroads into local
land ownership, with many of its more than 6,300 members living and serving
in the provinces by 1681.[18]

In the highest ranks of the Moscow-based elite, servitors responded by diver-
sifying their service, moving into bureaucratic service in addition to traditional
military roles.[19] They developed literacy and governing skills; they became
"noble servitors." Their numbers grew as much from political tensions as from
the increasing needs for administrative leadership. For about seven years after
Aleksei Mikhailovich's accession in 1645, the size of the conciliar elite steadily
grew, from about thirty to thirty-five in the early 1640s to sixty by 1652. The
number stayed roughly in the sixties until the mid-1670s when, with a severe
succession crisis, the numbers surged again. In the tense politics of succession
that followed Tsar Aleksei Mikhailovich's death in 1676 and endured until
Peter I consolidated power in 1689, the conciliar ranks burgeoned twice, first
in Fedor Alekseevich's reign (d. 1682), when the roughly sixty-five to seventy
boyars grew in number to eighty-seven in 1676 and to ninety-nine by 1681.
Precipitous growth then continued during the minority of the two boy tsars—

---

[15]1632: AMG 1, no. 322, p. 341. 1642: Blum, *Lord and Peasant*, p. 187. July 1, 1653: PSZ 1,
no. 100, p. 291. See also Kivelson, *Autocracy in the Provinces*, p. 44.

[16]On leniencies, see Hellie, *Enserfment*, pp. 48–50, 59–60. Return to status: ZA no. 66, p. 80
(between February 1613 and July 1615).

[17]John Keep, "The Muscovite Elite and the Approach to Pluralism," *Slavonic and East European Review* 48, no. 3 (1970):211; Kivelson, *Autocracy in the Provinces*, p. 44.

[18]Novosel'skii, "Feodal'noe zemlevladenie," p. 154.

[19]Robert O. Crummey, *Aristocrats and Servitors: The Boyar Elite in Russia, 1613–1689* (Princeton, N.J., 1983), and idem, "The Origins of the Noble Official: The Boyar Elite, 1613–1689," in
Walter M. Pintner and Don Karl Rowney, eds., *Russian Officialdom: The Bureaucratization of
Russian Society from the Seventeenth to the Twentieth Century* (Chapel Hill, N.C., 1980), pp.
46–75. See also Borivoj Plavsic's article in the same collection, "Seventeenth-Century Chanceries
and Their Staffs," pp. 19–45.

Ioann V and Petr Alekseevichi—and regency of Sofiia Alekseevna (1682–89), when the number of boyars rose from 107 in 1682 to 145 in 1686, peaking at 153 in 1690 after Peter began consolidating his power in 1689. Robert Crummey notes that this period not only brought in many families new to the highest ranks but also introduced a new phenomenon: favoritism. Many of the new appointments were young men from the highest families who occupied themselves only with attendance at court, not with productive service in the military or civil administration.[20] The net effect of the growing number of men in high ranks was to create an elite of relatively new families with power and status, but not "rank" in traditional genealogical or service terms.

A social fissure between the "aristocratic" clans and lesser families in the conciliar ranks was graphically attested to in a 1678 land survey. Of men in the conciliar ranks, "aristocratic" families possessed an average of 817.1 peasant households, while less eminent families averaged only 200.9 peasant households. These eminent families—one-seventh of the entire Moscow-based elite in 1678–81—owned 42.4% of all the land granted to these high ranks. Pavel Sedov's study of the Moscow-based elite in the 1670s starkly illustrates these trends. On one hand, untitled new families flooded into the Moscow-based nobility, with, for example, the number of *stol'niki* doubling from 1676 to 1681, primarily with men from new families. On the other hand, the conciliar ranks remained a preserve of the aristocrats: When the number of boyars tripled under Fedor Alekseevich (ruled 1676–82), only two of the new appointees came from nonaristocratic backgrounds.[21] The process continued into the 1690s, when laws (which proved difficult to enforce) in theory closed the aristocratic preserve by preventing men from the provincial ranks from entering the lower Moscow-based ranks of *stol'nik, striapchii,* and *dvorianin moskovskii.*[22]

A de facto aristocracy was being created, which, as we shall see, reflected itself in the reforms surrounding the abolition of precedence. One sees this fissure in changes in the style of governing and in heightened consciousness of social hierarchy. Affectations such as new titles that set apart the highest elite began to appear: Prince V. V. Golitsyn, regent Sofiia's closest advisor, styled himself the "privy counselor" (*blizhnii boiarin*) and took on the honorific title of "Guardian (*oberegatel'*) of the Tsar's Great Seal and of Great State Ambassadorial Affairs." Decrees established distinctions between social groups in

---

[20]Crummey, *Aristocrats and Servitors*, pp. 29–30, 175–77.

[21]P. V. Sedov, "Sotsial'no-politicheskaia bor'ba v Rossii v 70x–80x godakh XVII veka i otmena mestnichestva," Candidate dissertation, Leningrad State University, 1985, chap. 1, Table 2, Appendix 2, and the abstract for this dissertation, esp. pp. 5–7. For more on the landholding of the wealthiest, see Crummey, *Aristocrats and Servitors*, chap. 5.

[22]S. M. Troitskii, *Russkii absoliutizm i dvorianstvo v XVIII v. Formirovanie biurokratii* (Moscow, 1974), p. 41.

public ceremonies, official terminology, and the like, all with the effect of elevating the status of the highest ranks of the Moscow-based elite. A decree of 1668, for example, specified different degrees of ornamentation to be used for various ranks in land-grant charters (for only the highest ranks, for example, could cinnabar be used). In 1659, state secretaries (*dumnye d'iaki*) were declared to rank higher than privileged merchants; in 1677, *kravchie* (an honorific court rank) were decreed to be superior to *okol'nichie*. The lesser conciliar ranks of state secretaries and state gentrymen (*dumnye dvoriane*) had their dignity defended in laws of 1680 and 1685, which decreed that their names should be written with their patronymic in official records; in 1692, even nonconciliar state secretaries were given this honor.[23]

Rules, enunciated particularly in the 1670s and 1680s, graphically exhibited the hierarchy of ranks by decreeing what ranks should walk and what ranks had the right to ride on horseback or in carriages in the Kremlin grounds, and how far those who had the right to ride could go before dismounting, and by what gate which ranks should enter the Kremlin grounds and the palace itself, and the like. In 1681, it was decreed that homes of elite servitors should thereafter be built in stone, a physical representation of the owners' eminence as well as a fire prevention measure.[24] In the 1670s, for the first time in Russian history, sumptuary laws were enunciated to standardize public dress and to distinguish social groups and status. In 1675, it was decreed that no servitors were to wear foreign dress or foreign hairstyles, and laws of 1668 and 1675 defined the proper dress for each rank to wear on various ceremonial occasions. A law of October 23, 1680, decreed that all servitors should wear proper service garb, and another law of that year defined ceremonial clothing for various holy days for various ranks. A law of 1697 forbade the lower servitor ranks in Siberia to wear "luxury clothes."[25] A new elite was thus being forged. Concurrently, its mentality was being shaped in different ways than tradition had once mandated; new attitudes toward self and public life were emerging that prepared the grounds for political change.

---

[23]"Guardian": PSZ 2, no. 958 (1682); PSZ 2, no. 1134 (1685). 1668 charters: PSZ 1, no. 422. 1659 merchants: PSZ 1, no. 247. 1677 *kravchie*: PSZ 2, no. 701. 1680, 1685, patronymic: PSZ 1 nos. 851 and 1106. 1692: PSZ 3, no. 1436.

[24]Access to Kremlin: PSZ 1, nos. 116 (1654), 468 (1670); PSZ 2, nos. 901–2 (1681), 1064 (1684). See also Grigorii Kotoshikhin, *O Rossii vo tsarstvovanie Alekseiia Mikhailovicha*, 4th ed. (St. Petersburg, 1906), pp. 29–31 (chap. 2, arts. 14–16); I. E. Zabelin, *Domashnii byt russkikh tsarei v XVI i XVII st.*, 3 bks. (Moscow, 1990), bk. 1, pp. 320–31 (reprint publ. of 4th exp. ed., Moscow, 1918). Stone houses: PSZ 1, no. 892 (1681).

[25]1675: PSZ 1, no. 607. 1668, 1675, 1680: PSZ 1, nos. 429 and 609. 1680: V. K. Nikol'skii, "Boiarskaia popytka 1681 g.," *Istoricheskie izvestiia, izd. Istoricheskim obshchestvom pri Moskovskom universitete*, 1917, bk. 2, p. 75; PSZ 2, no. 850. 1697: PSZ 3, no. 1598. Peter reversed these sumptuary rules, mandating Western dress (see footnote 84 below).

Piety and a New Cultural Ethos

Unlike earlier Muscovite texts that preached preservation and avoidance of change,[26] seventeenth-century texts and cultural practices validate change, albeit within the Orthodox idiom. Slowly and narrowly—affecting the literate members of the landed elite—but unmistakably, elite Muscovites embraced new ways of thinking about self, state, and society, ways that shifted their focus from the collective to the individual and made precedence's defense of quintessentially clan behavior that much less immediate.

Historians have long explored Russia's contacts with the West in the seventeenth century, placing particular attention on the import of technical military expertise from Northern Europe and the influx of reformist trends in Orthodoxy from Ukraine and Belarus' that helped lead to the Schism in the Russian Orthodox Church.[27] Recent scholarship, however, has also explored the impact of European culture on piety and mentality. Paul Bushkovitch, for example, has shown how trends in religious thought encouraged the cultivation of the individual. In response to the Time of Troubles, to enserfment, and to state centralization, some in the elite turned to a more personal morality, focusing as early as the 1620s on the cultivation of the individual through learning and a pursuit of virtues such as charity and humility. These themes were taken up in the 1630s by the Zealots of Piety (*Bogoliubtsy*) and other later religious reformers who advocated a more personal experience of the faith. By midcentury, Ukrainian-trained scholars such as Epifanii Slavinetskii and Simeon Polotskii preached to the court elite a personal ethic of "virtue" construed in Renaissance terms. Virtue was embodied by learning, piety, probity, humility, charity, and public service. In identifying with an ethic that "moved beyond asceticism to a morality designed for action in the world," Bushkovitch argues, the elite created a social environment receptive to change in government and society.[28]

Trends in printing promoted more secular interests as well. From the 1630s on, printing expanded under the aegis of tsar and church. Liturgical and pietistic texts were in the forefront of published titles, but publications in history, science, military arts, and other fields also began to appear. Books published in the last half of the century included handbooks of modern military warfare; translations of classical authors, such as Thucydides and Pliny the Younger on

[26]This was a key theme in the Protocols of the 1551 *Stoglav* Church Council; see Jack E. Kollmann, Jr., "The Moscow *Stoglav* ('Hundred Chapters') Church Council of 1551," Ph.D. dissertation, University of Michigan, 1978. Ivan Timofeev similarly attributed the Time of Troubles to change in customs: *Vremennik* (Moscow and Leningrad, 1951), pp. 110–11.

[27]S. F. Platonov, *Moskva i zapad* (Leningrad, 1925); Georges Florovsky, *Ways of Russian Theology: Part One*, in idem, *Collected Works*, vol. 5 (Belmont, Mass., 1979).

[28]Paul Bushkovitch, *Religion and Society in Russia: The Sixteenth and Seventeenth Centuries* (New York, 1992), quote on p. 179.

law and civil administration; geographies of Europe and Asia; and medical textbooks.[29] A narrow literate elite developed. S. M. Solov'ev reported that in 1652, Prince Repnin-Obolenskii returned to Russia from Poland with the following books: a Slavic-Russian lexicon; a dictionary of German, Latin, and Polish; a Polish bible; Piasecki's *Chronicle*; and Guagnini's *History*.[30] Numerous individuals collected libraries of both religious and secular works. In 1689, Prince V. V. Golitsyn's library included works on diplomacy, history, military arts, architecture, medicine, and heraldry. He may not have read them all; we do know that he could read Latin. The library of Sylvester Medvedev (a pupil of Simeon Polotskii and member of Sofiia Alekseevna's court circle) was larger (651 books) and more scholarly.[31] Literate Muscovites were embracing a classical sense of military glory, associating virtue with public service and personal achievement. The Foreign Office (*Posol'skii prikaz*) library included books on the "history of Assyrian, Persian, Greek, Roman and Russian military campaigns," as well as lists of world rulers, historical and present.[32]

Further suggesting new attitudes toward self, the scope of scholarly and literary compositions expanded dramatically in the seventeenth century. The first evidence of secular poetry is witnessed: In verse form, state secretaries and clerics associated with the Printing Office (*Pechatnyi dvor*) in the 1630s through 1650s wrote about the importance of education as a path to morality, a source of praise for oneself, and a benefit to the tsar.[33] New genres were experimented with—the traditional annalistic form of history writing was supplemented with classical-style "histories," which were more narrative and interpretive. A. P. Bog-

---

[29]V. S. Rumiantseva, "Tendentsii razvitiia obshchestvennogo soznaniia i prosveshcheniia v Rossii XVII veka," *Voprosy istorii* 1988, no. 2:28; Lindsey Hughes, *Sophia, Regent of Russia, 1657–1704* (New Haven, Conn., and London, 1990), pp. 165–68; Gary J. Marker, *Publishing, Printing and the Origins of Intellectual Life in Russia, 1700–1800* (Princeton, N.J., 1985), pp. 19–20; A. S. Demin, *Pisatel' i obshchestvo v Rossii XVI–XVII vekov* (Moscow, 1985); L. N. Pushkarev, *Obshchestvenno-politicheskaia mysl' Rossii. Vtoraia polovina XVII veka* (Moscow, 1982); A. N. Robinson, *Bor'ba idei v russkoi literature XVII veka* (Moscow, 1974); D. S. Likhachev, *Razvitie russkoi literatury X–XVII vekov*, in his *Izbrannye raboty*, 3 vols. (Leningrad, 1987), vol. l.

[30]S. M. Solov'ev, *Istoriia Rossii s drevneishikh vremen*, 29 vols. in 15 bks. (Moscow, 1959–66), 13 (1962):142–44; Florovsky, *Ways of Russian Theology: Part One*, p. 105.

[31]Golitsyn was recorded as having 93 books in his Moscow home and 123 more at his other properties. His collection is discussed in Abby Finnogh Smith, "Prince V. V. Golitsyn: The Life of an Aristocrat in Muscovite Russia," Ph.D. dissertation, Harvard University, 1987, pp. 239–44; Hughes, *Sophia*, pp. 170–71; idem, *Russia and the West: The Life of a Seventeenth-Century Westernizer, Prince Vasily Vasil'evich Golitsyn (1643–1714)* (Newtonville, Mass., 1984), pp. 87–88; S. P. Luppov, *Kniga v Rossii v XVII veke* (Leningrad, 1970), pp. 107–10.

[32]Solov'ev, *Istoriia Rossii* 13:146–47; Hughes, *Russia and the West*, p. 88; David Das, "History Writing and the Quest for Fame in Late Muscovy: Andrei Lyzlov's *History of the Scythians*," *Russian Review* 51, no. 4 (1992):502–9.

[33]Bushkovitch, *Religion*, pp. 140–45; A. M. Panchenko, *Russkaia stikhotvornaia kul'tura XVII veka* (Leningrad, 1973).

danov argues that the last quarter of the seventeenth century witnessed the rise of modern historical research, based on classical models and a Renaissance-inspired critical approach to the sources and driven, as he puts it, by "the intense reflections of learned men on the paths of the country's further development."[34] By the end of the century, picaresque tales were being written; panegyrics and playful poetry testify to a new willingness to experiment and to explore personal feelings and secular themes.[35]

Schools were founded on the Jesuit model to train active citizens through the study of grammar, rhetoric, history, the sciences, and languages. In 1649, a Greek-Latin Academy was founded in Moscow by one of the leading Zealots of Piety, Archpriest of the Annunciation Cathedral Stefan Vonifat'ev. In 1650, a secular member of the Zealots, F. M. Rtishchev, founded such a school in the Andreevskii monastery in Moscow. In 1665, Simeon Polotskii founded an academy in the Zaikonospasskii Monastery, which taught Russian and Latin to state secretaries; in 1680, he authored a charter for a Slavonic-Greek-Latin Academy modeled on the Kievan Mohyla Academy, which was finally opened in 1687. In 1680, the Printing Office opened a secular school for its staff. The Jesuits even opened a school in Moscow in the 1680s. None of these endeavors survived long, but they are indicative of cultural ferment.[36]

What resulted from this ferment was not wholesale rejection of Muscovite values, but integration of new ideas into the old synthesis. These wide-ranging trends toward cultivation of the individual—so hailed by students of Russian literature and culture of the seventeenth century (D. S. Likhachev depicts the era as Russia's Renaissance)[37]—added new dimensions to personal lifestyle but

---

[34]A. P. Bogdanov, *Ot letopisaniia k issledovaniiu. Russkie istoriki poslednei chetverti XVII veka* (Moscow, 1995), quote on p. 503.

[35]On the range of literary activity, see William Edward Brown, *A History of Seventeenth-Century Russian Literature* (Ann Arbor, Mich., 1980); L. V. Cherepnin, *Russkaia istoriografiia do XIX veka. Kurs lektsii* (Moscow, 1957), chap. 5; S. A. Peshtich, *Russkaia istoriografiia XVIII veka*, 3 vols. (Leningrad, 1961–71), vol. 1 (1961), chaps. 2–3; M. A. Alpatov, *Russkaia istoricheskaia mysl' i Zapadnaia Evropa XII–XVII vv.* (Moscow, 1973); E. V. Chistiakova and A. P. Bogdanov, *"Da budet potomkam iavleno": Ocherki o russkikh istorikakh vtoroi poloviny XVII veka i ikh trudakh* (Moscow, 1988); A. P. Bogdanov, "Letopisnye i publitsisticheskie istochniki po politicheskoi istorii Rossii kontsa XVII veka," Candidate dissertation, Institute of the History of the USSR of the Academy of Sciences of the USSR, 1983; V. P. Grebeniuk, ed., *Panegiricheskaia literatura petrovskogo vremeni* (Moscow, 1979).

[36]Rumiantseva, "Tendentsii," pp. 39–40; Florovsky, *Ways*, pp. 112–13; Hughes, *Sophia*, pp. 161–66; C. Bickford O'Brien, *Russia under Two Tsars, 1682–1689: The Regency of Sophia Alekseevna* (Berkeley and Los Angeles, 1952), p. 55.

[37]See D. S. Likhachev, *Razvitie*, and his *Chelovek v literature drevnei Rusi* (Moscow, 1958); L. A. Chernaia, "Problema chelovecheskoi lichnosti v russkoi obshchestvennoi mysli vtoroi poloviny XVII–nachala XVIII veka," Abstract of candidate dissertation, Moscow State University, 1980. But see Victor M. Zhivov's relevant reflections: "Religious Reform and the Emergence of the Individual in Russian Seventeenth-Century Literature," in Samuel H. Baron and Nancy Shields Kollmann, eds., *Religion and Culture in Early Modern Russia and Ukraine* (DeKalb, Ill., 1997), pp. 184–98.

did not displace the old. Most written and visual expression and cultural practice retained the Orthodox idiom to explore new problems of personal virtue or new views of space and time, and those individuals who did explore new cultural practices in a more secular idiom—Prince V. V. Golitsyn and Tsar Aleksei Mikhailovich are notable examples[38]—remained devoted Orthodox believers and patrons at the same time. Meanwhile, the church was working to improve the moral and educational level of parish life, to regularize spiritual practices such as cults of saints and relics, and to bring religion closer to believers by expanding the number of dioceses.[39] The late seventeenth century integrated new concepts of self and society into traditional patterns of autocracy more organically than did Peter in the next generation.

Muscovites, however few, were carving out a "private sphere," whereas traditionally no such space had been recognized for private sensibilities. In traditional Muscovy, for the elite, private life was fused with public. Marriage, family, and clan structured politics, and clan status and Orthodox traditions constrained individuals' deportment. By the second half of the seventeenth century, power politics was still shaped by family, but individuals had more options in daily life. Aristocrats were seeking a sphere for the expression of individual interests and associations, a place where the ties of clan and tradition did not bind so tightly.[40] They cultivated a personal lifestyle, carving out niches of leisure time and developing summer residences luxuriously provisioned with libraries and imported furniture. Not only is Prince V. V. Golitsyn famed for summer residences and refined personal tastes, but so also were his contemporaries, such as Golitsyn's distant cousin Prince Boris Golitsyn, Bogdan Khitrovo, A. S. Matveev, and others in progressive elite circles.[41] They appointed their homes with luxury goods, demonstrating their sophistication, education, and personal taste. Prince V. V. Golitsyn assembled in his private homes portraits of contemporary and historical luminaries—Grand Prince Vladimir I of Kiev, Ivan IV and his successors through Petr and Ioann Alekseevichi, Patriarch Nikon, the King and Queen of Poland—as well as clocks, furniture, and mirrors of German, Italian, and Persian manufacture and ceilings decorated with signs of the zodiac.[42] On display in the State Armory Museum are some of Prince V. V. Golit-

---

[38]See V. O. Kliuchevskii's masterful portrayals of seventeenth-century men who straddled old and new (Tsar Aleksei Mikhailovich, Prince V. V. Golitsyn, F. M. Rtishchev, A. L. Ordin-Nashchokin): *Kurs russkoi istorii* in *Sochineniia*, 8 vols. (Moscow, 1956–59), vol. 3 (1957), lects. 56–58.

[39]Bushkovitch, *Religion*, chap. 3.

[40]This is a key theme of Abby Finnogh Smith's dissertation, "Prince V. V. Golitsyn," esp. chap. 6.

[41]On seventeenth-century boyars' residences, see Crummey, *Aristocrats and Servitors*, pp. 143–50; Smith, "Prince V. V. Golitsyn," pp. 228–38.

[42]On Golitsyn's portrait collection, see Hughes, *Sophia*, p. 145; idem, "The Moscow Armoury and Innovations in Seventeenth-Century Muscovite Art," *Canadian-American Slavic Studies* 13 (1979):207; and the inventory of Golitsyn's library and home in Hughes, *Russia and the West*, pp. 87–88, 94–96.

syn's German silver service (forty-six items) and two silver goblets from Germany presented to Aleksei Mikhailovich and to his son Aleksei by Boyar Boris Ivanovich Morozov. Bogdan Matveevich Khitrovo gave Tsar Aleksei Mikhailovich a small European-style carriage; A. S. Matveev gave him a black German coach with glass windows and a double roof, and to Tsar Fedor Alekseevich he gave a carriage with landscapes on the exterior and velvet interiors.[43]

A more modern consciousness of the self and the private is evidenced also in dress and self-image in this era. Contrary to his popular image, Prince V. V. Golitsyn wore Russian dress most often, but he had a wardrobe of luxurious examples of contemporary Western clothes as well. He dressed to suit his personal fancy, wearing European outfits on occasional hunting expeditions.[44] Men of these generations willfully fashioned their self-images as individuals, contrasting sharply with the sense of self exhibited earlier by the Muscovite elite in genealogical books, where individuals were subsumed into their clans. Late seventeenth-century elite men actively had their virtues exalted in panegyrics. Prince V. V. Golitsyn commissioned a panegyric to himself in 1689 by Karion Istomin, which praised his noble birth and personal deportment: "Among boyars the noble prince is famed; He [Golitsyn] is strong in courage and free in battle . . . for the eternal glory of the Golitsyn clan." Other contemporaries also commissioned panegyrics, such as Prince Boris Golitsyn and his wife and Prince M. A. Cherkasskii and his wife.[45]

In addition to collecting portraits of eminent personalities, individuals had their own likenesses reproduced, including Tsar Aleksei Mikhailovich. In 1671, he was depicted in oils, a departure from the egg-tempera paints of icons and a superior medium for reproducing the three-dimensional illusionism of post-Renaissance European art. In 1678, both Patriarch Ioakhim and Tsar Fedor Alekseevich sat for portraits; in 1682, Tsar Fedor Alekseevich commissioned an oil portrait of his father.[46] Prince V. V. Golitsyn commissioned his portrait at least twice, once to celebrate his role in forging the "eternal peace" treaty with Poland in 1686 and once to put a favorable spin (in modern-day parlance) on his participation in the disastrous Crimean campaigns.[47] His cousin Prince Boris Golitsyn also commissioned his own portrait, as did the diplomat A. L.

---

[43]Golitsyn's silver: V. N. Ivanov, ed., *Oruzheinaia palata* (Moscow, 1964), p. 249. Morozov's gift: V. S. Goncharenko and V. I. Narozhnaia, *Oruzheinaia palata. Putevoditel'* (Moscow, 1995), p. 188. Morozov was a boyar from at least January 1634 until his death in November 1661: Crummey, *Aristocrats and Servitors*, p. 184. Khitrovo and Matveev: Solov'ev, *Istoriia Rossii* 13:136.

[44]Smith, "Prince V. V. Golitsyn," pp. 238–39.

[45]Smith, "Prince V. V. Golitsyn," pp. 188–91; the poems to Princes V. V. and B. A. Golitsyn are published in A. P. Bogdanov, ed., *Pamiatniki obshchestvenno-politicheskoi mysli v Rossii kontsa XVII veka. Literaturnye panegiriki*, 2 vols. (Moscow, 1983), nos. 26 and 25, respectively.

[46]Hughes, "Armoury," p. 207.

[47]Hughes, *Russia and the West*, pp. 101–2; Smith, "Prince V. V. Golitsyn," pp. 178–79, 188–92.

Ordin-Nashchokin and the bureaucrats A. S. Matveev and V. S. Volynskii.[48] Such requests, and the use of secular painting to decorate private and tsarist residences, account for the increasing number of European painters in Moscow in the second half of the seventeenth century. Many of them worked in the Armory; by 1683, the Armory's icon-painting workshop had created a separate branch for such secular painting.[49]

Some of these court painters decorated regent Sofiia Alekseevna's quarters in 1686, painted frescos with the secular subject of "heavenly bodies with clouds" in the Palace of Facets (Faceted Chamber) in 1684, and provided the backdrops for theatrical productions at the Kremlin court, an unprecedented entertainment.[50] Such theatricals, first performed at the Kremlin court in the year of Peter I's birth (1672), often even used musical instruments, traditionally forbidden by the church. The church's disapproval of such Western pastimes—shown when six carriages of "diabolical" musical instruments were burned by the church in 1649—stayed constant, but the use of musical instruments nevertheless grew as the century developed. S. M. Solov'ev states that at a banquet in 1674, Tsar Aleksei Mikhailovich himself played the organ and pipes.[51] A school for acting was founded in 1673 in Moscow by A. S. Matveev, and plays were enjoyed regularly from Aleksei Mikhailovich's time.[52]

People were beginning to enjoy themselves in cultural practices and leisure activities that bespeak individual sensibilities and alternatives to old ways of doing things. This is not to say that autocracy and its cultural code were being replaced—rather, a more dynamic sense of self and state was being integrated into the autocratic idiom. Orthodoxy remained the cultural code for court ritual and the focus of spiritual practice for most subjects of the tsar; family and clan were still paramount referents for individuals. Abby Finnogh Smith makes this argument particularly forcefully concerning the quintessentially progressive man of the late seventeenth century, Prince V. V. Golitsyn: His political success and his eventual downfall were both predicated on familial and factional alliances, the likes of which had structured Muscovite politics for at least three centuries.[53] Nevertheless, more room was being accorded to individual differences, and more tolerance for change was being engendered. It is not surprising that these new trends are reflected in the evolving rhetoric and praxis of autocracy.

---

[48]Smith, "Prince V. V. Golitsyn," p. 178.

[49]Hughes, "Armoury."

[50]Hughes, "Armoury," pp. 205–12; Hughes, *Russia and the West*, pp. 2, 40.

[51]Hughes, *Russia and the West*, p. 1; Solov'ev, *Istoriia Rossii* 13:128.

[52]Solov'ev, *Istoriia Rossii* 13:137.

[53]Smith, "Prince V. V. Golitsyn," esp. pp. 63–77. Some of his correspondence is published in *Vremennik Imp. Obshchestva istorii i drevnostei rossiiskikh*, vols. 7 (1850) and 13 (1852). On Muscovite politics, see Nancy Shields Kollmann, *Kinship and Politics: The Making of the Muscovite Political System, 1345–1547* (Stanford, 1987).

A New Sphere for Politics

A spirit of change within traditional idioms took place in political life as well, with new emphases on the ability of the individual to contribute to society, the obligation of government to serve the common good, and the authority of the state as an abstract entity. All these concepts paved the way for Peter I. The traditional autocratic theory of a God-dependent realm was being revised in the late seventeenth century toward a more activist vision. Paralleling the expanding private sphere for the individual, government leaders began to carve out a public sphere, an arena in which the state intervened to tend the worldly needs of the realm. Thus the self-contained clan politics of traditional Muscovy, where public and private were fused, gave way to a more dynamic state. While never abandoning the goal of leading their people to salvation, rulers took on the responsibility of improving life for their subjects here on earth.

The epitome of more utilitarian views of state and society was Simeon Polotskii (d. 1680). Born in Belarus', educated in Jesuit-style schools in Ukraine, Polotskii came to Moscow in 1663 to tutor Tsar Aleksei Mikhailovich's sons Aleksei and Fedor and daughter Sofiia and became active in polemical and pedagogical activities at court.[54] While in sermons he advanced the cause of personal cultivation and education, in other writings he developed the concept of the state's obligation to the common good. His encyclopedia of knowledge, written in verse in articles arranged alphabetically—"The Many-Flowered Garden" (*Vertograd mnogosvetnyi*)—describes a secular vision of state and society. In another essay, Polotskii makes his debt to Aristotle explicit when he spells out the distinction between a just ruler and a tyrant: "If you wish to know who is a tsar and who is a tyrant, / try to read the books of Aristotle. / He thinks the difference is this: The tsar / wishes for and seeks benefits for his subjects, / While the tyrant serves only himself, showing little concern for society." In "The Leader" (*Nachal'nik*), Polotskii defines the obligations of a good ruler in a deft mixture of Christian and Aristotelian theory: "Shepherds walk together ahead of the sheep, / leading them to good pasture; / So also it is the duty of rulers / to go before their flock of subjects, / to lead them to the pasture [of] health, safety, and / divine law, not contrary [to the] laws of human society." In this poem, he melds new secular concepts of ruler and state with traditional Muscovite views. He goes on to define six virtues and expectations of a ruler: that he defend piety; that he be humble, understanding that he will not rule forever; that he not rely on himself alone, but always seek the advice of wise men; that he protect the truth and judge great and small equally; that he

---

[54]On his career and writings, see Florovsky, *Ways*, pp. 106–12; Solov'ev, *Istoriia Rossii* 13:149–54; Douglas J. Bennet, "The Idea of Kingship in 17th-Century Russia," Ph.D. dissertation, Harvard University, 1967, pp. 233–51.

not heed flatterers; and finally, that he be gentle and meek, for which qualities God loves men.[55] In a project for an academy styled on Jesuit schools, Polotskii further defined the duties of the ruler in a secular, utilitarian vein:

> The first and foremost duty [of the ruler] is defense of the eastern Orthodox faith, and that of expanding well-being. These two duties are related to zealous concern for the orderly direction of the state and for defense.[56]

In the late seventeenth century, knowledge of classical authors—previously not part of traditional Russian learning—was not limited to Polotskii. A. S. Matveev owned a copy of Aristotle's *Politics*; in 1676, Aristotle's *Economics* was translated from the Polish; in 1678, *On the Ordering of the Commonwealth*, by the classically inspired Polish humanist Andrzej Frycz-Modrzewski, was translated into Russian.[57]

On the broadest scale, rulers from Aleksei Mikhailovich on demonstrate an increasingly interventionist attitude toward society; the religious realm is a particularly good barometer of this. Although the state had always shared responsibility with the church for punishing heresy, the repression of the Old Belief exhibited a more activist conception of the state, for example. Although no doctrinal issue was at stake and therefore no heresy was involved, the government repressed the Old Believers for their *civil* disobedience. The church council of 1681/82 branded Old Believers civil criminals, and by 1684, they were being vigorously persecuted.[58] From the Old Believers' viewpoint, the state's more active role in spiritual life represented deep rupture with tradition.[59] The state, however, was acting on a reformed vision of self that demanded greater attention to society.

The tsars took other steps to promote religious life in the second half of the seventeenth century, paralleling the more activist policies characteristic of European absolutist states. Numerous laws introduced secular involvement in

---

[55]Aristotle: Simeon Polotskii, *Izbrannye sochineniia* (Moscow and Leningrad, 1953), pp. 15–16; English translation by Bennet in "The Idea of Kingship," p. 240. "The Ruler": Polotskii, *Izbrannye*, pp. 11–15; full translation in Bennet, "The Idea of Kingship," pp. 239–42. English translations of some of these texts can also be found in S. M. Solov'ev, *History of Russia, Vol. 24: The Character of Old Russia*, ed., trans., with intro. by Alexander V. Muller (Gulf Breeze, Fla., 1987), pp. 218–22.

[56]Bennet, p. 248 (his translation), quoting N. I. Novikov, ed., *Drevniaia rossiiskaia vivliofika* . . ., 2d ed., 20 vols. (Moscow, 1788–91), 6:398–99.

[57]Bennet, "The Idea of Kingship," pp. 251–52.

[58]PSZ 2, no. 1102 (1684).

[59]See Michael Cherniavsky, "The Old Believers and the New Religion," in idem, ed., *The Structure of Russian History: Interpretive Essays* (New York, 1970); Robert O. Crummey, *The Old Believers and the World of Antichrist: The Vyg Community and the Russian State, 1694–1855* (Madison, Wis., 1970), chap. 1; Florovsky, *Ways*, chap. 3.

religious observance: A law of 1649 decreed that bureaucrats not work from noon on Saturday through Sunday or on holy days; one from 1653 mandated that the land and property of some non-Orthodox Germans in Russian service be seized because they failed to allow their peasants to observe Orthodox holy days; one from 1659 required people of all ranks to go to confession and observe Holy Week fasts; one of 1660 decreed that the Monasterial Chancery be sent lists of those who failed to fulfill the above obligations; another from that year required all people to observe the fast of St. Filipp. An edict of 1668 ordered that individuals not ride or walk at night on Cheese Fast (*Syrnaia nedelia*) in Lent; numerous laws regulated respectful behavior during processions of the cross; a decree in 1669 ordered a man's peasants imprisoned for working on Sundays. The clergy were increasingly drawn into reporting to the government popular conformance with religious ritual.[60] The church as an institution was also not immune to increasing government involvement. Primarily to gain more revenues, but also to free the church from nonspiritual tasks, tsars attempted, not completely successfully, to assert greater control over its secular affairs, epitomized by the abortive formation of the Monastery Chancery in the midseventeenth century.[61]

Similar activist measures had emerged in post-Reformation Europe to fill the vacuum in social and cultural services left by the abandonment of Catholicism. They were legitimized by new ideologies—such as Lutheran Pietism—and paired with economic theories—such as mercantilism—that mandated that the state be dynamic and interventionist in the economic arena. These conjunctions of religious, social, and economic changes stimulated the construction of the so-called "well-ordered police state," the dynamic absolutist state.[62] Russia, pushed by many analogous social, economic, and ideational pressures, paralleled Europe in this development, drawing inspiration from its Ukrainian conduit to European ideas. Secular "police" measures are seen in Muscovy in, for example, a law of 1683 condemning unruly behavior in the streets, two laws of 1684 forbidding shooting inside one's home and defining orderly behavior in the Kremlin, and one of 1685 curbing litter on the public streets.[63] Neither in Europe nor in Muscovy did these measures mark a very radical departure

---

[60]1649: PSZ 1, no. 21. 1653: PSZ 1, no. 103. 1659–60: Solov'ev, *Istoriia Rossii* 13:127. 1668: PSZ 1, no. 423. Cross procession: PSZ 1, no. 430 (1668); PSZ 2, nos. 1089 and 1095 (both 1684). 1669: PSZ 1, no. 453. On early eighteenth-century edicts requiring the clergy to report to the state, see Cherniavsky, "The Old Believers," p. 171.

[61]Brown, "Early Modern Russian Bureaucracy," 2:588; Bennet, "The Idea of Kingship," pp. 217–18. The Monastic Chancery was abolished in 1677.

[62]See Marc Raeff, *The Well-Ordered Police State: Social and Institutional Change through Law in the Germanies and Russia, 1600–1800* (New Haven, Conn., 1983), and his "The Well-Ordered Police State and the Development of Modernity in Seventeenth- and Eighteenth-Century Europe: An Attempt at a Comparative Approach," *American Historical Review* 80, no. 5 (1975):1221–43.

[63]1683: PSZ 2, no. 984. 1684: PSZ 1, no. 1064, and PSZ 2, no. 1093. 1685: PSZ 2, no. 1181.

from traditional expectations of government, but rather an intensification of and greatly broadened scale for government activity, a step toward a more self-conscious and manipulative engagement with society.

We also see gradual changes in attitudes toward political actors. There was a trend away from a patrimonial vision of politics—one in which all are joined in a householdlike community linked by personal bonds of patrimonial authority and deference, and all are devoted to advising and leading, so that everyone from the tsar to the lowliest peasant will achieve salvation. The new trend, while still Orthodox in content, moved toward a more rational, socially stratified, and nonaffinitive image of who plays a role in political life, how that role is achieved, and how the political order is structured. There was some change in the image of the tsar. Starting in 1649, individuals were forbidden to petition the tsars directly.[64] According to a law in June 1680, the tsar was depicted as a less religious figure than previously: Petitioners were instructed not to address him in terms likening him to God; rather, they should simply "wish him long life and good health."[65] A similar decree in 1681 that boyars and men of conciliar (*dumnye*) ranks not be prostrated to likewise suggested a less patrimonial image of political actors.[66] It took decades for the underlying attitudes in these laws to be assimilated, but in theory, the tsar and his state were officially being depicted as more human, their concerns and obligations as more mundane.

The language and symbols of politics were wielded more aggressively in two ways. First, they were used to affirm the traditional message that the tsar and his religious and secular attendees symbolized God's blessing on the realm and the means by which the people would achieve salvation. Regent Sofiia Alekseevna was herself most assiduous in participating in public religious ceremony to legitimize her power in traditional terms. Although her very status as regent and de facto ruler was evidence of an opening of political opportunities, her political positioning was traditional. She presented herself as the "pious Sovereign Tsarevna" and persecuted religious dissent more forcefully than had her predecessors.[67] She was eulogized in a 1688 panegyric as "God-given" and praised for punishing the heresies of the Schism and the Uniate Church. Karion Istomin eulogized her in the same year: "Most virtuous maiden, chosen of God, most pious tsarevna . . . you are a source of great joy not only to all Russians . . . but also to many Christian peoples all over the world."[68]

---

[64]PSZ 1, no. 1 (1649: chap 10, art. 20; see also chap. 1, arts. 8–9); PSZ 2, no. 1092 (1684); PSZ 3, no. 1707 (1699); PSZ 4, no. 1748 (1700); PSZ 5, no. 3261 (1718); PSZ 6, nos. 3838 (1721), 3947 (1722).

[65]PSZ 2, no. 826.

[66]PSZ 2, no. 875.

[67]Lindsey A. J. Hughes, "Sophia, 'Autocrat of All the Russias': Titles, Ritual, and Eulogy in the Regency of Sophia Alekseevna (1682–89)," *Canadian Slavonic Papers* 28, no. 3 (September 1986):264–86; Hughes, *Sophia*, passim, esp. chap. 6.

[68]Both sources cited in Hughes, "Sophia, 'Autocrat'," p. 281.

Second, political language and symbolism were used to promote the concepts of virtue and morality in classical and Old Testament imagery. Sofiia Alekseevna, whose first name in Greek means "wisdom," was frequently personified allegorically as the Eastern Orthodox concept of "Sophia" or "Divine (God's) Wisdom"; in writers of her court, the theme of wisdom—connoting secular learning as opposed to tradition and piety—became prominent in discussions of good rulers. Here is Karion Istomin's tribute:

> For all rulers rule with wisdom; And all the elite commands well; And all is administered with wisdom; And all the people live in peace because of it. . . . All good things exist in the world because of it; The people gain reason and riches.[69]

The accent here is on the worldly accomplishments and fame of the ruler, rather than on heavenly goal and reward.

Public symbolism was also used to promote a more personal image of the ruler and of political actors, as seen in the tsars' distribution of commemorative medals. Fedor Alekseevich had engravings made to commemorate his marriage, and in 1678, he minted coins in celebration of a military victory. In 1683, Lazar Baranovych printed a panegyric to the two tsars. Regent Sofiia in particular understood the use of political propaganda to achieve political goals. She enhanced her claim to sovereignty by having realistic Western-style portraits painted of her in tsarist regalia with inscriptions extolling her virtues in terms drawn from classical imagery. One such picture—an engraving done in 1688 by Abraham Bloteling of Amsterdam, with inscriptions done in Latin of the regent's seven virtues (magnanimity, liberality, piety, prudence, chastity, justice, and hope in God)—was apparently executed for foreign consumption, while another by Tarasevich of 1687 was apparently for the local audience. In the late 1680s, Sofiia also minted coins and medals with her image alongside the two co-tsars (Ioann V and Petr) and commissioned panegyrics praising her peace treaty with Poland, her repression of the Old Believers, and the like.[70] Such political proselytizing exhibited a more secular political style and consciousness than anything Muscovy had ever seen, despite its Orthodox idiom.

Sofiia also used various media to rewrite the history of the failed Crimean campaigns in 1687–89. She had medals struck and distributed to the departing army; she greeted the returning troops with lavish receptions, banquets, and gifts; she disseminated in Western Europe a blatantly false composition

---

[69]S. K. Smirnov, *Istoriia Moskovskoi slaviano-greko-latinskoi akademii* (Moscow, 1855), p. 397.

[70]Hughes, *Sophia*, pp. 138–44, 163; A. P. Bogdanov, "Politicheskaia graviura v Rossii perioda regentstva Sof'i Alekseevny," in *Istochnikovedenie otechestvennoi istorii. Sbornik statei 1981* (Moscow, 1982), pp. 225–46; Hughes, "Sophia," pp. 278–82; Smith, "Prince V. V. Golitsyn," pp. 154–60.

praising the campaign. She was not alone: As indicated above, Prince V. V. Golitsyn had a panegyric to him written by the Likhudy brothers, a portrait done to praise his role in the Crimean War, and another portrait done to celebrate his rather more successful negotiations with Poland for peace in 1687.[71] So in 1699, when Peter I ordered the construction of a dozen monumental obelisks over the mass graves of the musketeers (*strel'tsy*) executed after the uprising earlier that year, and when he ordered hung on them twenty-four ponderous bronze tables condemning their sacrilege and treason, he was only following on a more grandiose scale the example set by his arch rivals Sofiia and Golitsyn.[72]

By such aggressive manipulations of political events and political discourse, these leaders stepped beyond the traditional Muscovite practice and concept of politics, even while maintaining the idiom of godly community. Politics was no longer just the pursuit of national salvation in theory or personal self-aggrandizement in practice, as it had been in Muscovy. Politics was that and more; it was also now a public sphere, created and manipulated by individuals with differing viewpoints, turned toward goals of societal welfare and change. It could be manipulated and created, just as in the growing private sphere individuals could shape their images according to their own advantage or tastes. The degree of volition political leaders assumed toward political events, the degree of publicity to which they subjected discussion, the variety of goals envisioned for state activity—all suggest a more modern and secular vision of political life developing within the framework of autocracy.

Absolutist Discourses and Practices

Thus the seventeenth century started a fundamental transformation in thinking about the ruler, the state, and society, parallel to European absolutist policies. The crucial step had been made of enunciating a more secular vision of society and the state, whose worldly needs required the attention of the ruler and which existed separate from the religious life of the individual. Ferment in church circles also produced rhetoric that empowered the ruler more explicitly

---

[71]Smith, "Prince V. V. Golitsyn," pp. 136–39, 178–79; Hughes, *Sophia*, pp. 216–17, 230–32; Bogdanov, "Politicheskaia graviura"; A. P. Bogdanov, "'Istinnoe i vernoe skazanie' o I krymskom pokhode 1687 g.—Pamiatnik publitsistiki posol'skogo prikaza," in *Problemy izucheniia narrativnykh istochnikov po istorii russkogo srednevekov'ia. Sbornik statei* (Moscow, 1982), pp. 57–84. The panegyrics are published in Bogdanov, ed., *Pamiatniki*, nos. 12–13, 15–16, 26–27.

[72]A. N. Kazakevich, "Novye dokumenty po istorii monumental'noi propagandy pri Petre I (Vosstanie moskovskikh strel'tsov 1698 g.)," in *Istochnikovedcheskie i istoriograficheskie aspekty russkoi kul'tury. Sbornik statei* (Moscow, 1984), pp. 53–58.

than ever before.[73] But Peter I culminated these processes even while he shifted the rhetorical base. He abandoned the Orthodox idiom in which the political theory imported from Ukraine had been recently couched and substituted a more thoroughly secular rhetoric with more categorical claims. Influences on him, however indirect, were primarily northern European and Protestant—Grotius, Pufendorf, Locke, and others.[74] Petrine theory brought the concept of autocracy much closer to a claim of total authority than it had been in Muscovy. Peter declared often and unequivocally that "the prince's will is law," acting on the claim in his unilateral assumption of the titles of "Emperor" and "Father of the Fatherland" in 1721 and his similarly unprecedented declaration in 1722 of the ruler's right to name his successor.[75] His military and naval law codes made this vision of absolute power explicit in a provision borrowed from Swedish sources:

For his Majesty is an autocratic monarch who is not obliged to answer for his acts to anyone in the world; but he possesses the force and the authority to rule his states and lands as a Christian sovereign, according to his will and best judgment.[76]

Peter justified his claim to absolute authority by equating his self-interest with that of the state. On the eve of the Poltava battle, he wrote:

[The Russian army] should not think that they have been armed and drawn up in battle array for the sake of Peter but for the state entrusted to Peter and for their kin and for the all-Russian people. . . . And about Peter, it should be known that his life is not dear to him, only that Russia and Russian piety, glory and prosperity should survive.[77]

[73]SGGD no. 27, p. 91. See also ibid., pp. 86–87, for their broad definition of the tsar's duties. Cf. Daniel Rowland, "Did Muscovite Literary Ideology Place Limits on the Power of the Tsar (1540s–1660s)?" *Russian Review* 49, no. 2 (1990):125–55.

[74]On political thought in Peter's time, see Sumner Benson, "The Role of Western Political Thought in Petrine Russia," *Canadian-American Slavic Studies* 8, no. 2 (1974):254–73; A. Lappo-Danilevskii, "Ideia gosudarstva i glavneishie momenty eia razvitiia v Rossii so vremeni smuty i do epokhi preobrazovanii," *Golos minuvshogo* 2, no. 12 (1914):24–31; Raeff, *The Well-Ordered Police State*; Michael Cherniavsky, *Tsar and People: Studies in Russian Myths* (New Haven, Conn., and London, 1961), chap. 3; Marc Raeff, "The Enlightenment in Russia and Russian Thought in the Enlightenment," in J. G. Garrard, ed., *The Eighteenth Century in Russia* (Oxford, 1973), pp. 25–47; James Cracraft, "Empire Versus Nation: Russian Political Theory under Peter I," *Harvard Ukrainian Studies* 10, nos. 3/4 (1986):524–41.

[75]Titles: PSZ 6, no. 3840 (1721). Succession law: PSZ 6, no. 3893 (1722).

[76]The Military Articles: PSZ 5, no. 3006, chap. 3, art. 20, Commentary, p. 325 (1716). The naval statute: PSZ 6, no. 3485, bk. 5, chap. l, par. 2, Commentary (1720).

[77]*Pis'ma i bumagi Imperatora Petra Velikogo*, 13 vols. in 16 pts. to date (St. Petersburg and Moscow, 1887–), vol. 9, pt. 1 (1950), no. 3251, p. 226.

Peter believed that a ruler's duty was to enhance his state's worldly stature and prosperity by developing its resources, human and natural. He made himself the first and most zealous worker toward that end. He bitterly remonstrated with his son and heir Aleksei, a man known for his piety and devotion to the church—in other words, a potential tsar of the old type—for his neglect of the secular learning and skills he would require for governing in the new Petrine style. In 1718, he deprived his son of the succession, with the following expressed concerns:

> We cannot in good conscience keep him as our successor to the Russian throne, knowing that through his disgraceful actions he would squander all the glory of our people and all the advantage to our state received of God's grace and our tireless labors, [all of] which we have received with such work—not only that we have regained from the enemy provinces torn away from our state, but also that we have brought to it many eminent cities and lands; and it is also known to all that we instructed our people in many military and civil sciences to the benefit and glory of the state.[78]

These trends are not new in Russian political discourse. Epifanii Slavinetskii and Simeon Polotskii from the 1650s to the 1680s had preached these same themes of service to society, but they took their inspiration from Renaissance texts via the Polish-Ukrainian cultural conduit. Peter's theorists took their inspiration from the "police state" of Prussia, where the combination of zealous reforming monarchs and Lutheran Pietism created a potent engine for nation-building.[79] In Peter's Russia, theoretical formulation of these views was entrusted to an erudite circle of Ukrainian, Russian, and Greek clergymen.[80] In "The Right of the Monarch's Will," written in 1722 to justify Peter's changing the rules of succession, Feofan Prokopovich and his circle elaborated a theory of absolute power heavily influenced by Grotius, based on natural law and a Hobbesian interpretation of the social contract:

> It is the duty of a tsar . . . to maintain his subjects free from affliction and to provide them all the best instruction, both for piety and for honorable living. And if his subjects fall into affliction, the tsar must respond so that there be true justice in the state, to protect his subjects who are injured from the offenders. Similarly he should provide a strong and efficient army to defend the whole fatherland from

[78]PSZ 5, no. 3151, p. 538 (1718). See also his angry letter in 1715 to Aleksei: N. G. Ustrialov, *Istoriia tsarstvovaniia Petra Velikogo*, 5 vols. in 6 pts. (St. Petersburg, 1858–63), vol. 6 (1859), no. 46, pp. 346–48.

[79]Raeff, "The Enlightenment in Russia," and *The Well-Ordered Police State*.

[80]James Cracraft, "Did Feofan Prokopovich Really Write *Pravda voli monarshei?*" *Slavic Review* 40, no. 2 (1981):173–93.

enemies. . . . The people must obey all the orders of the autocrat without contra-
diction or objection . . . the word of God and also . . . the interpretation of the
people's will . . . shows . . . clearly: for since the people have divested itself of its
general will and have transferred it to the monarch, then how can they not be
obliged to obey his orders, laws and statutes without any objection? [81]

Peter's goal was to cultivate social forces to contribute with him in the building of a stronger, more powerful state. Implicit in absolutist visions of the service state—whether in the new piety of Muscovite sermons of the 1680s or in
Peter's Lutheran-inspired rhetoric—was the enlistment in service to the state of
"virtuous" men, members of privileged social groups such as nobility or
bureaucracy capable of carrying out the state's program.[82] Education, merit,
and ability were required to serve, but granting such social groups hereditary,
privileged status did not contradict the goals of absolute rulers, as contradic-
tory as this idea seems to our modern sensibility. Peter simultaneously affirmed
both the concept of status based on merit and hereditary nobility in the Table
of Ranks of 1722: Nongentry people reaching the upper ranks were to receive
hereditary nobility.[83] Similar in concept to the reform projects of 1681, the
Table of Ranks completed the dual processes whereby civil and military service
was opened up in theory to all of the free populace and whereby the social elite
was formally designated and privileged.

To cultivate a new elite, to change people's thinking and social interactions,
Peter followed in his stepsister's footsteps by manipulating the symbolism of
political life. He did this not with medals and panegyrics, but with dress and
demeanor. Peter urged German, French, and Hungarian garb on his elite and
decreed that members of the upper ranks should shave their beards.[84] He man-

[81]PSZ 7, no. 4870, pp. 622, 625.

[82]On the crucial role of intermediary social bodies in the absolutist vision, see Raeff, *The Well-
Ordered Police State*; idem, *Understanding Imperial Russia*, trans. Arthur Goldhammer (New
York, 1984); idem, "The Well-Ordered Police State"; Hans-Joachim Torke, "Continuity and
Change in the Relations between Bureaucracy and Society in Russia, 1613–1861," *Canadian Slavic
Studies* 5 (1971):457–76. For further discusssions of the cultivation of social groups in absolutism,
see Hans Rosenberg, *Bureaucracy, Aristocracy and Autocracy* (Cambridge, Mass., 1958), and
Nicholas Henshall, *The Myth of Absolutism* (London, 1992).

[83]PSZ 6, no. 3890 (1722). Personal (nonhereditary) nobility was granted to all who achieved
any of the offices of the fourteen ranks. The ranks ascended from no. 14 to no. 1; hereditary nobility accrued to those who achieved rank no. 8 (no. 12 in the military ladder). In 1856, the rank levels at which an official won personal and hereditary nobility were raised (to the ninth rank for
personal nobility and to the fourth civil and sixth military rank for hereditary). See S. M. Troitskii,
"Tabel' o rangakh," *Sovetskaia istoricheskaia entsiklopediia*, 16 vols. (Moscow, 1961–76), 14 (1973):
cols. 15–16, and Evgenii V. Anisimov, *The Reforms of Peter the Great: Progress through Coercion
in Russia*, trans. John T. Alexander (Armonk, N.Y., 1993), pp. 188–91.

[84]Cherniavsky cites such a law of 1698 in "The Old Believers," p. 171. Others followed: PSZ
4, nos. 1741 (1700), 1887 (1701), 1898 (1702), 1999 (1704); PSZ 5, no. 2874 (1714).

dated that they entertain themselves, with their wives and daughters, at European-style soirées[85]; he founded a new capital city, modeled on Amsterdam and situated far from Muscovy's traditional heartland; he introduced classical architecture and new uses of private and public space.[86] He disseminated insignia and genres of political symbolism previously not widespread in Muscovy: the cults of Saints Peter and Paul and of Saint Andrew, complete with honorific orders in their names; coins and medals in honor of battles and ceremonial occasions; and banners and battle standards, secular processions, and court ceremony based on the European model. He bestowed European titles of nobility, such as "Maltese cavalier" and "count" (*graf*).[87] All these endeavors had the goal of shaping a vision of the state as an abstract entity embodying the will of educated society, whose representatives in turn regarded themselves as the state's worthy servants. Not surprisingly, Peter was as interested as his Muscovite predecessors had been in personal honor, and he used it to suit his new demand for cultivated individuals. Although he tried, with limited success, to inculcate a more socially exclusive sense of aristocratic honor, he and his successors also affirmed the traditional Russian consciousness of honor and its definition, fulfilling the autocrat's mandate to give justice to his people.

Peter's endeavors to create a new elite and inculcate a new attitude toward the state, building on changes in political thinking and the elite from the late seventeenth century, bore fruit throughout the eighteenth century. As Cynthia Whittaker has chronicled, the eighteenth century saw a self-conscious affirmation of autocracy, as reshaped in the Petrine idiom. By the end of the century, Russian historians and publicists had produced a "rich and nuanced understanding of the idea of autocracy," one that differed markedly from traditional Muscovite concepts of power. They proffered a secular rationale for power; they advocated progressive change over conservative tradition as the ruler's chief duty; and they presented the Russian tsar as one of the community of European leaders, not,

[85]PSZ 5, no. 3246 (1718).

[86]James Cracraft, *The Petrine Revolution in Russian Architecture* (Chicago, 1988); Priscilla Roosevelt, *Life on the Russian Country Estate* (New Haven, Conn., 1995), chap. 1.

[87]For coverage of some aspects of this vast field, see Richard Wortman, *Scenarios of Power: Myth and Ceremony in Russian Monarchy* (Princeton, N.J., 1995), chap. 2; Anisimov, *The Reforms of Peter the Great*, pp. 217–43; Lindsey Hughes, *Russia in the Age of Peter the Great* (New Haven, Conn., 1998), pt. 8, pp. 248–97; I. G. Spasskii, *Inostrannye i russkie ordena do 1917 goda* (Leningrad, 1963); G. V. Bilinbakhov, "Otrazhenie idei absoliutizma v simvolike petrovskikh znamen," in *Kul'tura i iskusstvo Rossii XVIII veka* (Leningrad, 1981), pp. 7–25, and "Gosudarstvennaia geral'dika Rossii kontsa XVII-pervoi chetverti XVIII veka (K voprosu formirovaniia ideologii absoliutizma v Rossii)," Abstract of candidate dissertation, Leningrad State University, 1982; N. A. Baklanova, "Otrazhenie idei absoliutizma v izobrazitel'nom iskusstve pervoi chetverti XVIII v.," in *Absoliutizm v Rossii (XVI–XVIII vv.)* (Moscow, 1964), pp. 492–507; I. Spasskii and E. Shchukina, comp. with intro., *Medals and Coins of the Age of Peter the Great* (Leningrad, 1974). Maltese cavalier: DAI 12 (1872), no. 97, p. 401 (1699).

The striking contrast between Peter I's chosen style for his new capital of St. Petersburg (a restrained northern European classicism) and traditional Muscovite architecture (exemplified by the Kremlin ensemble) epitomizes the emperor's radical break with Muscovite cultural patterns. (Photograph: Jack Kollmann.)

Whittaker points out, as "an isolated and unique Orthodox ruler." Paralleling political theory across the continent in the eighteenth century, they created a coherent but diverse argument in favor of autocracy, borrowing from *philosophes* the classical argument that autocracy was the preferable form of government for Russia, given its geography and social structures.[88] Russian political praxis and thought had fulfilled the promise implicit in the cultural ferment of Aleksei Mikhailovich's and Sofiia Alekseevna's reforming reigns.

The Abolition of Precedence

Peter's predecessors therefore were actively engaged in reforming government to reflect better the social elite with which they ruled and to accomplish better the tasks of a government envisioned in a more dynamic mode. The traditional institution for establishing hierarchy in the elite—precedence—fell vic-

[88]Cynthia Hyla Whittaker, "The Idea of Autocracy among Eighteenth-Century Russian Historians," *Russian Review* 55, no. 2 (1996):149–71, and "The Reforming Tsar: The Redefinition of Autocratic Duty in Eighteenth-Century Russia," *Slavic Review* 51, no. 1 (1992):77–98.

tim early to these energies. When Fedor Alekseevich published the manifesto abolishing precedence in 1682, he anticipated Peter's more explicit references to the common weal:

> It befits us according to God's command to anticipate, establish and decree so that all Orthodox Christians of every rank and age, placed under our governance for their peace, serenity and love can have the best conditions and security; and to root out and destroy that which tends to ruin and leads to a reduction of the general good.[89]

The declaration that precedence "leads to a reduction of the general good" demonstrates how much Muscovite politics had changed, even within the limits of Orthodox Muscovy. A public space was being cleared for the pursuit of social needs, as well as a private space for self-cultivation; an elite receptive to new ways of thinking and governing was evolving; rhetoric was becoming available to describe and validate change. The abolition of precedence in 1682 was part of an early program of reforms that demonstrated the directions that change would take for decades to come. And it could not have happened if the above-described social changes and transformations in the political order had not laid the groundwork for it.

Under Fedor Alekseevich (ruled 1676–82), a group of strong leaders around the tsar's Miloslavskie kinsmen[90] moved aggressively to increase revenues, streamline the government, and pursue ambitious foreign policy goals. They undertook a program of rationalization of resources: They ordered a census in 1678, introduced taxation by household in 1679, consolidated direct and indirect taxes in 1679, and consolidated the fiscal and military chanceries that collected taxes and oversaw the army in 1680.[91]

Attempting to centralize the central government and make it more efficient, a commission in 1681 led by Prince V. V. Golitsyn also considered a dramatic reform that would have transformed the highest echelons of government as they presently existed. It proposed a threefold parallel hierarchy of civil ranks (*namestniki*), military ranks (*voevody*), and court ranks (using titles generally derived from court practice); the scheme was similar to the Table of Ranks eventually adopted in 1722. The projected ninety-four members of these ranks constituted a relatively compact number, intended to staunch the explosion of men

[89]PSZ 2, no. 905, p. 371.

[90]During Sofiia's regency, the court was divided into two factions led by the clans of Aleksei Mikhailovich's two wives: Tsar Ioann V and Sofiia were of Miloslavskii heritage, Tsar Peter of the Naryshkin clan. The Miloslavskie were in the ascendancy under Fedor Alekseevich and until Sofiia was deposed in 1689.

[91]Brown, "Bureaucracy," pp. 485–500. For general surveys of these reforms, see Hughes, *Sophia*, chap. 5; Keep, "The Muscovite Elite"; O'Brien, *Russia under Two Tsars*.

in conciliar ranks and to create a small peerage-type enclave. The civil governors were to be given honorific titles associating them with specific regions, but they were to remain in Moscow as a broad consultative body, while the military governors were to rule in the military regions as the de facto heads of local government. The new governing edifice would have been capped by a twelve-man privy council and a prime minister.[92] In tandem with the consolidation of chanceries and army going on in these years, this plan would have streamlined central government (not decentralized it, as critics and some later scholars argued).

It would also have institutionalized a degree of political "pluralism" (in John Keep's phrase) never before spelled out in Muscovite law. But that pluralism was of a very elite type, because the beneficiaries of the project would have been the aristocrats—that evolving wealthy and favored narrow stratum of great old and new clans.[93] The ninety-four civil and military governors and court officials named in the reform plan were to have been chosen from the "noble" (*velikorodnye*) families and given their titles for life, an aristocratic model of government owing much to the contemporary Polish-Lithuanian one, in which great families dominated the honorific offices of senator, palatine, and castellan. The proposal reified the evident emergence of a privileged aristocracy whose claim to power and status was based on birth, wealth, and access.

The 1681 reform project apparently foundered initially on the opposition of the church, because a version of the proposal also suggested reorganizing the church hierarchy territorially in a manner parallel to the civil and military components of the plan. Patriarch Ioakhim rejected this part of the project, fearing that it would subordinate hierarchs to the local civil governors in their areas.

[92]Details of the plan are known mainly from two drafts of the project; there is disagreement about the relationship of those two texts. I tend to agree with those scholars (Keep, "Muscovite Elite" sums up the historiography) who view the longer text as a second draft of the original plan, written after a key provision about church offices had been eliminated, and who see the shorter text as simply a later report about the plan. The longer text is published in M. A. Obolenskii, ed., "Proekt ustava o sluzhebnom starshinstve boiar, okol'nichikh i dumnykh liudei po tridtsati chetyrem stepeniam . . .," *Arkhiv istoriko-iuridicheskikh svedenii, otn. do Rossii . . .* 1, sect. II (Moscow, 1850), pp. 20–40, and discussed in Georg Ostrogorsky, "Das Projekt einer Rangtabelle aus der zeit des Caren Fedor Aleksěevič," *Jahrbücher für Kultur und Geschichte der Slaven* n.f. 9 (1933):86–138. The shorter one is published in E. E. Zamyslovskii, *Tsarstvovanie Fedora Alekseevicha* (St. Petersburg, 1871), app. III, pp. xxxiv–xxxv.

[93]Discussions of the reform project and the abolition of precedence include Keep, "Muscovite Elite"; idem, *Soldiers*, pp. 53–55; Crummey, *Aristocrats and Servitors*, pp. 32–33; Sedov, "Sotsial'no-politicheskaia bor'ba"; Chernov, *Vooruzhennye sily*, chap. 7; Carol B. Stevens, "Honor and Precedence amongst Muscovy's Elite after 1682," unpubl. manuscript, 1986; A. I. Markevich, *Istoriia mestnichestva v Moskovskom gosudarstve v XV–XVII veke* (Odessa, 1888), pp. 550–611; M. Ia. Volkov, "Ob otmene mestnichestva v Rossii," *Istoriia SSSR* 1977, no. 2, pp. 53–67; L. V. Cherepnin, *Zemskie sobory Russkogo gosudarstva v XVI–XVII vv.* (Moscow, 1978), pp. 346–55; Nikol'skii, "Boiarskaia popytka"; Smith, "Prince V. V. Golitsyn," pp. 77–90.

More generally, he spoke out about the perils of granting too much authority to great aristocrats who will only "puff up with pride and enrich themselves" with lifetime offices to the detriment of the tsar's autocratic power and the unity of the realm. With the clerical sections eliminated, the reform apparently was moving forward when Fedor Alekseevich died in April 1682. In the intense political infighting of the subsequent decade, the Miloslavskii faction led by regent Sofiia and Prince V. V. Golitsyn was too politically isolated to carry it to fruition.

One offshoot of these reform activities was, however, put into life; it had to do with the regularization of the lesser ranks of the Moscow-based elite (from *stol'nik* to *zhilets*) in the framework of the reformed army. It was proposed in the commission led by Golitsyn—and rubber-stamped by a larger council—that these ranks would be turned into new-model regiments (*roty*) and that their officers (*rotmistry* and *porutchiki*) would be selected without regard to "place" (*mesto*). Some distinguished families protested, fearing that they would suffer insult in the future from service in these ranks. So the assembled delegates recommended the complete abolition of ranking by place—*mestnichestvo*—for all aspects of military and civil service, "so that in the future the tsar will suffer no detriment in military and all other service from precedence disputes." And the tsar, after consulting with the church hierarchy, called precedence "the work of the devil" and abolished it with a ceremonial burning of some of the records of service rankings. Precedence was abolished, then, as a step toward military modernization.[94]

Even though some families stubbornly sued for place for another decade, by and large precedence was abolished without protest. In fact, it had become moribund, as we have seen in Chapter 4; precedence had been declared null at most major military campaigns in the seventeenth century, and it had failed to prevent new families from penetrating to the apex of the elite as the leadership needs of the state exploded.[95] Most members of the late seventeenth-century elite were newcomers to genealogical rankings and not well served by the system. With the abolition of precedence, the elite did not lose a cherished perquisite, but rather gained in theory better instruments for affirming status. Not only was the abolition paired with reforms that would have created a House of Lords–type peerage of privileged families, the abolition decree itself also enshrined the principle of elite status. It explicitly allowed families to keep genealogical books at home and ordered new official genealogical records to be composed that would reflect the "new men" of the late seventeenth-century

[94]PSZ 1, no. 905 (January 12, 1682); also published in RZ 4:34–52. For historiography on precedence, see chap. 4.

[95]Iu. M. Eskin records nineteen suits from 1683–94: *Mestnichestvo v Rossii. XVI–XVII vv. Khronologicheskii reestr* (Moscow, 1994), pp. 208–10. On the absence of protest, see Keep, "Muscovite Elite," p. 217; Smith, "Prince V. V. Golitsyn," p. 83.

elite. The genealogies in the official 1550s *Sovereign's Genealogical Book* (*Gosudarev rodoslovets*) were to be updated for those families still surviving, and four more books were to be composed to include newer families. The first was to include all princely families and all those in conciliar rank, as well as those whose service in high ranks extended back to Ivan IV's time but who did not happen to have been included in the *Gosudarev rodoslovets*; the second was to include clans serving from the time of Mikhail Fedorovich (ruled 1613–45) in the next highest level of government service, such as generals of regiments and ambassadors and those in the first rank (*stat'ia*) of the elite muster books (*desiatni*); book three was to include the "middle" and "lesser" ranks of those muster books; book four was to include those who had been enrolled in the low Moscow-based ranks but who merited status because of their loyal service or that of their fathers. Because the only explanation given for these books was that they were to establish the "memory" of these families for future generations, what was being proposed here was in essence the registration of a nobility.[96]

The project was not completed as planned. The *Gosudarev rodoslovets* was updated ca. 1687 and came to be called the *Velvet Book* (*Barkhatnaia kniga*) after its binding and cover. But the four others were not compiled, owing not only to the downfall of the Miloslavskii faction in 1689, but probably also to the elite's uncertainty about the point of the exercise. No tangible rights and privileges had, after all, been associated with being enrolled in the new books. The records reemerged, however, in the late eighteenth century when aristocratic self-consciousness had matured and the 1785 Charter for the Nobility—which did grant explicit rights and privileges—mandated that official genealogical records of the newly defined corporate estate be kept.[97] Neither did Golitsyn's ambitious plan to reform central government succeed.

---

[96]RZ 4:44–45. Repeated orders to submit genealogical records include PSZ 2, nos. 1051 (1683), 1207 (1686; which decree explicitly mandates the inclusion of eminent Siberian, Tatar, and Georgian ruling clans), 1219 (1686). Already in the 1670s, Muscovite chanceries were developing interest in European genealogical record keeping and heraldry, evidence of increasing aristocratic sensibility: M. E. Bychkova, "Pol'skie traditsii v russkoi genealogii XVII veka," *Sovetskoe slavianovedenie* 1981, no. 5, pp. 39–50.

[97]On the gathering of genealogical materials after 1682, see M. E. Bychkova, *Rodoslovnye knigi XVI–XVII vv. kak istoricheskii istochnik* (Moscow, 1975), pp. 38–46, 180–81; idem, "Iz istorii sozdaniia rodoslovnykh rospisei kontsa XVII v. i Barkhatnoi knigi," *Vspomogatel'nye istoricheskie distsipliny* 12 (1981):90–109; A. Barsukov, *Obzor istochnikov i literatury russkogo rodosloviia* (St. Petersburg, 1887), pp. 3–11. On the revival of interest in these documents, see A. B. Kamenskii, "K istorii izucheniia genealogii v Rossii v XVIII veke," in *Istochnikovedcheskie issledovaniia po istorii feodal'noi Rossii* (Moscow, 1981), pp. 150–61, and idem, "Praviashchii klass-soslovie i gosudarstvennyi apparat Russkogo tsentralizovannogo gosudarstva v trudakh istorikov i arkhivistov vtoroi poloviny XVIII veka. Istochnikovedcheskoe issledovanie," Candidate dissertation, Moscow State Historical-Archival Institute, 1984.

But the elite weathered these inconveniences, maintaining its hold on high office well into the eighteenth century. While the old conciliar ranks existed (until 1713), the same families maintained primacy in that domain; they then made the transition to new Petrine structures and titles of government.[98] The abolition of precedence affirmed the privilege and status of Moscow's highest ranks and families and made no effort to substitute new value systems. Honor remained a key social value and practice for elite and populace alike after 1682.

[98]On continuity in the elite, see Robert O. Crummey, "Peter and the Boiar Aristocracy, 1689–1700," *Canadian-American Slavic Studies* 8 (1974):274–87; John P. LeDonne, "Ruling Families in the Russian Political Order, 1689–1825," *Cahiers du monde russe et soviétique* 28, nos. 3–4 (1987):233–322; Brenda Meehan-Waters, *Autocracy and Aristocracy: The Russian Service Elite of 1730* (New Brunswick, N.J., 1982); A. N. Medushevskii, "Boiarskie spiski pervoi chetverti XVIII v.," in *Arkheograficheskii ezhegodnik za 1981 god* (Moscow, 1982), pp. 158–63. Elite prosopography: *The Annual Composition of the Muscovite Boyar Duma, 1613–1713*, comp. The Muscovite Biographical Group [Ol'ga Kosheleva, Russell Martin, Boris Morozov, Marshall Poe], (Cambridge, Mass., 1995). See also A. N. Medushevskii, "Istochniki o sostave tsentral'nogo apparata upravleniia Rossii v pervoi chetverti XVIII v.," *Sovetskie arkhivy* 1981, no. 3, pp. 58–60, and idem, "Feodal'nye verkhi i formirovanie biurokratii v Rossii pervoi chetverti XVIII v. Istochnikovedcheskoe issledovanie," Abstract of candidate dissertation, Institute of the History of the USSR of the Academy of Sciences of the USSR, 1985.

The Endurance of Honor

Social change in the seventeenth century prepared the way for a more complex structuring of government, for the forging of a more explicitly privileged corporate elite, and for the mobilization of social forces for ambitious military and fiscal goals. Most of the reforms undertaken by Peter I (b. 1672, ruled 1682–1725) had their antecedents in Muscovite times: To a great extent, his contribution was to systematize and intensify reform.[1] He systematized, for example, the trend toward aristocratization in the elite by creating the terminology and status of nobility with the 1722 Table of Ranks. Moreso than had the abortive 1681 reform proposals, Peter's reforms created new institutions of governance: twelve "colleges" (to replace dozens of chanceries), a Senate, and a series of reforms of local and urban administration. More systematically than the legislation of the 1680s, Petrine laws set down rules for behavior in state institutions, defining the extent of government authority and rationalizing the bureaucratic service. Peter took the Muscovite army—by the 1690s essentially a modern one—and made it immense, thereby setting into motion reverberating forces of taxation, social regimentation, and peasant recruitment that changed the Russian countryside. In a purposeful manner, he gave the elite a new European vocabulary and new genres for cultural expression. Much of what he endeavored did not outlive him, his beloved navy being the prime example. And much of what had informed Muscovite society and politics endured beyond his reign.

---

[1]On Petrine reforms, see Marc Raeff, *Understanding Imperial Russia: State and Society in the Old Regime*, trans. Arthur Goldhammer (New York, 1984), chaps. 2–4; Evgenii V. Anisimov, *The Reforms of Peter the Great: Progress through Coercion in Russia*, trans. John T. Alexander (Armonk, N.Y., 1993); M. S. Anderson, *Peter the Great*, 2d ed. (New York, 1995); Richard Hellie, "The Petrine Army: Continuity, Change and Impact," *Canadian-American Slavic Studies* 8, pt. 2 (1974):237–53.

What makes Peter's endeavors and those of his successors most dramatic for observers—and perplexing for those engaged by the "continuity or change?/ reform or revolution?" conundrum—is the way in which Petrine reform turned Muscovite themes and traditions to its own use. Peter did this so emphatically, with such single-mindedness, that ultimately change was accomplished by riding the crest of continuity. The political system of late Muscovy that he carried to fruition paralleled the ideas of European absolutism. He introduced an even more explicit rhetoric of absolutism, capitalizing on the late seventeenth-century Russian embrace of the concept of "social good" and initiating a claim to unlimited power for an autocracy that theretofore had not known one. Peter adopted an aggressively secular rhetoric of power and an overtly secular program for the culture of the elite. Confronted with such intense stimuli, traditional Muscovite institutions—among them the theory and practice of honor—adapted. The state preserved the opportunity for individuals to defend honor, and individuals and families continued to seek public vindication for insult. But the emphasis of the concept of honor gradually changed from the collective to the individual.

Continuities in the Use of Honor

The abolition of precedence in 1682 did not abolish the defense of honor. Indeed, the abolition decree specifically mandated that anyone attempting to sue for precedence in the future should, in addition to suffering confiscation of property and loss of position, pay a dishonor fee (*beschest'e*) to each man in the clan whose member was being sued.[2] The decades between the abolition of precedence and Peter I's serious engagement in reform—that is, from the 1680s to 1690s—were so rife with dishonor litigation that suits from this era constitute a significant portion of our database and have been frequently referred to in the preceding text.[3] As suggested in Chapter 1, the proliferation of suits was likely a response to social change as much as a compensation to the upper ranks for their loss of precedence (after all, precedence suits had been curtailed over the seventeenth century). Legislatively, honor received the same sort of unsystematic treatment that had characterized the seventeenth century: Edicts established the dishonor compensation for new social groups and institutions (1684, 1699)[4];

---

[2]PSZ 2, no. 905, pp. 377–78 (1682).

[3]The published description of the Military Service Chancery, a major resource for dishonor suits through the 1690s, averages fewer than one hundred cases per decade from the sixteenth century through the 1660s, and then lists 178 in the 1670s, 445 in the 1680s, and 893 in the 1690s. Even accounting for better survival rates of later documents, this disproportion is striking.

[4]RGADA, f. 210, Moscow stol, stb. 717, pt. 1, ll. 23–24 (1684; dishonor value of Voskresenskii monastery); PSZ 3, no. 1731 (1699; dishonor value for Greeks insulted by foreigners).

enjoined musketeers not to dishonor people with rowdy behavior (1682)[5]; man-dated corporal punishment for peasants guilty of dishonor who lacked the wherewithal to pay a cash fine (1687); and even defined the dishonor fine (cal-culated in numbers of camels, horses, bulls, and sheep) that Mongol and Buriat tribal elders had to pay if they insulted Russian emissaries or soldiers (1689).[6] A decree of 1690 has a somewhat rationalizing character, inasmuch as it tried to distinguish intentional from unintentional mistakes in names and titles in official documents, allowing only intentional slights to be litigated as dishonor.[7]

Dishonor continued to capture legal attention in the first two decades of the next century. Two trends are evident. On the one hand, even while maintaining essentially Muscovite traditions regarding honor, edicts tended to limit slightly the scope of "dishonor," forbidding confiscation of land to pay a dishonor fine (1700), forbidding soldiers to sue merchants for dishonor (1700), and forbid-ding anyone to dishonor members of foreign embassies by trying them in chanceries other than the Foreign Affairs Chancery (1708).[8] An edict in 1700 tried to limit frivolous suits over colorful epithets, the likes of which earlier would have qualified as actionable insults (e.g., "little gentryman," "assaulter," "baby," "coward"). In that same year, a suit was thrown out as frivolous when a man complained that another had leered at him "in a beastlike way" (*zveroo-brazno*).[9] In 1719, precedence-type quarrels over place in state service were again resolutely forbidden.[10] During Peter's reign, the term for insult began to change: *obida* and *oskorblenie* were used interchangeably with *beschest'e*. In 1721, for example, laws clarified that church people should sue for *obida* or for verbal insult (*bran'*) in church, not civil, courts. In 1722, General Procurators were enjoined from causing dishonor (*beschest'e*) to anyone through careless consideration of cases. Change and continuity are evident in an edict of 1723. Paralleling the 1649 Conciliar Law Code, it prohibited disorderly behavior and insulting language in the Senate and before judges in courtrooms. The punish-ments prescribed were a combination of Muscovite penalties (paying a fee based on the annual salary of the aggrieved party, brief imprisonment, confis-cation of property) and penalties from the new military ordinances (military trial, public petition for forgiveness).[11] Legislation in 1724 continued Mus-covite traditions by affirming that judges were entitled to collect dishonor pay-

[5]PSZ 2, no. 963 (1682).
[6]PSZ 2, no. 1238 (1687); PSZ 3, no. 1329, sect. IX, arts. 2–4 (1689).
[7]PSZ 3, no. 1374 (1690).
[8]Land: PSZ 4, no. 1796 (1700). Soldiers: PSZ 4, no. 1785 (1700). Embassies: PSZ 4, no. 2206 (1708).
[9]Epithets: DR 4: cols. 1132–33 (1700). Beastlike: DR 4: cols. 1136–38, and PSZ 4, no. 1809 (1700).
[10]PSZ 5, no. 3384 (1719).
[11]1721: PSZ 6, no. 3718, art. 10, p. 345 (the Spiritual Regulation); *Polnoe sobranie postanovlenii i rasporiazhenii po vedomstvu pravoslavnogo ispovedeniia Rossiiskoi imperii*, 19 vols. (St. Peters-burg, 1869–1915), vol. 1 (1869), no. 150 (1721). 1722: PRP 8 (1961):217; PSZ 6, no. 3979, art. 2. 1723: PSZ 7, no. 4337.

ments (*beschest'e*) from accusers if they were falsely accused of favoritism. Even after Peter, Muscovite terminology and practice endured: In the 1730s and 1740s, the Cossack officer corps of various parts of Ukraine were allowed to use local legal norms in resolving disputes over dishonor (*beschest'e*).[12]

On the other hand, Peter tried to inculcate a sense of personal honor on a European model, honor that was "highly individualized,"[13] based on a person's cultivated self, rather than on heritage and clan. He declared in the 1720 General Regulation: "No reward so leads people to do good than the love of honor (*chest'*), in the same way that no punishment is so feared as its loss."[14] While Muscovite honor was a collective, family possession, here the accent is on the individual.[15] Although it took decades for such a concept to be internalized, the sorts of cultural changes the elite was undergoing in the late seventeenth century made educated people receptive to these ideas.

Peter also introduced the concept of "defamation" of military officers or civil servants found guilty of treasonous harm to the state. This was a concept of "political death," by which guilty parties were deprived of all property and of civil rights (access to the legal system, for example), publicly labeled "defamed person[s]" (*shel'm*), and expelled from "the society of good people." If the crime was serious enough, they could be executed.[16] There are some Muscovite precedents for such exclusion of criminals from society: "Disgrace" (*opala*) banished an individual from the tsar's presence (literally, "from before his bright eyes"), and, as I have noted, perpetrators of high crimes were excluded from honor. Muscovite law also implicitly treated some sanctions as shaming to the person. It was an insult, for example, to accuse someone of having been flogged, and corporal punishments were reserved for lower social ranks in punishment for dishonor. According to the Conciliar Law Code of 1649, for example, in one instance in which beating was mandated, imprisonment could be substituted for men of high birth.[17] Public shaming rituals, such as the humiliation of the elite in precedence litigation (*vydacha golovoiu*) or public beatings ("punishment in the marketplace," or *torgovaia kazn'*), combined shame with the intent to deter

[12]1724: PSZ 7, no. 4593. Ukraine: PSZ 9, no. 6578, no. 14 (1734); PSZ 12, no. 9062 (1744).

[13]Edward Muir's phrase, discussing new concepts of honor in Renaissance Italy: *Mad Blood Stirring: Vendetta and Factions in Fruili during the Renaissance* (Baltimore, 1992), p. 256.

[14]PSZ 6, no. 3534, chap. 53 (1720) (also published in PRP 8:102).

[15]V. Spasovich rather quaintly argued that true honor is individual honor and thus couldn't exist in Muscovy's patriarchal society: "O prestupleniakh protiv chesti chastnykh lits po ulozheniiu o nakazaniiakh 1845 goda," *Zhurnal Ministerstva iustitsii* 3, pt. 2 (1860):5–13.

[16]Various references to defaming sanctions: PSZ 6, no. 3006 (Voinskie artikuly, chap. 12, arts. 98, 99, chap. 15, art. 123, chap. 16, arts. 124–25) (1716) (also published in PRP 8:342–43, 348–49); PSZ 7, no. 4460 (1724). My thanks to Irina Reyfman for raising these issues to me in a personal communication.

[17]RZ 3: 105 (chap. 10, art. 20).

or to reconcile. Peter's "political death" conveyed more systematically than had Muscovite law a vision of society as a sphere of honorable individuals from which people could be excluded by their unworthy behavior.[18]

Other Petrine legislation demonstrates this more personalized image of honor. The 1716 Military Articles, for example, labeled the author of anonymous defamations "dishonorable" (*beschestnyi*); they and the Naval Ordinance of 1720 put the same label on anyone who committed a crime while using a false name. The Table of Ranks of 1722 branded a man as "dishonorable" if he falsely claimed noble heritage.[19] In Courland, later in the century, being forced to "stand by the pillar of dishonor" (*stoianie u beschestnogo stolba*) was listed as among the "shameful" (*postydnye*) criminal punishments sufficient to allow a spouse to sue for divorce.[20]

Even as these changes occurred, however, the popular conception of honor remained traditional and inclusive, as we can see in attitudes toward dueling. Dueling, generally by sword rather than pistols in the seventeenth and eighteenth centuries, came to Russia as a foreign import and got a cold reception. The elite apparently perceived it as a foreign affectation made unnecessary by traditional Muscovite protections of honor. A Prussian ambassador, Johannes Gottgilf Vockerodt, who had lived in St. Petersburg for several years under Peter I, wrote in 1737:

> Generally, for Russians, of all the foreign ideas nothing is more amusing than . . . the concept of honor. . . . Thus Peter found in no other of his laws no more such eager acquiescence than in the prohibition on dueling, and to this day no Russian officer considers demanding satisfaction in the case of insult (*beschest'e*) to him by a man of equal standing but, rather, assiduously follows the prescriptions of the Edict on Duels which orders the injured side to submit a complaint to the proper courts.[21]

These attitudes persisted: Irina Reyfman argues that many late eighteenth-century Russians found dueling a barbaric practice, at odds with their Enlight-

---

[18]A rare Muscovite instance of implicit definitions of community is the clause of the 1589 law code that deprives only the worst of criminals of honor: PRP 4 (1956):421 (art. 71).

[19]Defamation: PSZ 5, no. 3006, chap. 18, art. 150 (1716); see a similar usage in the Patent on Duels (chap. 49, art. 11), labeling someone a "good for nothing" or "unworthy" (*negodnyi*) for hitting another man or for challenging another to a duel. Military and Naval Ordinances on false name: PSZ 5, no. 3006, chap. 22, art. 202 (1716), and PSZ 6, no. 3485, chap. 18, art. 137 (1720); see a similar clause in the 1832/1842 edition of the Criminal Code (*Svod zakonov Rossiiskoi imperii, poveleniem Imperatora Nikolaia Pavlovicha sostavlennyi. Vol. 15. Zakony ugolovnye* [St. Petersburg, 1832], 15, art. 660; repeated as art. 768 in ibid. [St. Petersburg, 1842]). Table of Ranks: PSZ 6, no. 3890, arts. 16, 18 (1722).

[20]This punishment may be a sort of stocks: PSZ 25, no. 18,517 (1798).

[21]"Rossiia pri Petre Velikom," trans. A. N. Shemiakin, *Chteniia*, 1874, bk. 2, pp. 109–10.

enment desire to create a rational society ruled by law. It is not surprising that dueling was almost exclusively the preserve of foreigners in Russia from the mid-seventeenth to at least the mideighteenth century.[22]

Despite Peter's commitment to a more individualized style of honor, he wanted to avoid the extreme aristocratization that dueling represented. He and subsequent Russian rulers, like their European counterparts, perceived dueling as a threat to the public order. In 1702, Peter I issued an edict forbidding dueling among foreigners in Russian service on pain of death, "despite the customs of all neighboring states,"[23] and in 1716, extensive legislation on dueling was included in the Military Ordinance (*Ustav voinskii*) as the "Patent on Dueling" (chapter 49).[24] It set harsh sanctions and mandated the use of the courts for insult (*obida*)—defined as verbal assault, humiliating blows, or threats, essentially equivalent to Muscovite concepts of *beschest'e*.[25] All insults had to be reported promptly, either by the insulted party or witnesses; failure to do so incurred punishment. Similarly, judges would be fined if they did not resolve a case promptly—within six weeks, preferably three to four. The law emphatically declared the tsar's willingness to defend honor: "So that an insulted party . . . should not have the least cause to seek satisfaction himself and avenge himself, We here announce and assure that We will never for any intercession or considerations fail to give anyone the required satisfaction according to this Our edict" (art. 10). Those who persisted in defiance of the law faced loss of rank and large fines for summoning someone to a duel and execution for actually unsheathing swords or exchanging blows. These strictures applied to all participants, including seconds, go-betweens, and witnesses.

The Military Ordinance went on in its "Military Articles" (*Artikuly voinskie*) to prescribe harsh punishments for any disturbance of public order by any mili-

---

[22]Irina Reyfman, "The Emergence of the Duel in Russia: Corporal Punishment and the Honor Code," *Russian Review* 54, no. 1 (1995):26–43; see also Abby A. McKinnon [Abby Finnogh Smith], "Duels and the Matter of Honor," in R. P. Bartlett, A. G. Cross, and Karen Rasmussen, eds., *Russia and the World of the Eighteenth Century* (Columbus, Ohio, 1988), pp. 229–42, and Iu. M. Eskin, "Duel' v Moskovii 1637 goda," *Arkheograficheskii ezhegodnik za 1997 god* (Moscow, 1997), pp. 456–63.

[23]PSZ 4, no. 1890 (1702).

[24]PSZ 5, no. 3006, chap. 49 (1716); also published in PRP 8:457–60. The Patent had been formulated ca. 1708–11: PRP 8:460–66, commentary.

[25]*Obida* and *oskorblenie* began around this time to join the term *beschest'e* to indicate insult to honor, but they also bore the more general meaning of affront or injury. The word *beschest'e* continued to be used as a verb and particularly as a noun indicating the cash payment for dishonor. See usages of *beschest'e* through the eighteenth century in SRIa 1 (1975):179–80, and *Slovar' russkogo iazyka XVIII veka*, 8 vols. to date (Leningrad, 1984–) 2 (1985):17. On *obida*, see SRIa 12 (1987):49–50; *Slovar' Akademii rossiiskoi*, 7 vols. (St. Petersburg, 1789–94), 4 (1793): cols. 584–86, and its next edition, the *Slovar' Akademii rossiiskoi po azbuchnomu poriadku razpolozhennyi*, 7 vols. (St. Petersburg, 1806–22), 4 (1822): col. 41. On *oskorblenie*, see SRIa 13 (1987):95–97, and *Slovar' Akademii rossiiskoi po azbuchnomu poriadku* 4: col. 401.

tary men—"quarrel, verbal insult, fistfight" (which would have generated suits for dishonor in the civilian world).[26] The Articles also addressed the topic of intentional false allegations,[27] either in the form of pasquinades (anonymous written denunciations) or disparagement of another's honor behind his back or to his face. Interestingly, in addition to harsh corporal punishments, this code introduced a new ritual for intentional disparagement behind someone's back and for direct verbal abuse: public recantation and request for forgiveness from the victim on bended knee (as well as a prison term). This form of supplication was a novelty drawn from European practice but served the purpose of bringing closure to antagonisms and publicly restoring reputation—just as had Muscovy's "surrender by the head" ritual.[28] Subsequent Petrine Laws—the Naval Ordinance of January 1720[29] and the General Regulation of February 1720—echoed these concerns. The General Regulation, for example, prescribed harsh punishment—corporal punishment, confiscation of property, and/or loss of rank determined "according to the circumstances, the issues and the people involved"—for saying insulting or abusive (*rugatel'nye*) words in the Colleges (state ministries), because such behavior disturbs "good order and general calm."[30]

Petrine law of this kind essentially codified Muscovite practice more systematically, offering redress for insult in the interest of avoiding public disorder. These laws did not supersede the norms of the Conciliar Law Code of 1649, but supplanted them (despite repeated attempts, Peter never succeeded in codifying a new law code, and the Conciliar Law Code of 1649 remained in force through the eighteenth century[31]). The harshness of the sanctions was necessary for the inculcation of military discipline in the new Petrine army and bureaucracy, but the overall intent was also to cultivate a new kind of elite—educated, confident, and dignified. Peter also introduced new precedents and emphases. He accentuated the Muscovite practice of punishing more harshly insult to public places and officers of the state than insults to private individuals; he set statutes of limitations on reporting and adjudicating insult and introduced sanctions based in part on the offense as well as on the rank of the disputants. Peter introduced a public ritual, less elaborate than "being sent by the head" and not limited to the elite, that served the same purpose. Eventually

[26]Quarrels: PSZ 5, no. 3006, chap. 17, arts. 133–48 (1716).

[27]On later codifications of these ideas, see G. Sl. [Sliuzberg, G. B.], "Kleveta," *Entsiklopedich-eskii slovar'* 15 (1895):332–33, and K. K. [Krasuskii, K. A.], "Obida lichnaia . . . (v uglov. prave)," ibid., 21a (1897):505–7.

[28]Pasquinades: PSZ 5, no. 3006, chap. 18, arts. 149–53 (1716).

[29]PSZ 6, no. 3485, bk. 5, chap. 1, arts. 4–7, and note included in art. 7 (1720).

[30]PSZ 6, no. 3534, chap. 55 (1720).

[31]Peter's directives to compile a new legal codex: PSZ 4, no. 1765 (1700); PSZ 5, no. 2819 (1714); PSZ 6, no. 3661 (1720); PSZ 7, no. 4658 (1725). In addition to references to the Conciliar Law Code in cases discussed below, see the edict of 1724, which Peter signed with the notation, "enter into the *Ulozhenie*" (PSZ 7, no. 4460).

these trends toward harsher sanctions for insult to officials and a more individualized sense of personal honor found their way into civil legislation.

New Petrine ideas and laws coexisted with older norms for many decades. Essentially similar to Muscovite cases are those from Peter's lifetime. In September 1701, for example, a peasant from the Komaritskii commune area of the Upper Oka region won a suit against another peasant for the dishonor of being called a murderer and thief; the defendant refused to pay the fine because he insisted that the victim *was* "a murderer and a thief." But investigation proved him wrong, and in February 1702, the court upheld the original verdict. In February 1704, a *stol'nik* won a suit against the governor of Shatsk for arresting his man without cause and ordering his men to assault the plaintiff's home, during which assault they insulted him with a mother oath. He won his suit because the defendant failed to appear at trial and then absconded without paying the dishonor fees of more than five hundred rubles.[32] In a similar case in 1716, a *stol'nik* sued a mayor for calling him a slanderer. The defendant delayed by various familiar stratagems (outright refusal, accusing the judge of favoritism and winning a change of venue, and petitioning for delay because of service obligations) and finally settled the case in 1722 when it had been transferred a second time, this time to the Moscow appellate court (*Nadvornyi sud*). A suit of 1700 regarding official abuse of power strikes similar chords. A group of undersecretaries and judicial personnel charged that a bailiff in service to the patriarch of the church had insulted an official document and had beaten, verbally abused, and unjustly imprisoned them. The bailiff denied all, feebly claiming that he pulled a man by the hair because of the latter's "impoliteness" and that he had insulted not the document but only those who had written it. The result is unknown, but the case followed Muscovite and Petrine precedent in its concern with representations of the state and with abuse of power.[33]

Even in the middle of the century, legal precedents continued to refer to Muscovite norms as well as newer Petrine ones. A suit of 1746, for example, punished a man for affronting the dignity of his office by working without proper uniform and for verbally insulting a subordinate with a mother oath; the decision invoked the General Regulation (1720) and the Military Ordinance (1716) in fining him for "the affront to the court room" and "for the dishonor" (*beschest'e*) to the man, but a comparable case of 1744 turned to the 1649 Conciliar Law Code for norms of sanction. In 1765, a court found "abusive words" (*rugatel'nye slova*) to be insult (*obida*) worthy of legal punishment, and in 1769,

---

[32]1701: RGADA, f. 210, Prikaznyi stol, stb. 2690, ll. 1–56. 1704: K. P. Pobedonostsev, ed., *Istoriko-iuridicheskie akty perekhodnoi epokhi XVII–XVIII vekov* (Moscow, 1887), pp. 5–41.

[33]1716: K. P. Pobedonostsev, ed., *Materialy dlia istorii prikaznogo sudoproizvodstva v Rossii* (Moscow, 1890), viazka 771, delo 40, pp. 115–16. 1700: RGADA, f. 210, Prikaznyi stol, stb. 2702, ll. 1–102.

the Conciliar Law Code's ruling on insult to parents by children (chap. 22, art. 4) was explicitly cited in a case against a nobleman for insult to his mother.[34]

The Catherinian era (1762–96) did not create significantly new standards regarding honor, but in typical Enlightenment fashion, it systematized the law.[35] Muscovite norms of compensation were upheld. The Charter to the Cities of 1785 and the unpromulgated Charter to State Peasants, also of 1785, both specifically defined the dishonor fine (*beschest'e*) for these groups in traditional ways—as equivalent to their annual tax obligations—and repeated the Muscovite norm that wives should be recompensed for dishonor with twice their husband's fine, unmarried daughters with a fourfold fine, and minor sons half the fine.[36] In 1797, legislation regarding state peasants set cash compensation rates for various ranks of village officials who suffered insult while on duty, adding a brief prison or labor term and threefold fines for insult with the blow of a hand.[37] Catherinian legislation also maintained the Muscovite and Petrine preoccupation with proper conduct, both public and private. The 1782 Ordinance of Good Order or "Police" Ordinance, for example, forbade insulting language, quarrels and fights, slander, threatening letters and duels, and disorder in public places, and it imposed stiff fines on transgressors.[38] Catherine also added to traditional concerns about judicial corruption (a theme sounded since the 1497 law code) other aspects of abuse of power, such as insulting behavior by officials during lawful searches of private property, and unlawful and improper searches and seizure of property. Victims of such abuse were allowed to collect dishonor from the insulting officials.[39]

---

[34]1746: PSZ 12, no. 9335. 1744: PSZ 12, no. 8968. 1765: PSZ 17, no. 12,523. 1769: PSZ 18, no. 13,262 (this case also echoes Muscovite practice in that the Empress interceded to reduce the sentence).

[35]See Richard Wortman's discussion of eighteenth-century legal culture for background: *The Development of a Russian Legal Consciousness* (Chicago and London, 1976), chap. 1.

[36]Townsmen: PSZ 22, no. 16,188, art. 91. Peasants: David Griffiths and George E. Munro, trans. and eds., *Catherine II's Charters of 1785 to the Nobility and the Towns* (Bakersfield, Calif., 1991), art. 62, p. 75.

[37]PSZ 24, no. 17,906, par. 187, p. 563; PSZ 24, no. 18,082, art. 12, p. 674 (1797). See N. A. Minenko on peasants' consciousness of honor in the eighteenth and early nineteenth centuries: *Zhivaia starina. Budni i prazdniki Sibirskoi derevni v XVIII—pervoi polovine XIX v.* (Novosibirsk, 1989), pp. 91–100.

[38]PSZ 21, no. 15,379, esp. arts. 222, 264. Russian codes affirmed the dignity of judges also in non-Russian colonial areas: In the 1818 charter for the Bessarabian territory, fines are defined for insulting the dignity of the local court and judge (PSZ 35, no. 27,357, paragraphs 4 and 75, pp. 251–52, 263 [1818]).

[39]Corrupt adjudication: PSZ 17, no. 12,710, arts. 8, 10, 11 (1766). Unlawful searches: PSZ 19, no. 14,172, art. 13 (1774); PSZ 21, no. 15,174, art. 88 (1781)—the latter ruling is significant in that it suggests that insulted parties from all social groups were eligible for compensation, whereas the 1774 ruling exempted peasants.

In its treatment of insult to honor, Catherine II's Manifesto on Duels (1787) fully reflected Enlightenment systematizing and European rhetoric. For the first time in Russian law, there was an actual definition of insult (here the preferred terms were *obida* and *oskorblenie*): "If someone causes a damage to someone either materially or subjectively, that is, if he shames, slanders, treats with contempt, humiliates or provokes someone, that is *oskorblenie* or *obida*" (art. 8). Insult could take three forms—"word, letter, or action"—and the element of intent to insult was necessary. Insult by blow was distinguished from a wound (*ran'*, *uvech'e*) by its lesser severity: "If someone threatens or actually hits someone with a hand, leg, or weapon, or pulls hair, that is *obida* by deed. Note: If someone draws blood or causes a black and blue spot or pulls out hair, then that is called a wound" (art. 14). Wounds were punished more harshly.

Following Petrine precedent, the Manifesto on Duels forbade private vengeance by dueling, referring victims of insult to the courts. For the first time in Russian law, it distinguished between civil and criminal jurisdictions for insult to honor, based on the severity of the insult itself. Those guilty of "serious insult" (*tiazhkaia obida*), such as dangerous blows or blows to the head or face (which were intrinsically humiliating), faced criminal punishment. So did those whose insults were associated with public space: "An insult is magnified (*otiagoshchaetsia*) according to its accompanying circumstances." Such offenses included insults such as those taking place "in a public place, in church, in the Emperor's palace, in a state office, or if someone is insulted during the performance of his duties, or in the presence of people in authority." "Serious" insult also involved issues of social hierarchy: If someone insulted a natural superior (such as a parent, a landlord or serf owner, or an official or commanding officer), that too merited criminal sanctions. The Manifesto devoted little attention to sanctions, compensation, or procedure. It left the impression that for minor insults, the traditional pattern of compensation based on social status would be followed, whereas "serious" insults would merit criminal penalties such as those contained in Petrine military codes. And indeed, cases of 1800 and 1820 for less than "serious" verbal insult and threats cited norms, "dishonor" (*beschest'e*) fines, and court fees that had been stipulated in the 1649 Conciliar Law Code.[40]

Nevertheless, the seeds planted in Peter's time bore fruit in Catherine's with the emergence of a more individualized sense of honor. In his play *The Brigadier* (1769), Denis Fonvizin satirized a provincial gentryman's preoccupation with a seemingly Muscovite-style of honor. The lampooned character insists on his "honor" even when he has been made totally ridiculous:

---

[40]Manifesto on Duels: PSZ 22, no. 16, 535 (1787). PSZ 24, no. 19,552 (1800); PSZ 37, no. 28,121 (1820).

COUNCILOR: No, my lord. I know what to do with your son. He has dishonored (*obeschestil*) me and I will sue him for as much dishonor fine (*beschest'e*) as I am due by law.
BRIGADIER'S WIFE: What! We should pay you for dishonor? For Heaven's sake, what for?
COUNCILOR: Because, my good lady, honor is more valuable to me than anything. I will sue him for every cent due to me according to my rank, not begrudging him even a penny.

In contrast to these sentiments evoking Muscovite terminology and dishonor fees, Fonvizin puts a more modern standard of honor in the words of the same character who, abashed and repentant, ends the play thusly: "They say it is hard to live with your conscience. But I have now learned for myself that to live without a conscience is the worst of all." Indeed, at the end of the eighteenth century, a widely distributed didactic handbook listed "the love of *honour*" as second in the "virtues of men" and stressed that "Honour is not in the power of the one who wishes to be honoured, rather it lies in the hands of those who honour us"; if others remain blind to one's good behavior, the honorable man pays no heed, confident in his own virtue. This 1783 publication also associates honor especially with the nobility: "Honour and the desire to preserve their acquired privileges without any suspicion ought to be the incentive for all the noblemen's deeds." Also in this century, the verb "to dishonor" took on the new meaning of "to take away one's good name."[41] More lethally, Russian noblemen began to identify with a code of individualized honor that led them to dueling. By the first third of the nineteenth century, aristocrats often dueled to avenge their honor—this, despite a century of legislation that assured them the state would be solicitous about such affronts. Irina Reyfman argues that the trend is evidence of a disillusionment by educated society with the willingness of the state to protect its rights[42]; more significantly, it also manifests a more individual sense of dignity.

The trend of late eighteenth-century legislation was to focus more attention on the content and consequences of an insult and to distinguish criminal from civil degrees of insult, steering Russia in the direction of European legislation on libel and slander. From the point of view of honor, the 1832 Digest of the Laws of the Russian Empire (*Svod zakonov Rossiiskoi imperii*), compiled by Count Mikhail Speranskii, essentially repeated existing precedent without

[41]Play: D. I. Fonvizin, *Brigadir. Nedorosl'* (Moscow and Leningrad, 1963), pp. 77, 80. Handbook: *Book on the Duties and Rights of Man and Citizen*, trans. Elizabeth Gorky, in J. L. Black, ed., *Citizens for the Fatherland* (New York, 1979), pp. 216–17, 252. Verb: *Slovar' russkogo iazyka XVIII veka* 2:17.
[42]Reyfman, "The Emergence of the Duel."

tying up loose ends, particularly regarding norms of compensation.[43] Its Criminal Code (vol. 15) devoted a chapter to insult—repeating the definitions of honor in the 1787 Manifesto on Duels[44]—and followed Petrine precedent on insults to officials, offenses in public places, slander in pasquinades, defamation of the law, and dueling.[45] The Civil Code of Speranskii's Digest (*Svod zakonov* 10), meanwhile, made no effort to define "minor" insult except in contrast to "serious" offenses, but it did try to systematize compensation norms, without great success. Noting that the norms of the 1649 Conciliar Law Code were outdated, it declared the precedents established by Peter to be operative. However, these—presumably the principle of criminal sanction for offenders according to the severity of the insult—seemingly coexisted with compensation fines called *beschest'e*. Recalling the 1649 Law Code, it specifically defined the dishonor fine for noblemen and bureaucrats as equal to their annual salary and affirmed the 1785 edicts equating fines for townsmen with their annual tax burden and setting the dishonor fines for wives, unmarried daughters, and minor sons as fixed proportions of their husband's or father's fee. Regarding civil compensation for peasants, the Code cited the Conciliar Law Code provision that levied a cash fine on all peasants for insult (art. 386) and mentioned earlier laws for cash compensation to insulted village elders in state peasant communities and in colonies of foreign settlers.[46]

In laws of 1845 and 1851, the issue of honor was codified for criminal and civil injuries in a relatively new and much more systematic way. The 1845 criminal code, for example, devoted an entire section to "crimes against the life, health, freedom, and honor of private persons," with chapters on the sorts of "serious" insults that were punishable with criminal sanctions: direct personal insult by blows, threats of physical assault, dishonorable deeds and verbal insult, slander (*kleveta*), unlawful seizure, violent assault, and threats. It set up escalating "levels" of severity of punishment depending on prior intent, the

---

[43]On Speranskii's work of compilation, see Marc Raeff, *Michael Speransky: Statesman of Imperial Russia, 1772–1839*, 2d rev. ed. (The Hague, 1969), chap. 11, and Wortman, *Development*, chap. 2.

[44]*Svod zakonov* 15 (1832): arts. 367–88; repeated, with three new articles (arts. 419, 426–27) as arts. 404–28 in *Svod zakonov* 15 (1842).

[45]Defamation of the law and officials, slander: *Svod zakonov* 15 (1832): arts. 229–45, 388, repeated as arts. 247–63, 428 in *Svod zakonov* 15 (1842). Dueling: *Svod zakonov* 15 (1832): arts. 349–56, repeated as arts. 381–88 in *Svod zakonov* 15 (1842).

[46]*Svod zakonov* . . . Vol. 10: *Zakony grazhdanskie i mezhevye*, 3d ed. (St. Petersburg, 1835), arts. 380–87. The earlier laws are cited in two other codes in the 1832 Digest. The first was the law on service by peasant representatives ("Ustav o sluzhbe po vyboram"), which set payments for insult to elected commune officials: *Svod zakonov* . . . Vol. 3: *Svod uchrezhdenii gosudarstvennykh i gubern-skikh. Pt. III. Ustavy o sluzhbe grazhdanskoi* (St. Petersburg, 1832), pt. 3, bk. 2, arts. 1139, 1166, 1192, 1210. The other code was the regulation for foreign colonists ("Svod postanovlenii ob inos-trannykh koloniiakh"), which listed fines for insult to officials in colonies in Saratov, Novorossiia, and other colonies: *Svod zakonov* . . . Vol. 12: *Svod ustavov gosudarstvennogo blagoustroistva*, pts. 4 and 5 (St. Petersburg, 1832), pt. 5, bk. 3, arts. 964–65.

location of the insult, or the social status of its target (e.g., parent, senior kinsman).[47] The lowest level of sanction involved public recantation and request for forgiveness as well as a brief prison term and compensation called by the Muscovite term, *beschest'e*; more serious offenses merited longer imprisonment, confiscation of property, corporal punishment, even exile. The 1845 Criminal Code frequently stipulated that individuals had the right to request civil compensation (*beschest'e*) in addition to the criminal punishment an offender would face for "serious" dishonor.

In other chapters, the 1845 Criminal Code went into greater depth than had the 1832/1842 Criminal Code to identify what constituted insult to representations of the tsar, insults long deemed "serious." Such insults included disrespecting the public announcement of a law, defacing a posted law, disseminating pasquinades about state officials or the laws themselves, and so on.[48] Conversely, it repeated the criminal sanctions and civil compensation for unlawful seizure and misbehavior by officials that were familiar from Catherinian times (arts. 376–78). The 1851 civil code removed much of the Muscovite complexity about sanction for insult, setting a narrow range of fines, from one to fifty rubles, depending on the relationship between the insulter and the aggrieved party.[49]

By the nineteenth century, law specific to peasants was being codified, including provisions for defense of honor. The 1832 Civil Code (in its article 386) had repeated the 1649 Conciliar Law Code's norms regarding dishonor for peasants; later codes refer to article 386 as precedent for peasant litigation on dishonor. In 1839, the Rural Judicial Charter for State Peasants explicitly amplified the provisions of the 1832 Civil Code by defining a state peasant's dishonor fine (it was made equivalent to the annual tax obligation of a man in the community to which the insulted party belonged) and specifying (as had the 1832 Civil Code, the 1785 Charter to the Towns, and earlier Muscovite law codes) that wives, daughters, and minor sons would receive, respectively, twice, four times, and one-half their husband's or father's dishonor fee. The 1839 Charter also mandated harsher sanctions, in addition to dishonor fines, when insults took place in public places or were directed at officials.[50] These provisions were repeated in the 1857 Code for the Good Ordering of State Peasant

---

[47]*Ulozhenie o nakazaniiakh ugolovnykh i ispravitel'nykh 1845 goda* (St. Petersburg, 1845), arts. 2008–39; included in *Svod zakonov . . . izdaniia 1857 goda. Vol. 15. Zakony ugolovnye* (St. Petersburg, 1857), arts. 2086–2117.

[48]*Ulozhenie o nakazaniikh*, arts. 301–16, 376–78; published also in RZ 6:245–49, 268–70 (a partial publication of the 1845 *Ulozhenie*); included as arts. 313–28 in *Svod zakonov* 15 (1857).

[49]PSZ, series 2, 55 vols. (St. Petersburg, 1830–84), vol. 26 (1852), no. 25,055, pt. III, arts. 60–63 (1851, March 21). Also published in I. M. Tiutriumov, ed., *Zakony grazhdanskie*, 5th ed., 2 vols. (Petrograd, 1915–), vol. 1 (1915), arts. 667–70. On the 1851 law, see V. N. [Nechaev, V. M.], "Obida lichnaia," *Entsiklopedicheskii slovar'* 21a (1897):504–5.

[50]"Sel'skii sudebnyi ustav dlia gosudarstvennykh krest'ian": PSZ, series 2, 14 (1840), pt. 1, no. 12,166, arts. 196–202.

Communities, which also incorporated norms from the 1851 civil law on compensation for insult.[51] As for criminal law, state peasants were not covered by the 1845 Criminal Code but remained under the jurisdiction of the 1839 Rural Judicial code until 1864.[52] The 1857 statute for foreign agrarian colonies did incorporate criminal penalties for insult to village officials based on the 1845 Criminal Code: It imposed harsher punishments for verbal insults to local officials, including public recantation before the assembled villagers (*na obshchem skhode*) and sanctions as decreed in the 1845 Criminal Code (namely, brief imprisonment and a fine according to the circumstances of the insult).[53] A new criminal code for the recently emancipated peasants was issued in 1864: the Code of Punishments to be Handed Down by Communal Judges. This law included provisions for insult (*obida*) by word, deed, and in writing.[54] From 1832 on, such laws for peasants specifically applied to state peasants. However, given that the 1832 Civil Code referred to the 1649 law covering all peasants, and that after emancipation all peasants were given the right to defend their honor, one can surmise that throughout the eighteenth and nineteenth centuries private (enserfed) peasants at least in principle had the right to seek compensation for insult, presumably in village and landlords' courts. Case law indeed shows that honor remained a high social value, and frequent issue for disputes, among peasants in Imperial Russia.[55]

By 1851, honor was prosecuted more systematically under civil and criminal law. Punishment and compensation were based on the circumstances of the insult as well as on social status; insult to public officials and flagrant insults were singled out for particular sanction. But the evolution of the law remained

---

[51]1839 provisions in 1857 "Ustav o blagoustroistve v kazennykh i kazach'ikh seleniiakh": *Svod zakonov, izd. 1857 goda. Vol 12, pt. 2* (St. Petersburg, 1857), arts. 515–19. 1851 norms in 1857 "Ustav": ibid., art. 516.

[52]On peasants' exclusion, see introduction to the 1845 *Ulozhenie o nakazaniiakh*. On the continued relevance of the 1839 Rural Judicial Code, see the provisions appended on March 31, 1863, to the 1861 decree emancipating serfs: "Osoboe prilozhenie k tomu IX Zakonov o Sostoianiiakh . . . Polozheniia o krest'ianakh," in *Prodolzhenie Svoda zakonov Rossiiskoi imperii, izd. 1857 goda po 31 marta 1863 goda, pt. 3: Stat'i k IX tomu Svoda* (St. Petersburg, 1863), arts. 24, 102 (repeated in *Svod zakonov* 9 [St. Petersburg, 1876]).

[53]"Ustav o koloniiakh inostrantsev v Imperii": *Svod zakonov, izd. 1857 goda. Vol. 12, pt. 2* (St. Petersburg, 1857), arts. 444–46. 1845 code: *Ulozhenie o nakazaniiakh*, art. 316; also published in RZ (1988) 6:249.

[54]"Ustav o nakazaniiakh, nalagaemykh mirovymi sud'iami": PSZ, series 2, vol. 39, no. 41,478, arts. 31, 130–38. This law was thereafter included in editions of *Svod zakonov* 15 with the same article numbers; see, for example, the 1914 edition: *Svod zakonov 15, pt. 1* (Petrograd, 1914).

[55]On nineteenth-century peasants' defense of honor, see Minenko, *Zhivaia starina*, pp. 91–100; M. M. Gromyko, *Traditsionnye normy povedeniia i formy obshcheniia russkikh krest'ian XIX v.* (Moscow, 1986); and Christine Worobec, *Peasant Russia: Family and Community in the Post-Emancipation Period* (Princeton, N.J., 1991), chap. 4.

true to Muscovite precedents: All social groups could still litigate to defend honor (even serfs), and the honor of the state still functioned as a metaphor linking individuals and ruler.

Conclusion

Peter Berger suggests that the obsolescence of traditional concepts of honor in modern times is not necessarily a good thing. Once communities cease defining honor in terms of adherence to community institutions and values and celebrate the dignity of the individual instead, social behavior enjoys fewer constraints and wider latitude. In the European tradition, this course of development has generally been praised as progress toward democracy and the realization of personal capacities, but it comes at the cost of community and connection. "Modern man, almost inevitably it seems, is ever in search of himself," Berger observes.[56] Honor may traditionally have played the conservative role of upholding established social institutions and precluding change, but it also provided individuals a sense of belonging and a blueprint for negotiating the challenges of life. Berger laments the atomization of individuals and communities that comes with the waning of honor and the rise of individualism and opines that inevitably individuals will again come to identify themselves with new collective practices and institutions and new concepts of honor. He hopes, however, that such institutions and values will be based on a regard for human dignity.

Berger's nostalgia for a perhaps idealized past is driven by a philosopher's concern with the harsh edges of modern society. In considering the past, however, we might be wary of equating the existence of a coherent society-wide honor code with personal contentment; certainly, many other forces conspired to make premodern societies alienating places in which to live. Still, Berger's point is compelling. There is something in honor that holds a society together.

Honor does so not only because it prescribes behavior; that is the least of it. Rather, it provides a flexible code with which to handle the structures and tensions of daily life. We have seen how in Muscovy honor was an idiom for resolving and pursuing conflict, how it was a discourse that infused the way people interacted in their homes, families, and villages. It also gave people an idiom with which to relate to the powers that be—a sense that their honor was part of a larger social reserve that linked them with tsar and thus God through officials and other representations of the state. It was not a highly articulated vision of society, nor necessarily a deeply compelling one—most individuals

---

[56]Peter Berger, "On the Obsolescence of the Concept of Honour," in Michael J. Sandel, ed., *Liberalism and Its Critics* (New York, 1984), pp. 149–58, quote on p. 156.

probably regarded the local tax collector and military governor with scant appreciation. Honor's defense provided institutions and norms that linked people with their society, however, as well as a strategy for perceiving coherence in one's surrounding world. This would become particularly useful as bureaucracy and reform brought individuals more and more in contact with the "imagined community" of the absolutist state.

I have argued that the defense of honor was systematized during the sixteenth century in Muscovy because two processes came together at that time. One was the complex social tension arising from tremendous social mobility, social change, and social disruption experienced in virtually all corners of the realm. Such circumstances put people in competition with others for status, threw people into new settings where relations needed to be established from scratch, and cast prevailing norms into doubt. In similar circumstances in other early modern societies, defamation and pursuit of redress from insult both became tools for negotiating social change. And that spelled increased litigation.

The second process that helped to systematize honor in sixteenth-century Muscovy was the state's single-minded project of mobilizing social and natural resources to increase the expanse, power, and wealth of the grand prince's realm. In this project, offering individuals protection from insult served several goals. It punished disruptive behavior among neighbors, within regiments, or in any corporate group, and thus contributed to social order. It provided an alternative to private vendetta and feud. It reinforced the social status quo with sanctions pegged to social rank. It also disseminated an idealized vision of the state as united by honor from the tsar down to the humblest person, and this constituted a mechanism of social cohesion. It was probably not a terribly effective mechanism, given the weak development of communication, of central government at the local level, and of literacy. Cohesion, however, was an elusive goal for all premodern states. Finally, in offering to provide a legal defense of honor, the state created a tangible link between community and state, individual and tsar. This was a service from which individuals and clans benefited; in showing the sovereign to be a just judge and patron of his people, it helped to legitimize his government. For all these reasons, the latent consciousness of personal dignity evident in Muscovite society and its Rus' antecedents was crystallized in the sixteenth century into two judicial institutions and practices, the redress of dishonor (*beschest'e*) and precedence (*mestnichestvo*).

I have also explored the social aspects of Muscovite honor, arguing that Moscow's discourse and practice of honor were remarkably inclusive, both socially and geographically. Not only were all social ranks, even enslaved people, deemed to have honor defensible in court (the only people excluded were those guilty of the most serious crimes). In addition, all the tsar's subjects, regardless of religion and ethnicity, were included in the legislative provisions on dishonor; many foreigners, non-Slavs, and non-Orthodox litigated over honor. Cases studied here come from all corners of the empire, even Siberia. In this, Muscovite codes of honor differed from those in many contemporaneous European countries, where the tendency by the early modern period was for corporate groups—guilds, nobilities—to define separate codes of honor and thus to safeguard entrenched social positions. In Muscovy, in contrast, a shared understanding of dignity provided a putative unity.

At the same time, Muscovite practices in defense of honor—inasmuch as they linked compensation with social rank—reinforced social hierarchy. The landed military elite was valued far more than taxed people; ecclesiastical hierarchs and monks at the greatest monasteries enjoyed far greater compensation than did humble parish priests and monks at poor monasteries. The institutions of Muscovite honor reinforced the corporate structure of society: Compensation scales identified such corporate groups as provincial gentry, Moscow-based officers, boyar clans, Cossacks, new model army regiments, townsmen, merchants, Siberian native tribes, and enserfed peasants. All could defend their social status from defamation.

Moscow's discourse about honor—the definition of what constituted an honorable person—complemented the preachings of Orthodox didactic works and put forward a vision of dignity particularly attractive to the sort of government Moscow had. It was a social code that encouraged social conformity and order. It stressed the inviolability of marriage and family, the respect of social hierarchy, the avoidance of violence in word and deed in family and community, loyal service to the state, and identification with one's born social position. It was not a social code that validated change, innovation, or social mobility, and that was precisely what the state would have wanted. It was particularly strict on women, prescribing extreme subservience to male authority and strict control over sexual activity. Meekness and obedience were virtues that brought honor to women and presumably—by quelling the autonomy of half the population—that also decreased the potential for social disruption.

Not all was so tranquil in the actual practice of defense of honor, of course. Individuals, clans, and communities aggressively wielded the ideas and judicial instance of honor litigation to serve their purposes. They insulted in order to torment neighbors, they harassed rivals with interminable suits, they used honor as a lever to pressure community members to toe the line morally and legally, they used dishonor suits to bring long-standing quarrels to closure. The state may have had a conservative interest in entertaining litigation over reputation, but communities negotiated this discourse in their own ways.

As suggested above, the Muscovite state seems to have used honor as one of many mechanisms to promote a vision and reality of social cohesion. I surveyed here the range of those mechanisms—coercive force and the threat thereof; co-opting social groups, especially elites, with rewards in the form of land, serfs, wealth, and status; ideas expressed in writing, in ritual, and in symbol, as in art and architecture; and practices such as defense of honor. The way in which honor promoted social cohesion in Muscovy was particularly interesting. The tsar styled himself as the center of a community of honor and imbued all his institutions and representations with honor. Insults that took place in his presence or chambers were doubly dishonoring to the recipient; insults to the tsar's judges, bailiffs, or documents were insults to him. Symbolically, the realm was a community of honor. On a narrower plane, the tsars used honor as an instrument of social control over the highest elite, adjudicating precedence disputes in such a way that social hierarchy was maintained and the tsar's authority demonstrated and affirmed.

I have also argued that the Muscovite use of honor changed with changing times. On the one hand, litigation over defamation escalated in the late seventeenth century in response to some significant social transformations—enserfment, the de facto transformation of the cavalry elite into a landed gentry, the emergence of aristocratic sensibilities, the expansion of bureaucracy and bureaucratic control, and the wholesale reform of the army. Russians continued to litigate to defend their honor well into the eighteenth and nineteenth centuries. At the same time, however, the content and practice of honor underwent a gradual change. Precedence was abolished in 1682 when the clan-based elite had been so transformed in membership and attitude that the system of reckoning hierarchy by clan heritage had become antiquated. Clan honor was yielding to a consciousness of aristocratic corporate honor by the end of the century. Simultaneously, attitudes toward state and society were changing, prompting more individually oriented social values, which we see emerging in the reigns of Aleksei Mikhailovich and Sofiia Alekseevna. These trends are most strikingly and forcefully demonstrated by Peter I's transformation of the discourse of autocracy, which now made an absolute claim of sovereign personal power. This claim was a far cry from Moscow's corporately defined political ideology, in which the tsar's power was limited by his obligations to be pious, just, caring of his people, attentive to their advice, and respectful of tradition—"changing nothing." Although codes of honor took several decades to catch up with Peter's bold pronouncements, the first hints of a more individualized honor and a more corporate sense of state and society can be discerned in the late Muscovite years.

This book has ranged widely to situate honor in the broad context of Muscovite social values, social structure, and political system. In doing so, it has opened up many issues that deserve further consideration. As the first large-scale effort to examine the defense of personal dignity from dishonor (*beschest'e*) and to assess the broadest patterns of precedence (*mestnichestvo*) litigation, it is certainly not the last word on either subject. Microhistorical studies of the workings of precedence, for example, may well yield interesting stories of how particular families used precedence litigation at particular times and circumstances; a local history of the workings of dishonor litigation in a defined geographical community could similarly yield important insights into the meaning of honor, the practice of the law, and the structure of society at the local level.

Several of the work's key themes go beyond honor and merit further explo-
ration. One is the issue of legal culture. Dishonor litigations are only one manifestation of how Muscovites used the courts, how the law was written and
applied, and how laws and litigation provided social mechanisms to individuals
and communities. Such themes could be pursued in seventeenth- and eighteenth-
century Moscow and provincial archives, which are teeming with court cases,
and such research would immeasurably expand our understanding of lived
experience on the local level in conditions of autocracy. The field of legal history—jurisprudence and practice, particularly in eighteenth-century Russia—is
greatly underdeveloped and awaits its historian. Another perspective opened
by this work involves concepts of society. I have only scratched the surface in
examining how Muscovites saw their place in their communities, how they
regarded the broader social collective, how prescriptive literature regarded
state and society, and how these concepts might have changed over time. I have
argued that Muscovites had little conceptual vocabulary for collective self-
understanding, but the nuances of how communities did understand themselves in so diverse a realm remain to be explored.

Throughout, I have also sought to demonstrate the value of viewing Muscovy in a comparative context, at least on issues such as social and political
practice. Interpretations of the practice of politics and the structure of society
in early modern Europe and Russia seem to be converging: Historians of
Europe are becoming less interested in juridical institutions and abstract theory
and more engaged in sorting out the messy diversity of social identity, community relations, and political administration. At the same time, historians of
Muscovy are looking beyond statist models to assess lived experience. Thus
contemporary historiography in each of these fields has much to offer the other.

This work also raises, if only implicitly, the question of periodization. It is
traditional to regard Peter I as a great divide in Russian history, and on some
grounds, there is good reason to continue to do so. The Petrine era's radical
break with traditional expectations about both political power and the relationship of corporate groups to the state certainly changed the course of Russian history over the long run. Our study of honor also shows, however, that
such changes came gradually and that they were prepared by political policies
and practices initiated a generation or more before Peter took power. Beneath
the obvious and dramatic changes in political ideology, institutions, and high
culture, much about Muscovy changed slowly, if at all. The life of the peasantry, for example, apparently got worse, but did not change fundamentally.
The content of the law and the nature of litigation also changed only slowly,
despite sporadic efforts at legal reform. Tracing the practice and discourse of
honor to the Imperial period shows strong continuities in practice and concepts, as well as gradual change. Implicitly, this study portrays the seventeenth
and eighteenth centuries as a unified and integral historical period for Russia,
and it is hoped that other historians will push their research across the great

Petrine divide—forward to include the eighteenth century for "Muscovite" historians, backward to embrace the seventeenth century for "Imperial" historians. We may in time conclude that Russia's "early modern" period stretches from roughly 1600 to 1800.

Finally, this study of honor sheds light on the most vexed question of Russian historiography of the pre-Petrine era: the relationship of the state to society and the nature of autocracy. That Muscovites enjoyed protections of personal honor, and that those protections became only more explicit in law and practice as the state embraced European absolutism, tells us much about society and government in Russia before the great reforms of the 1860s. Russia was not a totalitarian state, nor an Oriental despotism, nor even a "plain tyranny," despite what some theorists of state and society have been saying about it since the sixteenth century. The state did indeed have great authority, and society had relatively little, as far as legal privileges and institutionalized bases of power went. There were, however, equally great limits to the state's power, limits imposed by the practical exigencies of colonial administration, by the empire's multiethnic character, by geography and climate, by the dearth of literacy and education, and by available technology and means of communication. Even more significantly, the state took as its responsibility defending the honor not only of public offices, ranks, and institutions but also of private individuals No matter how pragmatic that practice, it was also an affirmation of deeply rooted cultural values. And because the state was responsive to some social needs and limited in its coercive power, individuals enjoyed a wide arena for local autonomies and self-direction. No matter how autocratic or absolutist were premodern rulers' claims to authority, the reality of social practice was more open, more varied, and less predictable and controllable than they would have wanted.

Honor is only one arena in which individuals, families, and communities in early modern Russia interacted with each other and with the government in ways that satisfied both sides. Local government, landholding patterns, religious observance, litigation over misdemeanors, even criminal litigation were arenas in which communities manipulated the laws and negotiated institutions even as they conformed to state demands. Muscovite society has perhaps been underestimated—dishonored, one might say—by our failure to appreciate how dynamic, diverse, and complex it was.

Glossary

batogi bastinadoes

beschest'e insult to honor; fine for such insult

bran' verbal abuse

deti boiarskie (sing.: syn boiarskii) gentry; provincial cavalrymen; those who serve "from the towns"; literally, "sons of boyars"

d'iak state secretary

dumnyi of the Council, Conciliar, referring to the council of advisors to the tsar, in four *dumnyi* ranks by the late sixteenth century: boyar, *okol'nichii*, *dvorianin*, and *d'iak*

dvorianin (plural: dvoriane) gentryman; provincial cavalryman

gubnoi starosta locally elected gentryman in charge of criminal affairs

guliashchie liudi vagrants; unregistered people

iasak tribute, often paid in furs

kruchinit' to distress; to anger

lai verbal insult

mestnichestvo precedence

namestnik governor, generally a sixteenth-century title

okol'nichii second conciliar rank, after boyar; no useful English equivalent; based on the word *okolo* (near, around), suggesting serving at the ruler's side

pod'iachii undersecretary

pomest'e   service-tenure estate, i.e., populated village or part of village given to cavalrymen in conditional tenure in exchange for service

posad   urban commune

poval'nyi obysk   inquest, community survey

Razriadnyi prikaz   Military Service Chancery

rodoslovnyi   high born; a member of the Moscow-based cavalry ranks

rynda   ceremonial bodyguard of tsar; etymology unknown

stol'nik   ceremonial rank for Moscow-based cavalrymen; first major rank below four conciliar ranks; no useful English translation; based on root word *stol* (table), initially implying serving at the grand prince's table

striapchii   ceremonial rank for Moscow-based cavalrymen; second major rank below four conciliar ranks; no useful English translation; based on the verb *striapat'* (to work, to serve)

uvech'e   mutilation, injury

voevoda   military commander; governor, generally in the seventeenth century

volost'   rural commune

votchina   estate held in hereditary or patrimonial possession

zhilets   ceremonial rank for Moscow-based cavalrymen; last major rank of Moscow-based cavalry; no useful English translation; based on the verb *zhit'* (to live), implying servitors resident at court

Bibliography

Primary Sources

Archival Materials

Rossiiskaia gosudarstvennaia biblioteka, Moscow:
  fond 256: Collection of N. P. Rumiantsev
  fond 303: Trinity St. Sergii Monastery
Rossiiskii gosudarstvennyi arkhiv drevnikh aktov, Moscow:
  fond 210: Razriadnyi prikaz
  fond 239: Sudnyi prikaz
  fond 1103: Arzamas prikaznaia izba
  fond 1167: Temnikov and Kadom prikaznaia izba
  fond 1175: Shatsk prikaznaia izba
  fond 1177: Iakutsk prikaznaia izba
St. Petersburgskii filial arkhiva Instituta rossiiskoi istorii Rossiiskoi akademii nauk, St. Petersburg:
  fond 62: Kablukov family archive
  koll. 9: Collection of A. I. Artem'ev

Published Sources

Akty istoricheskie, sobrannye i izdannye Arkheograficheskoiu kommissieiu. 5 vols. St. Petersburg, 1841–42.
Akty iuridicheskie. St. Petersburg, 1838.
Akty Moskovskogo gosudarstva. 3 vols. St. Petersburg, 1890–1901.
Akty, otnosiashchiesia do iuridicheskogo byta drevnei Rossii. 3 vols. and index. St. Petersburg, 1857–1901.
Akty, sobrannye v bibliotekakh i arkhivakh Rossiiskoi imperii Arkheograficheskoiu ekspeditsieiu Imp. akademii nauk. 4 vols. and index. St. Petersburg, 1836, 1838.

Akty sotsial'no-ekonomicheskoi istorii severo-vostochnoi Rusi kontsa XIV–nachala XVI v. 3 vols. Moscow, 1952–64.

"Akty Tul'skogo gubernskogo pravleniia." LZAK *za 1910 god* 23 (1911), sect. III.

Almazov, A. *Tainaia ispoved' v pravoslavnoi vostochnoi Tserkvi.* Vol. III. *Prilozheniia.* Moscow, 1995.

Anpilogov, G. N., ed. *Novye dokumenty o Rossii kontsa XVI–nachala XVII v.* Moscow, 1967.

Berry, Lloyd E., and Robert O. Crummey, eds. *Rude and Barbarous Kingdom: Russia in the Accounts of Sixteenth-Century English Voyagers.* Madison, Wis., 1968.

Bogdanov, A. P., ed. *Pamiatniki obshchestvenno-politicheskoi mysli v Rossii kontsa XVII veka. Literaturnye panegiriki.* 2 vols. Moscow, 1983.

Bogoiavlenskii, S., ed. "Bran' kniazia Vasiliia Mikulinskogo. . . ." In *Chteniia* 1910, bk. 3, Miscellany, pp. 18–20.

Bond, Edward A., ed. *Russia at the Close of the Sixteenth Century: comprising, the treatise "Of the Russe Common Wealth," by Giles Fletcher; and the Travels of Sir Jerome Horsey, now for the first time printed entire from his own manuscript.* London, 1856.

"Book on the Duties and Rights of Man and Citizen." Trans. Elizabeth Gorky. In J. L. Black, ed., *Citizens for the Fatherland,* pp. 210–66. New York, 1979.

Bychkova, M. E., ed. "Novye rodoslovnye knigi XVI v." In *Redkie istochniki po istorii Rossii.* Fasc. 2. Moscow, 1977.

Chaadaev, P. Ia. *Peter Iakovlevich Chaadaev: Philosophical Letters and Apology of a Madman.* Trans. with intro. by Mary-Barbara Zeldin. Knoxville, Tenn., 1969.

Delovaia pis'mennost' Vologodskogo kraia XVII–XVIII vv. Vologda, 1979.

de Mayerberg, Augustin Baron. *Relation d'un voyage en Muscovie.* 2 vols. Paris, 1858.

Dewey, H. W., comp., ed., and trans. *Muscovite Judicial Texts, 1488–1556.* Michigan Slavic Materials, no. 7. Ann Arbor, Mich., 1966.

Dewey, H. W., and A. M. Kleimola, trans. and eds. *Russian Private Law in the XIV–XVII Centuries.* Ann Arbor, Mich., 1973.

Dmitrieva, R. P., ed. *Povest' o Petre i Fevronii.* Leningrad, 1979.

Dmytryshyn, Basil, ed. *Medieval Russia: A Source Book, 850–1700.* 3d ed. Fort Worth, Tex., 1991.

Doklady i prigovory sostoiavshiesia v Pravitel'stvuiushchem Senate v tsarstvovanie Petra velikogo. 6 vols. in 11 pts. St. Petersburg, 1880–1901.

Dopolneniia k Aktam istoricheskim. 12 vols. and index. St. Petersburg, 1846–75.

Druzhinin, V. G. "Neskol'ko neizvestnykh literaturnykh pamiatnikov iz sbornika XVI-go veka." LZAK *za 1908 god* 21 (1909):1–117.

Dvortsovye razriady. 4 vols. St. Petersburg, 1850–55.

Dukhovnye i dogovornye gramoty velikikh i udel'nykh kniazei XIV–XVI vv. Moscow and Leningrad, 1950.

Fonvizin, D. I. *Brigadir. Nedorosl'.* Moscow and Leningrad, 1963.

Got'e, Iu. V. *Akty, otn. k istorii zemskikh soborov.* Moscow, 1909.

Grekov, B. D., ed. *Sudebniki XV–XVI vekov.* Moscow and Leningrad, 1952.

Griffiths, David, and George E. Munro, trans. and eds. *Catherine II's Charters of 1785 to the Nobility and the Towns.* Bakersfield, Calif., 1991.

Gudzii, N. K. *Khrestomatiia po drevnei russkoi literature XI–XVII vekov*. 4th rev. ed. Moscow, 1947.

Hellie, Richard, trans. and ed. *The Muscovite Law Code (Ulozhenie) of 1649. Part 1: Text and Translation*. Irvine, Calif., 1988.

Herberstein, Sigismund von. *Description of Moscow and Muscovy, 1557*. Ed. Bertold Picard. Trans. J. B. C. Grundy. New York, 1969.

——. *Notes upon Russia*. Trans. and ed. R. H. Major. 2 vols. London, 1851–52.

Horsey, Jerome. "Travels." In Edward A. Bond, ed., *Russia at the Close of the Sixteenth Century: comprising, the treatise "Of the Russe Common Wealth," by Giles Fletcher; and the Travels of Sir Jerome Horsey, now for the first time printed entire from his own manuscript*. London, 1856.

Ianin, V. L., and A. A. Zalizniak. *Novgorodskie gramoty na bereste*. Moscow, 1986.

Ioasafskaia letopis'. Ed. A. A. Zimin. Moscow, 1957.

Justinian. *The Digest of Roman Law: Theft, Rapine, Damage and Insult*. Trans. C. F. Kolbert. Harmondsworth, England, and New York, 1979.

Knigi razriadnye po ofitsial'nym onykh spiskam. . . . 2 vols. St. Petersburg, 1853–55.

"Knigi rodoslovnye." *Arkhiv istoriko-iuridicheskikh svedenii, otn. do Rossii* 1, sect. III (1850):22–26.

Korkunov, M. A., ed. *Pamiatniki XV veka. Akty iz dela o mestnichestve Saburova s Zabolotskim*. St. Petersburg, 1857.

Kotoshikhin, Grigorii. "*On Russia in the Reign of Alexis Mikhailovich*: An Annotated Translation." Trans. with notes and intro. by Benjamin Uroff. Ph.D. dissertation, Columbia University, 1970.

——. *O Rossii vo tsarstvovanie Alekseia Mikhailovicha*. 4th ed. St. Petersburg, 1906.

Letopis' zaniatii Imp. Arkheograficheskoi kommissii. 35 vols. St. Petersburg and Leningrad, 1861–1928.

Likhachev, N. P., ed. "Inoka Fomy slovo pokhval'noe o blagovernom velikom kniaze Borise Aleksandroviche." *Pamiatniki drevnei pis'mennosti i iskusstva* 168 (1908): i–lx, 55 pp.

——, ed. *Mestnicheskie dela, 1563–1605 gg*. St. Petersburg, 1894.

Margeret, Jacques. *The Russian Empire and Grand Duchy of Muscovy: A 17th-Century French Account*. Trans. and ed. Chester S. L. Dunning. Pittsburgh, 1983.

Mitchell, Bonner, and Russell Zguta, trans. and eds. "A Sixteenth-Century 'Account of Muscovy' Attributed to Don Felippo Prenestain." *Russian History* 8, pt. 3 (1981): 390–412.

Moskovskaia delovaia i bytovaia pis'mennost' XVII veka. Moscow, 1968.

The Muscovite Biographical Group [Ol'ga Kosheleva, Russell Martin, Boris Morozov, Marshall Poe], comp. *The Annual Composition of the Muscovite Boyar Duma, 1613–1713*. Cambridge, Mass., 1995.

Nasonov, A. N., ed., with intro. "Letopisnyi svod XV v. (po dvum spiskam)." In *Materialy po istorii SSSR*. Vol. 2. Moscow, 1955:273–321.

Novgorodskaia pervaia letopis' starshego i mladshego izvodov. Eds. M. N. Tikhomirov and A. N. Nasonov. Moscow and Leningrad, 1950.

Novikov, N. I., ed. *Drevniaia rossiiskaia vivliofika*. . . . 2d ed. 20 vols. Moscow, 1788–91.

Obolenskii, M. A., ed. "Proekt ustava o sluzhebnom starshinstve boiar, okol'nichikh i dumnykh liudei po tridtsati chetyrem stepeniam. . . ." *Arkhiv istoriko-iuridicheskikh svedenii, otn. do Rossii* . . . 1, sect. II (1850):20–40.

Olearius, Adam. *The Travels of Olearius in Seventeenth-Century Russia.* Trans. and ed. Samuel H. Baron. Stanford, 1967.

Palitsyn, Avraami. *Skazanie.* Moscow and Leningrad, 1955.

Pamiatniki delovoi pis'mennosti XVII veka. Vladimirskii krai. Moscow, 1984.

Pamiatniki diplomaticheskikh snoshenii drevnei Rossii s derzhavami inostrannymi. Pt. 1: Snosheniia s gosudarstvami evropeiskimi. St. Petersburg, 1851.

Pamiatniki literatury drevnei Rusi. XIV–seredina XV veka. Moscow, 1981.

Pamiatniki literatury drevnei Rusi. XVII vek. 3 bks. Moscow, 1988–94.

Pamiatniki literatury drevnei Rusi. Konets XV–pervaia polovina XVI veka. Moscow, 1984.

Pamiatniki pis'mennosti v muzeiakh Vologodskoi oblasti. Katalog-putevoditel'. 5 vols. in 11 pts. Vologda, 1982–89.

Pamiatniki russkogo prava. 8 vols. Moscow, 1952–63.

Pamiatniki starinnoi russkoi literatury. 4 vols. St. Petersburg, 1860–62.

Pipes, Richard, ed. *Karamzin's Memoir on Ancient and Modern Russia: A Translation and Analysis.* New York, 1969.

Pis'ma i bumagi Imperatora Petra Velikogo. 13 vols. in 16 pts. to date. St. Petersburg and Moscow, 1887–.

Pobedonostsev, K. P., ed. *Istoriko-iuridicheskie akty perekhodnoi epokhi XVII–XVIII vekov.* Moscow, 1887.

——. *Materialy dlia istorii prikaznogo sudoproizvodstva v Rossii.* Moscow, 1890.

Pogodin, M. P. "Dela po mestnichestvu." *Russkii istoricheskii sbornik* 2, bks. 1–4 (1838); 5 (1842).

Polnoe sobranie postanovlenii i rasporiazhenii po vedomstvu pravoslavnogo ispovedeniia Rossiiskoi imperii. 19 vols. St. Petersburg, 1869–1915.

Polnoe sobranie russkikh letopisei. 41 vols. to date. St. Petersburg and Moscow, 1841–.

Polnoe sobranie zakonov Rossiiskoi imperii. Vol. 1 in 40 vols. with 5 additional vols. of indices. St. Petersburg, 1830.

Polnoe sobranie zakonov Rossiiskoi imperii. Series 2. 55 vols. St. Petersburg, 1830–84.

Polotskii, Simeon. *Izbrannye sochineniia.* Moscow and Leningrad, 1953.

"Poslednii pretendent mestnichestva. . . ." *Moskvitianin* 1841, pt. 1, nos. 1–2, pp. 476–81.

Possevino, Antonio, S. J. *The Moscovia.* Trans. Hugh F. Graham. Pittsburgh, 1977.

Pouncy, Carolyn Johnston, ed. and trans. *The Domostroi: Rules for Russian Households in the Time of Ivan the Terrible.* Ithaca, N.Y., and London, 1994.

Povest' vremennykh let. Ed. V. P. Adrianova-Peretts. 2 vols. Moscow, 1950.

Priselkov, M. D., comp. *Troitskaia letopis'. Rekonstruktsiia teksta.* Moscow and Leningrad, 1950.

Prodolzhenie Svoda zakonov Rossiiskoi imperii . . . po 31 marta 1863 goda. Pt 3: Stat'i k IX tomu Svoda. St. Petersburg, 1863.

Razriadnaia kniga 1475–1605 gg. Ed. N. G. Savich. Vol. 1 in 3 pts. Moscow, 1977–78. Ed. N. G. Savich. Vol. 2 in 3 pts. Moscow, 1981–82. Ed. L. F. Kuz'mina. Vol. 3 in 3 pts. Moscow, 1985–89. Ed. L. F. Kuz'mina. Vol. 4 in 1 pt. to date. Moscow, 1994–.

Razriadnaia kniga 1495–1598 gg. Ed. V. I. Buganov. Moscow, 1966.

Razriadnaia kniga 1550–1636 gg. 2 vols. in 3 pts. Ed. L. F. Kuz'mina. Moscow, 1975–76.

Razriadnaia kniga 1559–1605 gg. Ed. L. F. Kuz'mina. Moscow, 1974.

Razriadnye knigi 1598–1638 gg. Ed. V. I. Buganov. Moscow, 1974.

Rossiiskoe zakonodatel'stvo X–XX vekov. Ed. O. I. Chistiakov. 9 vols. Moscow, 1984–94.

Russkaia istoricheskaia biblioteka. 39 vols. St. Petersburg and Leningrad, 1872–1929.

Sbornik Imp. Russkogo istoricheskogo obshchestva. 148 vols. St. Petersburg and Petrograd, 1867–1916.

Serbina, K. N., ed. *Ustiuzhskii letopisnyi svod (Arkhangelogorodskii letopisets).* Moscow and Leningrad, 1950.

Shcherbatov, Prince M. M. *On the Corruption of Morals in Russia.* Ed. and trans. with intro. by A. Lentin. Cambridge, England, 1969.

Smirnov, P. P., ed. "Chelobitnye dvorian i detei boiarskikh vsekh gorodov i pervoi polovine XVII v." In *Chteniia* 1915, bk. 3, pp. 1–73.

———. "Neskol'ko dokumentov iz istorii Sobornogo Ulozheniia i Zemskogo Sobora 1648–1649 gg.," In *Chteniia* 1913, bk. 4, pp. 1–20.

Sobranie gosudarstvennykh gramot i dogovorov. 5 pts. Moscow, 1813–94.

Sochineniia I. Peresvetova. Ed. A. A. Zimin. Moscow and Leningrad, 1956.

Subbotin, N. I. *Materialy dlia istorii raskola za pervoe vremia ego sushchestvovaniia.* 9 vols. Moscow, 1875–86.

———. *Tsarskie voprosy i sobornye otvety o mnorazlichnykh tserkovnykh chinekh (Stoglav).* Moscow, 1890.

Svod zakonov Rossiiskoi imperii, poveleniem Imperatora Nikolaia Pavlovicha sostavlennyi. Vol. 3: Svod uchrezhdenii gosudarstvennykh i gubernskikh. Pt. III. Ustavy o sluzhbe grazhdanskoi. St. Petersburg, 1832.

Svod zakonov Rossiiskoi imperii, poveleniem Imperatora Nikolaia Pavlovicha sostavlennyi. Vol. 10: Zakony grazhdanskie i mezhevye. 3d ed. St. Petersburg, 1835.

Svod zakonov Rossiiskoi imperii, poveleniem Imperatora Nikolaia Pavlovicha sostavlennyi. Vol. 12: Svod ustavov gosudarstvennogo blagoustroistva. Pts. 4 and 5. St. Petersburg, 1832.

Svod zakonov Rossiiskoi imperii, izdaniia 1857 goda. Vol. 12. Pt. 2. Ustavy o gorodskom i sel'skom khoziaistve, o blagoustroistve v kazennykh i kazach'ikh seleniiakh, i o koloniiakh inostrantsev v Imperii. St. Petersburg, 1857.

Svod zakonov Rossiiskoi imperii, poveleniem Imperatora Nikolaia Pavlovicha sostavlennyi. Vol. 15. Zakony ugolovnye. St. Petersburg, 1832.

Svod zakonov Rossiiskoi imperii, poveleniem Imperatora Nikolaia Pavlovicha sostavlennyi. Vol. 15. Zakony ugolovnye. St. Petersburg, 1842.

Svod zakonov Rossiiskoi imperii, izdaniia 1857 goda. Vol. 15. Zakony ugolovnye. St. Petersburg, 1857.

Tatishchev, Iu. V. *Mestnicheskii spravochnik XVII veka.* Vilnius, 1910.

Tikhomirov, M. N., ed. *Zakon sudnyi liudem prostrannoi i svodnoi redaktsii.* Moscow, 1961.

Timofeev, Ivan. *Vremennik.* Moscow and Leningrad, 1951.

Titov, A. A., ed. *Kungurskie akty XVII veka. 1668–1699 g.* St. Petersburg, 1888.

Tiutriumov, I. M., ed. *Zakony grazhdanskie.* 5th ed. 2 vols. Petrograd, 1915.

Ulozhenie o nakazaniiakh ugolovnykh i ispravitel'nykh 1845 goda. St. Petersburg, 1845.

Valuev, D. A., ed. "Razriadnaia kniga ot 7067 do 7112 goda." In *Simbirskii sbornik*. Moscow, 1844.

Varentsov, V. A. "Zhalovannaia gramota na zvanie 'gostia' novgorodtsu Ivanu Kharlamovu." *Sovetskie arkhivy* 1979, no. 6:59–60.

Vockerodt, Johan Gottgilf. "Rossiia pri Petre Pervom." Trans. A. N. Shemiakin. In *Chteniia* 1874, bk. 2, sect. IV, pp. 1–120.

Zakonodatel'nye akty Russkogo gosudarstva vtoroi poloviny XVI–pervoi poloviny XVII veka. Kommentarii. Leningrad, 1987.

Zakonodatel'nye akty Russkogo gosudarstva vtoroi poloviny XVI–pervoi poloviny XVII veka. Teksty. Leningrad, 1986.

Zenkovsky, Serge A. *Medieval Russia's Epics, Chronicles and Tales.* Rev. ed. New York, 1974.

Zimin, A. A., ed. *Tysiachnaia kniga 1550 g. i dvorovaia tetrad' 50-kh godov XVI v.* Moscow and Leningrad, 1950.

Secondary Sources

Primarily Relevant to Russia

Abramovich, G. V. "Gosudarstvennye povinnosti vladel'cheskikh krest'ian severo-zapadnoi Rusi v XVI–pervoi chetverti XVII veka." *Istoriia SSSR* 1972, no. 3:65–84.

Absoliutizm v Rossii (XVII–XVIII vv.). Moscow, 1964.

Akhieser, A. S. *Rossiia: Kritika istoricheskogo opyta.* 3 vols. Moscow, 1991.

Aksakov, K. S. "On the Internal State of Russia." In Marc Raeff, ed., *Russian Intellectual History: An Anthology*, pp. 230–51. New York, 1966.

Alef, Gustave. "A History of the Muscovite Civil War: The Reign of Vasilii II (1425–62)." Ph.D. dissertation, Princeton University, 1956.

——. "Aristocratic Politics and Royal Policy in Muscovy in the Late Fifteenth and Early Sixteenth Centuries." *Forschungen* 27 (1980):77–109.

——. "Muscovite Military Reforms in the Second Half of the Fifteenth Century." *Forschungen* 18 (1973):73–108.

——. "The Origins of Muscovite Autocracy: The Age of Ivan III." *Forschungen* 39 (1986): 362 pp.

——. "Reflections on the Boyar Duma in the Reign of Ivan III." *Slavonic and East European Review* 45 (1967):76–123.

Alekseev, Iu. G. *Agrarnaia i sotsial'naia istoriia severo-vostochnoi Rusi XV–XVI vv. Pereiaslavskii uezd.* Moscow and Leningrad, 1966.

Alpatov, M. A. *Russkaia istoricheskaia mysl' i Zapadnaia Evropa XII–XVII vv.* Moscow, 1973.

Al'shits, D. N. "Razriadnaia kniga Moskovskikh gosudarei XVI v." *Problemy istochnikovedeniia* 6 (1958):130–51.

Anderson, M. S. *Peter the Great.* 2d ed. New York, 1995.

Andreyev, Nikolai. "Filofei and His Epistle to Ivan Vasil'yevich." *Slavonic and East European Review* 38, no. 90 (1959–60):1–31.

Anisimov, Evgenii V. *The Reforms of Peter the Great: Progress through Coercion in Russia.* Trans. John T. Alexander. Armonk, N.Y., 1993.

Armstrong, John A. "Old-Regime Governors: Bureaucratic and Patrimonial Attributes." *Comparative Studies in Society and History* 14 (1972):2–29.

Backus, Oswald P. *Motives of West Russian Nobles in Deserting Lithuania for Moscow, 1377–1514.* Lawrence, Kans., 1957.

Bakhrushin, S. K. "Komi." In *Ocherki istorii SSSR. Period feodalizma. Konets XV v.–nachalo XVII v.*, pp. 640–48. Moscow, 1955.

Baklanova, N. A. "Otrazhenie idei absoliutizma v izobrazitel'nom iskusstve pervoi chetverti XVIII v." In *Absoliutizm v Rossii (XVII–XVIII vv.)*, pp. 492–507. Moscow, 1964.

Baron, Samuel H. "Feudalism or the Asiatic Mode of Production: Alternative Interpretations of Russian History." In idem and Nancy Whittier Heer, eds., *Windows on the Russian Past: Essays on Soviet Historiography since Stalin*, pp. 24–41. Columbus, Ohio, 1977.

——. "Vasilii Shorin: Seventeenth-Century Russian Merchant Extraordinary." *Canadian-American Slavic Studies* 6, no. 4 (1972):503–48.

——. "Who Were the *Gosti?*" *California Slavic Studies* 7 (1973):1–40.

Baron, Samuel H., and Nancy Whittier Heer, eds. *Windows on the Russian Past: Essays on Soviet Historiography since Stalin.* Columbus, Ohio, 1977.

Baron, Samuel H., and Nancy Shields Kollmann, eds. *Religion and Culture in Early Modern Russia and Ukraine.* DeKalb, Ill., 1997.

Barsukov, A. *Ozbor istochnikov i literatury russkogo rodosloviia.* St. Petersburg, 1887.

Bazil'evich, K. V. "Novgorodskie pomeshchiki iz posluzhil'tsev v kontse XV veka." *Istoricheskie zapiski* 14 (1945):62–80.

Bennet, Douglas J. "The Idea of Kingship in 17th-Century Russia." Ph.D. dissertation, Harvard University, 1967.

Benson, Sumner. "The Role of Western Political Thought in Petrine Russia." *Canadian-American Slavic Studies* 8, no. 2 (1974):254–73.

Bernadskii, V. N. *Novgorod i novgorodskaia zemlia v XV veke.* Leningrad, 1961.

Bilinbakhov, G. V. "Otrazhenie idei absoliutizma v simvolike petrovskikh znamen." In *Kul'tura i iskusstvo Rossii XVIII veka*, pp. 7–25. Leningrad, 1981.

——. "Gosudarstvennaia geral'dika Rossii kontsa XVII–pervoi chetverti XVIII veka (K voprosu formirovaniia ideologii absoliutizma v Rossii)." Abstract of candidate dissertation, Leningrad State University, 1982.

Black, J. L. *Citizens for the Fatherland: Education, Educators, and Pedagogical Ideals in Eighteenth-Century Russia.* New York, 1979.

Blum, Jerome. *Lord and Peasant in Russia from the Ninth to the Nineteenth Century.* New York, 1969.

Bobrovskii, P. O. *Mestnichestvo i prestupleniia protiv rodovoi chesti v russkom voiske do Petra I.* St. Petersburg, 1888.

Bogdanov, A. P. "'Istinnoe i vernoe skazanie' o I krymskom pokhode 1687 g.—Pamiatnik publitsistiki posol'skogo prikaza." In *Problemy izucheniia narrativnykh istochnikov po istorii russkogo srednevekov'ia. Sbornik statei*, pp. 57–84. Moscow, 1982.

——. "Letopisnye i publitsisticheskie istochniki po politicheskoi istorii Rossii kontsa XVII veka." Candidate dissertation, Institute of the History of the USSR of the Academy of Sciences of the USSR, 1983.

——. *Ot letopisaniia k issledovaniiu. Russkie istoriki poslednei chetverti XVII veka.* Moscow, 1995.

———. "Politicheskaia graviura v Rossii perioda regentstva Sof'i Alekseevny." In *Isto-chnikovedenie otechestvennoi istorii. Sbornik statei. 1981*, pp. 225–46. Moscow, 1982.

Bogoiavlenskii, S. K. "Prikaznye d'iaki XVII veka." *Istoricheskie zapiski* 1 (1937):220–39.

Bogoiavlenskii, S. K, and S. B. Veselovskii. "Mestnoe upravlenie." In *Ocherki istorii SSSR. Period feodalizma. XVII vek*, pp. 384–94. Moscow, 1955.

Bogoslovskii, M. M. "Zemskie chelobitnye v drevnei Rusi." *Bogoslovskii vestnik* 1911, nos. 1:133–50; 2:215–41; 3:403–19; 4:685–96.

———. *Zemskoe samoupravlenie na russkom Severe v XVII veke*. 2 vols. In *Chteniia* 1910, bk. 1, and 1912, bks. 2 and 3.

Brown, Peter Bowman. "Early Modern Russian Bureaucracy: The Evolution of the Chancellery System from Ivan III to Peter the Great, 1478–1717." 2 vols. Ph.D. dissertation, University of Chicago, 1978.

———. "Muscovite Government Bureaus." *Russian History* 10 (1983):269–330.

———. "The *Zemskii sobor* in Recent Soviet Historiography." *Russian History* 10, pt. 1 (1983):77–90.

Brown, William Edward. *A History of Seventeenth-Century Russian Literature*. Ann Arbor, Mich., 1980.

Buganov, V. I. *Razriadnye knigi poslednei chetverti XV–nachala XVII v.* Moscow, 1962.

———. "'Vrazhdotvornoe' mestnichestvo." *Voprosy istorii* 1974, no. 11:118–33.

Bulanin, D. M. "Tainaia tainykh." In *Slovar' knizhnikov i knizhnosti drevnei Rusi*, 2, pt. 2 (1989):427–30. 3 vols. in 5 pts. to date. Leningrad, 1987–.

Bushkovitch, Paul. "The Epiphany Ceremony of the Russian Court in the Sixteenth and Seventeenth Centuries." *Russian Review* 49, no. 1 (1990):1–18.

———. "The *Life of Saint Filipp*: Tsar and Metropolitan in the Late Sixteenth Century." In Michael S. Flier and Daniel Rowland, eds. *Medieval Russian Culture, Vol. II*. California Slavic Studies XIX, pp. 29–46. Berkeley and Los Angeles, 1994.

———. *The Merchants of Muscovy, 1580–1650*. Cambridge, England, 1980.

———. *Religion and Society in Russia: The Sixteenth and Seventeenth Centuries*. New York and Oxford, 1992.

Bychkova, M. E. "Iz istorii sozdaniia rodoslovnykh rospisei kontsa XVII v. i Barkhatnoi knigi." *Vspomogatel'nye istoricheskie distsipliny* 12 (1981):90–109.

———. "Pervye rodoslovnye rospisi litovskikh kniazei v Rossii." In *Obshchestvo i gosudarstvo feodal'noi Rossii*, pp. 133–40 Moscow, 1975.

———. "Pol'skie traditsii v russkoi genealogii XVII veka." *Sovetskoe slavianovedenie* 1981, no. 5:39–50.

———. *Rodoslovnye knigi XVI–XVII vv. kak istoricheskii istochnik*. Moscow, 1975.

———. *Sostav klassa feodalov Rossii v XVI v. Istoriko-genealogicheskoe issledovanie*. Moscow, 1986.

Channon, John, and Robert Hudson. *The Penguin Historical Atlas of Russia*. London, 1995.

Cherepnin, L. V. *Russkaia istoriografiia do XIX veka. Kurs lektsii*. Moscow, 1957.

———. *Zemskie sobory Russkogo gosudarstva v XVI–XVII vv.* Moscow, 1978.

Cherepnin, L. V., and V. D. Nazarov. "Krestianstvo na Rusi v seredine XII–kontse XV v." In Z. V. Udal'tsova, ed., *Istoriia krest'ianstva v Europe. Epokha feodalizma* 2 (1986):250–86. 3 vols. Moscow, 1985–86.

Chernaia, L. A. "'Chest': Predstavleniia o chesti i beschestii v russkoi literature XI–XVII vv." In A. S. Demin, ed., *Drevnerusskaia literatura. Izobrazhenie obshchestva*, pp. 56–84. Moscow, 1991.

——. "Problema chelovecheskoi lichnosti v russkoi obshchestvennoi mysli vtoroi poloviny XVII–nachala XVIII veka." Abstract of candidate dissertation, Moscow State University, 1980.

Cherniavsky, Michael. "The Old Believers and the New Religion." In idem, ed., *The Structure of Russian History: Interpretive Essays*, pp. 140–88. New York, 1970.

——. *Tsar and People: Studies in Russian Myths.* New Haven, Conn., and London, 1961.

Chernov, A. V. "O klassifikatsii tsentral'nykh gosudarstvennykh uchrezhdenii XVI–XVII vv." *Istoricheskii arkhiv* 1, no. 1 (1958):195–202.

——. *Vooruzhennye sily Russkogo gosudarstva v XV–XVII vv.* Moscow, 1954.

Chew, Allen F. *An Atlas of Russian History.* Rev. ed. New Haven, Conn., and London, 1970.

Chistiakova, E. V., and A. P. Bogdanov. *"Da budet potomkam iavleno": Ocherki o russkikh istorikakh vtoroi poloviny XVII veka i ikh trudakh.* Moscow, 1988.

Chteniia v Imp. obshchestve istorii i drevnostei rossiiskikh pri Moskovskom universitete. Sbornik. 264 vols. Moscow, 1845–1918.

Cracraft, James. "Did Feofan Prokopovich Really Write *Pravda voli monarshei?*" *Slavic Review* 40, no. 2 (1981):173–93.

——. "Empire Versus Nation: Russian Political Theory under Peter I." *Harvard Ukrainian Studies* 10, nos. 3/4 (1986):524–41.

——. *The Petrine Revolution in Russian Architecture.* Chicago, 1988.

Crummey, Robert O. *Aristocrats and Servitors: The Boyar Elite in Russia, 1613–1689.* Princeton, N.J., 1983.

——. "'Constitutional' Reform during the Time of Troubles." In idem, ed., *Reform in Russia and the U.S.S.R.*, pp. 28–44. Urbana, Ill., and Chicago, 1989.

——. "Court Spectacles in Seventeenth-Century Russia: Illusion and Reality." In Daniel Clarke Waugh, ed., *Essays in Honor of A. A. Zimin*, pp. 130–58. Columbus, Ohio, 1985.

——. "The Miracle of Martyrdom: Reflections on Early Old Believer Hagiography." In Samuel H. Baron and Nancy Shields Kollmann, eds., *Religion and Culture in Early Modern Russia and Ukraine*, pp. 132–45. DeKalb, Ill., 1997.

——. *The Old Believers and the World of Antichrist: The Vyg Community and the Russian State, 1694–1855.* Madison, Wis., 1970.

——. "The Origins of the Noble Official: The Boyar Elite, 1613–1689." In Walter M. Pintner and Don Karl Rowney, eds., *Russian Officialdom: The Bureaucratization of Russian Society from the Seventeenth to the Twentieth Century*, pp. 46–75. Chapel Hill, N.C., 1980.

——. "Periodizing 'Feudal' Russian History." In R. C. Elwood, ed., *Russian and East European History: Selected Papers from the Second World Congress for Soviet and East European Studies*, pp. 17–42. Berkeley, 1984.

——. "Peter and the Boiar Aristocracy, 1689–1700." *Canadian-American Slavic Studies* 8, no. 2 (1974):274–87.

——. "Reflections on Mestnichestvo in the 17th Century." *Forschungen* 27 (1980):269–81.

——. "Reform under Ivan IV: Gradualism and Terror." In idem, ed., *Reform in Russia and the U.S.S.R.*, pp. 12–27. Urbana, Ill., and Chicago, 1989.

Dal', V. I. *Tolkovyi slovar' zhivogo velikorusskogo iazyka.* 4 vols. Moscow, 1863–66.
——. *Tolkovyi slovar' zhivogo velikorusskogo iazyka.* 4th ed. 4 vols. St. Petersburg, 1912–14.
Das, David. "History Writing and the Quest for Fame in Late Muscovy: Andrei Lyzlov's *History of the Scythians.*" *Russian Review* 51, no. 4 (1992):502–9.
Davies, Brian L. "The Politics of Give and Take: *Kormlenie* as Service Remuneration and Generalized Exchange, 1488–1726." In Ann M. Kleimola and and Gail Lenhoff, eds., *Culture and Identity in Muscovy, 1359–1584.* UCLA Slavic Studies, n.s. 3, pp. 39–67. Moscow, 1997.
——. *State Power and Community in Early Modern Russia.* Cambridge, England, forthcoming.
——. "Village into Garrison: The Militarized Peasant Communities of Southern Muscovy." *Russian Review* 51, no. 4 (1992):481–501.
de Madariaga, Isabel. "Autocracy and Sovereignty." *Canadian-American Slavic Studies* 16, nos. 3–4 (1982):369–87.
Demidova, N. F. *Sluzhilaia biurokratiia v Rossii XVII v. i ee rol' v formirovanii absoliutizma.* Moscow, 1987.
Demin, A. S. *Pisatel' i obshchestvo v Rossii XVI–XVII vekov. (Obshchestvennye nastroeniia).* Moscow, 1985.
d'Encausse, Hélène. *The Russian Syndrome: One Thousand Years of Political Murder.* Trans. Caroline Higgitt. New York, 1992.
Dewdney, John C. *A Geography of the Soviet Union.* 3d ed. Oxford, 1979.
Dewey, H. W. "The Decline of the Muscovite *Namestnik.*" *Oxford Slavonic Papers* 12 (1965):21–39.
——. "Defamation and False Accusation (*Iabednichestvo*) in Old Muscovite Society." *Etudes slaves et est-européennes/Slavic and East European Studies* 11, nos. 3–4 (1966/67):109–20.
——. "The 1550 *Sudebnik* as an Instrument of Reform." *Jahrbücher für Geschichte Osteuropas,* n.s. 10, no. 2 (1962):161–80.
——. "The 1497 Sudebnik—Muscovite Russia's First National Law Code." *The American Slavic and East European Review* 15 (1956):325–38.
——. "Immunities in Old Russia." *Slavic Review* 23, no. 4 (1964):643–59.
——. "Muscovite *Guba* Charters and the Concept of Brigandage (*razboj*)." *Papers of the Michigan Academy of Science, Arts and Letters. Pt. 2: Social Sciences* 51 (1966):277–88.
——. "Old Muscovite Concepts of Injured Honor (*Beschestie*)." *Slavic Review* 27, no. 4 (1968):594–603.
——. "Political *Poruka* in Muscovite Rus'." *Russian Review* 46, no. 2 (1987):117–34.
——. "Trial by Combat in Muscovite Russia." *Oxford Slavonic Papers* 9 (1960):21–31.
——. "The White Lake Charter: A Mediaeval Russian Administrative Statute." *Speculum* 32, no. 1 (1957):74–83.
Dewey, H. W., and A. M. Kleimola. "Promise and Perfidy in Old Russian Cross-Kissing." *Canadian Slavic Studies* 2, no. 3 (1968):327–41.
——. "Suretyship and Collective Responsibility in pre-Petrine Russia." *Jahrbücher für Geschichte Osteuropas* 18 (1970):337–54.
D'iakonov, M. A. *Ocherki obshchestvennogo i gosudarstvennogo stroia drevnei Rusi.* 4th ed. Moscow and Leningrad, 1926.
——. *Vlast' moskovskikh gosudarei.* St. Petersburg, 1889.

Diuvernua, A. L. *Materialy dlia slovaria drevnerusskogo iazyka.* Moscow, 1894.

Eck, Alexandre. *Le moyen âge russe.* Paris, 1933.

Entsiklopedicheskii slovar'. 41 vols. in 82 pts. plus 2 supplements. St. Petersburg, 1890–1907.

Eskin, Iu. M. "Duel' v Moskovii 1637 goda." In *Arkheograficheskii ezhegodnik za 1997 god,* pp. 456–63. Moscow, 1997.

——. "'I Vasilei skazal, to de Artemei zamyslil vorovski . . .'" *Istoricheskii arkhiv* 1993, no. 2:189–209.

——. "K voprosu o rekonstruktsii 'mestnicheskogo arhiva'." In *Vspomogatel'nye istoricheskie distsipliny: Vysshaia shkola . . . Tezisy dokladov,* pp. 155–56. Moscow, 1994.

——. "Mestnichestvo i maiorat." In *Chteniia pamiati V. B. Kobrina . . .,* pp. 203–5. Moscow, 1992.

——. *Mestnichestvo v Rossii. XVI–XVII vv. Khronologicheskii reestr.* Moscow, 1994.

——. "Mestnichestvo v sotsial'noi strukture feodal'nogo obshchestva." *Istoriia SSSR* 1993, no. 1:39–53.

——. "Smuta i mestnichestvo." In *Realizm istoricheskogo myshleniia . . . Chteniia, posv. pamiati A. L. Stanislavskogo,* pp. 266–68. Moscow, 1991.

Evraziiskie issledovaniia. Almanakh "forum." Moscow, 1994.

Evraziistvo: Rossiia mezhdu Evropoi i Aziei. Moscow, 1994.

Evreinov, N. N. *Istoriia telesnykh nakazanii v Rossii.* New York, 1979.

Fedotov, George P. *The Russian Religious Mind, Vol. II: The Middle Ages. The Thirteenth to Fifteenth Centuries.* Ed. with intro. by John Meyendorff. Cambridge, Mass., 1966.

——. *St. Filipp: Metropolitan of Moscow.* Belmont, Mass., 1978.

Flier, Michael S. "Breaking the Code: The Image of the Tsar in the Muscovite Palm Sunday Ritual." In Michael S. Flier and Daniel Rowland, eds. *Medieval Russian Culture, Vol. II.* California Slavic Studies XIX, pp. 213–42. Berkeley and Los Angeles, 1994.

——. "The Iconology of Royal Ritual in Sixteenth-Century Muscovy." In Speros Vryonis, Jr., ed., *Byzantine Studies: Essays on the Slavic World and the Eleventh Century,* pp. 53–76. New York, 1992.

Flier, Michael S., and Daniel Rowland, eds. *Medieval Russian Culture, Vol. II.* California Slavic Studies XIX. Berkeley and Los Angeles, 1994.

Floria, B. N. "'Beschest'e' russkogo feodala XV–XVI vv." In *Russkoe tsentralizovannoe gosudarstvo,* pp. 42–44. Moscow, 1980.

——. "Formirovanie soslovnogo statusa gospodstvuiushchego klassa drevnei Rusi (Na materiale statei o vozmeshchenii za 'beschest'e')." *Istoriia SSSR* 1983, no. 1:61–74.

——. "O putiakh politicheskoi tsentralizatsii Russkogo gosudarstva (na primere Tverskoi zemli)." In *Obshchestvo i gosudarstvo feodal'noi Rossii,* pp. 281–90. Moscow, 1975.

Florovskij, A. "Le conflit de deux traditions—la latine et la byzantine—dans la vie intellectuelle de l'Europe Orientale aux XVI–XVII siècles." *Zapiski nauchno-issledovatel'skogo ob'edineniia* [Prague] 5 (old ser. no. 10), no. 31 (1937):171–94.

Florovsky, Georges. *Ways of Russian Theology, Part One.* In idem, *Collected Works, Vol. 5.* Belmont, Mass., 1979.

Forschungen zur osteuropäischen Geschichte. 53 vols. to date. New series. Berlin, 1954–.

Frank, Stephen P. "Popular Justice, Community and Culture among the Russian Peasantry, 1870–1900." *Russian Review* 46, no. 3 (1987):239–65.

——. "'Simple Folk, Savage Customs?' Youth, Sociability, and the Dynamics of Culture in Rural Russia, 1856–1914." *Journal of Social History* 25, no. 4 (1992):711–36.

Freeze, Gregory L. "Bringing Order to the Russian Family: Marriage and Divorce in Imperial Russia, 1760–1860." *Journal of Modern History* 62 (1990):709–46.

——. "The *Soslovie* (Estate) Paradigm and Russian Social History." *American Historical Review* 91, no. 1 (1986):11–36.

Froianov, I. Ia. *Kievskaia Rus'. Ocherki sotsial'no-politicheskoi istorii.* Leningrad, 1980.

Gilbert, Martin. *Atlas of Russian History.* 2d ed. New York, 1993.

Goldfrank, David M. "Moscow, the Third Rome." *Modern Encyclopedia of Russian and Soviet History* 23 (1981):118–21.

Goncharenko, V. S., and V. I. Narozhnaia. *Oruzheinaia palata. Putevoditel'.* Moscow, 1995.

Got'e, Iu. V. *Ocherk istorii zemlevladeniia v Rossii.* Sergiev Posad, 1915.

——. *Zamoskovnyi krai v XVII veke.* Moscow, 1906.

Graham, Hugh F. "Mestnichestvo." *Modern Encyclopedia of Russian and Soviet History* 22 (1981):8–13.

Grebeniuk, V. P., ed. *Panegiricheskaia literatura petrovskogo vremeni.* Moscow, 1979.

Grekov, I. B., and F. F. Shakhmagonov. *Mir istorii. Russkie zemli v XIII–XV vekakh.* Moscow, 1986.

Griffiths, David. "Of Estates, Charters and Constitutions." In David Griffiths and George E. Munro, trans. and eds., *Catherine II's Charters of 1785 to the Nobility and the Towns,* pp. xvii–lxix. Bakersfield, Calif., 1991.

Gromyko, M. M. *Traditsionnye normy povedeniia i formy obshcheniia russkikh krest'ian XIX v.* Moscow, 1986.

Grossman, Joan Delaney. "Feminine Images in Old Russian Literature and Art." *California Slavic Studies* 11 (1980):33–70.

Gruzberg, A. A. *Chastotnyi slovar' russkogo iazyka vtoroi poloviny XVI–nachala XVII veka.* Perm', 1974.

Hammond, Vincent E. "The History of the Novgorodian *Pomest'e*: 1480–1550." Ph.D. dissertation, University of Illinois at Urbana-Champaign, 1987.

Hellie, Richard. "Early Modern Russian Law: The Ulozhenie of 1649." *Russian History* 15, nos. 2–4 (1988):155–80.

——. *Enserfment and Military Change in Muscovy.* Chicago and London, 1971.

——. "The Petrine Army: Continuity, Change, and Impact." *Canadian-American Slavic Studies* 8, pt. 2 (1974):237–53.

——. *Slavery in Russia, 1450–1725.* Chicago and London, 1982.

——. "Some Considerations on the Development of the Russian Mind and Culture (Especially Late Muscovy)." Unpubl. manuscript, June 1993.

——. "The Structure of Modern Russian History: Toward a Dynamic Model." *Russian History* 4, no. 1 (1977):1–22.

——. "Ulozhenie Commentary—Preamble." *Russian History* 15, nos. 2–4 (1988):181–224.

——. "Zemskii sobor." *Modern Encyclopedia of Russian and Soviet History* 45 (1987):226–34.

Hittle, J. Michael. *The Service City: State and Townsmen in Russia, 1600–1800.* Cambridge, Mass., and London, 1979.

Hoch, Steven L. *Serfdom and Social Control in Russia: Petrovskoe, A Village in Tambov*. Chicago, 1986.

Hughes, Lindsey A. J. "The Moscow Armoury and Innovations in Seventeenth-Century Muscovite Art." *Canadian-American Slavic Studies* 13 (1979):204–23.

——. *Russia and the West: The Life of a Seventeenth-Century Westernizer, Prince Vasily Vasil'evich Golitsyn (1643–1714)*. Newtonville, Mass., 1984.

——. *Russia in the Age of Peter the Great*. New Haven, Conn., 1998.

——. "Sophia, 'Autocrat of All the Russias': Titles, Ritual, and Eulogy in the Regency of Sophia Alekseevna (1682–89)." *Canadian Slavonic Papers* 28, no. 3 (1986):266–86.

——. *Sophia, Regent of Russia, 1657–1704*. New Haven, Conn., and London, 1990.

Ianin, V. L. *Novgorodskie posadniki*. Moscow, 1962.

Istoriia Moskvy. 6 vols. in 7 pts. Moscow, 1952–59.

Ivanov, P. I. "O mestnichestve." *Russkii istoricheskii sbornik* 2 (1838):i–xv.

Ivanov, V. N., ed. *Oruzheinaia palata*. Moscow, 1964.

K., K. [Krasuskii, K. A.] "Obida lichnaia . . . (v uglov. prave)." *Entsiklopedicheskii slovar'* (1897) 21a:505–7.

Kaiser, Daniel H. *The Growth of the Law in Medieval Russia*. Princeton, N.J., 1980.

——. "Law, Russian (Muscovite), 1300–1500." In Joseph R. Strayer, ed. *Dictionary of the Middle Ages* 7 (1986):506–12. 13 vols. New York, 1982–89.

——. "Vozrast pri brake i raznitsa v vozraste suprugov v gorodakh Rossii v nachale XVIII v." In *Sosloviia i gosudarstvennaia vlast' v Rossii. XV–seredina XIX vv.*, pp. 225–37. Moscow, 1994.

Kamenskii, A. B. "K istorii izucheniia genealogii v Rossii v XVIII veke." In *Istochnikovedcheskie issledovaniia po istorii feodal'noi Rossii*, pp. 150–61. Moscow, 1981.

——. "Praviashchii klass-soslovie i gosudarstvennyi apparat Russkogo tsentralizovannogo gosudarstva v trudakh istorikov i arkhivistov vtoroi poloviny XVIII veka. Istochnikovedcheskoe issledovanie." Candidate dissertation, Moscow State Historical-Archival Institute, 1984.

Kappeler, Andreas. *Ivan Groznyj im Spiegel der ausländischen Druckschriften seiner Zeit*. Bern and Frankfurt, 1972.

——. "Das Moskauer Reich des 17. Jahrhunderts und seine nichtrussischen Untertanen." *Forschungen* 50 (1995):185–98.

——. *Russlands erste Nationalitäten: Das Zarenreich und die Völker der mittleren Wolga vom 16. bis 19. Jahrhundert*. Cologne, 1982.

Karamzin, N. M. *Istoriia gosudarstva rossiiskogo*. Ed. I. Einerling. 12 vols. in 3 bks. 5th ed. St. Petersburg, 1842–43.

Kashtanov, S. M. *Finansy srednevekovoi Rusi*. Moscow, 1988.

——. "Iz istorii poslednikh udelov." *Trudy Moskovskogo gosudarstvennogo istoriko-arkhivnogo instituta* 10 (1957):275–302.

Kavelin, K. D. *Sobranie sochinenii. Vol. 1: Monografii po russkoi istorii*. Moscow, 1897.

Kazakevich, A. N. "Novye dokumenty po istorii monumental'noi propagandy pri Petre I (Vosstanie moskovskikh strel'tsov 1698 g.)." In *Istochnikovedcheskie i istoriograficheskie aspekty russkoi kul'tury. Sbornik statei*, pp. 53–58. Moscow, 1984.

Keenan, Edward L. "Muscovite Political Folkways." *Russian Review* 45, no. 2 (1986): 115–81.

Keep, John L. H. "The Muscovite Elite and the Approach to Pluralism." *Slavonic and East European Review* 48, no. 111 (1970):201–31.

——. *Soldiers of the Tsar: Army and Society in Russia, 1462–1874*. Oxford, 1985.

Khmyrov, M. D. *Mestnichestvo i razriady*. St. Petersburg, 1862.

Khoroshkevich, A. L. "Istoricheskie sud'by belorusskikh i ukrainskikh zemel' v XIV–nachale XVI v." In V. T. Pashuto, B. N. Floria, and A. L. Khoroshkevich, eds., *Drevnerusskoe nasledie i istoricheskie sud'by vostochnogo slavianstva*, pp. 69–150. Moscow, 1982.

Kireevskii, I. V. "On the Nature of European Culture and Its Relation to the Culture of Russia." In Marc Raeff, ed., *Russian Intellectual History: An Anthology*, pp. 174–207. New York, 1966.

Kivelson, Valerie A. *Autocracy in the Provinces: The Muscovite Gentry and Political Culture in the Seventeenth Century*. Stanford, 1996.

——. "The Devil Stole His Mind: The Tsar and the 1648 Moscow Uprising." *American Historical Review* 98, no. 3 (1993):733–56.

——. "Patrolling the Boundaries: The Uses of Witchcraft Accusations and Household Strife in Seventeenth-Century Muscovy." *Harvard Ukrainian Studies* 19 (1997):302–23.

Kleimola, Ann M. "Boris Godunov and the Politics of Mestnichestvo." *Slavonic and East European Review* 53, no. 132 (1975):355–69.

——. "The Changing Face of the Muscovite Aristocracy. The Sixteenth Century: Sources of Weakness." *Jahrbücher für Geschichte Osteuropas* 25 (1977):481–93.

——. "'In accordance with the Canons of the Holy Apostles': Muscovite Dowries and Women's Property Rights," *Russian Review* 51, no. 2 (1992):204–29.

——. "Justice in Medieval Russia: Muscovite Judgment Charters (*Pravye Gramoty*) of the Fifteenth and Sixteenth Centuries." *Transactions of the American Philosophical Society*, n.s. 65, pt. 6 (1975): 93 pp.

——. "*Kto kogo*: Patterns of Duma Recruitment, 1547–1564." *Forschungen* 38 (1986): 205–20.

——. "The Muscovite Autocracy at Work: The Use of Disgrace as an Instrument of Control." In William E. Butler, ed., *Russian Law: Historical and Political Perspectives*, pp. 29–50. Leyden, 1977.

——. "Patterns of Duma Recruitment, 1505–1550." In Daniel Clarke Waugh, ed., *Essays in Honor of A. A. Zimin*, pp. 232–58. Columbus, Ohio, 1985.

——. "Status, Place, and Politics: The Rise of Mestnichestvo during the *Boiarskoe Pravlenie*." *Forschungen* 27 (1980):195–214.

——. "Up Through Servitude: The Changing Condition of the Muscovite Elite in the Sixteenth and Seventeenth Centuries." *Russian History* 6, pt. 2 (1979):210–29.

Kleimola, Ann M., and Gail Lenhoff, eds. *Culture and Identity in Muscovy, 1359–1584*. UCLA Slavic Studies, n.s. 3. Moscow, 1997.

Kliuchevskii, V. O. *Boiarskaia duma drevnei Rusi*. 5th ed. Petrograd, 1919.

——. "Istoriia soslovii v Rossii." In *Sochineniia* 6 (1959):276–466.

——. *Kurs russkoi istorii*. In *Sochineniia*, vols. 1–5. Moscow, 1956–58.

——. *Sochineniia*. 8 vols. Moscow, 1956–59.

Kniaz'kov, S. E. "Sudnye prikazy v kontse XVI–pervoi polovine XVII v." *Istoricheskie zapiski* 115 (1987):268–85.

Kobrin, V. B. "Iz istorii mestnichestva XVI veka." *Istoricheskii arkhiv* 1 (1960):214–19.

——. *Vlast' i sobstvennost' v srednevekovoi Rossii (XV–XVI vv.)*. Moscow, 1985.

Kobrin, V. B., and A. L. Iurganov. "Stanovlenie despoticheskogo samoderzhaviia v srednevekovoi Rusi. (K postanovke problemy)." *Istoriia SSSR* 1991, no. 4:54–64.

Kochin, G. E. *Materialy dlia terminologicheskogo slovaria drevnei Rossii.* Moscow and Leningrad, 1937.

Kollmann Jr., Jack E. "The Moscow *Stoglav* ('Hundred Chapters') Church Council of 1551." Ph.D. dissertation, University of Michigan, 1978.

Kollmann, Nancy Shields. "The Boyar Clan and Court Politics: The Founding of the Muscovite Political System." *Cahiers du monde russe et soviétique* 23, no. 1 (1982):5–31.

——. "Collateral Succession in Kievan Rus'." *Harvard Ukrainian Studies* 14, no. 3/4: 377–87.

——. "Concepts of Society and Social Identity in Early Modern Russia." In Samuel H. Baron and Nancy Shields Kollmann, eds. *Religion and Culture in Early Modern Russia and Ukraine*, pp. 34–51. DeKalb, Ill., 1997.

——. "Consensus Politics: The Dynastic Crisis of the 1490s Reconsidered." *Russian Review* 45, no. 3 (1986):235–67.

——. "Honor and Dishonor in Early Modern Russia." *Forschungen* 46 (1992):131–46.

——. *Kinship and Politics: The Making of the Muscovite Political System, 1345–1547.* Stanford, 1987.

——. "Murder in the Hoover Archives." *Harvard Ukrainian Studies* 19 (1997):324–34.

——. "Muscovite Russia, 1450–1598." In Gregory L. Freeze, ed., *Russia: A History*, pp. 27–54. Oxford and New York, 1997.

——. "Pilgrimage, Procession, and Symbolic Space in Sixteenth-Century Russian Politics." In Michael S. Flier and Daniel Rowland, eds., *Medieval Russian Culture, Vol. II.* California Slavic Studies XIX, pp. 163–81. Berkeley and Los Angeles, 1994.

——. "Preface." In N. P. Voskoboinikova, ed., *Opisanie drevneishikh dokumentov arkhivov moskovskikh prikazov XVI–nach. XVII vv.* (RGADA f. 141. *Prikaznye dela starykh let)*, pp. xi–xiv. Moscow, 1994.

——. "Ritual and Social Drama at the Muscovite Court." *Slavic Review* 45, no. 3 (Fall 1986):486–502.

——. "The Rus' Principalities [in the Fourteenth Century]." In *The New Cambridge Medieval History, Vol. VI.* Cambridge, England, forthcoming.

——. "Russia." In *The New Cambridge Medieval History, Vol. VII, c. 1415–c. 1500*, pp. 748–70. Cambridge, England, 1998.

——. "The Seclusion of Elite Muscovite Women." *Russian History* 10, pt. 2 (1983):170–87.

——. "Was There Honor in Kiev Rus'?" *Jahrbücher für Geschichte Osteuropas*, 36, no. 4 (1988):481–92.

——. "Women's Honor in Early Modern Russia." In Barbara Evans Clements, Barbara Alpern Engel, and Christine D. Worobec, eds., *Russia's Women: Accommodation, Resistance, Transformation*, pp. 60–73. Berkeley, 1991.

——, ed. with intro. *Major Problems in Early Modern Russian History.* New York and London, 1992.

Kostomarov, N. I. *Sobranie sochinenii. Istoricheskie monografii i issledovaniia.* 21 vols. in 8 bks. St. Petersburg, 1903–6. Reprint ed.: The Hague, 1967–68.

Lange, Nikolai I. "O nakaniiakh [*sic*] i vzyskaniiakh za beschestie po drevnemu russkomu pravu." *Zhurnal Ministerstva narodnogo prosveshcheniia* 102 (1859):161–224.

Lantzeff, George V. *Siberia in the Seventeenth Century.* Berkeley, 1943.

Lappo-Danilevskii, A. S. "Ideia gosudarstva i glavneishie momenty eia razvitiia v Rossii so vremeni smuty i do epokhi preobrazovanii." *Golos minuvshogo* 2, no. 12 (1914):5–38.

Latkin, V. N. *Lektsii po istorii russkogo prava.* St. Petersburg, 1912.

Laucevicius, E. *Popierius Lietuvoje XV–XVIII a.* 1 vol. with album. Vilnius, 1967.

LeDonne, John P. *Absolutism and Ruling Class: The Formation of the Russian Political Order, 1700–1825.* New York and Oxford, 1991.

——. "Ruling Families in the Russian Political Order, 1689–1825." *Cahiers du monde russe et soviétique* 28, nos. 3–4 (1987):233–322.

Leont'ev, A. K. *Obrazovanie prikaznoi systemy upravleniia v Russkom gosudarstve.* Moscow, 1961.

Levin, Eve. "*Dvoeverie* and Popular Religion." In Stephen K. Batalden, ed., *Seeking God: The Recovery of Religious Identity in Orthodox Russia, Ukraine, and Georgia,* pp. 31–52. DeKalb, Ill., 1993.

——. *Sex and Society in the World of the Orthodox Slavs, 900–1700.* Ithaca, N.Y., and London, 1989.

——. "Supplicatory Prayers as a Source for Popular Religious Culture." In Samuel H. Baron and Nancy Shields Kollmann, eds. *Religion and Culture in Early Modern Russia and Ukraine,* pp. 96–114. DeKalb, Ill., 1997.

Levitsky, Serge L. "Protection of Individual Honour and Dignity in Pre-Petrine Russian Law." *Revue d'histoire du droit/Tijdschrift voor rechitsgeschiedenis* 40, nos. 3–4 (1972):341–436.

Levy, Sandry. "Women and the Control of Property in Sixteenth-Century Muscovy." *Russian History* 10, no. 2 (1983):201–12.

Likhachev, D. S. *Chelovek v literature drevnei Rusi.* Moscow, 1958.

——. *Izbrannye raboty.* 3 vols. Leningrad, 1987.

——. *Razvitie russkoi literatury X–XVII vekov.* In his *Izbrannye raboty* 1 (1987).

Likhachev, N. P. *Biblioteka i arkhiv moskovskikh gosudarei v XVI stoletii.* St. Petersburg, 1894.

——. *Bumaga i drevneishie bumazhnye mel'nitsy v Moskovskom gosudarstve. Istoriko-arkheograficheskii ocherk.* St. Petersburg, 1891.

——. "*Gosudarev Rodoslovets*" *i rod Adashevykh.* St. Petersburg, 1897.

——. *Paleograficheskoe znachenie bumazhnykh vodianykh znakov.* 3 vols. and addendum. St. Petersburg, 1899.

——. *Razriadnye d'iaki XVI veka. Opyt istoricheskogo issledovaniia.* St. Petersburg, 1888.

Luppov, S. P. *Kniga v Rossii v XVII veke.* Leningrad, 1970.

Lur'e, Ia. S. *Dve istorii Rusi XV veka.* St. Petersburg, 1994.

——. *Obshcherusskie letopisi XIV–XV vv.* Leningrad, 1976.

——. "Rol' Tveri v sozdanii Russkogo natsional'nogo gosudarstva." *Uchenye zapiski Leningradskogo gosudarstvennogo universiteta. Seriia istoricheskikh nauk,* no. 36 (1939):85–109.

Marker, Gary J. "Literacy and Literacy Texts in Muscovy: A Reconsideration." *Slavic Review* 49, no. 1 (1990):74–89.

——. "The Petrine 'Civil Primer' Reconsidered: A New Look at the Publishing History of the 'Grazhdanskaia Azbuka', 1708–1727." *Solanus* (1989):25–39.

——. "Printers and Literacy in Muscovy: A Taxonomic Investigation." *Russian Review* 48, no. 1 (1989):1–20.

——. *Publishing, Printing, and the Origins of Intellectual Life in Russia, 1700–1800.* Princeton, N.J., 1985.

Markevich, A. I. "Chto takoe mestnichestvo?" *Zhurnal Ministerstva narodnogo prosveshcheniia* no. 204 (1879):262–71.

——. *Istoriia mestnichestva v Moskovskom gosudarstve v XV–XVII veke.* Odessa, 1888.

——. *O mestnichestve.* Kiev, 1879.

Martin, Janet. "'Backwardness' in Russian Peasant Culture: A Theoretical Consideration of Agricultural Practices in the Seventeenth Century." In Samuel H. Baron and Nancy Shields Kollmann, eds., *Religion and Culture in Early Modern Russia and Ukraine,* pp. 19–33. DeKalb, Ill., 1997.

——. *Medieval Russia, 980–1584.* Cambridge, England, 1995.

——. "Mobility, Forced Resettlement and Regional Identity in Muscovy." In Ann M. Kleimola and Gail Lenhoff, eds., *Culture and Identity in Muscovy, 1359–1584.* UCLA Slavic Studies, n.s. 3, pp. 431–49. Moscow, 1997.

——. "Muscovite Frontier Policy: The Case of the Khanate of Kasimov." *Russian History* 19, nos. 1–4 (1992):169–80.

Martin, Russell. "Royal Marriage in Muscovy, 1500–1725." Ph.D. dissertation, Harvard University, 1996.

Maslennikova, N. N. *Prisoedinenie Pskova k Russkomu tsentralizovannomu gosudarstvu.* Leningrad, 1955.

McKinnon, Abby A.; *see* Smith, Abby Finnogh.

Medushevskii, A. N. "Boiarskie spiski pervoi chetverti XVIII v." In *Arkheograficheskii ezhegodnik za 1981 god,* pp. 158–63. Moscow, 1982.

——. "Feodal'nye verkhi i formirovanie biurokratii v Rossii pervoi chetverti XVIII v. Istochnikovedcheskoe issledovanie." Abstract of candidate dissertation, Institute of the History of the USSR of the Academy of Sciences of the USSR, 1985.

——. "Istochniki o sostave tsentral'nogo apparata upravleniia Rossii v pervoi chetverti XVIII v." *Sovetskie arkhivy* 1981, no. 3:58–60.

Meehan-Waters, Brenda. *Autocracy and Aristocracy: The Russian Service Elite of 1730.* New Brunswick, N.J., 1982.

——. "Elite Politics and Autocratic Power." In A. G. Cross, ed., *Great Britain and Russia in the Eighteenth Century: Contacts and Comparisons,* pp. 229–46. Newtonville, Mass., 1979.

Meier, D. I. *Russkoe grazhdanskoe pravo.* 5th ed. Moscow, 1873.

Mel'nikov, Iu. N. "Mestnicheskie dela v razriadnom sudoproizvodstve 80-x godov XVI v." *Vspomogatel'nye istoricheskie distsipliny* 9 (1978):222–36.

——. "Mestnichestvo i politicheskaia bor'ba v Rossii v 80-x godakh XVI v." Candidate dissertation, Institute of the History of the USSR of the Academy of Sciences of the USSR, Moscow, 1979.

——. "Opisanie mestnicheskikh del 80-kh godov XVI v." In *Arkheograficheskii ezhegodnik za 1977 god,* pp. 275–85. Moscow, 1978.

——. "O strukture i istochnike opisi dokumentov razriadnogo prikaza 1626 g." In *Arkheograficheskii ezhegodnik za 1983 god,* pp. 87–89. Moscow, 1985.

Meyendorff, John. "Law, Canon: Byzantine." In Joseph R. Strayer, ed., *Dictionary of the Middle Ages* 7 (1986):394–95. 13 vols. New York, 1982–89.

——. "Was There Ever a 'Third Rome'? Remarks on the Byzantine Legacy in Russia." In John J. Yiannias, ed., *The Byzantine Tradition after the Fall of Constantinople,* pp. 45–60. Charlottesville, Va., and London, 1991.

Michels, Georg Bernhard. "Muscovite Elite Women and Old Belief." *Harvard Ukrainian Studies* 19 (1997):428–50.

——. "Myths and Realities of the Russian Schism: The Church and Its Dissenters in Seventeenth-Century Muscovy." Ph.D. dissertation, Harvard University, 1991.

——. "The Solovki Uprising: Religion and Revolt in Northern Russia." *Russian Review* 51, no. 1 (1992):1–15.

——. "The Violent Old Belief: An Examination of Religious Dissent on the Karelian Frontier." *Russian History* 19, nos. 1–4 (1992):203–30.

Miller, David B. "The *Velikie Minei Chetii* and the *Stepennaia Kniga* of Metropolitan Makarii and the Origins of Russian National Consciousness." *Forschungen* 26 (1979):263–382.

Minenko, N. A. *Zhivaia starina. Budni i prazdniki Sibirskoi derevni v XVIII–pervoi polovine XIX v.* Novosibirsk, 1989.

N., V. [Nechaev, V. M.], "Obida lichnaia." *Entsiklopedicheskii slovar'* (1897) 21a:504–5.

Nazarov, V. D. "O strukture 'Gosudareva dvora' v seredine XVI v." In *Obshchestvo i gosudarstvo feodal'noi Rossii*, pp. 40–54. Moscow, 1975.

Nechaev, V. M. "Obruchenie." *Entsiklopedicheskii slovar'* (1897) 42:579–80.

Nikol'skii, V. K. "Boiarskaia popytka 1681 g." *Istoricheskie izvestiia, izd. Istoricheskim obshchestvom pri Moskovskom universitete*, 1917, bk. 2:57–87.

Nosov, N. E., "Boiarskaia kniga 1556. Iz istorii proiskhozhdenii chetvertchikov." In *Voprosy ekonomiki i klassovykh otnoshenii v Russkom gosudarstve XII–XVII v.*, pp. 191–227. Moscow and Leningrad, 1960.

——. *Ocherki po istorii mestnogo upravleniia Russkogo gosudarstva pervoi poloviny XVI veka.* Moscow and Leningrad, 1957.

——. *Stanovlenie soslovno-predstavitel'nykh uchrezhdenii v Rossii.* Leningrad, 1969.

Novombergskii, N. Ia. *Slovo i delo gosudarevy. Protsessy do izdaniia Ulozheniia Alekseia Mikhailovicha 1649 goda.* Vol. 1. Moscow, 1911.

Novosel'skii, A. A. "Feodal'noe zemlevladenie. Boiarstvo, dvorianstvo i tserkov'." In *Ocherki istorii SSSR. Period feodalizma. XVII vek*, pp. 139–63. Moscow, 1955.

——. "Kollektivnye dvorianskie chelobitnye o syske beglykh krest'ian i kholopov vo vtoroi polovine XVII v." In *Dvorianstvo i krepostnoi stroi Rossii XVI–XVIII vv.*, pp. 303–43. Moscow, 1975.

——. "Krest'iane i kholopy." In *Ocherki istorii SSSR. Period feodalizma. XVII vek*, pp. 164–98. Moscow, 1955.

——. "Praviashchie gruppy v sluzhilom 'gorode' XVII v.," *Uchenye zapiski RANION* 5 (1929):315–35.

Obolensky, Dimitri. "Russia's Byzantine Heritage." *Oxford Slavonic Papers* 1 (1950): 37–63.

O'Brien, C. Bickford. *Russia under Two Tsars, 1682–1689: The Regency of Sophia Alekseevna.* Berkeley and Los Angeles, 1952.

Obshchestvo i gosudarstvo feodal'noi Rossii. Moscow, 1975.

Ocherki istorii SSSR. 8 vols. Moscow, 1953–58.

Ogloblin, N. N. *Obozrenie stolbtsov i knig Sibirskogo prikaza (1592–1768 gg.).* 4 vols. Moscow, 1895–1901.

Oikonomides, Nicholas. "Law, Byzantine." In Joseph R. Strayer, ed., *Dictionary of the Middle Ages* 7 (1986):390–93. 13 vols. New York, 1982–89.

Okenfuss, Max J. *The Discovery of Childhood in Russia.* Newtonville, Mass., 1980.

Opisanie dokumentov i bumag, khran. v Moskovskom arkhive Ministerstva iustitsii. 21 vols. St. Petersburg–Moscow, 1869–1921.

Orchard, G. E. "The Eurasian School of Russian Historiography." *Laurentian University Review* 10, no. 1 (1977):97–106.

Ostrogorsky, Georg. "Das Projekt einer Rangtabelle aus der Zeit des Caren Fedor Aleksěevič." *Jahrbücher für Kultur und Geschichte der Slaven,* n.s. 9 (1933):86–138.

Panchenko, A. M. *Russkaia stikhotvornaia kul'tura XVII veka.* Leningrad, 1973.

Pavlov, A. P. *Gosudarev dvor i politicheskaia bor'ba pri Borise Godunove (1584–1605 gg.).* St. Petersburg, 1992.

Pavlov-Sil'vanskii, N. P. *Gosudarevy sluzhilye liudi. Proiskhozhdenie russkogo dvorianstva.* St. Petersburg, 1898.

———. *Sochineniia.* 3 vols. St. Petersburg, 1909–10.

Peshtich, S. A. *Russkaia istoriografiia XVIII veka.* 3 vols. Leningrad, 1961–71.

Pintner, Walter M. and Don Karl Rowney, eds. *Russian Officialdom: The Bureaucratization of Russian Society from the Seventeenth to the Twentieth Century.* Chapel Hill, N.C., 1980.

Pipes, Richard. *Russia under the Old Regime.* New York, 1974.

———. "Was There Private Property in Muscovite Russia?" *Slavic Review* 53, no. 2 (1994): 524–30.

Platonov, S. F. *Ivan the Terrible.* Ed. and trans. J. L. Wieczynski with intro. by Richard Hellie. Gulf Breeze, Fla., 1974.

———. *Lektsii po russkoi istorii.* 9th ed. Petrograd, 1915.

———. *Moskva i zapad.* Leningrad, 1925.

Plavsic, Borivoj. "Seventeenth-Century Chanceries and Their Staffs." In Walter M. Pintner and Don Karl Rowney, eds., *Russian Officialdom: The Bureaucratization of Russian Society from the Seventeenth to the Twentieth Century,* pp. 19–45. Chapel Hill, N.C., 1980.

Pobedonostsev, K. P. *Kurs grazhdanskogo prava. Pt. 3: Dogovory i obiazatel'stva.* St. Petersburg, 1896.

Poe, Marshall T. *Foreign Descriptions of Muscovy: An Analytic Bibliography of Primary and Secondary Sources.* Columbus, Ohio, 1995.

———. "'Russian Despotism': The Origins and Dissemination of an Early Modern Commonplace." Ph.D. dissertation, University of California, Berkeley, 1993.

———. "What Did Muscovites Mean When They Called Themselves 'Slaves of the Tsar'?" *Slavic Review* 57, no. 3 (1998):585–608.

Pogodin, M. P. "O mestnichestve." *Russkii istoricheskii sbornik* 3 (1838), bk. 1:268–83; bk. 2:370–97.

Pokrovskii, M. N. *Izbrannye proizvedeniia.* 4 vols. Moscow, 1965–67.

Ponomareva, L. V., ed. *Evraziia: Istoricheskie vzgliady russkikh emigrantov.* Moscow, 1992.

Pouncy, Carolyn Johnston. "The *Domostroi* as a Source for Muscovite History." Ph.D. dissertation, Stanford University, 1985.

Presniakov, A. E. *Moskovskoe tsarstvo.* Petrograd, 1918.

Priselkov, M. D. "Letopisanie Zapadnoi Ukrainy i Belorussii." *Uchenye zapiski Leningradskogo gosudarstvennogo universiteta. Seriia istoricheskikh nauk* 7, no. 67 (1940):5–24.

Prochazka, Helen Y. "On Concepts of Patriotism, Loyalty, and Honour in the Old Russian Military Accounts." *Slavonic and East European Review* 63, no. 4 (1985):481–97.

Protas'eva, T. N., ed. *Opisanie rukopisei Sinodal'nogo sobraniia (ne voshedshikh v opisanie A. V. Gorskogo i K. I. Nevostrueva). Pt. I: Nos. 577–819.* Moscow, 1970.

Pushkarev, L. N. *Obshchestvenno-politicheskaia mysl' Rossii. Vtoraia polovina XVII veka. Ocherki istorii.* Moscow, 1982.

Pushkareva, N. L. "Sem'ia, zhenshchina, seksual'naia etika v pravoslavii i katolitsizme: perspektivy sravnitel'nogo podkhoda." *Etnograficheskoe obozrenie* 1995, no. 3:55–69.

——. *Zhenshchiny drevnei Rusi.* Moscow, 1989.

Puti Evrazii: Russkaia intelligentsiia i sud'by Rossii. Moscow, 1992.

Putsillo, M. P. *Ukazatel' delam i rukopisiam otn. do Sibiri . . . .* Moscow, 1879.

Raeff, Marc. "The Enlightenment in Russia and Russian Thought in the Enlightenment." In J. G. Garrard, ed., *The Eighteenth Century in Russia*, pp. 25–47. Oxford, 1973.

——. *Michael Speransky: Statesman of Imperial Russia, 1772–1839.* 2d rev. ed. The Hague, 1969.

——. *Understanding Imperial Russia: State and Society in the Old Regime.* Trans. Arthur Goldhammer. New York, 1984.

——. "The Well-Ordered Police State and the Development of Modernity in Seventeenth- and Eighteenth-Century Europe: An Attempt at a Comparative Approach." *American Historical Review* 80, no. 5 (1975):1221–43.

——. *The Well-Ordered Police State: Social and Institutional Change through Law in the Germanies and Russia, 1600–1800.* New Haven, Conn., 1983.

Ransel, David L. "Character and Style of Patron-Client Relations in Russia." In Antoni Mączak, ed., *Klientelsysteme im Europa der frühen Neuzeit*, pp. 212–31. Munich, 1988.

Reyfman, Irina. "The Emergence of the Duel in Russia: Corporal Punishment and the Honor Code." *Russian Review* 54, no. 1 (1995):26–43.

Riasanovsky, Nicholas V. "The Emergence of Eurasianism." *California Slavic Studies* 4 (1967):39–72.

Robinson, A. N. *Bor'ba idei v russkoi literature XVII veka.* Moscow, 1974.

Roosevelt, Priscilla. *Life on the Russian Country Estate.* New Haven, 1995.

Rowell, S. C. *Lithuania Ascending: A Pagan Empire within East-Central Europe, 1295–1345.* Cambridge, England, and New York, 1994.

Rowland, Daniel. "Biblical Military Imagery in the Political Culture of Early Modern Russia: The Blessed Host of the Heavenly Tsar." In Michael S. Flier and Daniel Rowland, eds., *Medieval Russian Culture, Vol. II.* California Slavic Studies XIX, pp. 182–212. Berkeley and Los Angeles, 1994.

——. "Did Muscovite Literary Ideology Place Limits on the Power of the Tsar (1540s–1660s)?" *Russian Review* 49, no. 2 (1990):125–55.

——. "Muscovite Political Attitudes as Reflected in Early Seventeenth Century Tales about the Time of Troubles." Ph.D. dissertation, Yale University, 1976.

——. "The Problem of Advice in Muscovite Tales about the Time of Troubles." *Russian History* 6, pt. 2 (1979):259–83.

Rozhdestvenskii, S. V. *Sluzhiloe zemlevladenie v Moskovskom gosudarstve XVI veka.* St. Petersburg, 1897.

Rozhkov, N. A. *Sel'skoe khoziaistvo Moskovskoi Rusi v XVI veke.* Moscow, 1899.

Ruane, Christine, ed. "Current Problems of Historical Theory." *Russian Studies in History* 35, no. 3 (1996–97).

Rumiantseva, V. S. "Tendentsii razvitiia obshchestvennogo soznaniia i prosveshcheniia v Rossii XVII veka." *Voprosy istorii* 1988, no. 2:26–40.

Savin, A. N. "Mestnichestvo pri dvore Liudvika XVI." In *Sbornik statei, posv. V. O. Kliuchevskomu*, pp. 277–90. Moscow, 1909.

Scanlan, James P. "From Historical Materialism to Historical Interactionism: A Philosophical Examination of Some Recent Developments." In Samuel H. Baron and Nancy Whittier Heer, eds., *Windows on the Russian Past: Essays on Soviet Historiography since Stalin*, pp. 3–23. Columbus, Ohio, 1977.

——. *Marxism in the USSR: A Critical Survey of Current Soviet Thought*. Ithaca, N.Y., 1985.

Schaller, H. W., Karla Günther-Hielscher, and Victor Glötzner. *Real- und Sachwörterbuch zum altrussischen*. Neuried, 1985.

Sedov, P. V. "Sotsial'no-politicheskaia bor'ba v Rossii v 70x–80x godakh XVII veka i otmena mestnichestva." Candidate dissertation, Leningrad State University, 1985.

Sergeevich, V. I. *Lektsii i issledovaniia po drevnei istorii russkogo prava*. 3d ed. St. Petersburg, 1903. 4th ed. St. Petersburg, 1910.

Sergeevskii, N. D. *Nakazanie v russkom prave XVII veka*. St. Petersburg, 1887.

Ševčenko, Ihor. "A Neglected Byzantine Source of Muscovite Political Ideology." *Harvard Slavic Studies* 2 (1954):141–79.

Shashkov, S. S. *Istoriia russkoi zhenshchiny*. In idem, *Sobranie sochinenii*. 2 vols. St. Petersburg, 1898.

Shmidt, S. O. "Mestnichestvo." *Sovetskaia istoricheskaia entsiklopediia* 9 (1966): 382–83.

——. "Mestnichestvo i absoliutizm (postanovka voprosa)." In idem, *Stanovlenie rossiiskogo samoderzhaviia. Issledovanie sotsial'no-politicheskoi istorii vremeni Ivana Groznogo*, pp. 262–307. Moscow, 1973. Also publ. *Absoliutizm v Rossii, (XVII–XVIII vv.)*, pp. 168–205. Moscow, 1964.

Shott, Paul. "Transportation in Russia." *Modern Encyclopedia of Russian and Soviet History* 39 (1985):170–78.

Shtamm, S. I. "Sud i protsess." In V. S. Nersesiants, ed., *Razvitie russkogo prava v XV–pervoi polovine XVII v.*, pp. 203–51. Moscow, 1986.

Skrynnikov, Ruslan G. *Ivan the Terrible*. Ed. and trans. Hugh F. Graham. Gulf Breeze, Fla., 1981.

Sl., G. [Sliuzberg, G. B.], "Kleveta." *Entsiklopedicheskii slovar'* (1895) 15:332–34.

Slovar' Akademii rossiiskoi. 7 vols. St. Petersburg, 1789–94.

Slovar' Akademii rossiiskoi po azbuchnomu poriadku razpolozhennyi. 7 vols. St. Petersburg, 1806–22.

Slovar' russkogo iazyka IX–XVII vv. 23 vols. to date. Moscow, 1975–.

Slovar' russkogo iazyka XVIII v. 8 vols. to date. Leningrad, 1984–.

Smirnov, P. P. *Posadskie liudi i ikh klassovaia bor'ba do serediny XVII veka*. 2 vols. Moscow and Leningrad, 1947–48.

Smirnov, P. P., and A. N. Speranskii. "Posadskie liudi." In *Ocherki istorii SSSR. Period feodalizma. XVII vek*, pp. 198–220. Moscow, 1955.

Smirnov, S. K. *Istoriia Moskovskoi slaviano-greko-latinskoi akademii*. Moscow, 1855.

Smith, Abby Finnogh. "Duels and the Matter of Honor." In R. P. Bartlett, A. G. Cross, and Karen Rasmussen, eds., *Russia and the World of the Eighteenth Century*, pp. 229–42. Columbus, Ohio, 1988. [author listed as Abby A. McKinnon]

———. "Prince V. V. Golitsyn: The Life of an Aristocrat in Muscovite Russia." Ph.D. dissertation, Harvard University, 1987.

Smith, R. E. F. *Peasant Farming in Muscovy*. Cambridge, England, 1977.

Solov'ev, S. M. *History of Russia, Vol. 24: The Character of Old Russia*. Ed. and trans. with intro. by Alexander V. Muller. Gulf Breeze, Fla., 1987.

———. *Istoriia Rossii s drevneishikh vremen*. 29 vols. in 15 bks. Moscow, 1959–66.

———. "Neskol'ko ob'iasnitel'nykh slov po povodu drevneishogo mestnicheskogo dela." *Moskovskie vedomosti* 1857, no. 53.

———. "O mestnichestve." In *Moskovskii literaturnyi i uchenyi sbornik na 1847 god*, pp. 263–316. Moscow, 1847.

Spasovich, V. "O prestupleniakh protiv chesti chastnykh lits po ulozheniu o nakazaniiakh 1845 goda." *Zhurnal Ministerstva iustitsii* 3, pt. 2 (1860):3–44.

Spasskii, I. G. *Inostrannye i russkie ordena do 1917 goda*. Leningrad, 1963.

Spasskii, I. G., and E. Shchukina, comp. with intro. *Medals and Coins of the Age of Peter the Great*. Leningrad, 1974.

Sreznevskii, I. I., comp. *Materialy dlia slovaria drevne-russkogo iazyka po pis'mennym pamiatnikam*. 3 vols. and addenda. St. Petersburg, 1893–1912.

Stashevskii, E. D. *Ocherki po istorii tsarstvovaniia Mikhaila Fedorovicha. Pt. 1*. Kiev, 1913.

Stevens, Carol Belkin. "Honor and Precedence amongst Muscovy's Elite after 1682." Unpubl. manuscript, 1986.

———. *Soldiers on the Steppe: Army Reform and Social Change in Early Modern Russia*. DeKalb, Ill., 1995.

Stökl, Günther. "Staat und Kirche im Moskauer Russland. Die vier Moskauer Wundertäter." *Jahrbücher für Geschichte Osteuropas* 29 (1981):481–93.

Symons, Leslie. *The Soviet Union: A Systematic Geography*. 2d ed. London and New York, 1990.

Szeftel, Marc. "The Title of the Muscovite Monarch up to the End of the Seventeenth Century." *Canadian-American Slavic Studies* 13, nos. 1–2 (1979):59–81.

Thyrêt, Isolde. "Life in the Kremlin under the Tsars Mikhail Fedorovich and Aleksei Mikhailovich: New Perspectives on the Institution of the *Terem*." Unpubl. manuscript, 1996.

Tikhomirov, M. N. *Kratkie zametki o letopisnykh proizvedeniiakh v rukopisnykh sobraniakh Moskvy*. Moscow, 1962.

———. *Rossiia v XVI stoletii*. Moscow, 1962.

Tikhomirov, N. Ia., and V. N. Ivanov. *Moskovskii Kreml'. Istoriia arkhitektury*. Moscow, 1967.

Timofeev, A. G. *Istoriia telesnykh nakazanii v russkom prave*. St. Petersburg, 1897.

Torke, Hans-Joachim. "Continuity and Change in the Relations between Bureaucracy and Society in Russia, 1613–1861." *Canadian Slavic Studies* 5, no. 4 (1971):457–76.

———. "Reichsversammlung." In idem, ed., *Lexikon der Geschichte Russlands*, pp. 317–19. Munich, 1985.

———. *Die staatsbedingte Gesellschaft im moskauer Reich. Zar und Zemlja in der altrussischen Herschaftsverfassung, 1613–1689*. Leiden, 1974.

———. "Sudebnik." In idem, ed., *Lexikon der Geschichte Russlands*, pp. 370–71. Munich, 1985.

Toynbee, Arnold. "Russia's Byzantine Heritage." In his *Civilization on Trial*, pp. 164–83. New York, 1948.

Troitskii, S. M. *Russkii absoliutizm i dvorianstvo v XVIII v. Formirovanie biurokratii.* Moscow, 1974.

———. "Tabel' o rangakh." *Sovetskaia istoricheskaia entsiklopediia*, 16 vols. (Moscow, 1961–76), vol. 14 (1973), cols. 15–16.

Tromonin, K. Ia. *Iz'iasneniia znakov, vidimykh v pischei bumage . . . .* Moscow, 1844.

Tsamutali, A. N. *Bor'ba techenii v russkoi istoriografii v polovine XIX veka.* Moscow, 1979.

———. *Bor'ba techenii v russkoi istoriografii vo vtoroi polovine XIX veka.* Leningrad, 1977.

Ulashchik, N. N. *Vvedenie v izuchenie belorussko-litovskogo letopisaniia.* Moscow, 1985.

Ustiugov, N. V. "Evoliutsiia prikaznogo stroia Russkogo gosudarstva v XVII v." In *Absoliutizm v Rossii (XVII–XVIII vv.)*, pp. 134–67. Moscow, 1964.

———. "Finansy." In *Ocherki istorii SSSR. Period feodalizma. XVII vek*, pp. 411–39. Moscow, 1955.

Ustrialov, N. G. *Istoriia tsarstvovaniia Petra Velikogo.* 5 vols. in 6 pts. St. Petersburg, 1858–63.

Val'denberg, Vladimir. *Drevnerusskie ucheniia o predelakh tsarskoi vlasti.* Petrograd, 1916.

Valuev, D. A. "Vvedenie." In *Simbirskii sbornik*. Moscow, 1844.

Vasil'evskaia, E. A. "Terminologiia mestnichestva i rodstva." *Trudy Moskovskogo gosudarstvennogo istoriko-arkhivnogo instituta* 2 (1946):155–79.

Vel'iaminov-Zernov, V. V. *Issledovanie o kasimovskikh tsariakh i tsarevichakh.* 4 pts. St. Petersburg, 1863–87.

Veselovskii, S. B. *Issledovaniia po istorii klassa sluzhilykh zemlevladel'tsev.* Moscow, 1969.

———. *K voprosu o proiskhozhdenii votchinnogo rezhima.* Moscow, 1926.

———. "Poslednie udely v severo-vostochnoi Rusi." *Istoricheskie zapiski* 22 (1947):101–31.

———. *Selo i derevnia v severo-vostochnoi Rusi XIV–XVI vv.* Moscow and Leningrad, 1936.

———. *Soshnoe pis'mo.* 2 vols. Moscow, 1915–16.

Vladimirskii-Budanov, M. F. *Obzor istorii russkogo prava.* 6th ed. St. Petersburg and Kiev, 1909.

Volkov, M. Ia. "Ob otmene mestnichestva v Rossii." *Istoriia SSSR* 1977, no. 2:53–67.

Voronova, E. M. "Zhitie Evfrosinii Polotskoi." In *Slovar' knizhnikov i knizhnosti drevnei Rusi* 1:147–48. 3 vols. in 5 pts. to date. Leningrad, 1987–.

Walicki, Andrzej. *A History of Russian Thought from the Enlightenment to Marxism.* Trans. Hilda Andrews-Rusiecka. Stanford, 1979.

———. *The Slavophile Controversy: History of a Conservative Utopia in Nineteenth-Century Russian Thought.* Trans. Hilda Andrews-Rusiecka. Notre Dame, Ind., 1975.

Weickhardt, George G. "Due Process and Equal Justice in the Muscovite Codes." *Russian Review* 51, no. 4 (1992):463–80.

———. "Legal Rights of Women in Russia, 1100–1750." *Slavic Review* 55, no. 1 (1996):1–23.

———. "The Pre-Petrine Law of Property." *Slavic Review* 52, no. 4 (1993):663–79.

———. "Reply." *Slavic Review* 53, no. 2 (1994):531–38.

Whittaker, Cynthia Hyla. "The Idea of Autocracy among Eighteenth-Century Russian Historians." *Russian Review* 55, no. 2 (1996):149–71.

———. "The Reforming Tsar: The Redefinition of Autocratic Duty in Eighteenth-Century Russia." *Slavic Review* 51, no. 1 (1992):77–98.

Wittfogel, Karl. *Oriental Despotism*. New Haven, Conn., 1957.

Worobec, Christine D. *Peasant Russia: Family and Community in the Post-Emancipation Period*. Princeton, N.J., 1991.

———. "Temptress or Virgin? The Precarious Sexual Position of Women in Postemancipation Ukrainian Peasant Society." *Slavic Review* 49, no. 2 (1990):227–38.

Wortman, Richard S. *The Development of a Russian Legal Consciousness*. Chicago and London, 1976.

———. *Scenarios of Power: Myth and Ceremony in Russian Monarchy, Vol. 1: From Peter the Great to the Death of Nicholas I*. Princeton, N.J., 1995.

Yanov, Alexander. *The Origins of Autocracy: Ivan the Terrible in Russian History*. Trans. Stephen Dunn. Berkeley and Los Angeles, 1981.

Zabelin, I. E. *Domashnii byt russkikh tsarei v XVI i XVII st.* 3 bks. Moscow, 1990. Reprint publ. of 4th exp. ed. Moscow, 1918.

Zaionchkovskii, P. A., ed. *Istoriia dorevoliutsionnoi Rossii v dnevnikakh i vospominaniiakh*. 5 vols. in 13 pts. Moscow, 1976–89.

Zamyslovskii, E. E. *Tsarstvovanie Fedora Alekseevicha, Vol. 1*. St. Petersburg, 1871.

Zernin, A. P. "Sud'ba mestnichestva. . . ." In N. A. Kalachov, ed., *Arkhiv istoriko-iuridicheskikh svedenii, otn. do Rossii*, vol. 3, sect. 1 (1861), pp. 1–138.

Zhivov, Victor M. "Religious Reform and the Emergence of the Individual in Russian Seventeenth-Century Literature." In Samuel H. Baron and Nancy Shields Kollmann, eds., *Religion and Culture in Early Modern Russia and Ukraine*, pp. 184–98. DeKalb, Ill., 1997.

Zhuk, S. I. "Maks Veber i sotsial'naia istoriia." *Voprosy istorii* 1992, nos. 2–3:172–77.

Zimin, A. A. "Feodal'naia znat' Tverskogo i Riazanskogo velikikh kniazhestv i moskovskoe boiarstvo kontsa XV–pervoi treti XVI veka." *Istoriia SSSR* 1973, no. 3:124–42.

———. *Formirovanie boiarskoi aristokratii v Rossii vo vtoroi polovine XV–pervoi treti XVI v.* Moscow, 1988.

———. *I. S. Peresvetov i ego sovremenniki*. Moscow, 1958.

———. "Istochniki po istorii mestnichestva v XV–pervoi treti XVI v." In *Arkheografich-eskii ezhegodnik za 1968 god*, pp. 109–18. Moscow, 1970.

———. "Iz istorii pomestnogo zemlevladeniia na Rusi." *Voprosy istorii* 1959, no. 11: 130–42.

———. "K istorii voennykh reform 50-x godov XVI v." *Istoricheskie zapiski* 55 (1956): 344–59.

———. "Kniazheskaia znat' i formirovanie sostava boiarskoi dumy vo vtoroi polovine XV–pervoi treti XVI v." *Istoricheskie zapiski* 103 (1979):195–241.

———. "Namestnicheskoe upravlenie v Russkom gosudarstve vtoroi poloviny XV–pervoi treti XVI v." *Istoricheskie zapiski* 94 (1974):271–301.

———. "O politicheskikh predposylkakh vozniknoveniia russkogo absoliutizma." In *Absoliutizm v Rossii (XVII–XVIII vv.)*, pp. 18–49. Moscow, 1964. English trans. by Susan Zayer Rupp in Nancy Shields Kollmann, ed. with intro., *Major Problems in Early Modern Russian History*, pp. 79–108. New York and London, 1992.

———. "O slozhenii prikaznoi sistemy na Rusi." *Doklady i soobshcheniia Instituta istorii Akademii nauk* 3 (1955):164–76.

———. "O sostave dvortsovykh uchrezhdenii Russkogo gosudarstva kontsa XV–XVI v." *Istoricheskie zapiski* 63 (1958):180–205.

——. *Reformy Ivana Groznogo*. Moscow, 1960.

——. "Sostav boiarskoi dumy XV–XVI vekakh." In *Arkheograficheskii ezhegodnik za 1957 god*, pp. 41–87. Moscow, 1958.

——. "Suzdal'skie i rostovskie kniaz'ia vo vtoroi polovine XV–pervoi treti XVI v." *Vspomogatel'nye istoricheskie distsipliny* 7 (1976):56–69.

——. "V. I. Lenin o 'moskovskom tsarstve' i cherty feodal'noi razdroblennosti v politicheskom stroe Rossii XVI veka." In *Aktual'nye problemy istorii Rossii epokhi feodalizma. Sbornik statei*, pp. 270–93. Moscow, 1970.

Žužek, P. Ivan, S.J. *Kormčaja Kniga: Studies on the Chief Code of Russian Canon Law*. Orientalia Christiana Analecta, no. 168. Rome, 1964.

Of Comparative or Theoretical Relevance

Abel, Richard L. "A Comparative Theory of Dispute Institutions in Society." *Law and Society Review* 8, no. 2 (1973):217–347.

Abercrombie, Nicholas, Stephen Hill, and Bryan S. Turner. *The Dominant Ideology Thesis*. London, 1980.

Andrew, Donna T. "The Code of Honour and Its Critics: The Opposition to Duelling in England, 1700–1850." *Social History* 5, no. 3 (1980):409–34.

Angell, Robert Cooley. "Social Integration." *International Encyclopedia of the Social Sciences* 7 (1968):380–86.

Archer, Ian W. *The Pursuit of Stability: Social Relations in Elizabethan London*. Cambridge, England, 1991.

Bailey, F. G. "Gifts and Poison." In idem, *Gifts and Poison: The Politics of Reputation*, pp. 1–25. New York, 1971.

Barber, Charles Laurence. *The Idea of Honour in the English Drama, 1591–1700*. Goteborg, 1957.

Baroja, Julio Caro. "Honour and Shame: A Historical Account of Several Conflicts." In J. G. Peristiany, ed., *Honour and Shame: The Values of Mediterranean Society*, pp. 79–138. Chicago, 1966.

——. "Religion, World Views, Social Classes and Honor during the Sixteenth and Seventeenth Centuries in Spain." In J. G. Peristiany and Julian Pitt-Rivers, eds., *Honor and Grace in Anthropology*, pp. 91–102. Cambridge, England, 1992.

Barton, Richard E. "Lordship in Maine: Transformation, Service, and Anger." *Anglo-Norman Studies* 17 (1995):41–63.

——. "'Zealous Anger' and the Renegotiation of Aristocratic Relationships in Eleventh- and Twelfth-Century France." In Barbara H. Rosenwein, ed., *Anger's Past: The Social Uses of an Emotion in the Middle Ages*, pp. 153–70. Ithaca, N.Y., 1998.

Becker, Marvin B. *Civility and Society in Western Europe, 1300–1600*. Bloomington, Ind., and Indianapolis, 1988.

Beik, William. *Absolutism and Society in Seventeenth-Century France: State Power and Provincial Aristocracy in Languedoc*. Cambridge, England, 1985.

Berger, Peter. "On the Obsolescence of the Concept of Honour." In Michael J. Sandel, ed., *Liberalism and Its Critics*, pp. 149–58. New York, 1984.

Black, Antony. "The Individual and Society." In J. H. Burns, ed., *The Cambridge History of Medieval Political Thought, c. 350–c. 1450*, pp. 588–606. Cambridge, England, 1988.

Boehm, Christopher. *Blood Revenge: The Enactment and Management of Conflict in Montenegro and Other Tribal Societies*. Philadelphia, 1984.

Bogucka, Maria. "The Foundations of the Old Polish World: Patriarchalism and the Family. Introduction into the Problem." *Acta Poloniae Historica* 69 (1994):37–53.

———. "Spectacles of Life: Birth—Marriage—Death. Polish Customs in the 16–18th Centuries." *Acta Poloniae Historica* 70 (1994):29–48.

Bonney, Richard. *The European Dynastic States, 1494–1660*. Oxford, 1991.

Bossy, John, ed. *Disputes and Settlements*. Cambridge, England, 1983.

Bourdieu, Pierre. *Outline of a Theory of Practice*. Trans. Richard Nice. Cambridge, England, 1977.

Brown, Keith M. *Bloodfeud in Scotland, 1573–1625*. Edinburgh, 1986.

Brown, Peter. *Power and Persuasion in Late Antiquity: Towards a Christian Empire*. Madison, Wis., 1992.

Brunner, Otto. *Land and Lordship: Structures of Governance in Medieval Austria*. Trans. from 4th rev. ed. by Howard Kaminsky and James Van Horn Melton. Philadelphia, 1992.

Bryson, F. R. *The Point of Honor in Sixteenth-Century Italy: An Aspect of the Life of the Gentleman*. Chicago, 1935.

Burghartz, Susanne. "Rechte Jungfrauen oder Unverschämte Töchter? Zur weiblichen Ehre im 16. Jahrhundert." *Journal Geschichte* 1, no. 13 (1991):39–45.

Burke, Peter. *The Historical Anthropology of Early Modern Italy*. Cambridge, England, 1987.

———. *History and Social Theory*. Ithaca, N.Y., 1992.

Burns, J. H., ed. *The Cambridge History of Medieval Political Thought, c. 350–c. 1450*. Cambridge, England, 1988.

Bynum, Caroline Walker. *Jesus as Mother: Studies in the Spirituality of the High Middle Ages*. Berkeley and Los Angeles, 1982.

Chaytor, Miranda. "Household and Kinship: Ryton in the Late 16th and Early 17th Centuries." *History Workshop Journal* 10 (1980):25–60.

Clanchy, M. T. *From Memory to Written Record: England, 1066–1307*. 2d ed. Oxford and Cambridge, Mass., 1993.

Cohen, Anthony P. *The Symbolic Construction of Community*. London and New York, 1985.

Cohen, Elizabeth S. "Honor and Gender in the Streets of Early Modern Rome." *Journal of Interdisciplinary History* 22, no. 4 (1992):597–625.

Cohen, Thomas V. "The Lay Liturgy of Affront in Sixteenth-Century Italy." *Journal of Social History* 25, no. 4 (1992):857–77.

Cohen, Thomas V., and Elizabeth S. Cohen. *Words and Deeds in Renaissance Rome*. Toronto, 1993.

Collier, Jane F. "Legal Processes." *Annual Reviews in Anthropology* 1975:121–44.

Coser, Lewis A. "Conflict: Social Aspects." *International Encyclopedia of the Social Sciences* 3 (1968):232–36.

Dahrendorf, Ralf. *Class and Class Conflict in Industrial Society*. Stanford, 1959.

Davies, Wendy, and Paul Fouracre, eds. *The Settlement of Disputes in Early Medieval Europe*. Cambridge, England, and New York, 1986.

Davis, Natalie Zemon. "Charivari, Honor, and Community in Seventeenth-Century Lyon and Geneva." In John J. MacAloon, ed., *Rite, Drama, Festival, Spectacle: Rehearsals toward a Theory of Cultural Performance*, pp. 42–57. Philadelphia, 1984.

——. *Fiction in the Archives: Pardon Tales and Their Tellers in Sixteenth-Century France*. Stanford, 1987.

——. "The Reasons of Misrule." In idem, *Society and Culture in Early Modern France*, pp. 97–123. Stanford, 1965.

——. *The Return of Martin Guerre*. Cambridge, Mass., 1983.

——. *Society and Culture in Early Modern France*. Stanford, 1965.

——. "Women on Top." In idem, *Society and Culture in Early Modern France*, pp. 124–51. Stanford, 1965.

Dinges, Martin. "Die Ehre als Thema der historischen Anthropologie. Bemerkungen zur Wissenschaftsgeschichte und zur Konzeptualisierung." In Klaus Schreiner and Gerd Schwerhof, eds., *Verletzte Ehre. EhrKonflikte in Gesellschaften des Mittelalters und der frühen Neuzeit*, pp. 29–62. Cologne, 1995.

Donahue Jr., Charles. "Law, Civil." In Joseph R. Strayer, ed., *Dictionary of the Middle Ages* 7 (1986):418–25. 13 vols. New York, 1982–89.

Duby, Georges. *The Early Growth of the European Economy*. Trans. Howard B. Clarke. Ithaca, N.Y., 1974.

Durkheim, Emile. *The Division of Labor in Society*. Trans. George Simpson. New York, 1933.

——. *The Elementary Forms of the Religious Life*. Trans. Joseph Ward Swain. London, 1915.

Eckhoff, Torstein. "The Mediator, the Judge and the Administrator in Conflict-Resolution." *Acta Sociologica* 10 (1966):148–72.

Eley, Geoff. "Nations, Publics, and Political Cultures: Placing Habermas in the Nineteenth Century." Unpubl. manuscript, April 1990.

——. "Reading Gramsci in English: Observations on the Reception of Antonio Gramsci in the English-speaking World, 1957–82." *European History Quarterly* 14, no. 4 (1984):441–78.

Elias, Norbert. *The Court Society*. Trans. Edmund Jephcott. New York, 1983.

Farr, James R. *Hands of Honor: Artisans and Their World in Dijon, 1550–1650*. Ithaca, N.Y., and London, 1988.

Fichtenau, Heinrich. *Living in the Tenth Century: Mentalities and Social Orders*. Trans. Patrick J. Geary. Chicago and London, 1991.

Fletcher, Anthony, and John Stevenson. "Introduction." In idem, *Order and Disorder in Early Modern England*, pp. 1–40. Cambridge, England, 1985.

——, eds. *Order and Disorder in Early Modern England*. Cambridge, England, 1985.

Foucault, Michel. *Discipline and Punish: The Birth of the Prison*. Trans. Alan Sheridan. New York, 1977.

——. "The Subject and Power." In Hubert L. Dreyfus and Paul Rabinow, eds., *Michel Foucault: Beyond Structuralism and Hermeneutics*, pp. 208–26. Chicago, 1982.

——. "Truth and Power." In Paul Rabinow, ed., *The Foucault Reader*, pp. 51–75. New York, 1984.

Garrioch, David. *Neighbourhood and Community in Paris, 1740–1790*. Cambridge, England, 1986.

——. "Verbal Insults in Eighteenth-Century Paris." In Peter Burke and Roy Porter, eds., *The Social History of Language*, pp. 104–19. Cambridge, England, 1987.

Gauvard, Claude. *"De grace especial." Crime, état et société en France à la fin du Moyen Age*. 2 vols. Paris, 1991.

Geary, Patrick J. "Extra-Judicial Means of Conflict Resolution." In *La giustizia nell'alto medioevo. (Secoli V–VIII)* 1:569–601. 2 vols. Spoleto, 1995.

——. "Moral Obligations and Peer Pressure: Conflict Resolution in the Medieval Aristocracy." In G. Duhamel and G. Lobrichon, eds., *Georges Duby. L'Ecriture de l'Histoire*, pp. 217–22. Brussels, 1996.

Geertz, Clifford. "Centers, Kings, and Charisma: Reflections on the Symbolics of Power." In his *Local Knowledge*, pp. 121–46. New York, 1983. Also publ. in Sean Wilentz, ed., *Rites of Power: Symbolism, Ritual, and Politics since the Middle Ages*, pp. 13–40. Philadelphia, 1985.

——. "Deep Play: Notes on the Balinese Cockfight." In idem, *The Interpretation of Cultures: Selected Essays*, pp. 412–54. New York, 1973.

——. *The Interpretation of Cultures: Selected Essays*. New York, 1973.

——. *Local Knowledge: Further Essays in Interpretive Anthropology*. New York, 1983.

——. "Religion as a Cultural System." In idem, *The Interpretation of Cultures: Selected Essays*, pp. 87–125. New York, 1973.

Giddens, Anthony. *Capitalism and Modern Social Theory: An Analysis of the Writings of Marx, Durkheim and Max Weber*. Cambridge, England, 1971.

——. *A Contemporary Critique of Historical Materialism, Vol. 1: Power, Property and the State*. Berkeley, 1981.

——. *The Nation-State and Violence: Volume Two of A Contemporary Critique of Historical Materialism*. Berkeley and Los Angeles, 1987.

——. "'Power' in the Recent Writings of Talcott Parsons." *Sociology* 2, no. 3 (1968):257–72.

Gilmore, David D., ed. *Honor and Shame and the Unity of the Mediterranean*. Washington, D.C., 1987.

Ginzburg, Carlo. *The Cheese and the Worms: The Cosmos of a Sixteenth-Century Miller*. Trans. John and Anne Tedeschi. Baltimore and London, 1980.

——. *The Night Battles: Witchcraft and Agrarian Cults in the Sixteenth and Seventeenth Centuries*. Trans. John and Anne Tedeschi. New York, 1985.

Gluckman, Max. *Custom and Conflict in Africa*. Glencoe, Ill., 1959.

——. "The Peace in the Feud." In *Custom and Conflict in Africa*, pp. 1–26. Glencoe, Ill., 1959.

——. *Politics, Law and Ritual in Tribal Society*. Oxford, 1965.

Goffman, Erving. "On Face Work." In idem, *Interaction Ritual*, pp. 5–46. Chicago, 1967.

Gramsci, Antonio. *An Antonio Gramsci Reader: Selected Writings, 1916–1935*. Ed. David Forgacs. New York, 1988.

Gutierrez, Ramon A. "Marriage, Sex and the Family: Social Change in Colonial New Mexico, 1690–1846." Ph.D. dissertation, University of Wisconsin, 1980.

Habermas, Jürgen. *Communication and the Evolution of Society*. Trans. with intro. by Thomas McCarthy. Boston, 1979.

——. "The Public Sphere: An Encyclopedia Article (1964)." *New German Critique* 3 (1974):49–55.

Hanlon, Gregory. "Les rituels de l'agression en Aquitaine au XVIIe siècle." *Annales: E.S.C.* 1985, no. 2:244–68.

Hatch, Elvin. "Theories of Social Honor." *American Anthropologist* 91 (1989):341–53.

Heers, Jacques. *Family Clans in the Middle Ages*. Amsterdam, 1977.

Henshall, Nicholas. *The Myth of Absolutism: Change and Continuity in Early Modern European Monarchy*. London and New York, 1992.

Herrup, Cynthia B. *The Common Peace: Participation and the Criminal Law in Seventeenth-Century England*. Cambridge, England, 1987.

Herzfeld, Michael. "'As in Your Own House': Hospitality, Ethnography, and the Stereotype of Mediterranean Society." In David D. Gilmore, ed., *Honor and Shame and the Unity of the Mediterranean*, pp. 75–89. Washington, D.C., 1987.

——. "Honour and Shame: Problems in the Comparative Analysis of Moral Systems." *Man* n.s. 15 (1980):339–51.

Hobsbawm, Eric, and Terence Ranger, eds. *The Invention of Tradition*. Cambridge, England, 1983.

Horská, Pavla. "Historical Models of the Central European Family: Czech and Slovak Examples." *Journal of Family History* 19, no. 2 (1994):99–106.

Howard, Michael. *War in European History*. Oxford, 1976.

Humphreys, Sally. "Law as Discourse." *History and Anthropology* 1, no. 2 (1985):241–64.

Hyams, Paul R. "Feud in Medieval England." *The Haskins Society Journal* 3 (1991):1–21.

Ingram, Martin J. *Church Courts, Sex and Marriage in England, 1570–1640*. Cambridge, England, 1987.

——. "Communities and Courts: Law and Disorder in Early-Seventeenth-Century Wiltshire." In J. S. Cockburn, ed., *Crime in England, 1550–1800*, pp. 110–34. Princeton, N.J., 1977.

——. "Ridings, Rough Music and Mocking Rhymes in Early Modern England." In Barry Reay, ed., *Popular Culture in Seventeenth-Century England*, pp. 166–97. London and Sydney, 1985.

Jaeger, C. Stephen. *The Origins of Courtliness: Civilizing Trends and the Formation of Courtly Ideals, 939–1210*. Philadelphia, 1985.

James, Mervyn. "English Politics and the Concept of Honour, 1485–1642." *Past and Present, Supplement 3* (1978): 92 pp.

Johnson, Eric A., and Eric H. Monkkonen, eds. *The Civilization of Crime: Violence in Town and Country since the Middle Ages*. Urbana, Ill., and Chicago, 1996.

Jones, W. R. "'Actions for Slaunder'—Defamation in English Law, Language and History." *Quarterly Journal of Speech* 57, no. 3 (1971):274–83.

Jouanna, Arlette. "Recherches sur la notion d'honneur au XVI-ème siècle." *Revue d'histoire moderne et contemporaine* 15 (1968):597–623.

Keddie, Nikki, and Lois Beck. "Introduction." In idem, eds., *Women in the Muslim World*, pp. 1–34. Cambridge, Mass., 1978.

Kent, Francis W. *Household and Lineage in Renaissance Florence*. Princeton, N.J., 1977.

Kiernan, V. G. *The Duel in European History: Honour and the Reign of Aristocracy*. Oxford, 1988.

Kishlansky, Mark A. *Parliamentary Selection: Social and Political Choice in Early Modern England*. Cambridge, England, 1986.

Klassen, John M. "Marriage and Family in Medieval Bohemia." *East European Quarterly* 19, no. 3 (1985):257–74.

Koziol, Geoffrey. *Begging Pardon and Favor: Ritual and Political Order in Early Medieval France*. Ithaca, N.Y., 1992.

——. "Monks, Feuds, and the Making of Peace in Eleventh-Century Flanders." In Thomas Head and Richard Landes, eds., *The Peace of God: Social Violence and Religious Response in France around the Year 1000*, pp. 239–58. Ithaca, N.Y., 1992.

Kuehn, Thomas. "Reading Microhistory: The Example of *Giovanni i Lusanna*." *Journal of Modern History* 61 (1989):512–34.

Laslett, Peter. *The World We Have Lost*. 2d ed. New York, 1971.

Laslett, Peter, with Richard Wall. *Household and Family in Past Time*. Cambridge, England, 1972.

Leach, Edmund R. "Ritual." *International Encyclopedia of the Social Sciences* 13 (1968):520–26.

Le Roy Ladurie, Emmanuel. *Montaillou: The Promised Land of Error*. Trans. Barbara Bray. New York, 1979.

Levine, Donald N. "Cultural Integration." *International Encyclopedia of the Social Sciences* 7 (1968):372–80.

Leyser, Karl. "Ritual, Ceremony and Gesture: Ottonian Germany." In idem, *Communications and Power in Medieval Europe*, pp. 189–213. London, 1994.

Lovejoy, Arthur O. *The Great Chain of Being*. Cambridge, Mass., 1936.

Luebke, David Martin. "Serfdom and Honour in Eighteenth-Century Germany." *Social History* 18, no. 2 (1993):143–61.

Lynch, Katherine A. "European Style Family." In Stearns, Peter N., ed., *Encyclopedia of Social History*, pp. 247–249. New York and London, 1994.

McAleer, Kevin. *Dueling: The Cult of Honor in Fin-de-Siècle Germany*. Princeton, N.J., 1994.

Maddern, Philippa C. *Violence and Social Order: East Anglia, 1422–1442*. Oxford, 1992.

Major, J. Russell. "Bastard Feudalism and the Kiss: Changing Social Mores in Late Medieval and Early Modern France." *Journal of Interdisciplinary History* 17, no. 3 (1987):509–35.

——. *From Renaissance Monarchy to Absolute Monarchy: French Kings, Nobles, and Estates*. Baltimore and London, 1994.

Mann, Michael. *The Sources of Social Power, Vol. 1: A History of Power from the Beginning to AD 1760*. Cambridge, England, 1986.

Margolf, Diane Claire. "The Paris *Chambre de l'Edit*: Protestant, Catholic and Royal Justice in Early Modern France." Ph.D. dissertation, Yale University, 1990.

Medick, Hans, and David Warren Sabean. *Interest and Emotion: Essays on the Study of Family and Kinship*. Cambridge, England, 1984.

Mellinkoff, Ruth. "Riding Backwards: Theme of Humiliation and Symbol of Evil," *Viator* 4 (1973):153–79.

Miller, William Ian. "Avoiding Legal Judgment: The Submission of Disputes to Arbitration in Medieval Iceland." *The American Journal of Legal History* 28 (1984): 95–134.

——. *Humiliation: and Other Essays on Honor, Social Discomfort and Violence*. Ithaca, N.Y., 1993.

Miner, Horace M. "Community-Society Continua." *International Encyclopedia of the Social Sciences* 3 (1968):174–80.

Moogk, Peter N. "'Thieving Buggers' and 'Stupid Sluts': Insults and Popular Culture in New France." *The William and Mary Quarterly*, 3d ser. 36, no. 4 (1979):524–47.

Motley, Mark. *Becoming a French Aristocrat: The Education of the Court Nobility, 1580–1715*. Princeton, N.J., 1990.

Muir, Edward. *Mad Blood Stirring: Vendetta and Factions in Fruili during the Renaissance*. Baltimore, 1992.

Nader, Laura. "Conflict: Anthropological Aspects." *International Encyclopedia of the Social Sciences* 3 (1968):236–42.

——. "From Disputing to Complaining." In Donald Black, ed., *Toward a General Theory of Social Control* 1:71–94. 2 vols. Orlando, Fla., 1984.

——. *Harmony Ideology: Justice and Control in a Zapotec Mountain Village*. Stanford, 1990.

——. "Styles of Court Procedure: To Make the Balance." In idem, ed., *Law in Culture and Society*, pp. 69–91. Chicago, 1969.

Nader, Laura, and Henry F. Todd Jr., eds. *The Disputing Process: Law in Ten Societies*. New York, 1978.

Neuschel, Kristen B. *Word of Honor: Interpreting Noble Culture in Sixteenth-Century France*. Ithaca, N.Y., and London, 1989.

Nye, Robert A. "Honor Codes." In Peter N. Stearns, ed., *Encyclopedia of Social History*, pp. 325–27. New York and London, 1994.

——. *Masculinity and Male Codes of Honor in Modern France*. New York, 1993.

Ortner, Sherry B. "Theory in Anthropology since the Sixties." *Comparative Studies in Society and History* 26 (1984):126–66.

Parker, Geoffrey. *The Military Revolution: Military Innovation and the Rise of the West, 1500–1800*. Cambridge, England, 1988.

Parsons, Talcott. *The Evolution of Societies*. Ed. with intro. by Jackson Toby. Englewood Cliffs, N.J., 1977.

——. *The Social System*. Glencoe, Ill., 1951.

——. "Social Systems." *International Encyclopedia of the Social Sciences* 15 (1968):458–73.

Peristiany, J. G., ed. *Honour and Shame: The Values of Mediterranean Society*. Chicago, 1966.

Peristiany, J. G., and Julian Pitt-Rivers, eds. *Honor and Grace in Anthropology*. Cambridge, England, 1992.

Pitt-Rivers, Julian. "Honor." *International Encyclopedia of the Social Sciences* 6 (1968): 503–11.

——. "Honour and Social Status." In J. G. Peristiany, ed., *Honour and Shame: The Values of Mediterranean Society*, pp. 19–78. Chicago, 1966.

——. "Postscript." In J. G. Peristiany and Julian Pitt-Rivers, eds., *Honor and Grace in Anthropology*, pp. 215–44. Cambridge, England, 1992.

Plakans, Andrejs. "Extended Family." In Peter N. Stearns, ed., *Encyclopedia of Social History*, pp. 253–55. New York and London, 1994.

——. "Seigneurial Authority and Peasant Family Life: The Baltic Area in the Eighteenth Century." *Journal of Interdisciplinary History* 5, no. 4 (1975):629–54.

Pollock, Sir Frederick, and Frederick William Maitland. *The History of English Law before the Time of Edward I*. Cambridge, England, 1895.

Powis, Jonathan. *Aristocracy*. Oxford, 1984.

Quillet, Jeannine. "Community, Counsel and Representation." In J. H. Burns, ed., *The Cambridge History of Medieval Political Thought, c. 350–c. 1450*, pp. 520–72. Cambridge, England, 1988.

Radin, Max. *Handbook of Roman Law*. St. Paul, Minn., 1927.

Ralston, David B. *Importing the European Army: The Introduction of European Military Techniques and Institutions into the Extra-European World, 1600–1914*. Chicago, 1990.

Ranum, Orest. "Courtesy, Absolutism and the Rise of the French State, 1630–1660." *Journal of Modern History* 52 (1980):426–51.

Reynolds, Susan. *Kingdoms and Communities in Western Europe, 900–1300*. Oxford, 1984.

Roberts, Michael. "The Military Revolution, 1560–1660." In idem, *Essays in Swedish History*, pp. 195–225. London, 1953.

Roberts, Simon. *Order and Dispute: An Introduction to Legal Anthropology*. New York, 1979.

——. "The Study of Dispute: Anthropological Perspectives." In John Bossy, ed., *Disputes and Settlements*, pp. 1–24. Cambridge, England, 1983.

Roper, Lyndal. "Will and Honor: Sex, Words and Power in Augsburg Criminal Trials." *Radical History Review* 43 (1989):45–71.

Rosenberg, Hans. *Bureaucracy, Aristocracy and Autocracy: The Prussian Experience, 1660–1815*. Boston, 1958.

Ruggiero, Guido. "'More Dear to Me Than Life Itself': Marriage, Honor and a Woman's Reputation in the Renaissance." In his *Binding Passions: Tales of Magic, Marriage and Power at the End of the Renaissance*, pp. 57–87. Oxford and New York, 1993.

——. *Violence in Early Renaissance Venice*. New Brunswick, N.J., 1980.

Russocki, Stanisław. "The Parliamentary Systems in 15th-Century Central Europe." In *Poland at the 14th International Congress of Historical Sciences in San Francisco*, pp. 7–21. Wrocław, Warsaw, Cracow, and Gdańsk, 1975.

Schalk, Ellery. *From Valor to Pedigree: Ideas of Nobility in France in the Sixteenth and Seventeenth Centuries*. Princeton, N.J., 1986.

Schreiner, Klaus, and Gerd Schwerhof, eds. *Verletzte Ehre. EhrKonflikte in Gesellschaften des Mittelalters und der frühen Neuzeit*. Cologne, 1995.

Seed, Patricia. *To Love, Honor and Obey in Colonial Mexico: Conflicts over Marriage Choice, 1574–1821*. Stanford, 1988.

Sharpe, J. A. *Defamation and Sexual Slander in Early Modern England: The Church Courts at York*. Borthwick Papers no. 58. York, n.d. [1980?].

Shoemaker, Robert B. *Prosecution and Punishment: Petty Crime and the Law in London and Rural Middlesex, c. 1660–1725*. Cambridge, England, 1991.

Smith, T. V. "Honor." *Encyclopedia of the Social Sciences* 7 (1932):456–58.

Stearns, Peter N., ed. *Encyclopedia of Social History*. New York and London, 1994.

Stone, Lawrence. "Interpersonal Violence in English Society, 1300–1980." *Past and Present* 101 (1983):22–33.

Strayer, Joseph R., ed. *Dictionary of the Middle Ages*. 13 vols. New York, 1982–89.

Stuart, Kathleen E. "The Boundaries of Honor: 'Dishonorable People' in Augsburg, 1500–1800." Ph.D. dissertation, Yale University, 1993.

Thompson, E. P. "'Rough music': Le charivari anglais." *Annales: E.S.C.* 27 (1972): 285–312.

Tilly, Charles. *Coercion, Capital, and European States, AD 900–1992*. Cambridge, Mass., and Oxford, 1990.

Todorova, Maria N. *Balkan Family Structure and the European Pattern*. Washington, D.C., 1993.

Turner, Victor W. "The Center Out There: Pilgrim's Goal." *History of Religions* 12, no. 3 (1973):191–230.

——. *Dramas, Fields and Metaphors: Symbolic Action in Human Society*. Ithaca, N.Y., 1974.

——. *The Drums of Affliction*. Ithaca, N.Y., 1968.

——. *The Forest of Symbols*. Ithaca, N.Y., 1967.

——. *The Ritual Process*. Chicago, 1969.

Turner, Victor W., and Edith Turner. *Image and Pilgrimage in Christian Culture: Anthropological Perspectives*. New York, 1978.

Underdown, D. E. "The Taming of the Scold: The Enforcement of Patriarchal Authority in Early Modern England." In Anthony Fletcher and John Stevenson, eds., *Order and Disorder in Early Modern England*, pp. 116–36. Cambridge, England, 1985.

van Dülmen, Richard. *Kultur und Alltag in der frühen Neuzeit*, vol. 2. *Dorf und Stadt, 16.–18. Jahrhundert*. Munich, 1992.

Walker, Mack. *German Home Towns: Community, State, and General Estate, 1648–1871*. Ithaca, N.Y., and London, 1971.

Watson, Curtis Brown. *Shakespeare and the Renaissance Concept of Honor*. Princeton, N.J., 1960.

White, Stephen D. "'*Pactum . . . Legem Vincit et Amor Judicium*': The Settlement of Disputes by Compromise in Eleventh-Century Western France." *The American Journal of Legal History* 22 (1978):281–308.

Wiesner, Merry E. *Women and Gender in Early Modern Europe*. Cambridge, England, 1993.

Williams, Raymond. *Marxism and Literature*. Oxford and New York, 1977.

Wolff, Larry. *Inventing Eastern Europe: The Map of Civilization on the Mind of the Enlightenment*. Stanford, 1994.

Wuthnow, Robert. "The Critical Theory of Jürgen Habermas." In idem, James Davison Hunter, Albert Bergesen, and Edith Kurzweil. *Cultural Analysis: The Work of Peter L. Berger, Mary Douglas, Michel Foucault and Jürgen Habermas*, pp. 179–239. London and New York, 1984.

Wuthnow, Robert, James Davison Hunter, Albert Bergesen, and Edith Kurzweil. *Cultural Analysis: The Work of Peter L. Berger, Mary Douglas, Michel Foucault and Jürgen Habermas*. London and New York, 1984.

Wyatt-Brown, Bertram. *Honor and Violence in the Old South*. New York, 1986.

——. *Southern Honor: Ethics and Behavior in the Old South*. New York, 1982.

Wyrobisz, Andrzej. "Patterns of the Family and Woman in Old Poland." *Acta Poloniae Historica* 71 (1995):69–82.

Index